Zvi Eckstein (Ed.)

Aspects of Central Bank Policy Making

With 53 Figures

Springer-Verlag

Berlin Heidelberg New York
London Paris Tokyo
Hong Kong Barcelona
Budapest

Prof. Dr. Zvi Eckstein
Department of Economics
Tel Aviv University
Ramat Aviv 69978
Tel Aviv
Israel

and

Department of Economics
Boston University
Boston MA 02215
USA

ISBN 3-540-54281-7 Springer-Verlag Berlin Heidelberg New York Tokyo
ISBN 0-387-54281-7 Springer-Verlag New York Berlin Heidelberg Tokyo

Printed in Germany

Printing: Druckerei Schmidt u. Sohn GmbH, Mannheim 61
Bookbinding: J. Schäffer GmbH & Co. KG, Grünstadt
2142/7130-543210

CONTENTS

PART II. INSURANCE AND REGULATION OF COMMERCIAL BANKS

PART III. REVIEW OF MONETARY POLICY IN GERMANY AND ISRAEL

LIST OF PARTICIPANTS

Benjamin Bental	Technion, Haifa
Eitan Berglas	Tel-Aviv University
Horst Bockelmann	Bank for International Settlements
Michael Bruno	Bank of Israel
Andrew Crocket	Bank of England
Alex Cukierman	Tel-Aviv University
Allan Drazen	Tel-Aviv University
Hermann-Josef Dudler	Deutsche Bundesbank
Zvi Eckstein	Tel-Aviv University
Thomas Franzen	Bank of Sweden
Mordechai Fraenkel	Bank of Israel
Alberto Giovannini	Columbia University
Elhanan Helpman	Tel-Aviv University
Yehuda Z.Hershlag	Tel-Aviv University
Dale Henderson	Federal Reserve Bank, USA
Zvi Hercowitz	Tel-Aviv University
Leonardo Leiderman	Tel-Aviv University
David Levhari	The Hebrew University of Jerusalem
Nissan Liviatan	The Hebrew University of Jerusalem
Rafael Melnick	Bank of Israel
Allan Meltzer	Carnegie-Mellon University
Leora Meridor	Bank of Israel
Akiva Offenbacher	Bank of Israel
Yair Orgler	Tel-Aviv University
Tommaso Padoa-Schioppa	Bank of Italy
Dan Peled	Technion, Haifa
Shula Pessach	Bank of Israel
Assaf Razin	Tel-Aviv University
Arthur Rolnick	Federal Reserve Bank of Minneapolis
Efraim Sadka	Tel-Aviv University
Rusdu Saracoglu	Bank of Turkey
Meir Sokoler	Bank of Israel
Zvi Sussman	Tel-Aviv University
Vito Tanzi	International Monetary Fund

PREFACE

This volume is a collection of papers which were presented and discussed at a conference on "Aspects of Central Bank Policy Making" which took place in January 1990 at the Bank of Israel and Tel Aviv University. The conference marked the tenth anniversary of the passing of David Horowitz who was the first governor of the Bank of Israel. The conference was sponsored by the Bank of Israel and the David Horowitz Institute for the Research of Developing Countries at Tel Aviv University. Eitan Berglas, Zvi Eckstein and Mordechai Fraenkel served as organizing committee.

The volume has three parts. The first part deals with the rules and the constraints that are fundamental for central bank policy making. It starts with a critical review of 75 years of monetary policy of the U.S. Federal Reserve Bank, followed by several studies directed at the issues concerning the establishment of a European central bank. The second part deals with the insurance, regulation and safety of commercial banks. The last part contains analysis of monetary policies in Germany and Israel.

Part of the research included in this volume is the result of a two years research project on "Central Bank Policies, Disinflation and the Macroeconomy" conducted at the David Horowitz Institute. The contributors to this project were: the Bundesbank, the Bank of England, the Bank of Italy, the Bank of Israel, the Bank for International Settlements and the Bank of the Netherlands.

Financial support for the conference was given by the Bank of Israel, the Organization of the Israeli Banks and The David Horowitz Institute for the Research for Developing Countries. Financial support for the publication of this volume has been provided by the Public Finance Chair in honor of Henrique Mario Simonsen that is incumbent on Professor Eitan Berglas, Department of Economics, Tel Aviv University. We would like to thank Phyllis Avni, Ruth Brig and Renee Friedman for their excellent work in organizing the conference, and to Stella Padeh for her excellent work in typing and organizing the publication of this volume.

INTRODUCTION

Zvi Eckstein

Economic policies of central banks have been the focus of research by economists for about two centuries. Recent research follows the same questions as those presented by the early debates on the goals, the rules and the constraints faced by the central bank. A central part of the debate is devoted to asking whether the central bank could control the money supply and the interest rate. If the answer is yes, then the question is whether the central bank should, and at what rate, control the money supply and the interest rate. The debate among economists and policy makers is as lively today as it was seventy five and one hundred and fifty years ago. In this volume the reader can follow the arguments from different points of view in relation to several actual important policy considerations.

In the first chapter **Alan Meltzer** provides us with a very critical review of the monetary policy conducted by the Federal Reserve since it's birth seventy-five years ago. Meltzer's view is that the Fed policies actually determined the fluctuations of the interest rate and the growth rate of the money supply. His main criticism of the policies is that the main attention of the Fed is on the short term fluctuations of the interest rate rather than the control of the monetary base in order to maintain price stability. Moreover, Meltzer claims that the Fed follows a discretion policy that is not based on fundamental understanding of the economy and, therefore, it is an inferior policy to an alternative monetarist suggestion of a credible set of rules on the monetary growth targets. The paper is a survey of the debates, the arguments and the counter-arguments that have appeared in the literature during the last twenty years. It also provides an extensive set of figures and tables on the actual data and the empirical analysis in order to explain the different points of view.

In chapter 2 **Padoa-Schioppa** raises the question of whether a fiscal discipline coordination is required for the establishment of a European monetary union and active central bank. Padoa-Schioppa's answer is that setting of a fiscal policy rule by member states is not a required condition for a viable monetary union. Given a strong monetary constitution that sets very clear rules on monetary growth, the member states would have to set fiscal policies that are consistent with the union monetary policy. Fiscal coordination and discipline would reduce the potential frictions and crises among the member states of the union, and, therefore, they are a desirable, but are not preconditions for a successful implementation of a monetary union.

Drazen considers the implications of a monetary policy that try to impose constraints on the local banking system in order to generate additional revenues for the government in face of a monetary integration. The idea is that given the monetary union, some governments will replace the seigniorage with higher demand for their national debt by imposing constraints on financial intermediaries.

Drazen shows, in chapter 3, that this policy is certainly counter productive in the long run, but may also generate less revenues in the short run due to the reduction in aggregate savings. Drazen concludes that the European monetary union implies loss of seigniorage for most countries, and there can, therefore, be no escape from fiscal adjustment of primary deficits among the states that are members of the union.

Bockelman discusses the issue of credible policies as it is viewed by central bank policy makers and the way they try to implement it by adopting strategies which enhance the credibility of the monetary policy authority. The claim is that the effectiveness of the policy is higher when the policy maker has a higher degree of credibility which is measured by the distance between the declarations and the actual events.

In chapter 5 **Cukierman** compares between an adjustable peg system of currencies and a commonly managed currency for a monetary union of different states, such as the European Monetary System. Cukeirman uses a political economy model of game among nations that belong to a monetary union in order to compare the two monetary regimes. The conclusion of the analysis is that the benefits of a stage two, as proposed in the Delors Report, are not worth the risks that such a stage carries towards full monetary unification. On the other hand, a full monetary unification is preferred if it is politically feasible. The paper also contains a review of recent developments in the literature on the theory of political monetary policy within the framework of the model of monetary integration of several nations.

Helpman and Leiderman critically survey the recent literature of exchange rate systems of small open economies. The main goal of their survey is to compare exchange rates using standard welfare considerations. Since most of the literature is not based on models for which this criteria would be useful, the survey moves towards the analysis of fixed vs. floating exchange rates under the criteria of macro stability. In addition they discuss deeply the viability of exchange rate pegs under different economic conditions. Finally, the paper considers the recent literature on exchange rate bands. The survey concludes "that during the many years passed since the publication of Friedman's defense of floating exchange rates the debate has shifted from the narrow comparison of fixed vs. floating exchange rates to debates on much broader menus of choice. This outcome has resulted from the wide recognition that neither one of these polar regimes is perfect and that the best solution lies in an intermediate system".

The second part of the book contains two papers that deal with theory and practice of the insurance and the regulation of commercial banks. **Bental, Eckstein and Peled** survey recent developments in the literature on the potential instability of a competitive banking system and provide a model for analyzing the desirability of government intervention to prevent banking instability. It is shown that a government insurance program that guarantees the return on short term deposits and is backed by future taxes can restore optimal allocation.

Boyd and Rolnick start with a description of the failure of the current deposit insurance system in the US. They emphasis the "moral hazard" aspect of the current deposit insurance institution together with the recent banking deregulation as the main cause for the recent crisis of the FSLIC and the FDIC. They suggest a deposit insurance method which provide banks managers, banks stock holders and depositors the incentives to contain the potential moral hazard problem.

The last part of the book contains four papers that consider actual monetary policy in Israel and Germany. **Dudler** provides a very detailed analysis of the German monetary and exchange rate policy during the second half of the eighties. Three papers discuss the Israeli economy. **Meridor and Pessach** empirically analyze the interaction between the monetary policy and the exchange rate regime. They find that the monetary policy is significantly offset by capital flows, and the level of the effect depends on the money multiplier. **Razin and Sadka** analyze the main factors for the recession of the Israeli economy from mid 1987 to mid 1989. Their claim is that "the recession is deeply rooted in the pegged exchange rate policy and high rates of interest that prevailed in 1987 and 1988. Finally, in chapter 12 of the book **Offenbacher** tests the tax smoothing and the Ricardian Equivalence hypotheses using Israeli data from 1961 to 1988. He concludes that since the tax smoothing hypothesis is not rejected, one may assume that the strict Ricardian hypothesis does not hold.

1 THE FEDERAL RESERVE AT SEVENTY FIVE

Allan H. Meltzer[1]

On December 23, 1913, Congress approved the Federal Reserve Act. Passage came after lengthy dispute, many pages of testimony, and more than thirty volumes of reports containing the findings of the National Monetary Commission. Despite the detailed investigation of financial systems that preceded passage and the number of alternative bills drafted, considered and dismissed, the Act says very little about the purposes of the legislation. Decisions about how the central bank was to operate, and the objectives to be served, were left in large part to the organizers.

Decisions were not taken quickly. The new system took nearly eight months to get started. It was not until August 10, 1914 that Charles Hamlin, Paul Warburg, Frederic Delano, W.P.G. Harding, and Adolph Miller took their oaths of office as the first appointive members of the Federal Reserve Board. The two remaining members of the 7 person Board, Secretary of the Treasury McAdoo and Comptroller Williams, were ex officio members who had taken office earlier. Reserve Banks opened later.

The system had an unusual organizational structure, reflecting both ambivalence about the desirability of a central bank and beliefs about its functions. Carter Glass, the Chairman of the House Banking Committee, accepted the argument that there were advantages to the centralization of banking resources, but he believed that, in a country as large as the United States, there was no need for a single money center. Hence, the House report on the Glass bill favored regional banks that were expected to function cooperatively, but independently, to achieve the advantages of a central bank without acquiring the monopoly

[1]I am grateful to Anna Schwartz, William Poole, Tom Mayer, Raymond Lombra and George Benston for comments on an earlier draft. Helpful assistance was received from Ezra Angrist, Chris Bryan and Jeremy Fand. This paper appeared previously as Chapter 1 of Monetary Policy on the 75th Anniversary of the Federal Reserve System, M.T.Belongia (ed.), Kluwer (1990).

powers of a single bank of issue.[2] Also prominent in the discussion was the desire to reduce the frequency and severity of banking crises. The main remedies were found in providing discounts for bills of exchange (and other instruments) at the regional reserve banks and issuing Federal Reserve notes. The development of a market for bills of exchange and the use of open market operations were considered helpful also.

Very little is said about inflation, deflation or price stability in the Act or in the Congressional reports that preceded it. Many of the framers understood that money had an effect on prices. Silver agitation and banking crises had made this relation familiar. The silver issue had been settled politically in 1900, following William Jennings Bryan's second failure to win the Presidency, by passage of the Gold Standard Act in 1900, and by the rise in the world gold stocks and country price levels earlier in the century. The drafters of the Federal Reserve Act may have presumed that the long-term movement of prices would be determined by gold flows.

Looking back after seventy-five years, one finds that many of the issues faced by the drafters and organizers return. Development of the Federal Reserve as an institution reflects not only the history in which it has played a part but also changing views about the principles by which the Federal Reserve should operate, the objectives to be served by monetary policy, centralization or decentralization of the system between the Board in Washington and the Reserve Banks, the problems of avoiding recessions and financial failure, and the shifting emphasis given to price and exchange rate stability as a goal of public policy.

A seventy-fifth anniversary, a diamond jubilee, suggests a comfortable settling into a secure niche with many of these issues resolved, a time to reflect on past accomplishments and problems surmounted. This is hardly the appropriate picture of the Federal Reserve at seventy-five. Its history is not a record of continuous achievement of well understood goals. The seventy-five year record shows only two periods of sustained non-inflationary economic growth or low inflation, from 1923 to the summer of 1929 and, with some exceptions, from 1952 to 1965. In addition to wartime inflations in 1917-18, and

---

[2]For the report on the Glass bill, see House Report 1593, 62nd Congress, 3rd sess. (February 28, 1913) in Krooss (1969, vol.3, 2143-95).

1941-45 and 1951, the Federal Reserve record includes the most severe depression and the longest, most sustained, peacetime inflation in our history. If we date the period of below normal output as lasting from 1929 to the beginning of World War II in 1941 and the period of sustained inflation from 1966 or 1967 to 1989, these years, and the years of wartime inflation include more than two-thirds of the period since 1914.

Surveying this history and much more that Federal Reserve has done, or failed to do, in its seventy-five year history is a daunting task for a book, an impossible task for a single paper. Fortunately, Friedman and Schwartz (1963) have provided a landmark history of the years to 1960, and Brunner and Meltzer (1964/1989) have related some of the principal policy errors to the framework used to guide monetary policy from the 1920s to the end of the 1960s. This paper will concentrate on selected events since 1960. Extending earlier work is made easier by the availability of materials, including reports by insiders and the release of primary materials. Where once researchers had to reconstruct the decision process and some of the basic data, there is now abundant material describing that process in detail and its outcomes at various times. Where once the Federal Reserve could be described as operating secretly, there is now a wealth of information.

The first section picks up where the earlier discussion left off. I summarize some of the principal criticisms of the Federal Reserve by Friedman and Schwartz and Brunner and Meltzer in the 1960s and discuss the extent to which the criticisms remained valid in the years that followed. Much of the attention is on the choice of operating procedures and domestic policy. These issues were important in earlier work and received much attention both within and outside the Federal Reserve in the years since 1960. Two other prominent issues during this period are the use of Regulation Q and its effects on the financial industry, financial structure, and the economy, and the inter-national role of the dollar under Bretton Woods and fluctuating exchange rates. Neither of these issues was entirely the responsibility of the Federal Reserve, but the Federal Reserve had a major role in setting and implementing policies. Space and time permit only brief discussion of both issues. This is a serious omission that leaves the history incomplete.

In many places, I treat the growth rates of monetary base and M_2 as main indicators of the thrust of monetary policy. Both the base and measures of money are endogenous variables under an interest rate control procedure. As is well-known and extensively documented, the Federal Reserve used the federal funds rate as the main control variable throughout the period. The degree of control varied under the different experiments, or quasi-experiments, with operating procedures, but there was generally a funds rate target and usually the Manager of the System Open Market Account kept the funds rate close to the target. Often there were targets for M_2 growth and other monetary aggregates also, but relatively large differences of actual from target growth were permitted under all control procedures.

The base and M_2 growth permit comparison of rhetoric to reality about the Federal Reserve's aims. I do not doubt that the responsible officials at the Federal Reserve during these years were honest and sincere public officials. They did not desire many of the outcomes they caused, or to which they contributed, including a high and durable inflation, devaluation, the end of the Bretton Woods system, several deep recessions, historically high market interest rates, and weakening of the financial structure. Some of them understood that the goals which they accepted such as low inflation, growth of real output, a stable money market, a stable international value of the dollar, low unemployment, stable money market conditions, safety and soundness of financial institutions, and profitability of the housing industry could not be achieved simultaneously. At critical points, Federal Reserve decisionmakers gave greater weight to stable money market conditions and stable federal funds rate than to other, more distant goals, just as they had in the preceding 50 year period. With hindsight it seems clear, as it was to some at the time, that improved control of money and a lower growth rate of money would have lowered the rate of inflation and might have entirely avoided inflation and devaluation. Stable, non-inflationary monetary growth would have reduced the severity of recessions, many of which were induced by the monetary contractions introduced to lower inflation or slow its rise.

Charts 1 and 2 show the growth rate of the monetary base and the level of the federal funds rate monthly from 1960 to 1988. The base is the St. Louis measure, and the monthly growth rates are calculated from the preceding year to avoid short-term fluctuations. The federal funds rate is the principal indicator of monetary policy used by the Federal Reserve. The monetary base is the principal alternative, although other aggregates are introduced below.

If the Federal Reserve had controlled the monetary base, maintained price stability, and permitted more short-term variability in interest rates, inflation would have been lower, nominal and real interest rates would not have reached the levels of 1981-82, and the Bretton Woods system would have survived longer. Banks and thrift institutions would not have experienced alternating effects of inflation and disinflation on their asset portfolios and their liabilities, so it seems likely that there would have been fewer failures. The world economy would not have experienced the rapid disinflation of the 1980s. The international debt problem would not have been exacerbated by the disinflation, recession and the attendant decline in the relative prices of commodity exports.

Until the experiment is run, no one can be certain about the full effects of a different operating procedure and a consistent effort to achieve price stability. Since identical circumstances cannot be achieved, there are limits to our hypothetical experiments. Data from countries where the base has been controlled, such as Switzerland, or where monetary growth has been less inflationary, as in Germany and Japan, provide useful supplementary information to support or modify the conclusions drawn.

The Lucas critique warns us about the difficulty of drawing inferences about the consequences of alternative policy rules, but it does not apply equally to all inferences. The response of prices to money and the effects of inflation on interest rates and exchange rates depend on the distinction between nominal and real values; this is an implication of rational behavior,

Insert Charts 1a, 1b, 1c, 2a, 2b and 2c.

not of a particular institutional arrangement or policy rule. The short-run non-neutrality of money is a result of costs of acquiring accurate information, the existence of contracts and laws written with nominal values. These costs, contracts and laws arise under many different policy rules. The timing of the principal responses to money may depend importantly on the institutional structure and policy rules; many of the long-term effects do not.

An historical discussion has an inevitable bias. We observe some mistake and some achievements. We cannot observe what was prevented from happening. Our hypotheses can help draw inferences about such events, but their power is limited. If discretionary action raised inflation but

Chart 1a

ANNUAL GROWTH OF THE MONETARY BASE
DURING THE SIXTIES

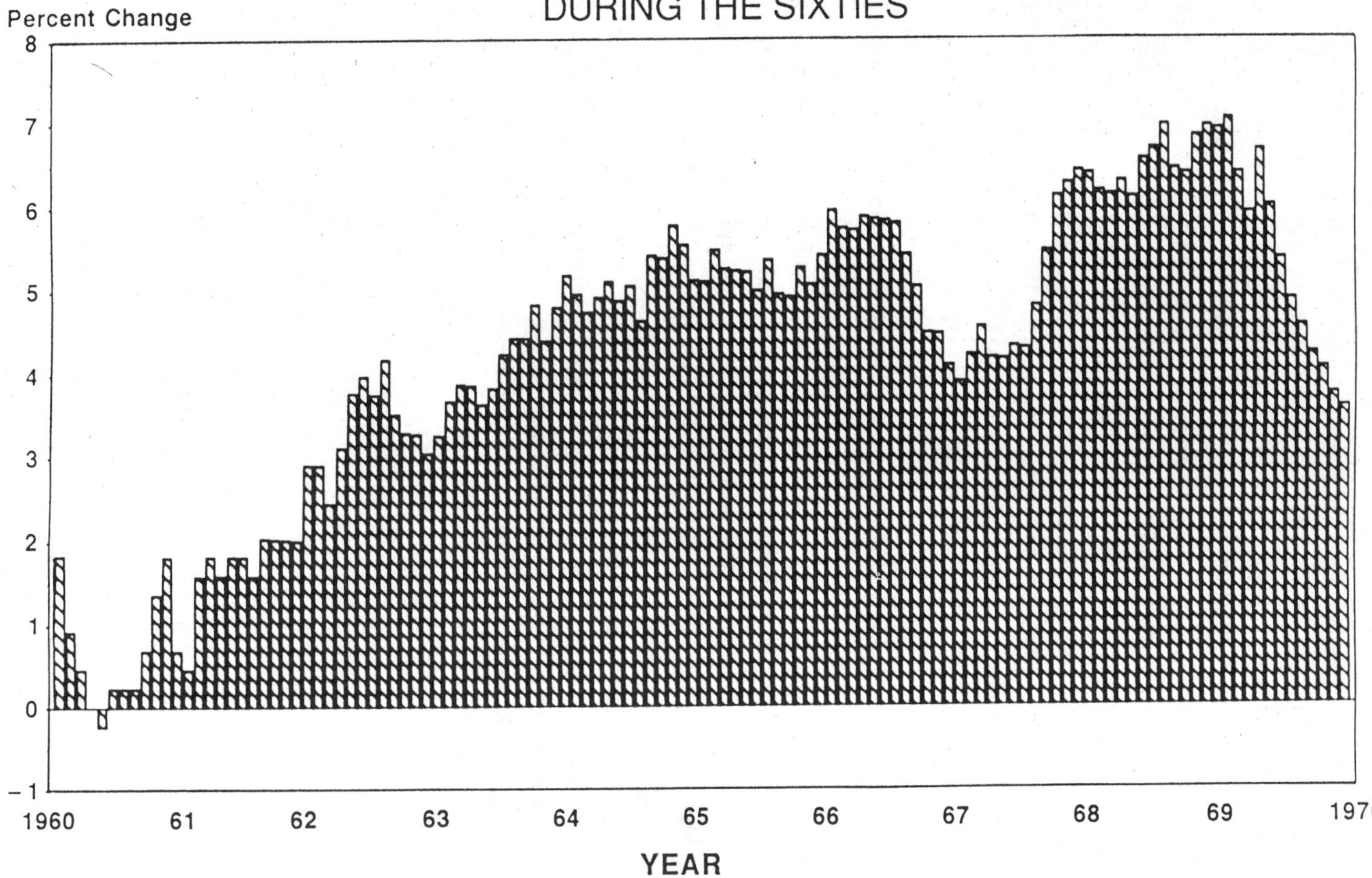

Chart 1b

ANNUAL GROWTH OF THE MONETARY BASE
DURING THE SEVENTIES

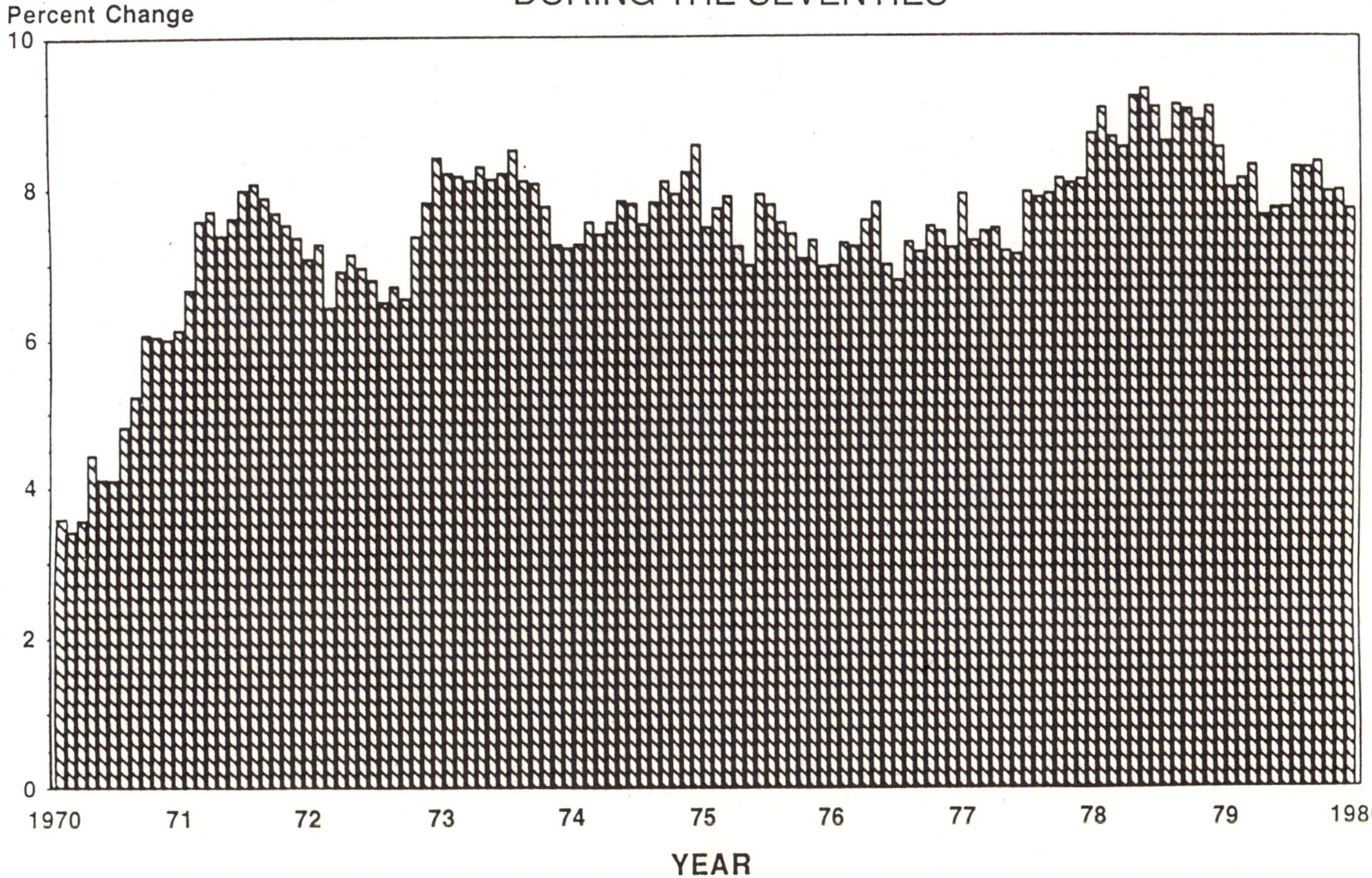

Chart 1c

ANNUAL GROWTH OF THE MONETARY BASE

DURING THE EIGHTIES

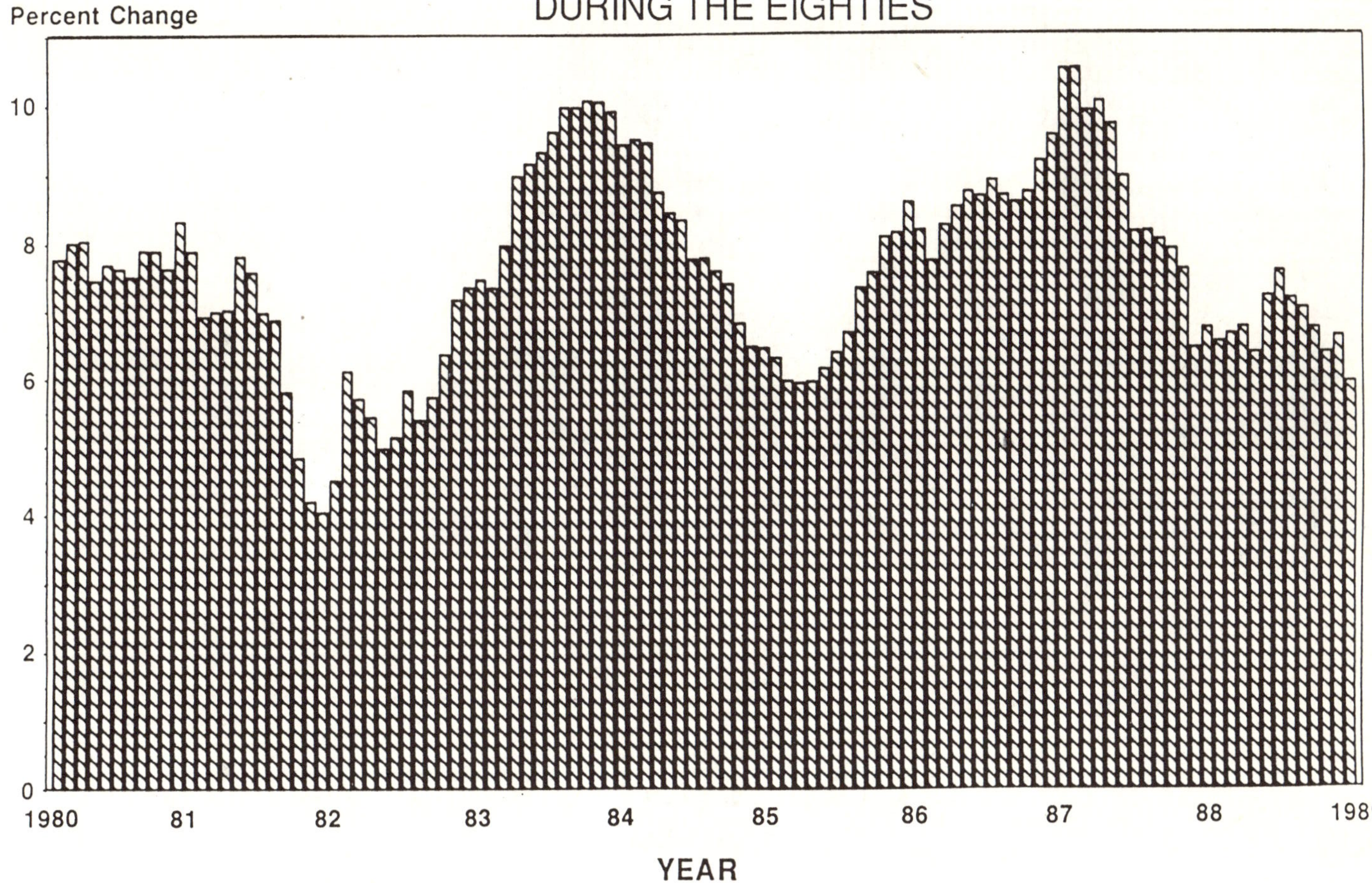

Chart 2a

FEDERAL FUNDS RATE
DURING THE SIXTIES

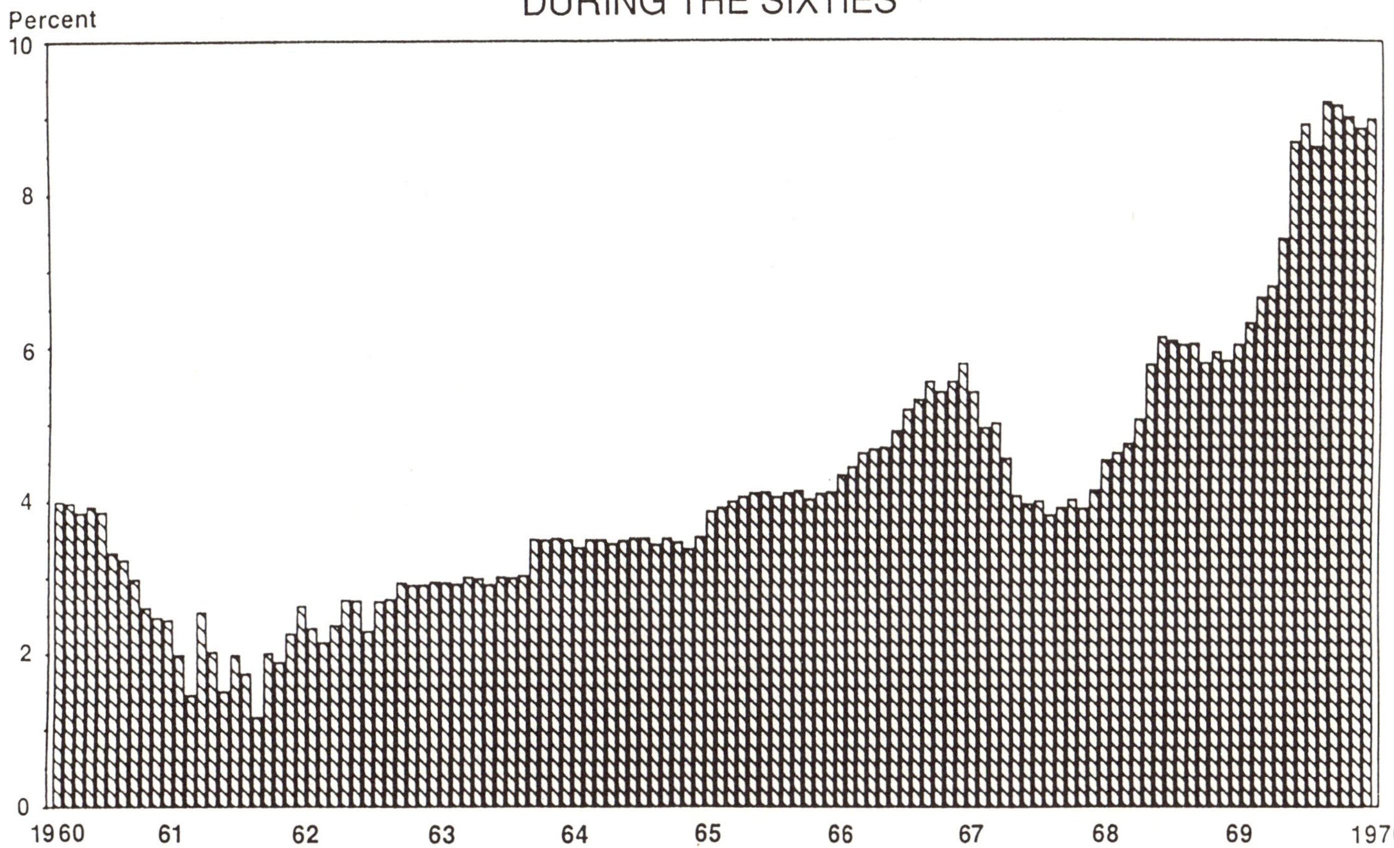

Chart 2b

FEDERAL FUNDS RATE

DURING THE SEVENTIES

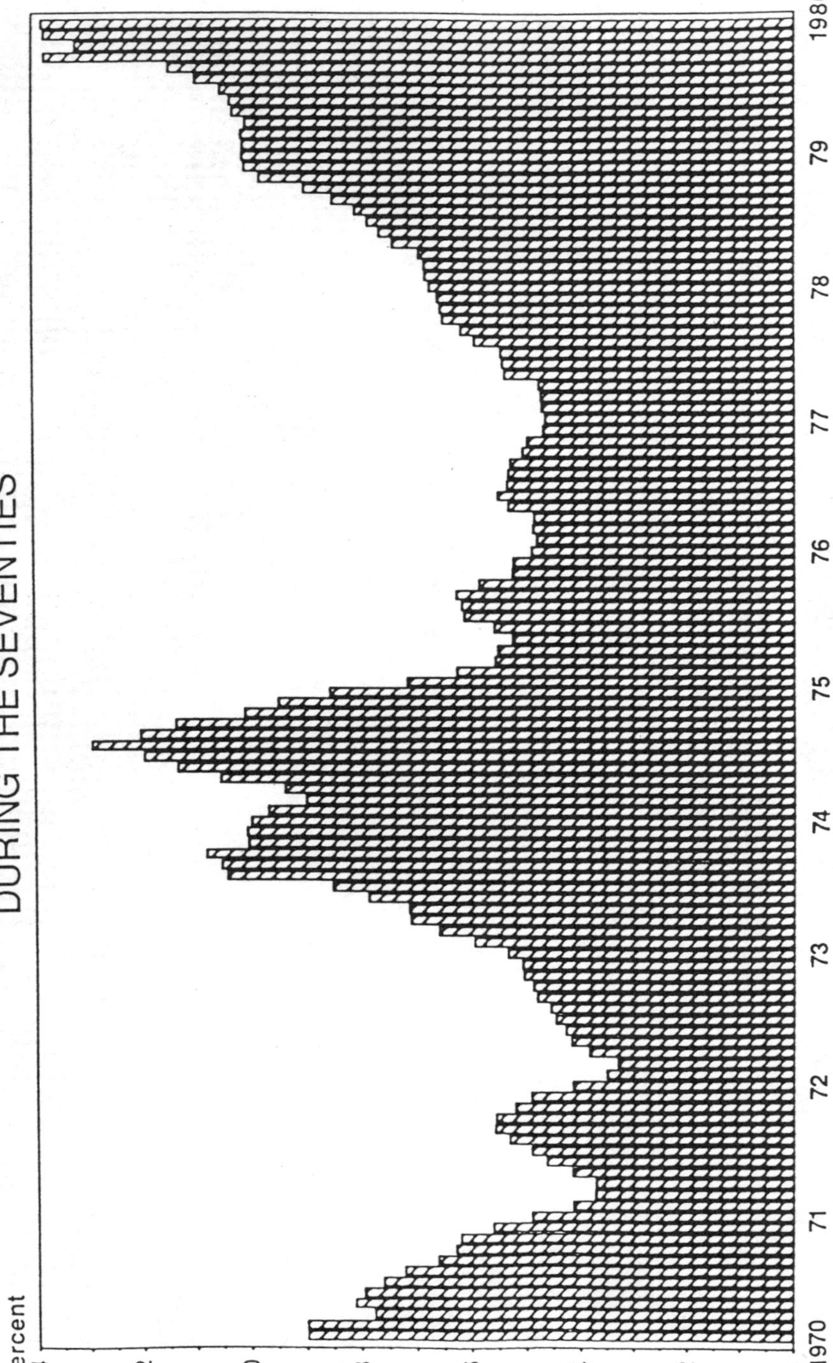

Chart 2c

FEDERAL FUNDS RATE
DURING THE EIGHTIES

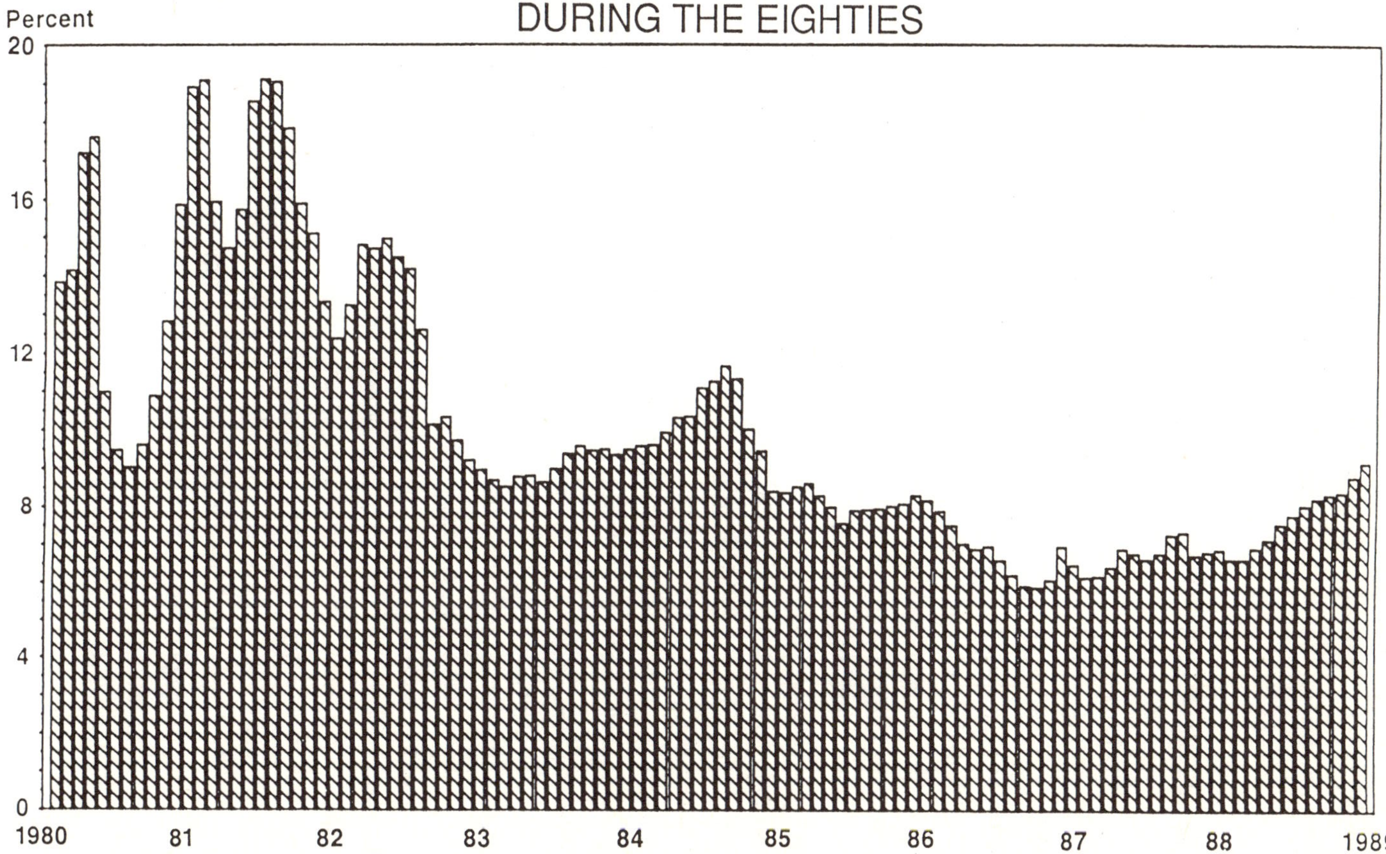

prevented or mitigated some problem, we can observe the inflation much more readily than the benefit achieved by discretionary action. This problem cannot be fully overcome in a study of this kind.

CRITICISMS AND RESPONSES

Criticisms of the Federal Reserve vary over a wide range. Many of the critics seek either to achieve different explicit or implicit objectives or to shift the distribution of costs and benefits resulting from policy actions. These criticisms of the effects of policy are part of the political process in democratic countries.

The monetarist critique, as it came to be known, had some of these features, but it concentrated much more on the process by which policy is made and implemented. The outcomes of policy actions were less than optimal, according to these critics, because the procedures for making policy were not well designed to achieve the objectives of relatively stable growth, at stable prices and high or maximum employment. The focus was on the choice of policy targets, the framework used to interpret or assess events, and reliance on discretion instead of rules for policy. Specific criticisms included the Federal Reserve's reliance on interest rates, "tone and feel" of the credit market, and free reserves, the latter defined as member bank excess reserves minus member bank borrowing from the Federal Reserve.

The critics argued that reliance on these measures led to systematic misinterpretation of the thrust of monetary policy and to a procyclical monetary policy; money growth rose faster in periods of expansion than in recessions. The procyclical movements of money contributed to higher inflation and deeper or more protracted recessions. Further, some of the critics claimed that the Federal Reserve's instructions to the Manager of the System Open Market Account were often vague, so that the Manager had considerable discretion about the thrust of policy.

Friedman and Schwartz's (1963) history documented the role of money in business cycles and provided evidence of the importance of money as a causal factor in fluctuations. These authors showed that the failure of the Federal Reserve to function as lender of last resort in 1929-33 contributed to the widespread failures of banks and to the depth and severity of the depression. Brunner and Meltzer (1964) concentrated on the framework guiding policy, particularly the use of free reserves as a target of policy, an indicator of the current thrust of policy, and as a causal variable in the transmission of monetary policy. These authors pointed out that systematic misinterpretation of policy was inherent in the use of free reserves as an indicator of the policy thrust. A rise in member bank borrowing lowered the level of free reserves but increased the amount of total reserves. The Federal Reserve interpreted a decline in free reserves as contractive (and a rise in free reserves as expansive). An increase in total reserves is expansive for the monetary system, so the interpretation based on free reserves led to misinterpretation. The Federal Reserve attempted to accommodate the conflict by arguing that banks borrowed only for short periods and only in case of need.[3] This argument is flawed; it relies on the fallacy of composition. Even if individual banks are reluctant to borrow, as Riefler (1930) attempted to show, the repayment by one bank, with the demand for bank credit and total reserves otherwise unchanged, shifts the demand to borrow to another bank. Total borrowing and total reserves do not contract. On the contrary, member bank borrowing is procyclical.

A related issue involved the interpretation of interest rates. The dominant interpretation in the System has been that a rise in interest rates is contractive for the economy; "money" is "tighter." A decline in interest rates is expansive; money is "easier." The relatively low interest rates in the 1930s were interpreted as a sign of easy policy.

There are two major problems with the Federal Reserve's interpretation. First is the failure to distinguish between nominal and real interest rates. With deflation, as in the early 1930s, nominal rates could be low or falling while (deflation adjusted) real rates were relatively high or rising. In the inflation of the 1960s and 1970s, the same problem arose again, but this time the problem was that historically high nominal rates were, in fact, associated with relatively low real rates. Second, reductions in the stock of base money raise interest rates, and increases in the base initially lower interest rates. Interest rates rise also, with continued growth in base money, if the public's supply of earning assets to banks increases or if the banks

---

[3]The interpretation was based on work done in the 1920s and reported in W.R.Burgess (1927) and W.W.Riefler (1930). Burgess and Riefler were economists in the Federal Reserve System at the time they wrote.

increase required reserves to support a higher level of bank deposits and, simultaneously, the public increases its currency holdings.

The critics claimed that concentration on short-term interest rates and money market conditions gave a narrow focus to policy operations. Friedman and Schwartz interpreted the historical evidence as showing that changes in money operated with a lag that varied in length. The response to policy actions spread from the money market to output, employment and prices with a delay measured in quarters or years, whereas the effects on the money market occur quickly. Brunner and Meltzer presented evidence suggesting that the Federal Reserve recognized turning points in the economy with little delay. The focus on money market conditions and short-term interest rates misled them into believing that effective action to expand or contract the pace of economic activity had been implemented.

The Federal Reserve's response to the monetarist critique was defensive to a degree but not entirely. Some staff members wrote memos summarizing the arguments and accepting some of the main criticisms.[4] The Federal Open Market Committee (FOMC) appointed a three man sub-committee, in 1964, to study the directive that the FOMC used to instruct the manager about policy. The sub-committee concluded that "the directive was incomplete, sometimes internally inconsistent, often too vague, and that it failed to show what policy was intended in explicit enough terms for the manager to follow the Committee's wishes." Maisel (1973, p. 168).[5] These were some of the same criticisms that had been made by the so-called monetarists.

By a vote of 9 to 3, the FOMC rejected the sub-committee report. At the time, William McChesney Martin was Chairman of the Board of Governors. Martin was a banker and the son of a former president of a Reserve bank. As Assistant Secretary of the Treasury, he had taken a leading role in negotiations leading to the 1951 accord between the Federal Reserve and the Treasury. Martin was market oriented and a firm adherent to the traditional approach of relying on the tone and feel of the money market and the use of free reserves as a target of policy and

---

[4]Examples are internal memos by Davis (1964) at the New York Federal Reserve Bank and Sigel (1964) at the Board of Governors.

[5]Sherman J.Maisel served as a member of the Board of Governors from 1965 to 1973.

an indicator of actions taken. Deficiencies in the conduct of monetary policy were to him unavoidable in a complex economy. They could best be handled by relying on the judgment of experienced people who respond flexibly to events as they unfold. In Martin's phrase, a flexible response leaned against the wind. See Maisel (1973, pp. 63, 81, 169-70; Brimmer (1971, p. 32).[6] With Martin opposed, major changes were unlikely.

Throughout its history, the Board of Governors and the FOMC had shown little interest in money or monetary aggregates. Data on money (M_1) was not collected and reported on a regular basis until monthly data appeared in the Federal Reserve Bulletin for February 1944. Daily average data began to be collected in 1947, but it was not until 1960 that the Bulletin began to publish data for the money stock based on daily averages. Further refinements to data on monetary aggregates were made periodically thereafter, and in February 1971 the Bulletin published data on M_2 and M_3 for the first time. In recent years, the data have been revised and the definitions changed to reflect innovations in banking and financial practices.

Maisel's report called for a break with past traditions that deemphasized or ignored money. A majority of the Board and many of the staff were opposed. Only one of the Reserve Banks, St. Louis, responded favorably. Under the leadership of Homer Jones, the St. Louis bank began to publish weekly and monthly releases showing growth rates of a number of monetary aggregates. Publishing these data in a form accessible to financial market participants helped to move the discussion into the public arena. Newspapers reported on the aggregates and the predictions of inflation or recession that gave considerable weight to changes in money. Further, research at the bank, Andersen and Jordan (1968), tested the influence of monetary and fiscal variables on nominal GNP and concluded that the effect of changes in money was larger and more reliable than the effects of fiscal variables. These and other activities, including a steady stream of research within parts of the System, helped to keep the criticisms from being shunted aside. Criticisms and discussion in the academic and semi-popular literature contributed also. Perhaps most important, however, were the rising rate

---

[6] Andrew F.Brimmer served as a member of the Board of Governors from 1966 to 1974.

of inflation, which gave substance to the criticisms, and the ineffectiveness of policies instituted to prevent inflation.

RESPONSE TO INFLATION

The Johnson administration's response to inflation relied heavily on the use of guideposts and guidelines. These were intended to limit price and wage increases in the private sector. Maisel (1973, p. 76) notes that the guidepost policy for wages and prices had been extended, de facto, to the prime lending rate. This encouraged borrowing and, in the opinion of several members of the Board, added to inflationary pressures. Maisel (1973, pp. 68-81) has a wide ranging discussion of the December 1965 decision to raise the discount rate from 4 to 4.5 per cent. By raising the discount rate, the Board intended to give the banks an opportunity to raise the prime rate and "tighten" money. At the same time, the Board voted to raise ceiling rates for time deposits by one percentage point (to 5.5 percent) under their authority to set Regulation Q ceiling rates. These actions touched off a dispute with President Johnson who interpreted the actions as a break with his policy.

The actions that followed the December decision raise some of the issues in the discussion of alternative policy procedures. Free reserves had been rising throughout the fall; they now reversed course and fell from $8 million in December to -$255 million by the following March. Member bank borrowing increased by a similar amount, and the federal funds rate rose. Judged by all of these measures, Federal Reserve policy had tightened. The seasonally adjusted monetary base continued to rise, however, and the stocks of money and credit rose also.

> "To those who adhered to the traditional doctrine and saw money market conditions tightening, the Fed was doing its part to fight inflation. But to those of us who saw the fast growth of the monetary aggregates and the rapid creation of money and credit, it seemed that the Fed, far from combatting inflationary forces, might even be adding to the inflation." Maisel (1973, p. 81).[7]

The result was another discussion of the directive that ended in a

[7]"As I gained more insight into the way monetary policy was being made, I began to suspect that the Fed might be committing some of the errors our critics accused us of." (<u>Ibid</u>, p.82). See also Brimmer (1971, 48-50).

compromise the following June (1966). The Committee continued to use money market conditions as the principal guide, but a proviso clause was added to the directive. If required reserves rose more rapidly than anticipated, the Manager was to lower free reserves and raise money market rates.

Neither at the time nor at subsequent meetings did the proviso clause have much effect. For the rest of the decade of the 1960s, free reserves and money market conditions remained the principal indicators and targets of monetary policy. As a result, the Federal Reserve continued to misinterpret its actions. An example is the period following the ten per cent income tax surcharge, passed in June 1968. The surcharge was intended to reduce the budget deficit, strengthen the dollar, and lower the inflation rate. The Federal Reserve responded to the surcharge by voting to ease monetary policy. From June to September, free reserves rose from -\$343 to -\$120 million; member bank borrowing declined, and federal funds moved down slightly (Chart 2a). The Federal Reserve believed that policy had eased. The growth of the monetary base shows a slight decline in rate of growth for the twelve months ending in September, from the rate achieved in the twelve months ending in June (Chart 1a). The monthly growth rates of M_1, shown in Chart 3, show little change in the maintained average rate in the summer and fall of 1968 and a decline in 1969.

(Insert Chart 3 here)

Partly in response to internal and external criticisms of this short-term focus, there was a change in policy procedures about this time. The staff began to make explicit forecasts of a number of variables and to include the forecasts as part of the information made available to the FOMC. The forecasts were obtained from a large scale econometric model, developed by the Board's staff with the assistance of some academic economists. Among the advantages of model forecasts is that the staff had to make explicit some assumptions about response lags and directions of influence, and the members were confronted with estimates of the effects on large numbers of variables estimated simultaneously. The forecasts encouraged the members to recognize that their actions had consequences for prices, output and inflation over a period much longer than the time between meetings. Also, the staff presented studies of the effects of different assumptions about policy action.

Chart 3

MONTHLY GROWTH OF M-1 (S.A.)

AUGUST 1965 - DECEMBER 1969

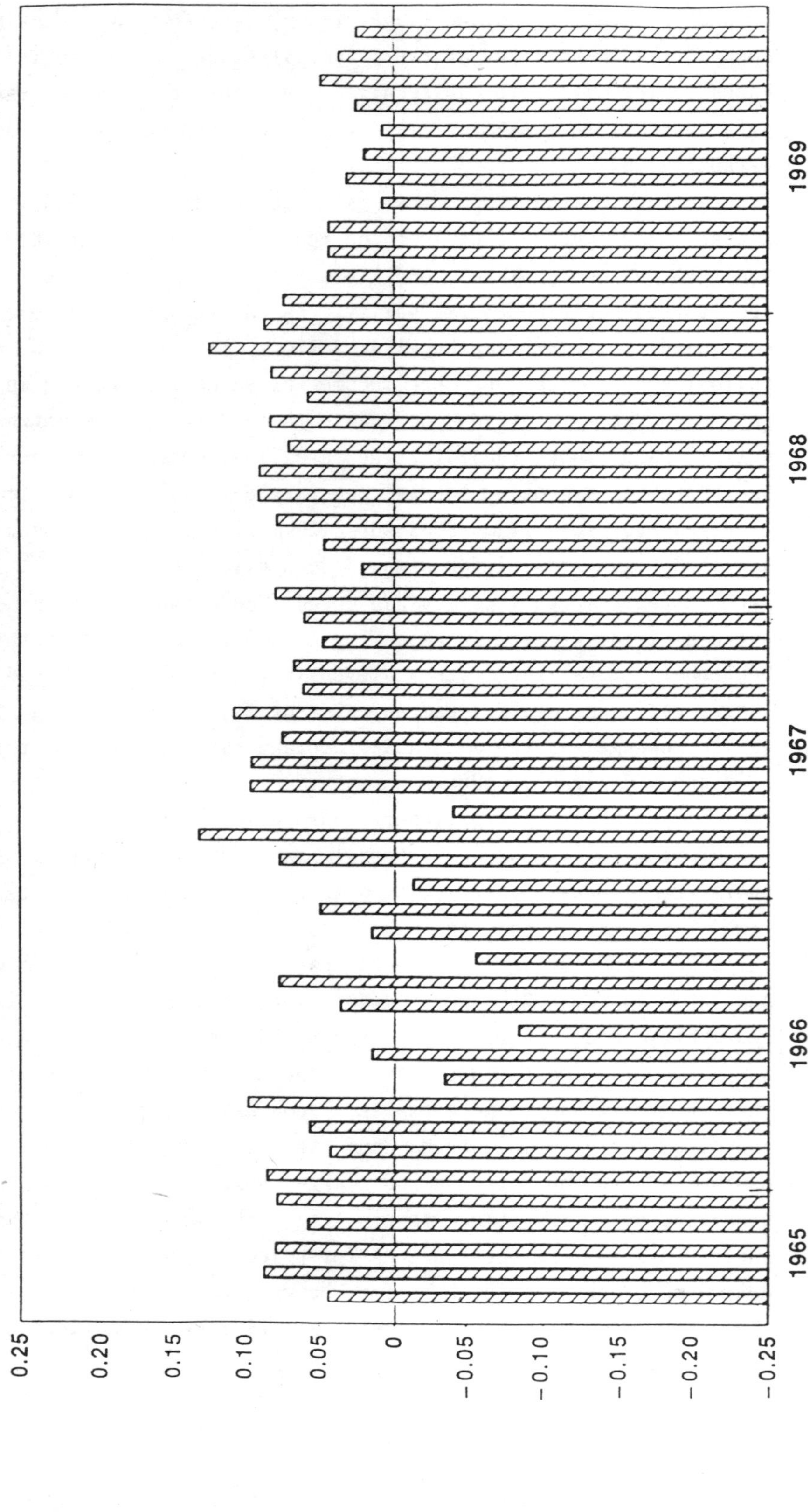

A principal problem soon became apparent. Relatively accurate forecasts proved difficult to achieve. Maisel (1973, p. 185) shows that the absolute percent forecast errors for the period 1967 to 1972 ranged from 16% to more than 30% for four quarter ahead forecasts of nominal and real GNP and the price deflator. Further, the errors were one-sided; the model or the assumptions gave a downward bias to inflation and nominal GNP, so these variables were typically underestimated. Projections for the monetary aggregates were subject to even larger errors than the GNP and price forecasts. Maisel (1973, pp. 184-86).

Reliance on forecasts and quantification may have lengthened the horizon for some members of the FOMC by encouraging them to consider long-term effects on prices and nominal values or to be more explicit about these effects. The main effect was in the opposite direction. Forecasts helped to sustain the entrenched belief that policy actions could adjust the economy's near-term path. If a mistake was made, it could be corrected later. Thus, the new procedures did not remove, but rather strengthened, the pressure for activist policies directed at current and near-term events.

This short-term focus is reflected in the events of 1969-70. Rising inflation, and rising public concern about inflation, precipitated a shift toward less expansive policy, a brief recession, and a turn back toward more expansive policy. A problem in this period, as in many others, was that policy was misinterpreted. The Federal Reserve had moved decisively toward restraint in the fall of 1968. From September 1968 to August-September 1969, free reserves fell by $800 million and the federal funds rate rose by more than three percentage points (Chart 2a), the most restrictive moves in the postwar period up to that time. However, through most of the period, the moving twelve month growth of the monetary base remained between 6% and 7% (Chart 1a). Judged by money market conditions, policy was contractive, but growth of the base indicated an expansive policy that added to inflationary pressures. In July 1969 growth of the base began to decline. At the start of the recession, in December, the moving twelve month growth of the base had fallen to 3.7%, half the growth rate reached in the previous December. Despite clear recognition by the FOMC in the winter of 1970 that a recession had started, and a decisive effort to reduce the funds rate and increase free reserves, annual growth of the monetary base remained about 4% until July 1970 (Chart 1b).[8]

The focus on financial market conditions and short-term interest rates remained. In the 1950s rates on federal funds had ranged between 1/2 and 4 percent. By the mid 1960s, federal funds reached 5 1/2%, and by 1969, this rate was above 9% (Chart 2a). Much of the increase reflected the higher rate of inflation in the late 1960s. To many members of the FOMC, however, the connections between money growth, inflation, and interest rates were obscure, and the pressures for lower interest rates from government, homebuilders and others were apparent. Also, there was considerable confusion or continued lack of clarity about the distinction between nominal and real interest rates. And, like many academicians, several members of the FOMC seem to have believed that expansive monetary policy could keep interest rates from rising at all maturities.

THE EARLY 1970s

The events of the late 1960s, and the impending change of chairman, brought another reexamination of operating procedures. Beginning in 1969, a new committee on the directive, chaired by Governor Maisel, restudied the old issues.

Maisel's views differed from those of the monetarist critics in several respects. He wanted an activist policy based on forecasts of the future path of the economy, and he believed that guideposts and incomes policy would be required to lower inflation. But, he accepted or shared many of the external criticisms of policy procedures. He recognized that the proviso clause, introduced to avoid excessive concentration on money market conditions, was ineffective because it was ignored. The Federal Reserve's public posture emphasized broad, wide ranging consideration of many tendencies in the economy, as reflected in statements about looking at many different variables. In practice, the focus was much narrower. Much of the concern remained on money market conditions. These did not reflect very accurately either changes in the principal monetary aggregates or, more importantly, changes in real GNP, inflation, and other variables of principal concern to households and businesses.

At the start of the 1970s, principal measures of inflation had

---

[8]Chart 3 above shows that growth of M-1 slowed beginning in January 1969.

reached annual rates between 5 and 6 percent. Moreover, whether measured by interest rates, money wages, or unit labor costs, there was increased evidence that the public anticipated continued inflation; the nominal values of each of these measures increased relative to the real values, reflecting current and anticipated inflation. One result was greater skepticism about policymakers commitments to price stability as shown by the response of inflation to policy changes. The brief slowing of the economy, following slower growth of money in 1966, had been followed by a sharp reduction in the rate of price increases. From a peak annual rate of increase of 7.2 percent in February, the (annualized) monthly CPI declined to -1.2 percent in January 1967. The six month moving average shows a similar but smaller decline from a peak of 4% (annual rate) in January 1966 to a trough of 1.3% (annual rate) in February 1967. In less than a year, inflation had been nearly eliminated without a recession. The 1969-70 recession also produced disinflation, but only for a short time. The peak six-month moving average of the CPI reached 6.6% in November 1969. A trough at 3.5% in March and April 1971 was short-lived. By May this measure of inflation was back to 4%, the peak rate reached in the 1966-67 experience.

The Nixon administration came into office in January 1969, promising to lower inflation without a recession. President Nixon's memory of his narrow defeat in the 1960 election in which recession was believed to have played a part, public memories of Republican policies in 1929 to 1933, and a desire to avoid incomes policies were important for this commitment. Alas, no one had a clear idea about how it was to be done. Stein (1988, pp. 148-54).[9]

The FOMC shared the administration's goal of lower inflation but differed both about treatment and procedures. Some believed that anticipations had become firmly rooted and could be removed only by decisive action. Others thought, or hoped, that a moderate policy would work or believed it would work if accompanied by some informal system of price and wage controls or incomes policy that the administration opposed. Maisel (1973, p. 232). In addition to this difference in beliefs, there were continuing differences about the relative importance to be given to monetary aggregates, interest rates and money market conditions. To resolve some of these differences, the Board voted in

[9]Herbert Stein was a member of the Council of Economic Advisers at the time. He became chairman in 1971 following the resignation of Paul McCracken.

April 1969 to raise reserve requirements, hoping to give a shock to expectations while leaving policy unchanged. The reserves removed by the change in the reserve requirement ratio were to be restored by open market operations. The effect of these changes was to leave the growth of the monetary base (St. Louis) unaffected, but to change the relative growth rates of money and bank credit (bank earning assets). By August, it was clear from data published at the time that money growth was continuing to expand but bank credit had slowed. Maisel (1973, p. 242). The difference in response is consistent with the expected effects of an increase in reserve requirement ratios on money and bank credit. Throughout the summer and fall, the FOMC continued to vote for "maintaining prevailing firm conditions." Free reserves of -$850 and -$1000 million, and a monthly average federal funds rate of 8.6 to 9.2 show this policy (Chart 2a). As noted earlier, the monetary base shows a highly expansive policy until June followed by a shift toward contraction.

Regulation Q ceilings added to the problem of interpreting some principal monetary aggregates. With market rates far above the 5.5% ceiling rate on time deposits, banks and thrifts lost time deposits to competing instruments. Some of the deposits returned as demand deposits. The substitution of demand for time deposits raised the amount of reserves that banks were required to hold and appeared as an increase in M_1, currency and demand deposits, relative to M_2, which included time deposits. At the time, the ceiling on interest rates applied to all time deposits, irrespective of denomination, so large depositors held Euro-dollar deposits in foreign branches in place of negotiable certificates of deposits at domestic branches. This substitution lowered average reserve requirements at money center banks, so banks facilitated the substitution.

The January 15, 1970 meeting of the FOMC was the last meeting chaired by Martin. The directive prepared at that meeting, for the first time, mentioned monetary aggregates as a target of policy. The directive expressed a "desire to see a modest growth in money and bank credit", but the following sentence called for the maintenance of firm conditions in the money market.

The directives for the rest of 1970 appear to give about equal weight to monetary aggregates and financial market conditions. A typical directive called for maintaining money market conditions consistent with moderate growth in money and bank credit. The directives did not specify what was meant by moderate growth and did not single out any particular monetary aggregate that the Manager was supposed to monitor. Maisel (1973, p. 254) notes that the intention was to pay attention to a three month average growth of money and credit, with main emphasis on M_1. Between meetings the Manager was to use money market conditions as an operating target. The staff was responsible for reconciling the operating target and the monetary indicator by relating the two empirically. At FOMC meetings, the members were to choose consistent targets based on staff estimates and other data. "[A] movement in money market conditions would not mean that monetary policy had changed. Policy was to be measured by movements in the monetary aggregates." (Ibid, p. 254).

The change in the directive to recognize monetary aggregates was not reversed. From 1970 on, with few exceptions, one or more monetary aggregates is mentioned in the directions to the Manager. By the mid-1970s, the FOMC chose explicit numerical targets for one or more monetary aggregates at every meeting. There were also numerical targets for the federal funds rate, and these continued to serve as an operating target for the Manager.

Three difficulties soon became apparent. First, the federal funds target specified a narrow band within which the Manager was supposed to keep the funds rate. This was an operationally feasible task. If the rate was too high, the Manager bought securities and increased reserves; if it was too low, he sold securities, reducing reserves. The growth of the monetary aggregates became available only after a lag, and short-term changes were not easy to interpret. There were always two or more aggregates mentioned, and their monthly or quarterly changes would often go in different directions. Changes were subject to large seasonal and random variation. Hence, judgment often had to be used to decide whether to adjust the federal funds rate target or permit the growth rate of one or more of the monetary aggregates to remain above or below the specified range. Second, forecasts of the future path of the economy and of the monetary aggregates are subject to large errors. Adjusting policy in response to forecasts may add rather than reduce variability (Friedman, 1953). This difficulty does not arise from the use of monetary aggregates. It is inherent in any discretionary policy based on forecasts, if the absolute size of forecast errors is sufficiently large or if the forecasts are biased, as the inflation forecasts proved to be. The low reliability of the forecasts provided a reason for delaying or for making very small, cautious adjustments in the funds rate. Third, neither the FOMC, nor the Congress, nor successive administrations was clear about the goals of monetary (or economic) policy. There were frequent changes in the real and nominal variables of interest, and the weight given to a particular variable shifted. Prices, the balance of payments, interest rates, housing, unemployment, economic growth, and money market conditions are prominent in the discussion at different times. Neither the Manager nor the FOMC had a clear vision about the interrelation of these goals or the precise way in which they could be affected by changes in money and interest rates. A short-run focus could account for the choice of real variables as targets, but there is not much recognition of the relation of the short-run changes to longer-term changes in prices and nominal values.

This uncertainty was not confined to the Federal Reserve. Academic economists and other outsiders who urged activist discretionary policies often minimized the longer-term consequences, perhaps because they thought inflation could be prevented "later" or because they expected to trade off unemployment for inflation. The Federal Reserve staff had to face the problem. The old procedures used judgments about tone, feel and their relation to free reserves; the new procedures required the staff to supply estimates of the demand for money, and the magnitude and timing of the responses of unemployment, output, prices, housing, balance of payments and many other variables to policy actions.

There is no indication that the Fed considered an explicit policy rule. Two options were available for discretionary policy. One, based on the supply function of money, would have controlled the monetary base, or total reserves, and allowed interest rates and later exchange rates to vary as required to keep some measure of money growth near the prescribed path. The second required estimates of the demand for money and the links between the money market interest rate that the Federal Reserve could control and interest rates on a broad spectrum of assets of different duration and risk.

The Fed chose the latter course and began to implement what is known as the two-stage procedure.[10] Under this procedure, there are

---

[10]There are many descriptions of this procedure. I follow Lombra and Moran (1980). See also Karamouzis and Lombra (1989). The two-stage procedure has

short- and long-term targets. Twice a year the FOMC chooses monetary targets that are thought to be consistent with its longer-term objectives, such as lower inflation or stable economic growth at relatively stable prices. Stage one is the choice of a strategy or path for the economy for the next 4 to 6 quarters and the set of monetary targets consistent with this path. The choice is based on information that each member brings to the meeting and on forecasts of the consequences of alternative policies prepared by the Board's staff. At each subsequent meeting, the FOMC chooses a short-term target, usually the federal funds rate, and the associated target for various definitions of money (or monetary aggregates) that are believed to lie on the path leading to the longer-term monetary target. The choice of the short-term targets is the second stage of the procedure.

Prior to each meeting the staff uses the longer-term growth rates of money chosen by the FOMC, and assumptions about fiscal policy and other predetermined variables, as policy inputs to develop forecasts of the principal non-financial variables. These forecasts take the financial variables as givens. At the same time, other staff members at the Board, assisted by the staff of the New York bank, develop forecasts of financial variables taking the forecasts of real variables as givens. Short-term interaction, or simultaneity, between deviations of monetary and real variables from their anticipated paths are presumed to be small.

During the 1970s and 1980s, the Federal Reserve maintained the two stage procedure but changed the implementation on two occasions. From 1970 through September 1979, implementation and control centered on the federal funds rate. From October 1979 to sometime in the summer or fall of 1982, non-borrowed reserves received increased emphasis, and the federal funds rate was changed more frequently and, at times, by larger amounts in response to deviations of non-borrowed reserves from the path

---

been criticized not only by those who wanted to control money but also by those who favored discretionary policy based on forecasts. See especially Friedman (1975) who used a Poole (1970) type analysis to show that the choice between the use of targets for reserves or interest rates depends on the variance of errors in equations relating each of these variables to nominal output. Analysis of this kind assumes more reliable knowledge of structure than economists have been able to provide. Friedman criticized the two-stage procedure on several grounds, including dependence on tight control of money and the assumption that current output is independent of current monetary policy action. See also Friedman (1977).

believed to be consistent with short-term policy. Borrowed reserves replaced non-borrowed reserves in 1982 and has retained a role in the implementation of short-run policy since that time.

Problems with Federal Reserve Procedures

Many critics have concentrated on the inefficiency of the two stage procedure. Benjamin Friedman (1975, 1977) develops these criticisms fully. The implicit or explicit suggestion in many of the criticisms is that a more efficient procedure for linking short- and long-term forecasts would make a substantial difference. Many of the critics favored replacement of the two stage procedure with a procedure that relied on a simultaneous solution for money, output, prices and interest rates. Karamouzis and Lombra (1989) found, however, that neglect of simultaneity was not a major source of error. They report that the Federal Reserve reacted to the lagged deviations of money growth from target, but the response was relatively small and was delayed. A principal reason for the delayed reaction is that, typically, the Fed's initial interpretation of the deviation of money from target is that the demand for money shifted. They act on the assumption that the monetary deviation is largely transitory and can be ignored when setting the federal funds rate. Their interpretation is correct at times, incorrect at others. The problem is to distinguish the two. Simultaneous estimation procedure would not separate permanent and transitory deviations. The problem of interpretation would remain.

A more basic problem lies in the use of a money market rather than a monetary strategy. In the money market strategy the control process centers on the federal funds rate. This rate is considered a principal determinant of other interest rates and the prices of assets relative to the prices of corresponding outputs. The transmission of monetary policy spreads, after a lag, from the federal funds rate to other interest rates, to asset prices, output and the demands for money and other assets. deLeeuw and Gramlich (1969). Changes in the federal funds rate are thought to be significant policy actions; changes in money are often interpreted either as random changes in the demand for money or as lagged responses to prior changes in interest rates. In common with the older, Riefler-Burgess tradition, the Federal Reserve observes the demand for borrowed (or non-borrowed) reserves at the posted federal funds rate. If deposit growth increases, the demand for reserves rises.

At first, the Federal Reserve satisfies demand by supplying reserves at the going federal funds rate. Persistent increases in the demand for reserves, to meet required reserves, may be followed by a decision to raise the federal funds rate. Following the decision, market interest rates would be expected to rise, slowing the growth of reserves relative to demand. The increase in the funds rate also increases member bank borrowing and, according to the hypothesis, subsequently reduces the quantity of money demanded.

As presented by Tinsely et al. (1982), the main features of the money market model can be reduced to a relation between the change in non-borrowed reserves, DNBR, and the change in the federal funds rate, DFF, given the discount rate. See, also, Karamouzis and Lombra (1989, Table 6). In simulations that study the longer-term consequences of various actions, the discount rate adjusts to the federal funds rate; in the short-term it is a policy variable that is fixed. Changes in the demand for money, time deposits and reserves are determined, up to a stochastic component, by DFF. The effect of changes in relative prices, income and wealth on the demand for these financial assets is shown as a shift in the intercept of the (linear) equations. This recursive model is not consistent with the best available theory and evidence.

A further deficiency of the money market model is the neglect of the broad spectrum of interest rates and asset prices that affect the demands for money and other financial assets. If changes in relative prices are tested one at a time, none may have a significant effect in a particular sample, yet the combined effect may influence the demand for money or change the supply of earning assets offered to banks. Anticipations change the relative yields on short- and long-term securities, changing the term structure of interest rates, desired money balances and the public's supply of earning assets to banks. These and other changes in relative prices are often a response to prior changes in money or to the anticipations of future changes or to the future effects of those changes. In the Board's short-term model, anticipations, relative prices and real wealth affect desired financial asset holding only by shifting the demand for money (or a monetary aggregate). Typically, these shifts are accommodated at an unchanged federal funds rates by supplying or withdrawing reserves and money.[11]

---

[11]Some Governors now regard changes in the term structure as an indicator of inflation, contrary to the staff model where long rates depend only on short

Further, it is incorrect to assume that interest rate changes spread from the federal funds rate to other interest rates. Often, the opposite is true; the Federal Reserve may be slow to respond to the forces changing open market rates. Changes in the expected rate of inflation, the productivity of capital, the public's supply of earning assets to banks, or firms' desired leverage can change longer-term rates relative to the Federal funds rate. As these examples suggest, the change in the term structure can have a real or nominal impulse. By fixing the federal funds rate and supplying or withdrawing base money, the Federal Reserve procedure assures that all real and nominal changes have a monetary effect.

To pursue one example, suppose the public, anticipating an increased return to capital or higher inflation, decides to borrow more. The public's supply of earning assets to banks increases, raising interest rates on the credit market. The Federal Reserve interprets the change as an increase in the demand for money. Typically, it treats the change in demand as transitory, so it holds the federal fund rate by supplying additional reserves and money, thereby reinforcing the initial anticipation and encouraging additional borrowing. Similarly, reductions in the public's supply of earning asset to banks are interpreted as unanticipated shifts in the demand for money and are matched by reductions in the stock of money at an unchanged federal funds rate.

Failure to distinguish changes in the demand for money and changes in the public's supply of earning assets to banks is a main reason that money typically has increased relatively faster during periods of economic expansion than during recessions. Money growth has been procyclical, often reinforcing recessions and inflations. Charts 4a and 4b show that except for M_2 in the 1980s money growth is higher in each expansion than in the preceding recession. Also, from peak to peak, the rate of money growth increased, raising the average rate of inflation; the highest rates of growth occurred during expansions.

(Insert Charts 4a and 4b here)

In principle, it is entirely possible to avoid procyclical money growth using an interest rate target. If the target is adjusted promptly in response to changed anticipations of inflation and changes in

---

rates. I do not believe that this conflict has been resolved or that real and nominal changes in the term structure have been recognized in either the staff's or the Governors' interpretation.

Chart 4a
MEAN GROWTH RATE OF M-1
1960-1988

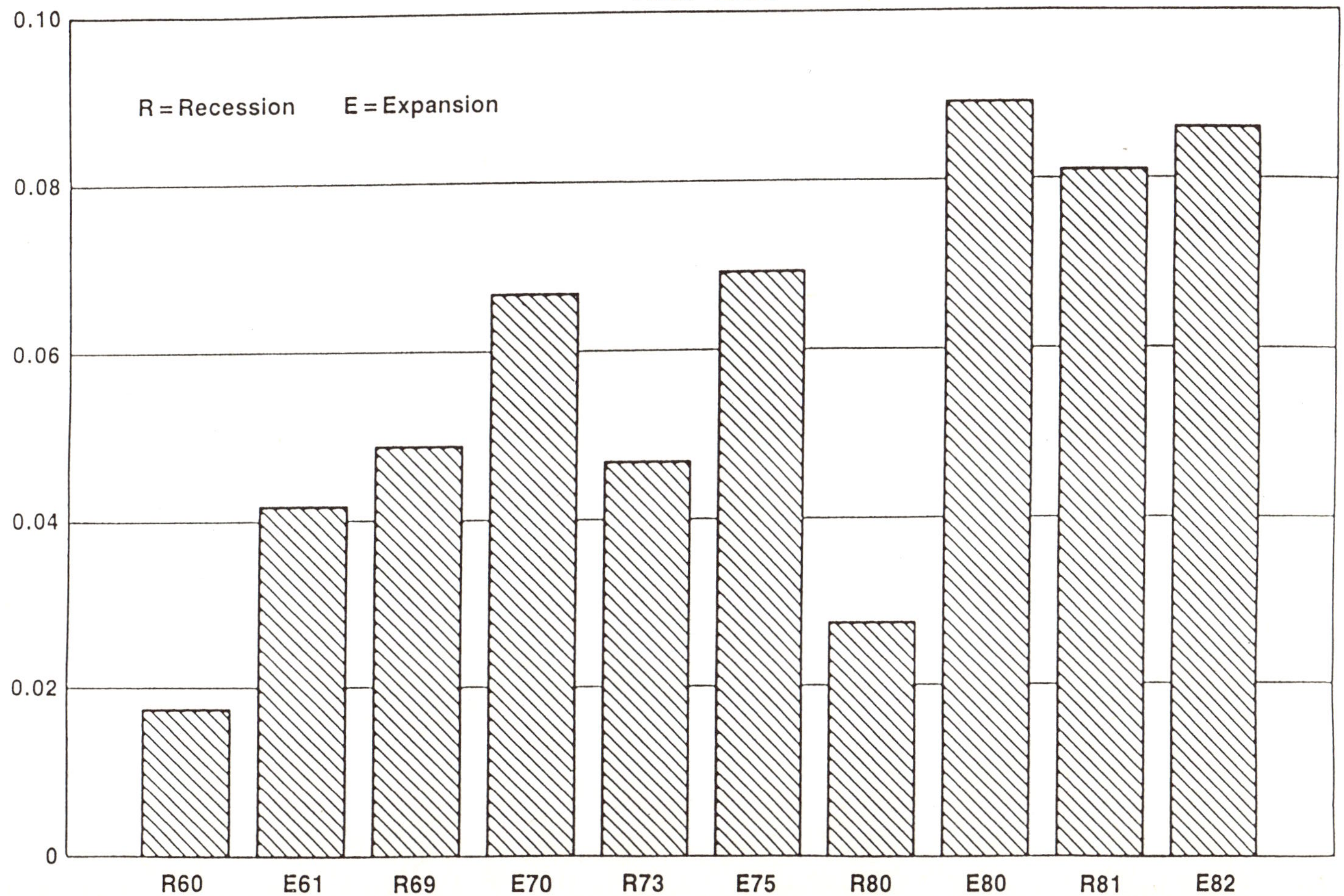

Chart 4b

MEAN GROWTH RATE OF M-2

1960-1988

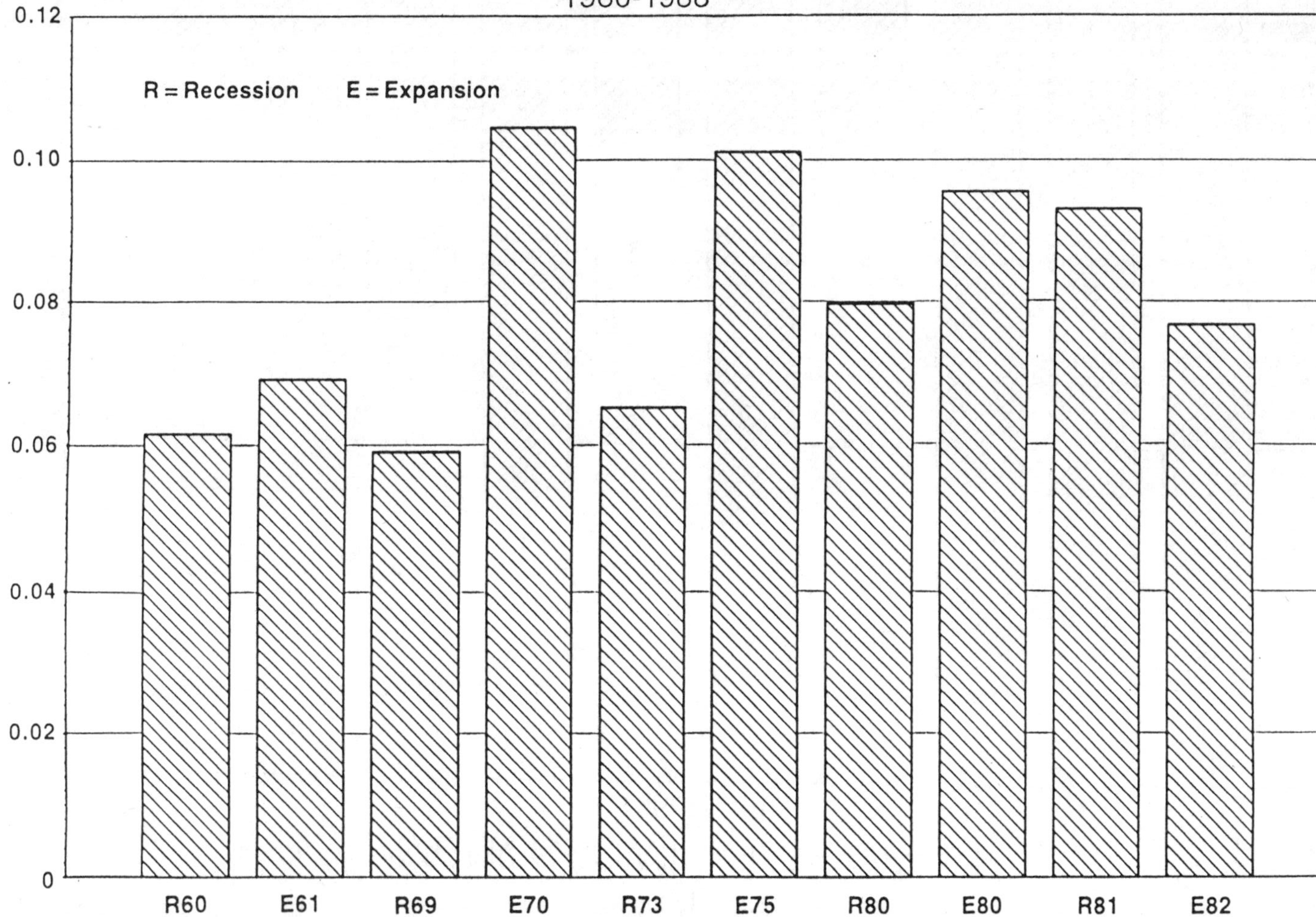

anticipated real returns, money growth responds less to procyclical changes in anticipated inflation and expansion. A central bank can, in principle, implement a stabilizing policy of this kind by giving greater weight to deviations of money growth from a non-inflationary path. In practice, it is difficult, but not impossible, to know how much the short-term interest rate should change. Evidence on inflation in Germany and Japan after the middle 1970s suggests that these countries have controlled inflation more successfully than the United States while implementing policy actions by setting short-term interest rates. And, Japan has achieved price stability or low inflation in recent years without experiencing a recession.

<u>On Hitting The Targets</u>

Charts 5a to 5c bring out the difference between the Federal Reserve's response to the federal funds target and the response to one of the money growth targets.[12] The federal funds (Chart 5a) rate is a monthly average. Chart 5b shows deviations of monthly growth of M_2 from the target. The fluctuations are large and erratic. During much of the period, the Federal Reserve relied on two or three month averages of money growth, so three-month moving averages of actual money growth in Chart 5c give a better indication of the Federal Reserve's response to deviations of money growth from short-term targets during the period 1974-78 than the monthly data in Chart 5b.

(Insert Charts 5a to 5c)

Two features stand out. First, almost all the deviations of money growth from target are positive during the period shown, and some are relatively large. Second, the Federal Reserve appears to have held to its federal funds rate targets and largely ignored the monetary targets throughout the period.

Why did the asymmetry in the responses of money and interest rates

---

[12]Targets were chosen for M_1, M_2 and M_3 and other aggregates at various times. I have used M_2. The detail would change, but the main conclusions here would be unchanged if I used M_1. In months when the Federal Reserve did not meet, the targets were unchanged; targets for these months are reported at the value for the previous month. Some of the data for actual values differ from data observed at the time because of revisions to the data. Data for the targets are taken from periodic Federal Reserve reports of its decisions.

Chart 5a

ACTUAL vs. PLANNED FED FUNDS RATE

3/1974 - 12/1978

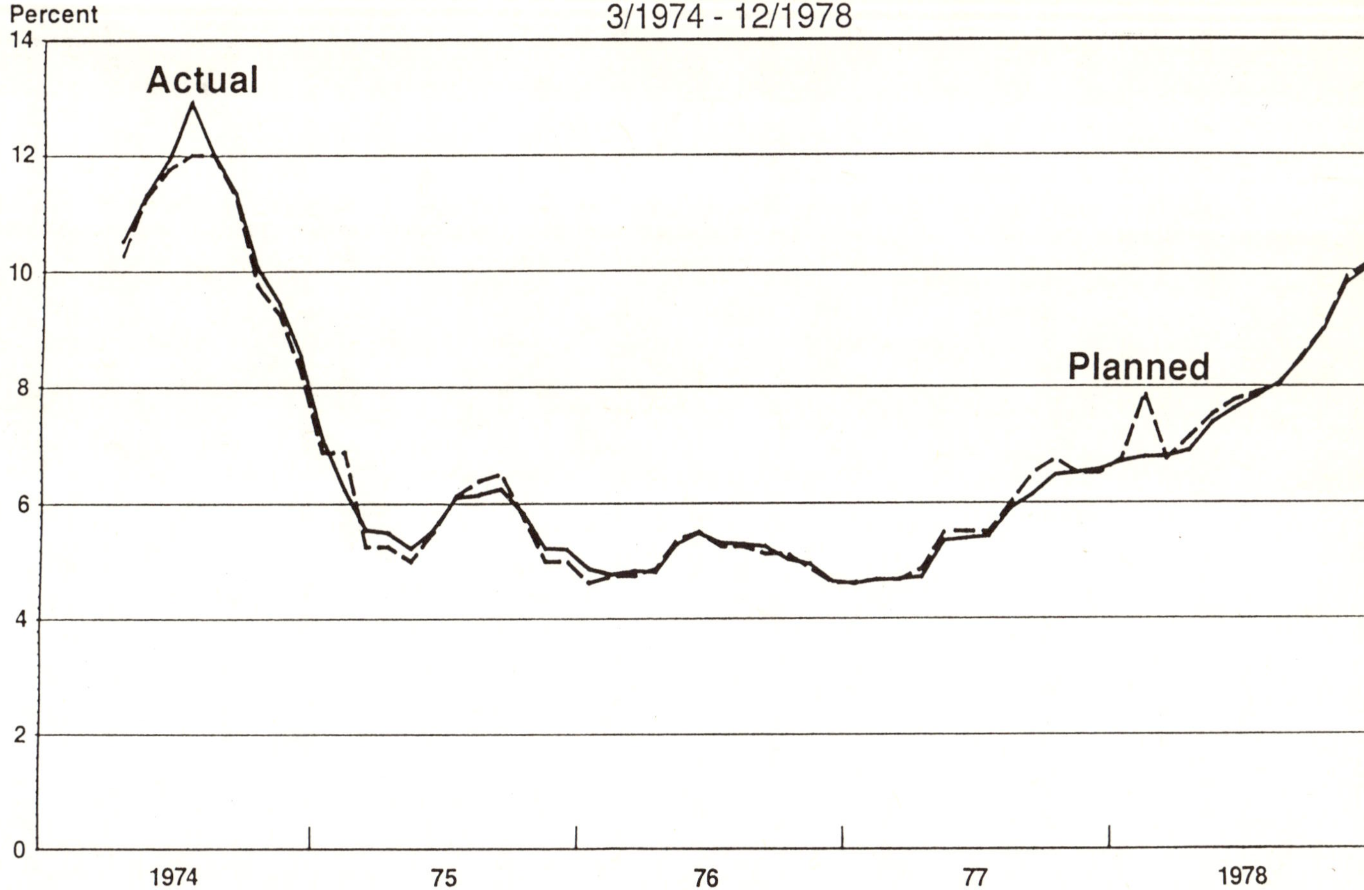

Chart 5b

ACTUAL vs. PLANNED GROWTH OF M-2

3/1974 - 12/1978

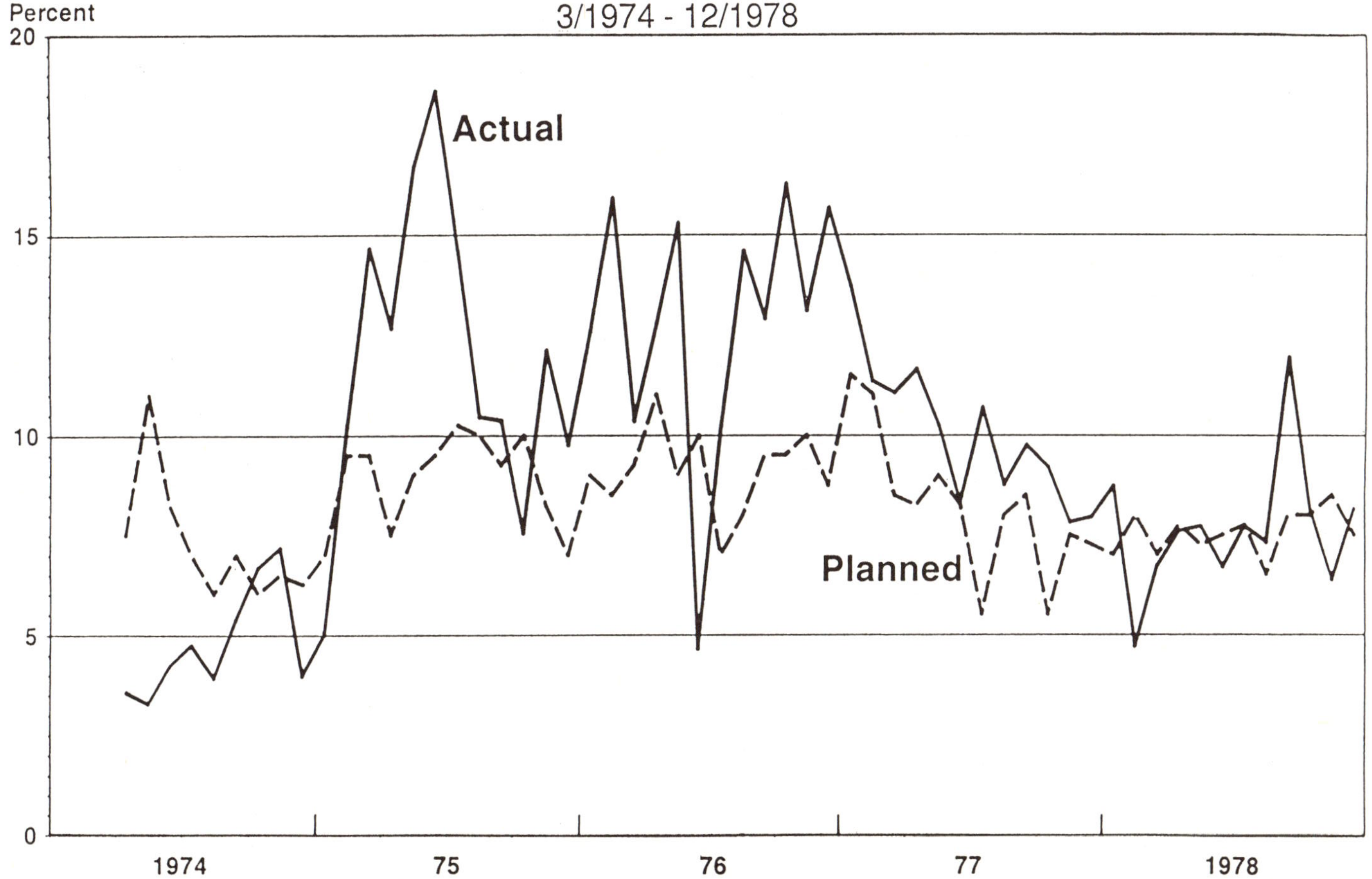

Chart 5c

ACTUAL vs. PLANNED M-2, 3 MONTH AVG.

5/1974 - 12/1978

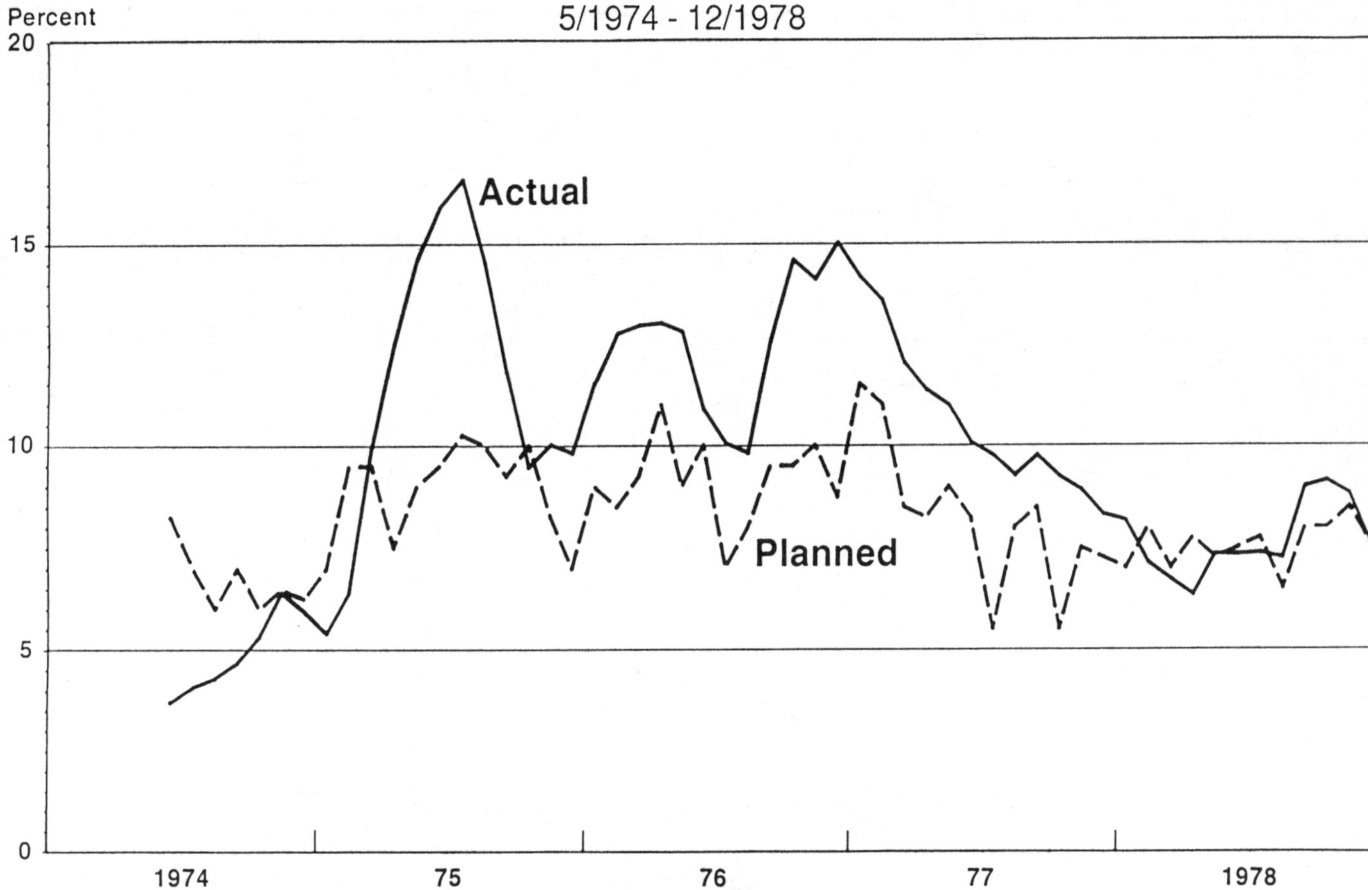

and the inflationary policy persist? The persistence of the deviations and their timing rule out unanticipated shocks, like the oil embargo of 1973 or the oil price increases of 1974 as a full explanation. An obvious explanation is that the Federal Reserve ignored the targets for money growth and concentrated on the federal funds rate. This would explain the comparative size of the deviations from targets, but it does not explain the systematic excess supply of money (relative to the target). A likely reason is that the public's supply of earning assets to banks and government borrowing to finance deficits was satisfied at unchanged interest rates. The Federal Reserve's analysis neglects the public's supply of earning assets to banks, so these changes would be a surprise. Evidence in charts 11a and 11b (below) shows that the Federal Reserve financed a higher share of the Federal debt in the 1970s than in earlier or later years.

The Federal Reserve would offer a different interpretation. On their interpretation of deviations of money growth from target, a persistent excess supply of money (and relatively small deviations from the funds rate target) suggests that the Federal Reserve repeatedly underestimated the demand for money during this period. On this interpretation, higher than expected money growth results from repeated upward shifts in the demand for money. We know that the Federal Reserve systematically underestimated inflation and growth of nominal GNP. The Federal Reserve continued to treat persistent increases in the demand for money as transitory changes (or as a permanent shift in desired portfolio unrelated to spending); by holding to the interest rate target, the Federal Reserve allowed the stock of money to increase with demand. Inflation rose more than their forecast.

The Federal Reserve hypothesis does not explain the errors adequately. Although the inflation forecast errors are consistent with the observed errors, estimates of the demand for money are not. Karamouzis and Lombra (1989, p. 43) computed the implied rates of change of actual and forecast values of output per unit of money, or monetary velocity, using staff forecasts of the demand for money. From 1973 to 1976, the Federal Reserve generally overestimated, and from 1976 to 1979 generally underestimated, velocity. This pattern of errors does not correspond to the errors in money growth, so neither unanticipated shifts in the demand for money (per unit of output) nor underestimation of the effects of inflation fully explain the errors in money growth.

We note, however, that the share of the debt financed by issuing base money rose when velocity was overestimated and declined when velocity was underestimated. If the changes in debt were unanticipated, they would explain some of the underestimate of earning asset supply and a slowly adjusting federal funds rate.

The most remarkable feature of the errors in forecasts of inflation and control of money growth is their persistence. The Federal Reserve permitted errors in the same direction to continue from meeting to meeting for years without recognizing that their procedures were flawed. Their narrow focus on interest rates and money market conditions appears to have misled them in the great inflation of the 1960s and 1970s as in the great depression of the 1930s.

Contributions of Discretionary Policy

The forecast errors for velocity and money provide a check on the contributions made by Federal Reserve discretionary policy. A main argument for discretionary policy is that the Federal Reserve can offset shifts in the demand for money by changing the stock of money. We have seen that this analysis fails if there are unanticipated permanent and transitory shifts in the demand for money, e.g. if the demand for money can be approximated by a random walk with drift. Karamouzis and Lombra (1989, pp. 41-2) computed the correlation between deviations of money and velocity from their respective target or anticipated paths to learn how serious the failure is. For the period 1973-82 the correlation based on quarterly data is -0.65, so the percentage of the variance explained is about 42%. This overstates the effectiveness of policy. Part of the correlation is unrelated to efforts to offset shifts in the demand for money; it is a result of the gradual adjustment of desired money balances. Unanticipated increases in money growth temporarily increase money balances relative to output and lower velocity and its growth rate; unanticipated reductions in money growth temporarily increase velocity growth.

Like the changes in money, the combined effect of changes in money and velocity is procyclical. Unanticipated money growth has a positive effect on nominal GNP growth, as is well-known from many studies. This suggests that tighter control of money would have avoided some of the procyclical and inflationary consequences of discretionary policy.

Brunner and Meltzer (1983, pp. 88-94) used ARIMA models for money

(M_1), base money (B) and their respective velocities (V_1 and V_B) to test whether Federal Reserve discretionary actions are stabilizing or destabilizing on average. The ARIMA models decompose measures of money and velocity into systematic and random components. The formula for the variance of a sum can be exploited.

$$\text{Var } y = \text{Var } m + \text{Var } v + 2 \text{ cov}(m, v)$$

where y, m, and v are first differences in the logarithms of nominal GNP, money and velocity. Brunner and Meltzer (1983, Table 1) report that for 1953-80 and for the sub-period 1969-80, the covariance of the systematic components of M and V is positive using both M_1 and B as measures of money. A rule calling for constant money growth would have zero values for Var m and cov(m, v), so Federal Reserve actions appear to have increased variability in these periods relative to a rule calling for constant growth of M_1 or B. If we assume that Var v would be unaffected by reliance on a rule, the data suggest that a rule requiring constant growth of the base would have eliminated three-fourths of the variance of the systematic components. The variance of actual nominal GNP would have been reduced, but the reduction would have been smaller. The reason is that the random (or unanticipated) changes in velocity must be added to the variability of the systematic component. That is,

$$\begin{aligned}\text{Var } y = {} & \text{Var } m^* + \text{Var } v^* + 2 \text{ cov}(m^*, v^*) + \\ & \text{Var } e + \text{Var } q + 2 \text{ cov}(e, q)\end{aligned}$$

where e and q are the random components and m*, v* are the systematic components.

Under a rule requiring constant growth of the base, unavoidable variability in nominal GNP growth would be the sum of the systematic and random components of base velocity. We cannot be certain how the variability of base velocity growth would change under a monetary rule. The evidence in the cited study suggests that, under the assumptions made, a rule for constant base growth would have produced an error variance of 1.6% to 2.1% during the period 1953-80.[13]

---

[13]Three caveats should be mentioned. First, the Lucas critique applies. We cannot know how much the variance of velocity would change with a change in the monetary rule, but there is no reason to presume it would increase.

Federal Reserve Forecasts

An obvious comparison is between a hypothetical rule that has an error variance of 1.6% to 2.1% and the errors in Federal Reserve forecasts. Unfortunately, the time periods that have been studied are not identical, so the comparison is at best suggestive. The difference in the variances or root mean square errors is sufficiently large and the time periods overlap sufficiently to make the comparisons useful, however. Table 1 compares the variances of the hypothetical, constant base rule to the root mean square errors of Federal Reserve forecasts reported by Lombra and Moran (1980) and Karamouzis and Lombra (1989). The variance of actual GNP growth shown in the table is computed as the sum of the variances and covariances estimated by the ARIMA model used in Brunner and Meltzer (1983).

The data suggest that the variance of Federal Reserve forecast errors is lower than the variance of GNP growth but generally higher than the variance produced by a rule for constant base growth. Although one comparison cannot be decisive, the data provide no evidence that discretionary policy is more stabilizing than a rule.

TABLE 1: QUARTERLY ERROR VARIANCES FOR NOMINAL GNP GROWTH

Source	Period	Variance (%)
Federal Reserve	1973-82	4.2
Federal Reserve	1970-73	2.0
Constant Base Rule	1953-80	1.6
Constant Base Rule	1969-80	2.1
Actual GNP Growth	1969-80	5.9

Additional evidence supporting this conclusion is reported by McCallum (1988). McCallum compared adaptive rules that achieved price stability. His rule adjusts monetary base growth in response to past changes in velocity growth and past deviations of real output growth

---

Second, a constant growth rule may not be optimal. There is some evidence that an adaptive rule is superior. McCallum (1988). Third, ex-post separation into random and systematic components may be more reliable than can be done at the time. If so, the procedure overstates what can be achieved by discretion.

from a 3% trend. For the period 1954-85 (quarterly), the rule had a root mean square error of 2% while holding inflation close to zero. For comparison, McCallum reports that the variance of deviations of actual GNP growth from trend is 8.5% for this period.

Two possible sources of Federal Reserve errors are the model used to generate forecasts and the judgments used to adjust the model forecasts. Federal Reserve forecasting models have retained the IS-LM framework. The models have not incorporated rational expectations, open economy dynamics and other recent developments. Nor has the model incorporated a credit market. Comparison suggests, however, that Fed forecasts of GNP are as accurate as the forecasts from other models, including time series models that do not have any structure, IS-LM or other. Karamouzis and Lombra (1989), Meltzer (1987). Alternative models that incorporate recent developments may produce smaller errors, but it is not clear how much room exists for improvement in the quality of forecasts. The similarity of mean absolute errors from different models suggests that much of the remaining average error may be random variation. Some tests of the forecast errors support the conclusion that most of the remaining errors are random. Random variation is more likely to be reduced by a change in the policy rule that reduces variability by changing the variances and covariances of money and other variables than improvements in forecasting.[14]

TABLE 2: FORECAST ERRORS 1970-82

1970-73	Mean		MAE		RMSE	
	y	p	y	p	y	p
Current Quarter	0.4	-0.9	1.6	1.2	2.1	1.4
Next Quarter	0.8	-1.2	2.2	1.6	2.9	1.9
Four Quarters	1.6	-3.9	2.5	4.0	3.4	4.8
1973-82						
Current Quarter	0.0	0.5	3.1	1.4	3.7	1.9
Next Quarter	-0.5	0.9	3.5	1.7	4.4	2.3
Four Quarters*	-0.7	0.9	2.0	1.6	2.5	2.0

y and p are real GNP growth and inflation as measured by the GNP deflator
*For 1973-82, the errors are for the full four quarters ahead; for 1970-73, the error is for the particular quarter.
Source: Lombra and Moran (1980); Karamouzis and Lombra (1989).

[14]This should not suggest that all forecasts have the same errors. Robinson (1989) studied the properties of forecasting models for the demand for money, including models similar to the Fed staff model. She found significant differences, but none of the models produced errors that are small relative to the variance of nominal GNP.

Real GNP grows at an annual of 2 1/2% to 3 on average.[15] During the years 1970-73 and 1973-82, the GNP deflator rose at average rates of 5.7% and 8.1%. Table 2 shows the mean and mean absolute error (MAE) and the root mean square error (RMSE) for the Fed's quarterly forecasts for these periods. Forecast errors for the current quarter, the following quarter and the next four quarters are large relative to the average rates of change. It seems clear that the Federal Reserve forecast errors, like those of other forecasters, are large relative to the changes they attempt to forecast. Moreover, the forecasts appear to be biased. This is particularly true of the inflation forecasts; the mean error and the mean absolute error are similar, again indicating that the Federal Reserve persistently underestimated inflation during the period of rising inflation. The errors in the forecasts of real GNP suggest, as in Meltzer (1987), that on average the Federal Reserve cannot distinguish in the current quarter whether the economy is in a boom or recession in that quarter. With a mean absolute error of 3.1% and a mean long-term growth rate of 3%, on average forecasts would not be able to detect differences between zero and 6%. Much the same is true for forecasts four quarters ahead, a period more relevant for Federal Reserve discretionary action.

Errors in forecasting nominal GNP growth lie in the same range as the errors for real GNP growth. For 1973-82, Karamouzis and Lombra (1989, p. 21) show a mean absolute error for current quarter nominal GNP growth of 3.3% and a RMSE of 4.2%. The latter is more than twice the RMSE obtained for a similar period using a monetary rule that keeps the base rising at a constant rate.

The quality of the staff inflation forecast is shown in Chart 6. The chart shows the persistent bias in the forecasts that was discussed earlier. During the period of rising inflation, inflation was underestimated, and during the period of disinflation, inflation was overestimated.

(Insert Chart 6 here)

Forecasts of Money Growth

Each month the Federal Reserve staff forecasts the money stock using their model of the demand for nominal money. Evidence is now

---

[15]Actual growth 1973-82 is estimated to have been 1.6% compounded annually.

Chart 6

FORECAST ERRORS FOR GNP DEFLATOR

ONE AND FOUR QUARTERS AHEAD
ACTUAL - PREDICTED

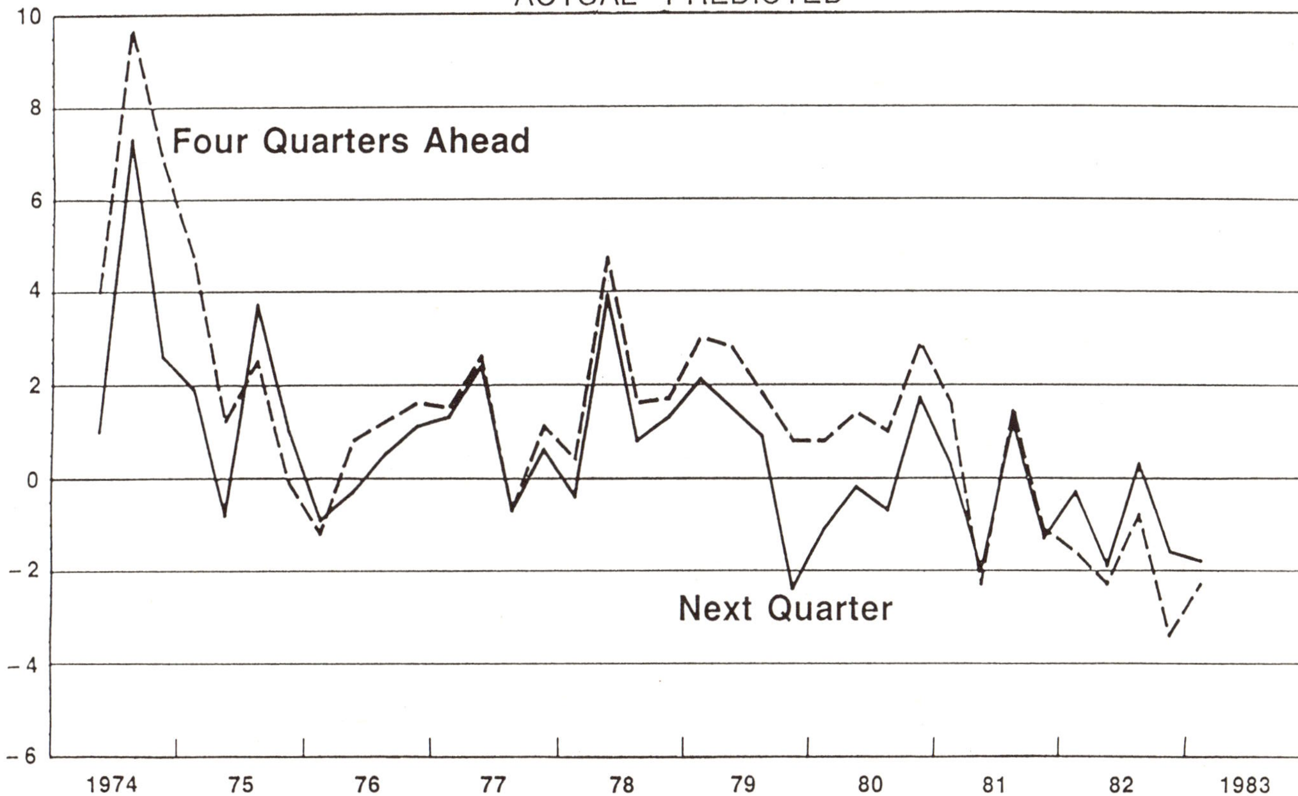

Source: Karamouzis and Lombra (1989) based on Federal Reserve greenbooks.

NEXT QUARTER ______

available on the quality of these forecasts and the quality of alternative forecasts based on the money supply model of Brunner and Meltzer (1964a, 1989) as developed by Rasche and Johannes (1987). Forecasts by the Board's staff and by Rasche and Johannes are actual forecasts made in advance of the events.

The principal conclusions to be drawn from this work are summarized by Rasche and Johannes (1987) and by Brunner and Meltzer (1983). First, monetary control is technically feasible for one or two quarter periods. An acceptable degree of control can be achieved using either the Board's procedure or the Johannes-Rasche procedure. Second, during much of the period, lagged reserve requirements increased the difficulty of controlling money growth. This conclusion is accepted by the Board's staff. Lindsey <u>et al</u>. (1981). Lagged reserve requirements have been all but abandoned. Third, traditional operation of the discount window lowers the degree of monetary control. A penalty rate system for discounting would enhance control. Fourth, long-run control can be achieved about as well by controlling either the monetary base or bank reserves. Control of the monetary base increases control of money in the short-run (relative to control of bank reserves). Fifth, forecast errors are not substantially different following the 1979 and 1982 changes in control procedures or before and after deregulation. The Rasche-Johannes procedure appears to be robust to these changes. Rasche and Johannes (1987, p. 12).

<u>Why Is Monetary Control So Poor?</u>

Rasche and Johannes (1987, p. 187) conclude that, by using a time series forecasting procedure, errors in controlling M_1 can be reduced to two-thirds of one percent per annum and for M_2 to one-half of one percent. To achieve these results, the Federal Reserve would have to control the monetary base; that is, they would have to maintain tight control of the size of their balance sheet. These results are based on data for the relatively variable period 1979-85, when the financial system experienced deregulation and deep recession. The Federal Reserve staff does not challenge these results, but they claim that better control can be obtained using judgment and the demand side model.[16]

[16]The Board staff criticizes the Rasche-Johannes procedure for using an endogenous variable, the base, as the control variable. They do not establish a bias but limit their criticism to a potential bias. Rasche and

Lindsey et al. (1981).

Actual control errors are much larger than the errors shown in these studies. According to staff estimates in Lindsey et al. and to Rasche and Johannes the Federal Reserve could achieve better control of money growth. Two complementary explanations of their failure to improve control have been offered. One focuses on the perceived short-term cost. The other raises broader issues about the use of discretionary policy. I discuss each in turn.

Charts 5a to 5c, above, show that the Federal Reserve kept the actual level of the federal funds rate close to the target level but tolerated relatively large deviations from the money growth target. The degree of control of interest rates and money differ in other periods, but the general pattern repeats. There is considerable evidence that this pattern reflects the Fed's reluctance to permit relatively short-term changes in credit market interest rates. Lombra and Moran (1980) report that, at times, the FOMC chose targets for money and the federal funds rate that were inconsistent with the staff's forecasting model. A principal reason appears to be that the members were reluctant to allow interest rates to rise as much as required by staff forecasts. They hoped to achieve lower inflation by reducing money growth but were reluctant to let interest rates rise by relatively large steps.

This is an example of money market myopia. With hindsight there is little doubt that neither long nor short-term nominal rates of interest would have reached the levels experienced in 1981-82 -- 15% to 20% -- if the Federal Reserve had prevented inflation. The same is true of ex post real rates, since the first effects of the monetary contraction of the early 1980s raised real rates of interest. During the early 1980s, ex post real rates of interest reached the highest levels in this century. Failing to permit market rates to rise sufficiently in the 1960s and 1970s required larger increases in nominal and real rates later. The levels reached by these rates could not have been predicted at the time, but it must have become clear that the level of interest rates increased with inflation. Yet, the Federal Reserve continued its policy procedure until 1979.

A second reason for continued use of inefficient control procedures and imprecise announcements has been suggested by Cukierman and Meltzer

---

Johannes carry out detailed tests that suggest that any bias is trivial.

(1986) and by Stein (1989). These authors show analytically that, at times, central banks prefer arrangements that obscure current or planned actions. The reason is that the central bank may wish to change policy without announcing or revealing the change. This is particularly true when the central bank desires an expansion of real activity. Unanticipated changes in money can be made larger and more potent for real variables if the public has difficulty interpreting central bank actions and announcements. If the public can accurately forecast policy or readily distinguish between permanent and transitory changes in money growth, opportunities to affect the pace of real activity would be severely limited. However, there are limits to the central bank's ability to exploit its opportunity to mislead the public. When the central bank chooses to reduce inflation, costs of disinflation depend on past performance and on the credibility of its statements. The more skeptical the public is about the central bank's commitment to disinflation, the higher the cost of disinflation. Hence, maintaining a stock of credibility for the future restricts the tolerable inefficiency of control procedures and the imprecision of announcements today.

THE INFLATION PROBLEM

The decade of the 1970s was a period of unprecedented inflation for the (mainly) peacetime U.S. economy. The average rate of increase of the GNP deflator from 1969 to 1979, 7.0%, is above the 6.1% average for the 1940s that includes a major war. Growth of money remained high, on average, for the decade. The monetary base rose at a compound annual rate of 7.7%, and M_2 rose at a compound rate of 9.3 from December 1969 to December 1979.

In Martin's last year as Chairman, the GNP deflator rose by 5.5%. Arthur Burns' public statements before taking office as Chairman showed him to be not only opposed to inflation but opposed to policies that produced inflation. In office, he behaved very differently. The inflation rate averaged 7.0% during his seven years as chairman. As a professor, he had criticized the Kennedy and Johnson administrations' reliance on wage-price guidelines. In office, he became a leading advocate of informal controls on prices and wages. Stein (1988, p. 155).

In the 1968 campaign, President Nixon had promised to reduce inflation with only a moderate rise in unemployment. Since economists are far from certain about how to deliver that result, the administration was unable to announce and follow a coherent policy. At the Fed, Burns preached against inflation and the problem of inflationary anticipations while conducting a monetary policy that increased inflation and sustained the anticipation that inflation would increase. As we have seen, the Federal Reserve raised the growth rates of the base and money within a few months of Burns' appointment as Chairman (February 1970), so at the time monetary policy did not contribute to the administration's desired reduction in inflation. Chart 1b shows that, during Burns' term in office, the annual growth rate of the monetary base remained above 7% most of the time. Burns' (1978) speeches show a clear understanding of the critical role of price and wage anticipations in the inflation process, but he attributed the failure of anticipations to decline in periods of unemployment to recent changes in the wage-price process and ignored inflationary monetary policy. To counter these changes, Burns (and many others) believed government had to intervene with guidance or control of wages and prices.

Burns' study of the business cycle at the National Bureau of Economic Research gave him an eclectic view of economic processes that fits harmoniously with the eclectic view at the Federal Reserve. He found it easy to argue publicly that fiscal policy, full employment, the spread of unemployment compensation, cost-push, a general inflationary bias in the economy and other forces were the main causes of inflation. He seemed to find no inconsistency in warning about the dangers of inflation, while claiming that "monetary policy has provided the funds needed for a good expansion of production and employment." (1978, p. 152) His speeches from his years as Chairman are filled with discussions of the various causes of inflation and warnings about the costs of inflation. If he believed that the Federal Reserve had an important influence on inflation, he was reluctant to say so.[17]

A further problem in the early 1970s was that Burns had accepted the Chairmanship of the Committee on Interest Rates and Dividends and membership on the Cost of Living Council. Both had been established under the wage and price control program. The Committee was supposed to

---

[17]Stein (1988, p.154) states that Burns believed that monetary policy could facilitate expansion if other conditions were "right."

monitor interest rates and dividends but had no authority to control them, whereas the Council had authority to control wages and prices. If interest rates rose, Congress was likely to press for more binding controls. Burns (1978, p. 139) opposed mandatory controls on interest rates. One way to avoid controls was to restore the policy followed during the early Johnson administration--keep interest rates from rising, at least for a time, by a combination of monetary growth and direct pressure on banks. That may explain why the Federal Reserve increased the growth rate of money during the price control period in 1972 and early 1973. Since the expansive monetary policy was in accord with the administration's desire to lower unemployment in an election year, no criticism came from that side. Stein (1988, p. 184). The growth rate of money in the second half of 1972 was the highest in the postwar period up to that time.

The experiment with controls failed to lower inflation. By hiding the inflation, it may have encouraged the Federal Reserve to follow more expansive monetary policies, adding to subsequent inflation. What is certain is that after controls were removed, broad based measures of inflation were higher in every year from 1974 through 1982 than before controls were in place. Countries that followed less expansive monetary policies and avoided price controls--notably Japan, Germany and Switzerland--did not share this fate. In these countries inflation rates declined in the late 1970s and by the end of the decade were below the rates at the start. These foreign economies were subject to many of the same shocks that affected the U.S. economy, particularly the rise in oil and food prices in the 1970s that were often blamed for U.S. inflation. They experienced currency revaluation, not devaluation, at the start of the fluctuating exchange rate period. This difference was a consequence of the inflation, not as is often suggested, the cause of a change in relative prices and country price levels.

The oil embargo in the fall of 1973, and the subsequent oil price increases in 1974, struck an economy that had been stimulated by rapid expansion of the monetary aggregates in earlier years. In the winter of 1973, prior to the oil shock, the FOMC directives called for slower growth in the monetary aggregates. M_2 growth fell from a peak rate of 12.2% for the twelve months ending in January 1973 to 6.2% for the twelve months ending January 1974. M_2 growth continued to fall slowly in 1974 until it reached a trough of 5.25% in January 1975. (See Chart 5c)

Twelve month growth of the monetary base shows a small decline at the end of 1973 and a rise in 1974 (see Chart 1b). The movement of the base is more consistent with the intent of Federal Reserve policy, as expressed in the minutes of the period. By the fall of 1974, the Fed was seeking faster growth of the monetary aggregates despite the high rate of price increase for the year.

One problem with the conduct of policy in 1974 arose from confusion between levels and rates of change of prices and output. An increase in oil prices raises costs of production and lowers the efficient level of output. Once the price level increase is absorbed, the measured rate of price change returns to the path consistent with monetary growth and the growth rate of output. The shock reduces the level of output; since the decline in output (and rise in prices) does not occur instantly, measured rates of change are affected temporarily. The loss of output is a permanent change in level, but there should be no lasting effect on the growth rate of output.

Most policy discussions ignored the difference between inflation--defined as the maintained rate of price change--and the one-time increase in the price level that caused a temporary increase in reported measures of monthly or annual rates of price change. Also ignored was the distinction between a cyclical recession and a permanent reduction in the level of output.[18] Those who were most concerned about "recession" favored a more expansive monetary policy, although they failed to explain how the creation of money to increase nominal aggregate demand could offset the effects on output and employment of a reduction in the supply of oil. Those who were most concerned about the "inflation" induced by the rise in oil prices favored a reduction in money growth. They failed to explain why one-time changes in the price level--up or down--should not be permitted to stand. The change in price level is part of the means by which the community adjusted money wages, money balances and other nominal values to the wealth transfer that society had to bear. By shifting aggregate demand, changes in money growth made the adjustment to the supply shock more difficult to interpret. The reason is that, in the present state of knowledge, the

---

[18]One exception is a group of non-government economists known as the Shadow Open Market Committee. At its meeting on September 12, 1975, the Committee pointed out that the supply shock was not a recession so the losses could not be avoided by expansive policy.

effects of the change in aggregate demand on prices and output are difficult to separate from the responses to the supply shock.

Judging by the growth rate of nominal M_2, money growth first reinforced the shock then tried to offset it. The Fed kept on the brakes in 1974, then stepped on the accelerator in 1975. Between January 1975 and January 1976, the twelve month rate of increase in money rose from 5.25% to 12.5%. The National Bureau (NBER) dates the recession from November 1973 to March 1975. Using these dates, seasonally adjusted monthly M_2 growth falls during the recession until December 1974, then rises two months before the trough (Charts 5b and 5c).

Burns' tenure at the Federal Reserve ended with inflation higher than when he assumed office. For the eight years 1970-77 inclusive, the GNP deflator rose at a compound rate of 6.8% and the consumer price index by 6.5%. In his last speech as Chairman, Burns (1978, pp. 255-6) recognized the failure to control inflation, but he placed the blame on the policies of the 1960s and the lack of political will.

Burns replacement as Chairman was a successful businessman, G. William Miller. Miller lacked Burns' command of economic data and its interpretation, and he also lacked any clear view about what monetary policy should do or how it should be conducted. During Miller's relatively brief tenure -- February 1978 to August 1979 -- the Federal Reserve maintained an expansive policy, perhaps reflecting administration policy. The Carter administration was anxious to avoid recession and to reduce unemployment. It tried a number of informal controls on wages and prices and maintained controls on energy prices to control "inflation". Its major policy initiative was an effort to achieve a coordinated increase in aggregate demand by major industrial countries. At first, this initiative was not accepted by foreign governments; the rate of inflation rose in the U.S. relative to inflation rates abroad, and the dollar declined on the currency markets. By the last year of the Carter administration, 1980, broad based measures of inflation in the U.S. were at least twice the rates in Germany and Japan.

The decline in the dollar, rising inflation and rising criticism at home and abroad brought a change in policy at the end of the decade. In August 1979, with the measured rate of consumer price increase between 13% and 15% for the year, Miller became Secretary of the Treasury and Paul Volcker became Chairman of the Board of Governors.

<u>The 1979-82 Experiment</u>

On October 6, 1979, after a Saturday meeting, the Federal Reserve announced a change in the method used to conduct monetary policy. The new procedure was intended to be a better means of achieving previously announced growth rates of monetary aggregates. Greater emphasis was given to "the supply of bank reserves" and less emphasis to "confining short-term fluctuations in the federal funds rate" Federal Reserve (1979, p. 1). At the same time, the discount rate was increased by a full percentage point and some technical adjustments in reserve requirements were introduced.

The announcement was widely interpreted as the beginning of a "monetarist" experiment. In fact, the change in procedure was intended to be relatively modest, as the announcement hinted. Control of market interest rates was not abandoned, nor was tight control of total reserves or the monetary base considered. Two principal changes were made. A relatively large, one-time increase in market interest rates followed the announcement. The federal funds rate was raised from a mean of 11.5% at the September meeting to a range of 11.5% to 15.5% on October 6 (Chart 2b). Greater emphasis was given to the growth of non-borrowed reserves and less emphasis to tight control of the federal funds rate, as suggested by the wider range for federal funds agreed to at the meeting.

The experiment ended late in the summer of 1982. Chart 7a shows absolute deviations of actual from the planned or target federal funds rate and absolute deviations of actual from planned growth of M_2 for the period of the experiment. Federal funds rate deviations are measured as the difference between the average monthly rate and the mean target reported in the minutes for the same month. Deviations of M_2 growth are differences between a three month moving average and the mean of the high and low targets selected at each meeting. For comparison, Chart 7b shows the same two measures for the period preceding the policy shift.

(Insert Charts 7a & 7b here)

Comparison of the two charts shows the change in policy. In the earlier period, departures of the federal funds rate from its target, shown by the solid line, are much smaller and less frequent than in the subsequent period. Deviations of M_2 growth from target are not noticeably different under the new policy regime. The change in procedures appears to have increased the variability of the federal

Chart 7a

M2 vs. FED FUNDS DEVIATIONS

10/1979 - 10/1982

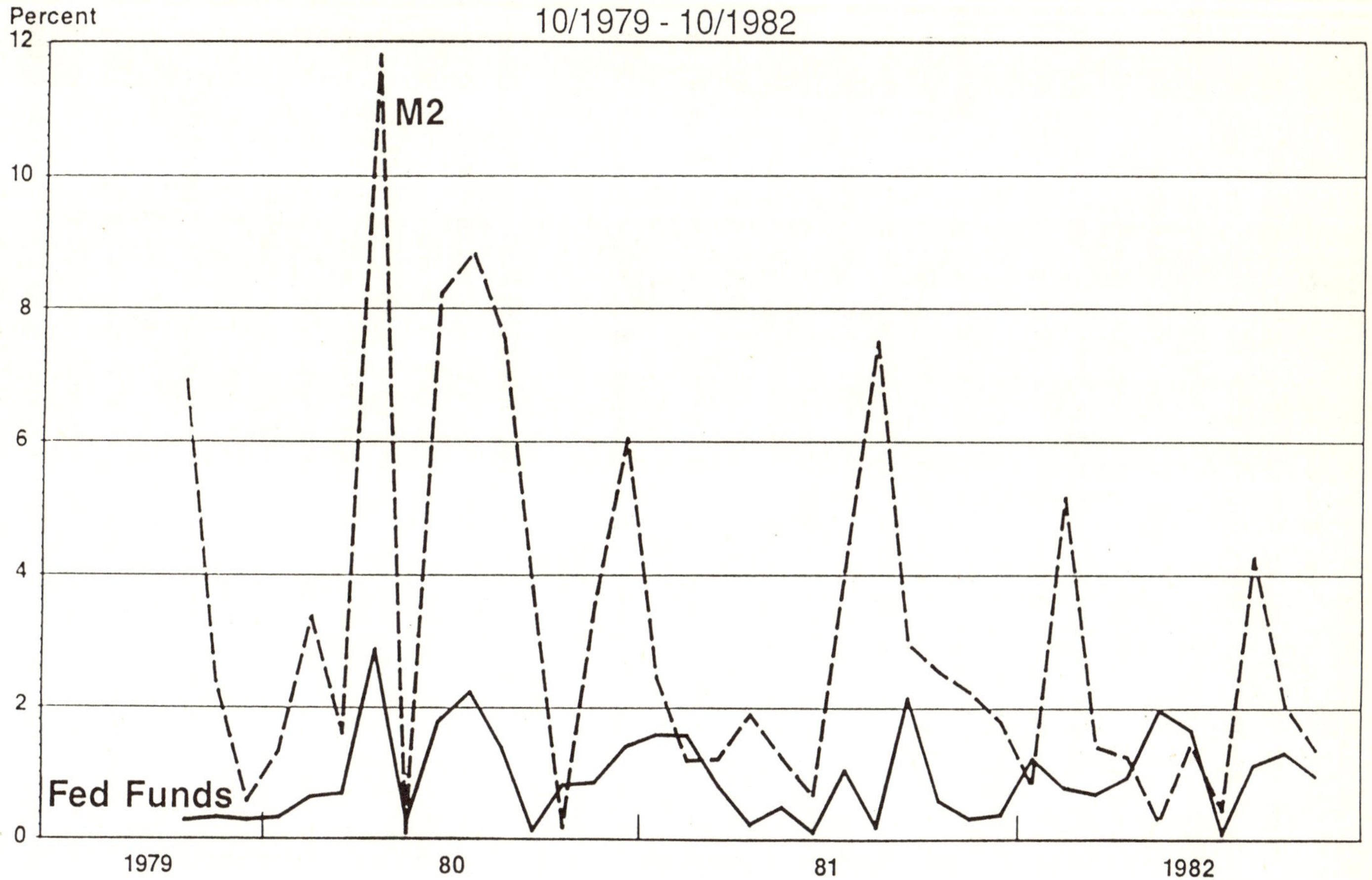

Chart 7b

M2 vs. FED FUNDS DEVIATIONS

3/1974 - 10/1979

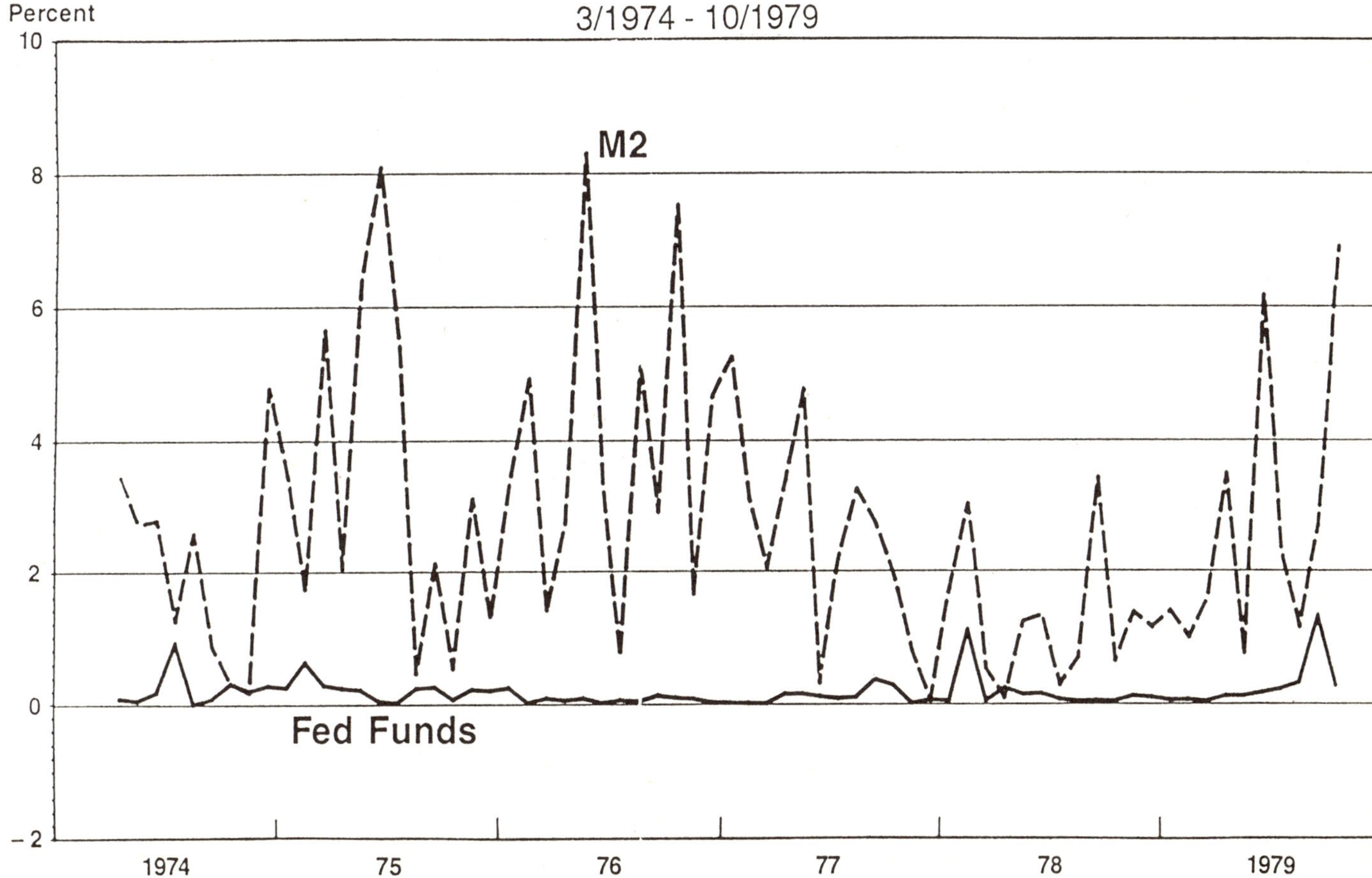

funds rate without reducing the variability of money growth (as measured by M_2). Large deviations from the planned targets for M_2 growth are common during the 1979-82 period. A considerable body of research suggests that these findings hold using other measures of interest rates and money. Table 3 reports comparative values of mean absolute deviations and standard deviations of the difference between the series shown in the two charts for several periods.

The table makes clear what the charts suggest. The new procedure was inefficient. Variability of the federal funds rate increased, but variability of money growth increased also. At least partly attributable to the change in policy procedures, the variability of ex post real rates of interest rates rose at all maturities. Table 4 shows 1 year and 10 year real rates computed by subtracting the rate of change of the GNP deflator.

The similarity of the standard deviations of real rates for 1 and 10 year securities is puzzling. The similarity persists during each sub-period. In part, the similarity reflects the use of a common measure

TABLE 3: DEVIATIONS FROM MONTHLY TARGETS

Period	Mean Absolute Difference		Standard Deviation	
	fed funds	M^2 growth[a]	fed funds	M^2 growth[a]
1/74 - 10/79	0.2	2.7	0.2	2.0
10/79 - 10/82	0.9	3.1	0.7	2.9
10/82 - 11/88	0.7	2.6	0.5	3.1
All months	0.6	2.7	0.6	2.7

[a] Actual growth is a three month average

of inflation, but this is far from a complete explanation.[19]

Several studies of the experiment are now available. See, inter alia Cook (1989), Karamouzis and Lombra (1989). From them, we learn that the experiment did not involve any major change in the staff's analysis of money and interest rates. To accommodate the change, the staff reversed the direction of causality between money and interest

[19]The relatively high average value of the ex post rates reflect some extreme values during the disinflation. For third quarter 1988, the values are 2.0% and 2.9%.

rates. Where the staff previously chose the desired change in the federal funds rate and accepted the associated change in money, they

TABLE 4: MEAN AND STANDARD DEVIATION (QUARTERLY) EX POST REAL RATES OF INTEREST (PERCENT)

Period	Means		Standard Deviation	
	1 year	10 year	1 year	10 year
1960/1 - 1973/1	1.8	2.2	1.2	1.2
1973/2 - 1979/3	-0.8	-0.5	2.2	2.8
1979/3 - 1982/3	4.2	3.7	4.3	4.8
1982/4 - 1988/3	5.0	6.5	2.5	2.6

now specified the target change in money and, in principle, accepted the associated change in the federal funds rate. Using the change in the federal funds rate obtained from their money model, the staff derived the changes in total reserves and member bank borrowing. Non-borrowed reserves (nbr) is the difference between total (tr) and borrowed reserves (br). The change in non-borrowed reserves, obtained in this way, became the operating target.

$$\Delta_{nbr} \equiv \Delta_{tr} - \Delta_{br}$$

Under the old operating procedure, changes in the demand for money were satisfied by changes in non-borrowed reserves and money at an unchanged federal funds rate. Under the revised procedure, non-borrowed reserves remained fixed (in principle), so the federal funds rate changed. In the short-run, ceteris paribus, an increase in the federal funds rate reduces the banks' quantity of borrowed reserves demanded; total and borrowed reserves fall, and the money stock falls. A reduction in the federal funds rate has the opposite effect.

The Federal Reserve continued to maintain the system of lagged reserve requirements under which banks used deposits held two weeks earlier as the base for computing required reserves on settlement dates. Given the stock of non-borrowed reserves, banks could obtain additional required reserves only by borrowing. Since the discount rate was often considerably lower than the federal funds rate and other market rates, banks had an incentive to delay adjustment of assets and deposits.[20]

In practice, the new control method proved to be a relatively modest change from past procedure . At each meeting, the Federal Reserve chose an average growth of nbr between meetings to meet the target for money growth. However, the federal funds rate did not vary to continually adjust the demand for reserves to the nbr target; the supply of non-borrowed reserves was not held at the level consistent with the target for money. Instead, the federal funds rate was allowed to rise or fall only when the Federal Reserve decided not to modify its nbr target, and nbr was allowed to deviate from target when the Federal Reserve did not choose to accept the required change in the federal funds rate. Cook (1989) notes that there were two types of discretionary change in the funds rate. One type of adjustment changed the distribution of Δnbr within the period without changing the average; the second adjusted the average growth of nbr to allow for unanticipated changes in reserves that occurred independently of money growth.[21]

Cook (1989) estimates that approximately two-thirds of the changes in the federal funds rate were discretionary during the 1979-82 period. This estimate is based on the average relation between changes in the federal funds rate and changes in borrowing, so the point estimate may be misleading. However, Cook shows that his model predicts movements of the federal fund rate during the period. If we accept his estimate, it follows that the change in control procedure was a smaller departure from previous practice than many observers believed at the time.

The new procedure added to uncertainty about what the Federal Reserve was doing. As noted earlier, variability of money, reserves and interest rates increased in part as a result of the uncertain and inefficient control procedure. Karamouzis and Lombra (1989, p. 51) report that "several members of the FOMC (in private communications) have indicated that the details and full ramifications of the changes in procedures...were not clear to them nor, in their judgment, to most FOMC members at the time [October 1979] or for months thereafter." A usual source of information, the speeches and writing of officials, did not

---

[20]In February 1984, after the experiment ended, the lag was reduced from two weeks to a few days.

[21]Examples are an increase in required reserves against liabilities not included in the money stock or an increase in excess reserves.

function or, worse, was unintentionally misleading.

One technical reason for the heightened variability and uncertainty was that the relation of borrowed reserves to interest rates is relatively unstable. Increases in borrowing were often difficult to interpret, so it was easy for the FOMC members and the staff to be skeptical of recommendations for action that depended on the borrowing equation. Under the federal funds targetting procedure, shifts in borrowing were accommodated most or all of the time; under the nbr procedure, shifts in borrowing were accommodated much of the time. This meant that the money target was an unreliable guide to desired Federal Reserve policy.

It should not be surprising that interest rates showed substantial response to deviations of money supply from target during the nbr targetting period. Market participants could not know, because the Federal Reserve did not usually know, how much of an observed change in money was a permanent change. The announced targets for money had generally not been achieved prior to 1979, and they were not generally achieved during the period 1979 to 1982. Hence, the information content of recent movements was high relative to the information in announcements or past averages. Rational behavior implies that current changes would have great influence on market participants' anticipations under the circumstances. Cukierman and Meltzer (1986).

At first, the experiment had little effect on the maintained rate of increase in the monetary base. The twelve month growth rate of the monetary base remained in the 7% to 8% range until 1981 (Chart 1c). By October 1981, the twelve month growth rate had fallen to 3.8%. The decline in base money growth, and a sharp fall in the growth of velocity for all monetary aggregates was followed by a decline in inflation. From the peak rate of 9.7% in 1981, inflation, as measured by the GNP deflator, fell to 6.4% in 1982 and 3.9% in 1983.

The Federal Reserve's experiment succeeded in lowering the inflation rate. Inflation (GNP deflator) fell from an average rate of 8.7% for the five years ending in 1981 to 3.2% for the five years ending in 1988. The costs of the reduction were larger than necessary. The 1981-82 recession is often described as the most severe in 50 years. This is an overstatement. The increase in unemployment and the decline in real growth are both smaller than in the 1973-75 decline. Nevertheless, for the year 1982 industrial production was below the level reached in 1978, and payroll employment was below the 1979 level. Unemployment rose 3.2 percentage points and real GNP fell 3.2% from the NBER expansion peak, in third quarter 1981, to the recession trough in fourth quarter 1982. Some of the cost of disinflation was a consequence of the uncertainty surrounding the policy rule, but much of the cost probably reflected prevailing skepticism about administration, Congressional and public tolerance for unemployment rates above 10%.

Although the recession receives most of the attention, it is not the only cost of the disinflation. Inflation and disinflation interacted with institutional arrangements such as ceilings on saving and time deposit interest rates, prohibition of interest payments on demand deposits, income tax rates based on nominal values and other restrictions to permanently alter the financial system. Sustained losses by financial firms and government intermediaries imposed large costs on taxpayers and solvent firms. The disinflation was worldwide, so it resulted in a marked fall in commodity prices (including petroleum prices), thereby contributing to the problem of developing country debt. As is often the case, a robust recovery in the U.S. followed the steep decline. By 1984, employment and production were above their previous peaks. The consequences of changes in asset values proved more durable. It seems likely that, absent the twenty year cycle of inflation and disinflation, the problems of the thrift industry, of international debt of developed countries and of government intermediaries in agricultural and mortgaging lending would have been smaller or largely avoided.

After 1982

Although inflation remained well above the rate of the early 1960s and was high by historical standards, the disinflation policy ended in the fall of 1982. The Federal Reserve did not announce the shift in policy. The initial announcement referred to some technical difficulties in interpreting monetary aggregates arising from the expiration of special tax exempt accounts at financial institutions. Money growth surged. Chart 8 shows the extraordinary increase in M_2 growth late in 1982.

(Insert Chart 8 here)

The Federal Reserve abandoned the efforts to implement control by means of the non-borrowed reserves procedure. The new procedure exploits the relation between the level of member bank borrowing (br) and the

Chart 8

ACTUAL vs. PLANNED GROWTH OF M2

10/1982 - 11/1988

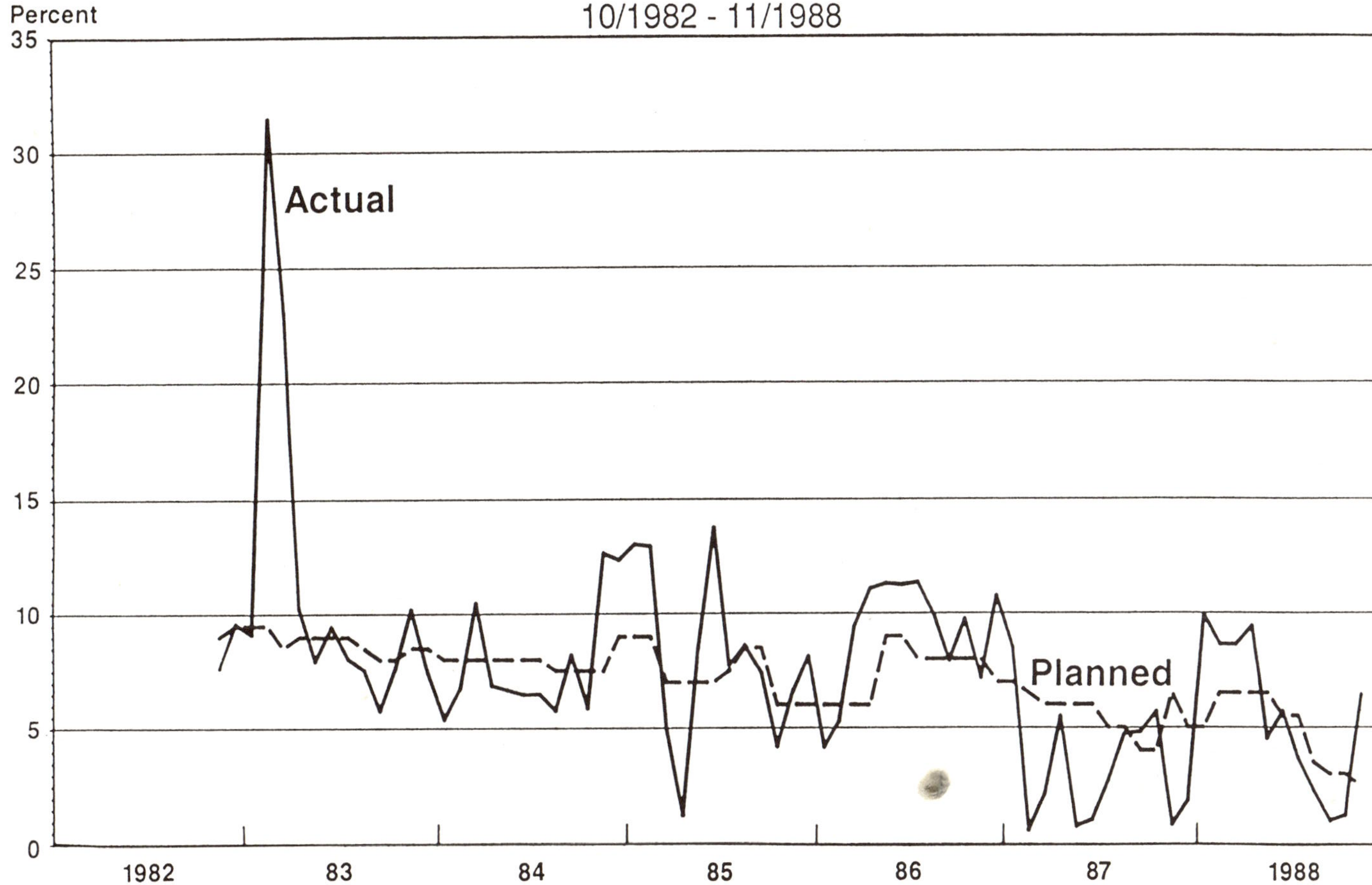

difference between the federal funds rate and the discount rate (d). If br is a linear function of d, we can write

$$br = a_0 + a_1 d + u$$

where u is a random variable. Changes in a_0 represent permanent shifts in the relation of br to d, and changes in u are presumed to be transitory. Thornton (1988) suggests that the federal funds rate is assumed to depend on the volume of non-borrowed reserves (nbr). This relation also is subject to permanent and transitory changes. If the br and nbr functions remain stable -- particularly if there are no permanent shifts in the relations -- the Federal Reserve can control the federal funds rate and br by varying nbr and the discount rate. Since br + nbr equal total reserves, the volume of total reserves is determined by supplying nbr up to the point at which the federal funds rate determines a level of br consistent with the Federal Reserve's choice of total reserves.

The central role assigned to borrowing in the control procedure represents a partial return to the Riefler-Burgess framework. Earlier work, Brunner and Meltzer (1964/89), and more recent work, Thornton (1988), suggest that changes in member bank borrowing are not closely related to changes in money. The borrowing relation is subject to permanent and transitory changes that are difficult to identify when they occur.[22] Hence, the Federal Reserve faces the same problem as under the nbr procedure; they must decide whether to hold the level of borrowing and let the funds rate adjust or to stabilize interest rates and permit total reserves and the money stock to deviate from their target. Chart 8 shows that there were frequent, large deviations of M_2 growth from target.

Chart 9 shows corresponding data for the federal funds rate. These data suggest that until late 1984, the Federal Reserve allowed relatively large deviations from the monthly funds rate target. After 1984, the deviations decline. They remain larger in absolute value than was true before 1979. Table 4 above confirms this impression.

---

[22] Thornton (1988, p.37) used a variable coefficients model to estimate the br relation. He found that there was considerable variability in the intercept. The Federal Reserve usually responded by reducing the size of the change in the funds rate.

(Insert Chart 9 here)

Not all of the variability in measures of monetary policy arises from the control procedure. The FOMC continues to shift the goal of policy. Table 5 shows that there were 12 reorderings of policy goals in three and one-half years. One occurred after the stock market crash in October 1987. This shift in objectives recognized the Fed's role as lender of last resort. Other changes are more difficult to interpret. We know very little about what the changes mean in practice. It may be that the changes in objective have no content. Analysis is difficult, given the relatively imprecise control of reserves and monetary aggregates. Reluctance to permit sufficient variability of the federal funds rate casts doubt on the importance the Federal Reserve attaches to the stated objectives or their ordering. Further, it is difficult to relate current actions to inflation, the pace of economic activity, or the exchange rate.

(Insert Table 5 here)

Comparison of periods in which monetary aggregates were placed first with other periods in which they were placed fourth or fifth shows no clear evidence of a change in the degree of control. In Chart 8, the deviations of M_2 growth from target early in 1985 are not much different from the deviations from target in 1987-88. Nor are the latter very different from the deviations from July 1986 to July 1987 when monetary aggregates were placed first or second.

The years 1982 to 1988 show no major break from the past in the conduct of monetary policy. Statements of intention to use monetary policy to control monetary aggregates or inflation seem unrelated to the actual growth rates of the monetary base, M_2, or other monetary aggregates. Announced targets for monetary growth were missed more often than they were achieved. The Federal Reserve announced multiple targets but typically gave little attention to any of them. Control of the federal funds rate remained the principal short-term focus of policy action, although larger deviations from target were permitted than in the 1960s and 1970s.

In August 1987, Alan Greenspan replaced Paul Volcker as Chairman of the Board of Governors. Greenspan has reduced the growth of the monetary aggregates. His public statements emphasize the importance of restoring and maintaining price stability. He responded promptly to the stock market crash by providing reserves for a brief period, and he made clear

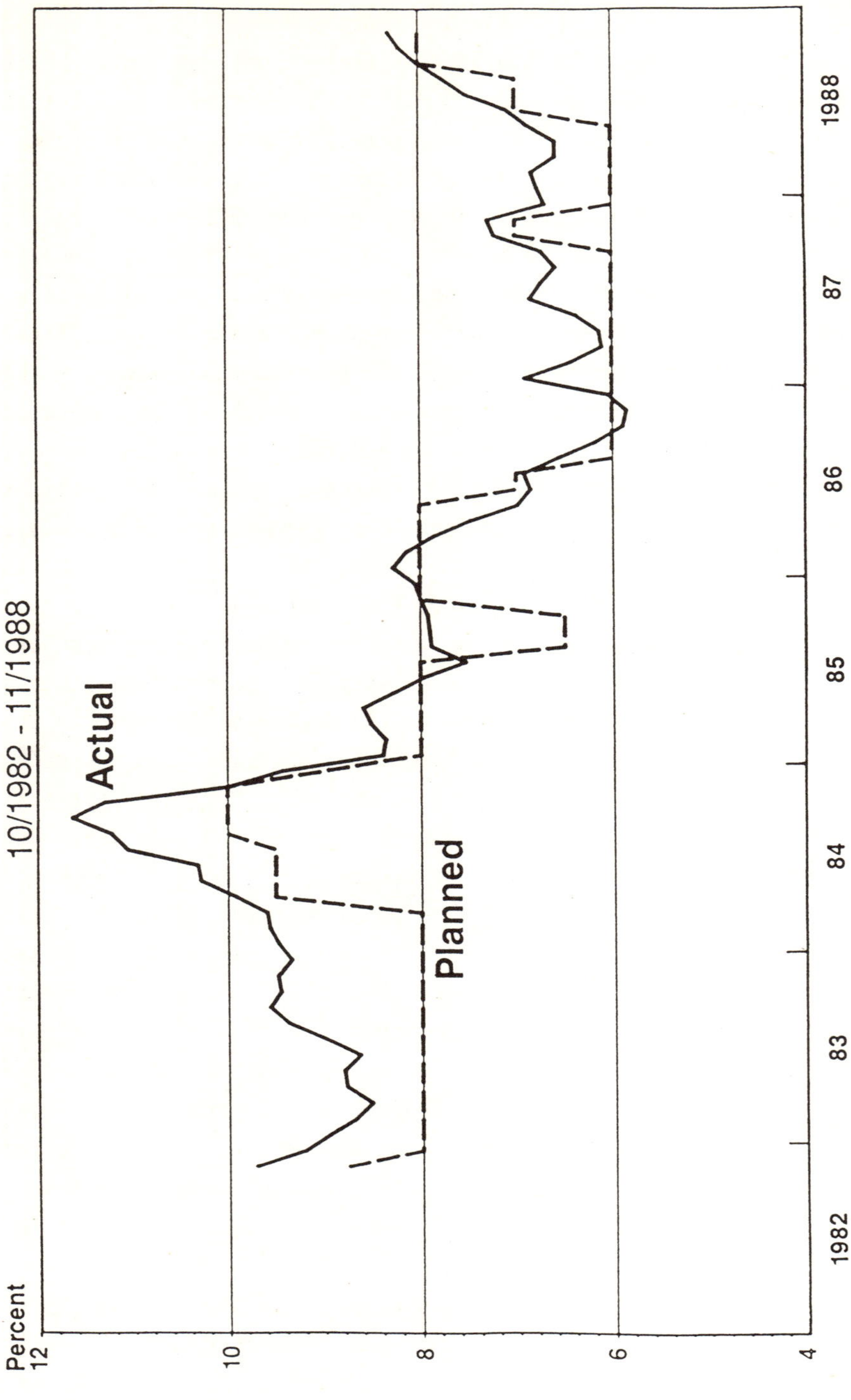

Chart 9
ACTUAL vs. PLANNED FED FUNDS RATE
10/1982 - 11/1988

TABLE 5

Order in which Policy Variables Appeared in the FOMC Directive

MEETING	FIRST	SECOND	THIRD	FOURTH	FIFTH
3/85 to 7/85	MONETARY AGGREGATE	STRENGTH OF EXPANSION	INFLATION	CREDIT MARKET CONDITIONS	EXCHANGE RATES
8/85 to 4/86	MONETARY AGGREGATE	STRENGTH OF EXPANSION	EXCHANGE RATES	INFLATION	CREDIT MARKET CONDITIONS
5/86	MONETARY AGGREGATE	STRENGTH OF EXPANSION	FINANCIAL MARKET CONDITIONS	EXCHANGE RATES	—
7/86 to 2/87	MONETARY AGGREGATE	STRENGTH OF EXPANSION	EXCHANGE RATES	INFLATION	CREDIT MARKET CONDITIONS
3/87	EXCHANGE RATES	MONETARY AGGREGATE	STRENGTH OF EXPANSION	INFLATION	CREDIT MARKET CONDITIONS
5/87	INFLATION	EXCHANGE RATES	MONETARY AGGREGATE	STRENGTH OF EXPANSION	—
7/87	INFLATION	MONETARY AGGREGATE	STRENGTH OF EXPANSION	—	—
8/87 to 9/87	INFLATION	STRENGTH OF EXPANSION	EXCHANGE RATES	MONETARY AGGREGATE	—
11/87	FINANCIAL MARKET CONDITIONS	STRENGTH OF EXPANSION	INFLATION	EXCHANGE RATES	MONETARY AGGREGATE
12/87 to 5/88	FINANCIAL MARKET CONDITIONS	STRENGTH OF EXPANSION	INFLATION	EXCHANGE RATES	MONETARY AGGREGATE
7/88	MONETARY AGGREGATE	STRENGTH OF EXPANSION	INFLATION	FINANCIAL MARKETS	EXCHANGE RATES
8/88 to 11/88	INFLATION	STRENGTH OF EXPANSION	MONETARY AGGREGATE	EXCHANGE RATES	FINANCIAL MARKETS

Source: Economic Review, Federal Reserve Bank of San Francisco, Spring 1989, p. 11.

that the Federal Reserve would serve as lender of last resort to the financial system. When the risk of an increased demand for money appeared to subside, the growth rate of money was reduced, and the policy of disinflation resumed.

WHAT HAS CHANGED?

At the end of the 1980s, the Federal Reserve was still searching for a reliable method of control that would stabilize the domestic money market without sacrificing longer-term control of the price level. The most recent effort to limit inflation and deflation depends on a construct known as p* that was developed at the urging of Chairman Greenspan. Increases in p* relative to p indicate that inflation will rise, and a reduction in p* relative to p signals disinflation. The computation of p* starts from the quantity equation and the assumption that the velocity of M_2 is trend stationary. Hallman, Porter and Small (1989).[23] The assumption that velocity is trend stationary runs counter to a large body of recent work suggesting that measures of monetary velocity are subject to permanent shocks and that velocity is well modeled as a random walk. If velocity is (approximately) a random walk, the actual price level will not return to p*, as required for the model to be a reliable guide to inflation control. The reason is that permanent deviations of velocity from a fixed trend will be mirrored by deviations of p from p* in the same direction.

Nevertheless, the introduction of p* marks a new effort to consider the longer-term implications of policy. Also, the computation of p* does not depend on forecasts from a large scale model. The problem is the Federal Reserve has announced, and subsequently ignored, many indicators of inflation that are as reliable as p*. It remains to be seen whether this new effort to find a price anchor will be another in the line of indicators that the Fed announced and subsequently ignored, starting with reserves against private deposits (RPDs) in the 1960s and including various monetary aggregates, measures of debt, borrowed reserves, non-borrowed reserves, and others. The answer will depend much more on the decision to allow sufficient flexibility of short-term interest

---

[23]The discussion of the p* model in this paragraph is based on Rasche (1989).

rates (and other money market targets) than on the choice of a particular indicator of inflation.

Chart 9 above shows that the Federal Reserve permitted increased interest rate flexibility in the 1980s. This change enabled the Fed to lower money growth after mid 1987. Experience is too brief to draw any general conclusion about whether this policy will remain in effect.

One of the main criticisms of past Federal Reserve policy is that money growth has been procyclical. Recent experience suggests that this, too, may have changed. Charts 4a and 4b above showed that for the 1980s, there is some evidence that this pattern no longer holds for M_2. Chart 10 shows more detail about the cyclical pattern of monthly M_1 growth. Each half cycle is divided into two equal parts. During the 1960s and 1970s, the data show that M_1 growth on average rises in the latter part of an expansion and falls in the latter part of a recession; M_1 growth is not only lower in the depth of the recession than at the peak of the expansion, but it falls during the recession and rises during the expansion. In the 1980s, this pattern vanishes. M_1 growth is highest late in the 1981-82 recession and declines, slightly, late in the 1982 recovery.[24]

(Insert Chart 10)

The problem is to decide whether the recent pattern reflects a change in disintermediation, a change in Federal Reserve behavior, or is mainly a chance event. The mean monthly growth of the monetary base is higher in the current expansion than in the preceding recession. This is consistent with past Federal Reserve policy; it suggests that no change in behavior has occurred. Working in the opposite direction is the slower growth of the monetary base and other monetary aggregates after the summer of 1987 (Chart 1c). If the duration of the economic expansion had been equal to the postwar average, growth of principal monetary aggregates would be higher than in the preceding recession. A further complication in interpreting M_1 is that the end of regulation Q ceilings changed the pattern of disintermediation. In previous postwar expansions, the rise in market rates induced the public to shift from commercial bank time deposits to open market paper and other, less regulated instruments, thereby reducing time deposits relative to demand

[24]All data end in November 1988.

Chart 10

MEAN GROWTH RATE OF M1
BY HALF RECESSION & HALF EXPANSION

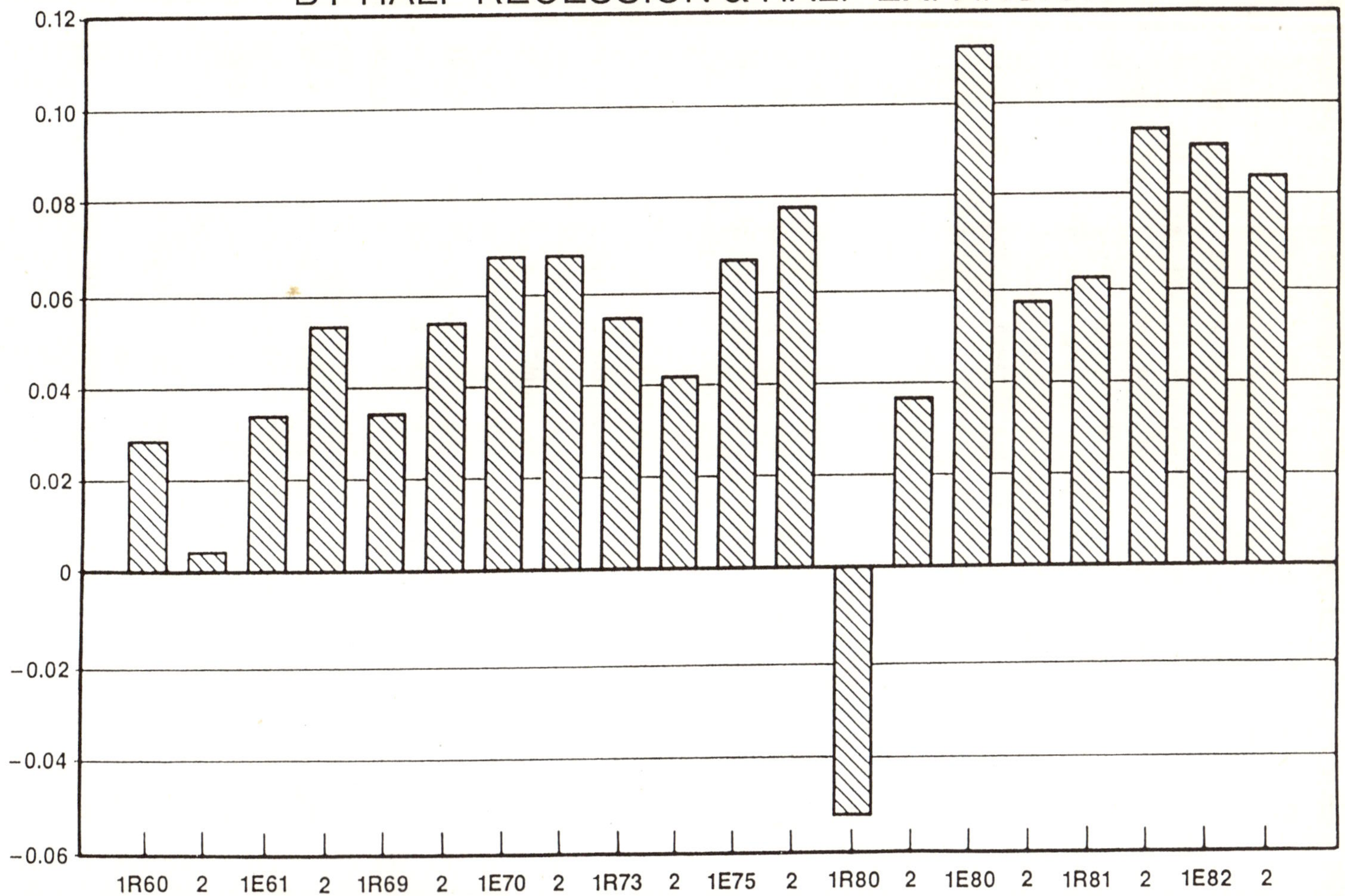

deposits. The change in disintermediation lowers the growth of M_1 late in the expansion relative to its previous norm. It is, therefore, difficult to draw a firm conclusion from the available data on M_1 about whether Federal Reserve actions remain procyclical.

One change in Federal Reserve policy action, or perhaps an outcome of their actions, is the decline in the share of debt financed by issuing base money. In Brunner and Meltzer (1976), the role of monetary policy in the financing of the government budget is summarized by the ratio of the stock of base money to the sum of the base plus the debt. In a closed economy, the denominator of the ratio is the cumulated value of past government deficits. In an open economy, the base includes the cumulated sum of foreign exchange (and gold) purchases. For the United States, the foreign component is a relatively minor sum, so I use the ratio to summarize the role of monetary policy in financing deficits contemporaneously or by subsequent open market operations. Charts 11a and 11b show the ratio for the years 1960 to 1988. There is a transition quarter in 1976 when the fiscal year changed; the 1976 data are for the fiscal year ending in June. The St. Louis version of the monetary base is used throughout.

(Insert Charts 11a & 11b)

A deficit financed by issuing debt lowers, and debt retirement raises, the ratio. Open market purchases increase, and open market sales reduce, the ratio. A rise in the ratio indicates that relatively more of the cumulated deficit has been financed by the monetary authority.

Chart 11b makes clear that the ratio has been falling during the years of relatively high budget deficits. If the ratio had remained at the average value for the 1970s, (.158) in the 1980s, the stock of base money would have been more than 30% higher for the decade. The resulting increase in average base growth would have produced higher inflation. The Federal Reserve avoided the inflationary potential of a large deficit by slowing base money growth absolutely and relative to the growth of the cumulated deficit.

In recent years, careful analysis of the relation of monetary to fiscal policy in an intertemporal context shows that fiscal policy has implications for monetary policy. Some of this work implies that continued deficits necessarily induce inflation. Sargent and Wallace (1981). In analyses where money, debt and capital are distinct assets, the long-run response of the price level to fiscal deficits depends on

Chart 11a

BASE/(DEBT + BASE)

1960 - 2Q 1976

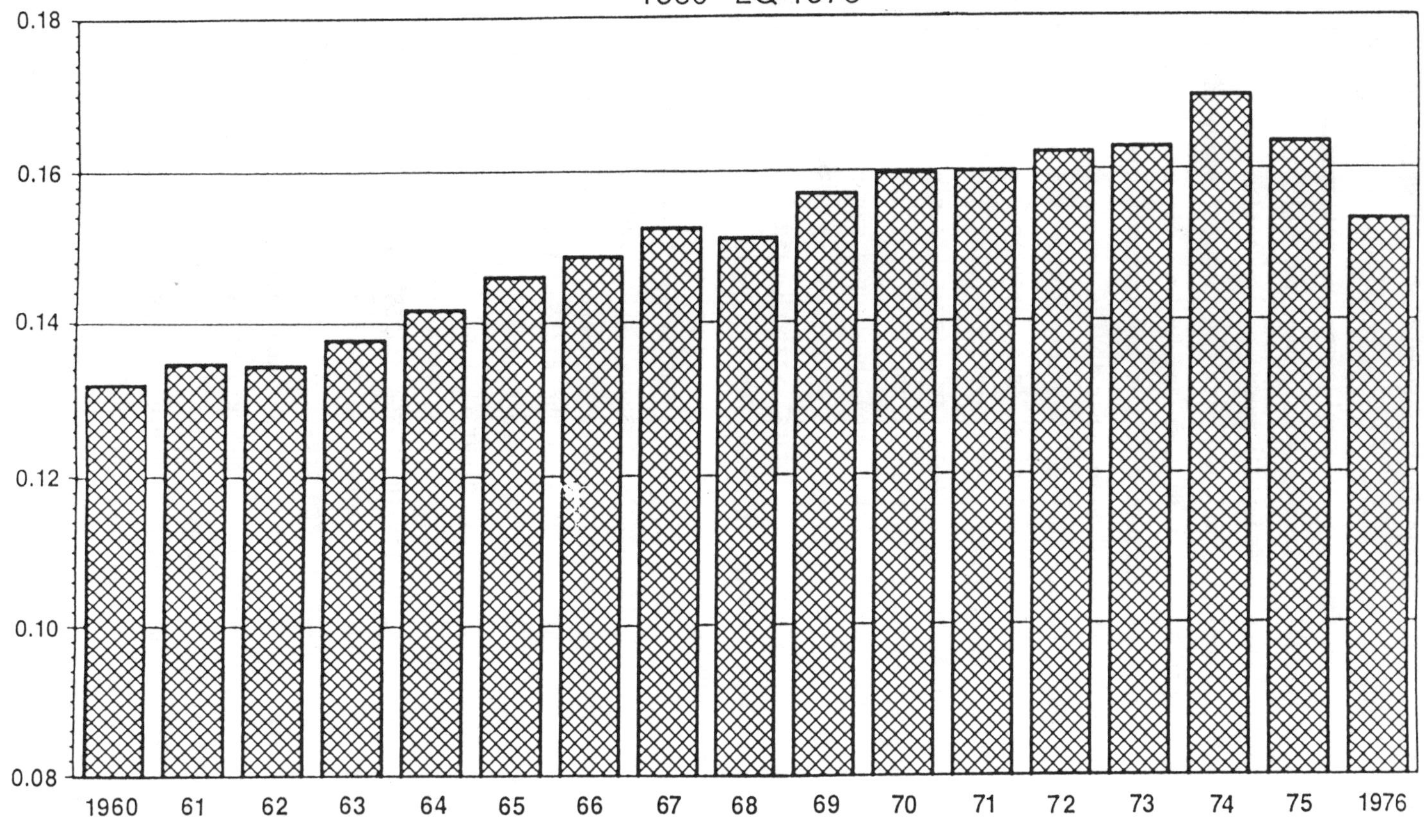

Chart 11b

BASE/(DEBT + BASE)

1977 - 3Q 1988

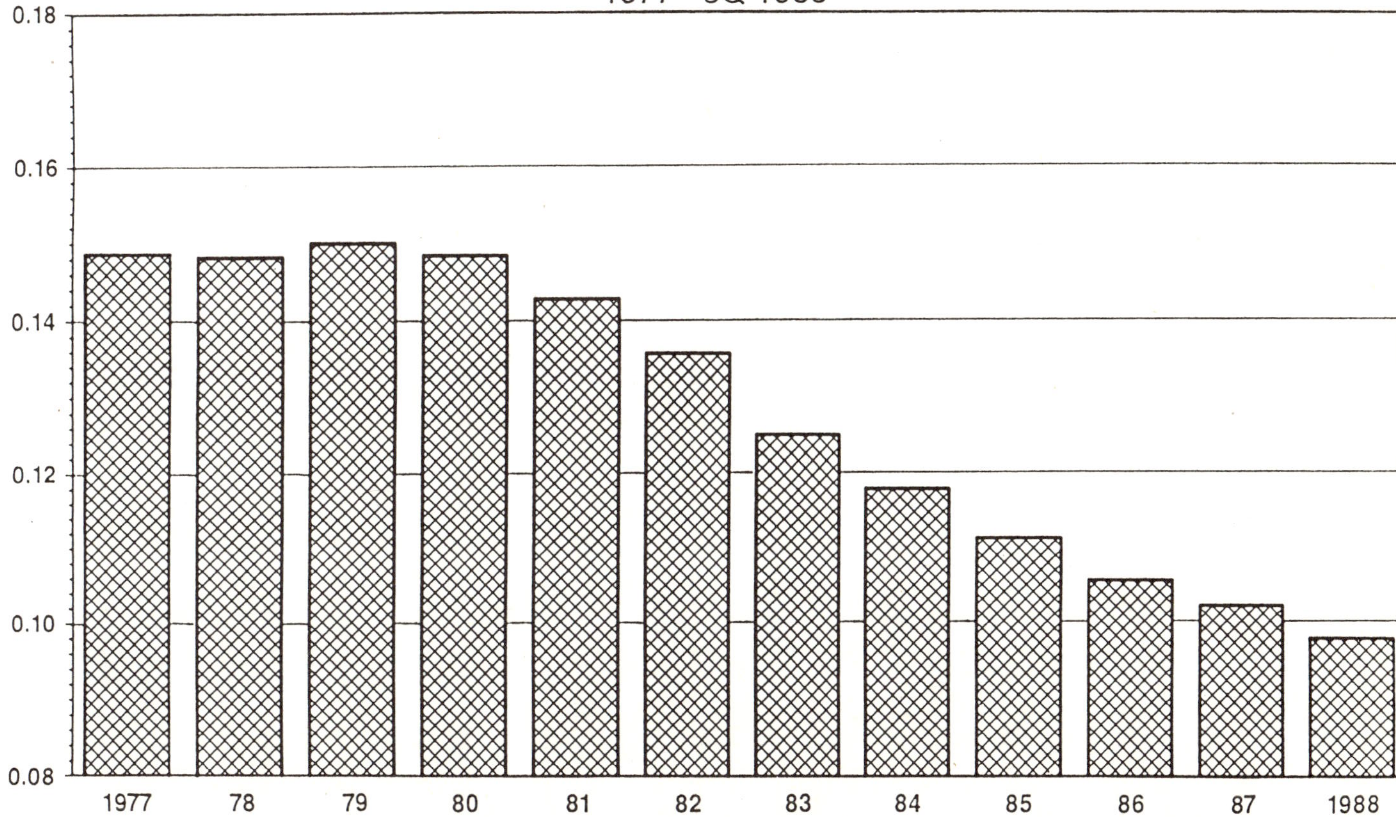

the ratio of base money to the cumulated deficit. In a closed economy (or in an open economy with a fluctuating exchange rate), the monetary authority can influence the long-term result.[25] The data for the 1980s suggest that the numerator of the ratio declined and the denominator increased. Within the ranges observed, the monetary authority has been able to lower inflation by lowering the growth rate of the base despite the continuation of relatively large measured budget deficits.

In addition to the changed relation of fiscal to monetary policy, there have been major changes in the relation of the Board in Washington to the Reserve Banks and changes in the Federal Reserve's understanding of its role as lender of last resort. From the start of the system through the 1930s, much of the authority for decisions resided in the Reserve Banks, as Friedman and Schwartz (1963) note. In the postwar period, and particularly in the 1970s and 1980s, the Board has held the dominant role. In the early years, the Governor (later President) of the New York Federal Reserve Bank had a major role in the formulation of monetary policy; now, his power is limited by the tighter control exercised by the Board and its staff.

Friedman and Schwartz (1963) document the failure of the Federal Reserve System to serve as lender of last resort to the banking system in the 1930s. The Fed responded differently in the 1970s and 1980s. Following the failure of the Penn Central Railroad in June 1970, the Federal Reserve notified banks that it was prepared to lend in an emergency. Similar actions were taken in other periods of financial distress that followed the failures of several large banks in the 1970s and 1980s. Following the October 1987 stock market decline, the Federal Reserve again recognized that it is the lender of last resort to the entire financial system; it provided reserves and expanded the monetary base promptly and maintained growth of money until the risk of a forced contraction subsided.

So great is the change that a new problem has arisen: the Fed often fails to distinguish between its responsibility toward the financial system and the failure of an individual bank. The Federal Reserve made loans, or encouraged bankers to lend, directly, to First Pennsylvania, Continental Illinois and other failing banks. This pattern of behavior

---

[25]Some qualifications are required. As shown in Brunner and Meltzer (1976) at low values of the ratio, stability of the model is not assured.

encourages banks to undertake risks that they could have avoided.

Recently the Federal Reserve has recognized in its public statements that the principal goal of a central bank is to achieve and maintain price stability. Central banks in Europe and Japan took a similar position earlier. Central bankers in developed countries appear to be much less confident that they can adjust aggregate demand, output and employment or that attempts to do so contribute to economic stability. If this change persists, it will be a significant departure from past belief and practice.

One result of the change would be a more stable monetary policy. In earlier work, I estimated the effect of unanticipated changes in base money, base velocity, and real GNP using a multi-state Kalman filter on each of these series separately. Meltzer (1986).[26] The unanticipated changes in each variable are obtained as the difference between actual values and the values predicted by the multi-state filter. Bomhoff (1983) describes the filter process. The time series are quarterly data from 1960 through 1984. The shocks to real GNP at or near business cycle turning points, chosen by the National Bureau of Economic Research, show the size and direction of change near the start of an expansion or contraction. The mean absolute value of the shocks at turning points is 2.25 times larger than the mean absolute error for the period as a whole. These data are shown in Table 6.

(Insert Table 6 here)

The table shows that unanticipated changes in the base typically lead shocks to real output by one to three quarters--three to nine months. This is consistent with several studies using different methods to measure changes and their timing. Shocks to base velocity are, most often, contemporaneous with the shock to real GNP.

Table 6 characterizes shocks to base money and velocity as weak or strong. This characterization is based on a comparison to the mean absolute error (or unanticipated change) for the period as a whole. The mean absolute errors are shown in the last row of the table.

---

[26]This section follows Meltzer (1986, pp.175-6). Table 6 is taken from that source. Additional evidence on monetary policy as a cause of fluctuations is given in Romer and Romer (1989) using historical data and Fair (1989) using a structural model. See also Stock and Watson (1987) for recent evidences on the relation of money to income and a brief summary of some of the issues in that large literature.

TABLE 6

Shocks to the base and base velocity at cyclical turning points in the U.S.

Quarter of NBER turning point[a]	Forecast error in percent per annum: Shock to real GNP	Shock to base	Shock to base velocity	Comment
1960/4		−0.20	−1.16	*B* leads
1961/1 T		+1.05	−0.76	*VB* contemp.
1961/2	+1.80	−0.44	+2.52	
1969/2		−0.95	+0.66	*B* leads
1969/3		−0.80	+0.59	*VB* contemp.
1969/4 P	−1.26	+0.51	−1.43	
1970/1		−0.14	−0.69	
1970/3		+0.63	−0.13	*B* leads
1970/4 T		+0.31	−1.11	*VB* contemp.
1971/1	+2.52	+0.34	+2.07	
1973/2		−0.26	−0.86	*B* leads (weak)
1973/3		−0.29	−0.46	*VB* leads (weak)
1973/4 P		−0.38	+0.71	*VB* contemp.
1974/1	−1.85	+0.56	−2.14	
1974/4		−0.26	−0.86	*B* lags (weak)
1975/1 T		−0.29	−0.46	*VB* contemp.
1975/2	+2.48	−0.38	+0.71	(weak)
1975/3		+0.56	−2.14	
1979/3		−1.25	+1.82	*B* leads (weak)
1979/4		+1.42	−1.41	*VB* contemp.
1980/1 P		−0.10	+0.20	
1980/2	−3.17	−0.26	−2.70	
1980/3 T		+0.85	−0.49	*B* leads
1980/4	+0.71	+0.88	+0.75	*VB* contemp.
1981/2		0	−0.79	*VB* leads (weak)
1981/3 P		+0.49	+0.41	*B* + *VB* contemp.
1981/4	−1.61	−0.60	−1.05	
1982/2		+0.12	−0.44	*B* leads
1982/3 T		+0.30	−0.88	
1982/4	+0.87	+0.98	−0.23	
Mean absolute error (percent) 1960/2–1984/4	0.8	0.4	1.0	

[a] P = peak. T = trough.

Source: Meltzer (1986).

Shocks to the monetary base lead the shock to output at seven of the nine turning points, but two of the leads are relatively weak. The base lags at the turning point only in one case, the 1974-75 recovery. Unanticipated changes in base velocity are usually contemporaneous with the shock to output and often follow a prior shock to the base. The principal exceptions are the declines following the oil shock of 1973-74, when velocity has a weak lead over output, and following the introduction of credit controls in March 1980, when the prior unanticipated change in the base is small. In 1973-74, the shock to the base and to base velocity were in the same direction; Federal Reserve actions augmented the real shock. This finding, using a very different procedure, reinforces the conclusion reached in the discussion of Table 1 above; monetary policy was destabilizing. In the 1980s, prior unanticipated movements in the base and base velocity are offsetting; the decisive shock is the shock to base velocity resulting from the imposition of credit controls.

The shocks to money are, by construction, impulses that cannot be anticipated using the past history of the series. The lead of the base at turning points may, therefore, suggest causation running from the unanticipated change in the base to the subsequent change in output. Many of the largest shocks to output in this period are preceded by relatively large unanticipated changes in the base that are in the same direction. Further, the nine business cycle turning points include six of the ten largest shocks to output during the period and the preceding shocks to the base are relatively large or cumulative. However, the interaction between money and output is almost certainly more complex than suggested by the lag structure used to construct the table, so I regard the evidence as a supplement to the evidence in earlier studies. Stock and Watson (1987) summarizes this literature and contribute evidence of an effect of past changes in money on output (industrial production).

The conclusion to be drawn from Table 6 and other past and recent evidence is not that all fluctuations are monetary in origin. Unanticipated changes can be real or nominal. Presumably institutional changes could reduce the size of unanticipated changes in both series, say by changing patent policy or increasing mobility of labor and capital in one case and by instituting a monetary rule (or changing the rule) in the other. A monetary rule that reduces variability, uncertainty and fluctuations would be socially beneficial even if, as seems likely, real shocks would remain.

Conclusion: Was the Experiment Successful?

This lengthy examination of the Federal Reserve's operations and actions has pursued two main themes. One reconsiders the criticisms of Federal Reserve operations, actions and policies made at about the time of the fiftieth anniversary and the Federal Reserve's responses. The other brings the analytic history of domestic policy operations up to the present. In the past twenty five years there have been intermittent changes in operating techniques and frequent changes in objectives. After seventy-five years, the Federal Reserve System still has not formulated coherent attainable long-term objectives or developed efficient operating procedures related to those objectives. The focus remains principally on short-term considerations, principally those affecting the money market.

The seventy-fifth anniversary of an institution is a time for assessing its contributions to wealth and welfare. For the Federal Reserve, issues of this kind, though related to the themes of the paper, are broader. They include an assessment of international operations, regulatory arrangements affecting the financial system, its safety and efficiency, and the Federal Reserve's contribution to economic stability, price stability and perhaps to the level or growth of output.

Advocates of a central bank early in this century argued that British exporters had a competitive advantage because they were able to discount bills that could be rediscounted at the Bank of England. Access to central bank rediscounts was expected to supplement the market, create a broader, more liquid market for bills of exchange, and reduce risk for individual holders and for the market. If we interpret the mandate to provide an elastic currency as more than Federal Reserve note issuance, bill purchases and discount operations are part of that mandate. In the early years, these operations were a major activity, but their importance declined in the 1930s. Few would now rest the case for a central bank or assign much significance for welfare to the existence and operations of the discount mechanism. Markets developed to provide these services.

The Federal Reserve got underway slowly in 1914, and it has been slow to change. It was slow to permit interest rates to adjust enough to prevent inflation. It was slow to recognize that regulation Q did not protect existing financial institutions. The U.K., Canada, and other countries learned to avoid financial panics much earlier than the United States. Schwartz (1986). The Federal Reserve was slow to recognize its responsibilities as lender of last resort in periods of panic, and its policies were at times a factor contributing to panics. Friedman and Schwartz (1963) note that, prior to the establishment of the Federal Reserve, the clearinghouses and banks performed some of the functions of a lender of last resort that the Federal Reserve failed to provide in the 1930s. Until the 1970s, and perhaps after, it was not clear when or whether the Federal Reserve would perform these functions. The existence of the Federal Reserve may have deterred the market from finding alternative solutions.

The costs of the 1930s mistakes did not end with the wartime recovery. The depression left a residue of legislation and regulation affecting banks, financial institutions and financial markets. Banking problems of the 1930s were wrongly interpreted as a consequence of interest payments on deposits, so interest payments were prohibited on demand deposits and restricted on time deposits. Benston (1964). Failures were also blamed on speculation, so investment and commercial banking were separated and mandatory margin requirements were introduced. Benston (1989). Some of these restrictions were removed slowly; others remain nearly sixty years later.

The Federal Reserve was slow to urge Congress to remove the restrictions on interest payments and slow to raise the ceilings so that the restrictions were not binding. In the 1960s, they acquiesced in, or perhaps encouraged, the extension of the ceilings to other financial instruments including deposits at thrift institutions. During the years of high inflation, the real losses suffered by depositors at banks and thrift institutions and by the institutions eventually led to repeal of most of the restrictions. But the losses also contributed to a weakening of the financial structure and to the failure of more than one-third of the thrift institutions and many banks.

Many of the losses and many of the continuing problems of financial fragility are the result of the Federal Reserve's failure to control inflation in the 1960s and 1970s and to the rapid disinflation of the early 1980s. By the 1980s prices of land and other inflation hedges rose to anticipate continued U.S. inflation of 8 or 9 percent. Disinflation lowered the values of these assets, in some cases below the value of the loans or mortgages which they supported. Absent the inflation and disinflation, much of the variability and many of the losses would have been avoided.

The inflation of the 1960s and 1970s and non-indexation of tax rates financed expansion of the welfare state and a burdensome system of income redistribution. Research has not established that these transfer programs would have been smaller or less costly if their costs had been financed by explicit taxes. Casual, but persuasive, evidence from the elections of the 1980s, however, suggests that the voters would have opposed increased taxes to pay for these programs. Hence, some of the programs may not have been approved or extended in the 1960s and 1970s absent the tax revenues from inflation.

Under the Bretton Woods agreement, U.S. inflation spread to much of the rest of the world, just as U.S. deflation had spread under the fixed exchange rates of the early 1930s. The spread of inflation under fixed exchange rates lowered the real wealth of foreign oil producers by reducing the value of their holdings of dollars. Research has not established that losses arising from world inflation strengthened the producer's cartel and encouraged them to respond by raising the relative price of oil. Again, it would not be surprising if inflation contributed to the oil shocks in this way.

Offsetting these actual or potential burdens is the increased stability of U.S. real output in the postwar period. Meltzer (1986a) shows a substantial reduction in the size of unanticipated shocks to output and inflation in the postwar years under fixed and fluctuating exchange rates. Federal Reserve actions may have contributed to the increased stability. Similar reductions in unanticipated variability are found for other countries. Bomhoff (1983) Meltzer (1986). DeLong and Summers (1986) suggest that the reasons for the increased stability of postwar output are not well understood, however, so the relative contributions of the Federal Reserve and other institutions or their policies remain an open issue.

These comments suggest that the losses resulting from Federal Reserve actions, slow responses, and inaction outweigh the benefits. The great depression, the great inflation, and the costs of interest rate regulation imposed large losses, social as well as private. Since many of the benefits of Federal Reserve actions -- recessions prevented, inflation avoided -- are unobservable, summarizing benefits is more difficult. These benefits would have to be large, however, to offset the more easily observed costs. It seems unlikely that benefits comparable to the losses can be found.

The losses arising from the great depression, the great inflation and other actions were not malicious or wilful acts. Many were the result of mistaken beliefs about the way policy works, or reliance on forecasts and judgments that were faulty. Some were the result of deliberate attempts to trade higher inflation for lower unemployment, attempts that continued long after research had established that there was no long-term tradeoff. Some, particularly in the postwar, were the result of the slow response characteristic of a government organization pressured by farmers, homebuilders, Congressmen and others who wanted interest rates to remain low or to rise, if they must, slowly. The Federal Reserve's status as an independent agency does not remove pressures of this kind. The pressures can be reduced, only if at all, by reducing opportunities for discretionary action or by strengthening incentives to maintain price stability.

Not all of the problems and errors were the result of pressures to pursue multiple goals or to change objectives. Some were the result of incorrect forecasts. Federal Reserve forecasts of output appear to be neither worse, nor demonstrably better, than other forecasts. Federal Reserve forecasts of inflation were consistently biased downward throughout the 1970s, however. On average for the postwar, the non-forecastable variability in U.S. real growth and inflation is a relatively large fraction of the average quarterly or annual change. Hence, policies based on forecasts are necessarily subject to large errors, even if the forecasts are up to the highest standard that economists can provide. Some evidence, Brunner and Meltzer (1983) and McCallum (1988), suggests that variability would be reduced and stability enhanced by following an adaptive rule that does not rely on forecasts.

The Federal Reserve has experimented with alternative control procedures and has shifted the weight on explicit forecasts and implicit judgments about the future many times. As far as we know, they have never tested an explicit rule that relies only on past information. In public statements, rules have been rejected as inflexible and inefficient because they do not use available information. This criticism does not apply to adaptive rules. Further, it is disingenuous. The Federal Reserve does not behave haphazardly; it follows some, possibly complex, rule to implement its free reserve or interest rate policy procedure. The strategy and perhaps the rule change periodically. The rejection of "rules" should be seen as an attempt to maintain opportunities for shifting the weights in its objective function, which is to say pursuing more variable policies. These shifting objectives produce higher inflation and increase variability Cukierman and Meltzer (1986).

I have suggested that the costs of Federal Reserve policy have outweighed the benefits in the first 75 years of Federal Reserve history. In the 1960s many economists believed that the future of discretionary policy was much better than its past. They expected that an explicit econometric model, with a well specified structure, would provide useful forecasts, improve policy operations and increase policymakers contribution to the stability of real and nominal values. This has not happened. Economists have not been successful in identifying stable structural parameters within broad ranges, and we have not discovered in any precise way how the structure responds to anticipations, taxes, age distribution, regulation and other institutional changes. Efforts to identify the length of response lags have been unsuccessful. Partly as a result, forecast errors have been large relative to average changes, and the results of discretionary policy action, based on forecasts, have disappointed central bankers. Yet, the Federal Reserve has continued to rely on forecasts and to undertake discretionary actions based on forecasts.

One reason for continued reliance on forecasts and sub-optimal procedures may be the low level of accountability. The major errors made in the 1930s, 1960s and 1970s did not lead to major reforms that increase accountability. To improve accountability, while retaining independence of the Federal Reserve within government, incentives must be changed. In New Zealand, the Governor's salary is now tied to his performance. In the past I have urged, a different system for the U.S. The Federal Reserve would be allowed to choose policies and procedures. They would announce explicit targets for money growth as at present. Since research at the Federal Reserve and elsewhere shows that annual targets can be achieved with relatively small errors, the Federal Reserve would be required to explain failures to keep money growth within (say) one percent of the target annually. The President would have the option of accepting the explanation or requiring the resignation of the Board.

This proposal may not be ideal. Perhaps more effective or more attractive proposals will be forthcoming. Without institutional change that increases incentives for achieving price stability and reducing variability, there is no reason to be confident that at 100th or 150th anniversary, future writers will have an empirical basis for believing that the experiment has been successful--that the Federal Reserve has contributed positively to wealth and welfare.

REFERENCES

Andersen, L. and Jordan, J.L. (1968) "Monetary and Fiscal Actions: A Test of their Relative Importance in Economic Stabilization," *Review*, Federal Reserve Bank of St.Louis (Nov.), 11-24.

Benston, G. (1964) "Interest Payments on Demand Deposits and Bank Investment Behavior," *Journal of Political Economy*, 72 (October), 431-49.

——— (1989) *The Separation of Investment and Commercial Banking: The Glass-Steagall Act Revisited and Reconsidered*, London, Macmillan.

Bomhoff, E.J. (1983) *Monetary Uncertainty*, Amsterdam, North-Holland.

Brimmer, A.F. (1971) "The Political Economy of Money," Washington Board of Governors (multilithed).

Brunner, K. and Meltzer, A.H. (1964-1989) *The Federal Reserve's Attachment to the Free Reserve Concept*. Washington: House Committee on Banking and Currency, reprinted in K.Brunner and A.H.Meltzer (eds.) Monetary Economics, London, Basil Blackwell.

——— and ——— (1964a) "Some Further Investigations of Demand and Supply Functions for Money," *Journal of Finance*, 19, 240-83.

——— and ——— (1976) "An Aggregative Theory for a Closed Economy," in *Monetarism*, J.Stein (ed.) Amsterdam, North Holland, 69-103.

——— and ——— (1983) "Strategies and Tactics for Monetary Control," *Carnegie-Rochester Conference Series on Public Policy*, 18, 59-103.

——— and ——— (1989) "Money Supply Theory" in *Handbook of Monetary Economics*, B.M.Friedman and F.H.Hahn (eds.) Amsterdam, Elsevier (forthcoming).

Burgess, W.R. (1927) *The Reserve Banks and the Money Market*, New York, Harper.

Burns, A.F. (1978) *Reflections of an Economic Policymaker*, Washington, American Enterprise Institute.

Cook, T. (1989) "Determinants of the Federal Funds Rate: 1979-1982" *Economic Review*, Federal Reserve Bank of Richmond, 75 (Jan.-Feb.), 3-19.

Cukierman, A. and Meltzer, A.H. (1986) "A Theory of Ambiguity, Credibility and Inflation under Discretion and Asymmetric Information," *Econometrica*, 54 (September), 1099-128.

Davis, R. (1964) "Research Memorandum: An Alternative Approach to the Monetary Mechanism," Federal Reserve Bank of New York, unpublished memo, November 30, 1964.

deLeeuw, F. and Gramlich, E. (1969) "The Channels of Monetary Policy: A Further Report on the Federal Reserve-MIT Model," *Journal of Finance*, 24, 265-90.

deLong, J.B. and Summers, L.H. (1986) "The Changing Cyclical Variability of Economic Activity in the United States," in R.J.Gordon, ed. *The American Business Cycle: Continuity and Change*, University of Chicago Press for the National Bureau of Economic Research, 679-734.

Fair, R.C. (1989) "Does Monetary Policy Matter? Narrative versus Structural Approaches," NBER, Working Paper No.3045.

Federal Reserve (1979), Press Release, October 6, 1979.

Friedman, B.M. (1975) "Targets, Instruments and Indicators of Monetary Policy," *Journal of Monetary Economics*, 1 (October), 443-73.

—————— (1977) "The Inefficiency of Short-Run Monetary Targets for Monetary Policy," *Brookings Papers on Economic Activity*, 2, 293-335.

Friedman, M. (1953) "The Effects of Full Employment Policy on Economic Stability: A Formal Analysis," in M.Friedman, ed. *Essays in Positive Economics*, Chicago, University of Chicago Press.

————— and Schwartz (1963) A Monetary History of the U.S., 1867-1960, Princeton, Princeton University Press for the National Bureau of Economic Research.

Hallman, J., Porter, R.D., and Small, D.H. (1989) "M_2 per Unit of Potential GNP as an Anchor for the Price Level," Staff Study, Board of Governors, Washington.

Karamouzis, N. and Lombra, R. (1989) "Federal Reserve Policymaking: An Overview and Analysis of the Policy Process," *Carnegie-Rochester Conference Series on Public Policy*, 30, 9-68.

Krooss, H. (1969) *Documentary History of Banking and Currency in the United States*, New York, Chelsia House in association with McGraw-Hill.

Lindsey, T. et al. (1981) "Monetary Control Experience under the New Operating Procedures," *New Monetary Control Procedures II*, Washington, Board of Governors.

Lombra, R. and Moran, M. (1980) "Policy Advice and Policymaking at the Federal Reserve," *Carnegie-Rochester Conference Series on Public Policy*, 13, 7-62.

Maisel, S.J. (1973) Managing the Dollar, New York, Norton.

McCallum, B. (1988) "Robustness Properties of a Rule for Monetary Policy," *Carnegie-Rochester Conference Series on Public Policy*, 29, 173-203.

Meltzer, A.H. (1986) "Size, Persistence and Interrelation of Nominal and Real Shocks," *Journal of Monetary Economics*, 17 (Jan.), 161-94.

——————— (1986a) "Some Evidence on the Comparative Uncertainty Experienced under Different Monetary Regimes," in C.D.Campbell and W.R.Dougan, eds.

——————— (1987) "Limits of Short-Run Stabilization Policy," *Economic Inquiry*, 25 (Jan.), 1-14.

Poole, W. (1970) "Optimal Choice of Monetary Policy Instruments in a Simple Stochastic Macro Model," *Quarterly Journal of Economics*, 84 (May), 197-216.

Rasche, R. (1989) "p* Type Models: Evaluation and Forecasts," Background paper prepared for Shadow Open Market Committee meeting, September 18 and 19th.

Rasche, R.H. and Johannes, J.M. (1987) *Controlling the Growth of Monetary Aggregates*, Boston, Kluwer.

Riefler, W.W. (1930) *Money Rates and Money Markets in the United States*, New York, Harper.

Robinson, S. (1989) "Empirical Evidence on the Accuracy of Money Demand Forecasts and their Importance to the Success of Discretionary Monetary Policy," unpublished dissertation, Carnegie-Mellon University.

Romer, C. and Romer, D. (1989) "Does Monetary Policy Matter? A New Test in the Spirit of Friedman and Schwartz," NBER Working Paper No.2966 (May).

Sargent, T. and Wallace, N. (1981) "Some Unpleasant Monetarist Arithmetic," *Federal Reserve Bank of Minneapolis Quarterly Review*, 5 (Fall), 1-17.

Schwartz, A.J. (1986) "Real and Pseudo-Financial Crises," in F.Capie and G.E.Wood, (eds.) *Financial Crises and the World Banking System*, London, Macmillan, 11-31.

Sigel, S. (1964) "Brunner and Meltzer's Alternative Approach to the Monetary Mechanism," unpublished memorandum, Washington, Board of Governors.

Stein, H. (1988) *Presidential Economics*, 2nd edition, Washington, American Enterprise Institute.

Stein, J.C. (1989) "Cheap Talk and the Fed," *American Economic Review*, 79 (March) 32-42.

Stock, J.H. and Watson, M.W. (1987) "Interpreting the Evidence on Money-Income Causality," NBER Working Paper No.2228 (April).

Thornton, D. (1988) "The Borrowed Reserves Operating Procedure: Theory and Evidence," *Review*, Federal Reserve Bank of St.Louis, 70 (Jan.-Feb.), 30-54.

Tinsley, P., Farr, H., Fried, G., Garrett, B., and von zur Muehlen, P. (1982) "Policy Robustness: Specification and Simulation of a Monthly Money Market Model," *Journal of Money, Credit and Banking*, 14, 829-56.

THE FEDERAL RESERVE SYSTEM AT SEVENTY FIVE

by: Allan Meltzer

Discussant: Andrew Crockett

1. Those of us brought up in parliamentary democracies have been taught to appreciate the value of an active opposition. Constant criticism and debate sensitizes a government to the consequences of its actions, and induces it to consider constantly how to improve its performance. The U.S. administration does not have the inestimable advantage of a "shadow government." But, as Allan Meltzer once more shows, this is no reason why the Federal Reserve System should be similarly deprived.

2. Meltzer has eloquently and thoroughly put the ease for the prosecution. IN the short time available to me, I will try and sketch some elements of the case for the defense. Not, I hasten to add, that the Federal Reserve has been without fault. Far from it. My purpose today will be to suggest that monetary policy making is more complex than some of the statements in Meltzer's paper seem to imply. These complexities mean that simple solutions are rarely available, and occasions will often arise in which judgements are avoidable. Judgements, as we know, will sometimes be wrong. But these mistaken judgements have not, as Meltzer suggests arisen from a failure to recognize certain simple relationships, reliance on which would alone solve the most difficult problems of macroeconomic management.

3. In these comments, I will select several simple propositions that emerge from Meltzer's analysis and analyze their validity. Some of the experience I will draw on is that of the United Kingdom rather than the United States, but for the purpose of the points I will try to make, that need not matter unduly.

4. The propositions I wish to examine - which I am deliberately putting more starkly than Meltzer does - are the following:

(1) Central Banks can choose to control either the monetary base (or some comparable aggregate) <u>or</u> short-term interest rates. By choosing one variable, the path taken by the other can be regarded as fully endogenous for analytical purposes.[1]

---

[1]I treat the growth rates of monetary base and M2 as main indicators of

as fully endogenous for analytical purposes.[1]

(2) The Federal Reserve has, for most of its history, chosen to control money market conditions (i.e., short-term interest rates), thus rendering the money supply endogenous.[2]

(3) This choice has mainly been responsible for a higher and more variable rate of inflation than necessary, and for various other ills in the financial system.[3]

(4) If low and stable monetary growth had been pursued, inflation would have been lower or non-existent and output growth would have been largely unimpaired.[4]

(5) Stable monetary growth can be attained through short term control of the liabilities of the Central Bank held by the rest of the banking system.

Consider each of these propositions in turn:

5. First, do central banks have to choose to control either a monetary aggregate or money market condition to the exclusion of the other variable. It seems clear to me that they do not, other than in the trivially short run. It is quite possible to operate on one variable, say short-term interest rates, but to modify the objective for short-term interest rates in the light of what is happening to the monetary aggregate. Most central banks pay relatively more attention to money market conditions in their day-to-day operations, and relatively more attention to other indicators (including the behavior of the money stock) in the longer run.

6. This is no more than a pragmatic reflection of the nature of the disturbance impinging on money markets. In the very short run,

---

[1]I treat the growth rates of monetary base and M_2 as main indicators of the thrust of monetary policy. Both the base and measures of money are endogenous variables under an interest rate control procedure (p.4).

[2]The federal funds rate is the principal indicator of monetary policy used by the Federal Reserve. The monetary base is the principal alternative... .

[3]The outcomes they (Federal Reserve policy) caused include[d] a high and durable inflation, devaluation, the end of the Bretton Woods system, several deep recessions, historically high market interest rates, and weakening of the financial structure (p.5).

[4]If the Federal Reserve had controlled the monetary base.... inflation would have been lower, nominal and real interest rates would not have reached the levels of 1981-82 and the Bretton Woods system would have survived longer.

movements in the demand for funds can occur in largely random fashion. To require that supply and demand be equilibrated at a given quantity would require short-term fluctuation in price (that is, in interest rates) that would impose costs without any significant compensating benefits. (The greater the distributed lag with which money demand adjusts to its determinants, the greater the movement in current interest rates needed to offset a short-term disturbance to demand.) In the medium and longer run, systematic factors are more important than random ones. So it is appropriate that the management of money market conditions should be adapted over time so as to achieve a path for monetary growth that is consistent with the intended evolution of nominal GNP.

7. This leads to the <u>second</u> of the five propositions that I have noted: namely, that the Federal Reserve has in fact focused on controlling money market conditions to the exclusion of a proper concern over the money supply. Meltzer suports this view by citing the continued frequent references to money market conditions in FOMC directives, and by noting that money supply targets are often missed. Neither of these pieces of evidence can be regarded as particularly persuasive on closer examination.

8. It is quite feasible to pursue a monetary growth objective through operating on interest rates: quantity is, after all, the dual of price, given stable demand and supply functions. Central Banks (for reasons I will arrive at later) generally find it easier to fix the interest rates at which they deal, rather than the quantities they buy and sell. It is natural, therefore, that even when their basic objective is to control monetary aggregates, they should give effect to this objective by adjusting prices.

9. But if monetary targets are missed, it could be asked, surely that means that the Central Bank cannot be paying much attention to them? Yes and no. That depends on how much the target has been missed by, and how hard the Central Bank has tried, through adjustments in policies, to limit the divergence from the target. In most cases where monetary growth has departed from its target, interest rates have tended to move too. In other words, central banks <u>have</u> responded to the departure from the monetary objective and <u>have</u> acted to limit it. The fact that they have not fully and immediately restored monetary growth to the original

path means, of course, that the monetary target has not taken predominance over all other objectives. Those who believe the money-income relationship is sufficiently stable to justify a unidimensional policy rule would doubtless condemn this. But since most evidence suggests that this relationship is subject to considerable instability, and since the authorities have at their disposal other pieces of evidence on how the economy is evolving, it is not surprising that Central Banks should be prepared to implement the monetary guidelines they set themselves in a flexible manner.

10. The <u>third</u> proposition I want to examine is that the failure to pursue a monetary rule has been responsible for a higher and more variable rate of inflation than would otherwise have occurred. Few central banks would nowadays dispute that inflation is largely the result of monetary policy. Or that the undesirably rapid inflation of the 1960s and 1970s reflected excess money creation.

11. The question, however, is whether these policy errors, which were serious ones, were errors of technique or strategy. In the 1960s, it is true, many policymakers were insufficiently aware of the importance of monetary growth as an indicator of the ease or tightness of monetary policy. By the 1970s, I would argue, there was much less room for doubt about this link. Most central banks accepted the proposition that there was some long-run rate of growth of the money stock that would be consistent with the desired degree of price stability. The problem, however, was that monetary authorities were either insufficiently ambitious in their anti-inflationary objectives, <u>or else</u> they made wrong judgements about the trend of velocity <u>or else</u> they took an excessively sanguine view of the consequences of a gradual rather than a direct approach to price stability.

12. The <u>fourth</u> proposition I have identified is expressed more positively. It is that low and stable monetary growth would enable the simultaneous achievement of low inflation and steady growth. This falls into the category of improvable assertions, and the Lucas critique should make us wary of accepting it on the basis of relationships estimated in a different policy regime. However, it is an assertion that clearly depends on the stability of the money demand function. It is therefore surprising that the issue of the stability of the demand for money is hardly touched on in Meltzer's critique of Federal Reserve

policy.

13. In the United Kingdom we have devoted considerable effort to the task of identifying a stable money demand function, and have had little success. This does not mean, of course, that such a function does not exist provided enough variables were included. The problem, however, is that successive institutional changes have caused the coefficients of the determinants of the demand for money to alter in ways that we have not yet been able to measure ex post, let alone identify ex ante.

14. To illustrate the magnitude of the difficulties we have faced, let me note that the annual velocity of 3 million pounds sterling, the monetary aggregate that had the most stable relation to income in the 1970s rose from 2.4 in 1973 to almost 3.5 in 1980, an increase of almost 50 percent. It subsequently fell back by some 20 percent over the ensuing six years.

15. What has caused these changes? During the decade of the 1980s, the financial system in the United Kingdom underwent a process of deregulation, disinflation and financial innovation. It was also subject to the consequences of growing integration in global financial markets. These changes clearly brought about important changes in the underlying relationship between money, incomes and interest rates. None of this undermines the essential truth that money causes inflation. But during the period in which an economy is adjusting to fundamental changes in its financial system, there are clearly limits to the extent with which policy can be based on the pursuit of monetary targets alone.

16. Fifth, and last, is the more technical question of the feasibility (as distinct from the desirability) of controlling the money stock through precise control of the reserve base of the banking system. The proposition that control of the monetary base is a necessary and sufficient condition to achieve adequate control of the money stock depends on the existence of a reasonably stable relationship between the reserve base of the banking system and the overall monetary stock. In a system without reserve requirements, the volume of non-interest bearing deposit banks willingly choose to hold with the central bank is very small. Moreover, it is likely to vary from day to day depending on the confidence with which banks can predict inflows and outflows from their accounts at the Central Bank. On the supply side, in a system in which the Central Bank acts as banker to the Government, the volume of central

bank liabilities available at the end of each day depends on elements not completely within the central banks control, such as the timing of large expenditures or tax payments by or to the Government. In such circumstances, the Central Bank cannot precisely control the reserve base of the banks on a daily basis, nor can it precisely predict the response of the banks to small changes in reserve holdings.

17. Of course, it would be possible to have a more reliable fulcrum for controlling aggregate bank deposits by decreasing that banks had to hold a much larger proportion of their assets in required reserves, and creating a deeper market in these central bank funds. This might make control of central bank deposits more predictable, but only at the cost of imposing what would in effect be a tax on intermediation through the banking system. This would create distortion and inefficiency and thus be undesirable in its own right. Moreover, it would have unpredictable consequences for the ultimate variable it was intended to control as it would encourage disintermediation (or intermediation through non-controlled institutions) and thus undermine the stability of the relation between money and income.

18. The problem of the "implicit tax" imposed by reserving holding could perhaps be met by paying interest on compulsory reserves. A more fundamental point is that the effectiveness of reserve-based monetary management depends on the demand for excess reserves, something that is not affected by the absolute level of reserves.

19. In the light of the foregoing, how should Allan Meltzer's dyspeptic assessment of the achievements of the Federal Reserve be viewed? There have, of course, been important failures in the record. There can be little doubt that the failure to control the acceleration of inflation in the 1970s contributed to the length and severity of the recession in the early 1980s. But the 1970s was a turbulent decade in which to make economic policy. The breakdown of the Bretton Woods system, the first oil price shock, and the 1974-75 recession created an environment in which there was a strong climate of opinion against taking deflationary risks. I would argue that the lessons of the failures of the seventies have, to a large extent, been learned. The 1980s have been more significant for the dogs that haven't barked: no recession, no financial crisis, no upsurge in inflation. This is not to deny that errors of judgement have occurred or that important problems still

remain. But overall the Fed's record in the 1980s, especially given the fiscal context in which monetary policy has had to be made, is quite a creditable one.

2 TOWARDS A EUROPEAN CENTRAL BANK: FISCAL COMPATIBILITY AND MONETARY CONSTITUTION[1]

Tommaso Padoa-Schioppa

1. INTRODUCTION

This paper deals with the issue of how much fiscal discipline and coordination among member states' budgets are necessary for the viability of a monetary union. This is one of the key open issues in the European agenda both at the political and at the technical level.

The "Report on European Economic and Monetary Union" (Delors Report) stresses the importance of fiscal coordination; it states that, although this objective should be achieved as much as possible through voluntary cooperation, there is a need for "binding rules" and for a transfer of some decision-making power from member states to the Community to avoid unsustainable differences in public sector borrowing requirements (par.19).

This position has been strongly endorsed by several countries after the publication of the Report of the Delors Committee. It was instead met with skepticism and recently with outright opposition by the UK Treasury and by a certain number of academic economists (see, in particular, Goodhart, 1989). According to the "counterplan" published by the British government last November, binding Community rules on the size of budget deficits are neither necessary nor desirable. They are unnecessary because "fixed exchange rate regimes have in the past operated successfully without such rules, as do the overwhelming majority of federal states today. Market pressures and multilateral surveillance will prevent deficits becoming unsustainable or unneighborly." Moreover, such rules are undesirable "because they infringe on the principle of subsidiarity and could lead to acute political difficulties within member states" (HM Treasury, 1989).

To put this debate in perspective, it is useful to recall two key features of the Delors Report.

Firstly, the project that has been proposed is more than a gradual

---

[1]I would like to thank Giampaolo Galli for valuable help in the preparation and drafting of this paper; sections 5 and 6 owe largely to his contribution.

strengthening of the existing exchange rate agreements in Europe. Although the Report borrows from the 1970 Werner Plan a definition of monetary union in terms of irrevocable fixing of parities and complete and irreversible mobility of capital, the key feature of the monetary union is that of a common monetary policy.

Secondly, following the model of the Bundesbank statute, the mandate of the European Central Bank (ECB) is defined as being that of ensuring price stability; only "subject to the foregoing - the Report states in para.32 - the System should support the general economic policy set at the Community level by the competent bodies."

Both features clearly require a high degree of consensus about the conduct of monetary policy; the question, that the Committee could not avoid, is whether they also require convergence and/or a degree of centralization of decision making powers in other areas of economic policy. Although the Report deals with a broad range of policies (the single market, competition, regional and structural policies, wage and price formation), it is unquestionably fiscal policy that receives the greatest attention.

In this paper I will argue that the preoccupations of the Delors Report are justified, but that the argument that a fiscal rule is a logical prerequisite for the viability of a monetary union is not compelling.[2] It is instead of the greatest importance that a strong monetary constitution be designed, providing for a clear separation between monetary and fiscal policy; in this regard I will try to go somewhat beyond the Delors Report, both in terms of analysis and proposals.

2. PRELIMINARY REMARKS ON FISCAL DISCIPLINE

Before going into the main issue, I should make my position clear on two preliminary points.

First, much greater fiscal discipline than we have seen so far in some European countries is necessary in its own right and would facilitate the transition towards greater exchange rate stability. Among the major countries, Italy has to take a decisive step to turn its

---

[2] A view that I have already expressed in Padoa-Schioppa (1988).

primary deficit into a surplus and start to repay the public debt. Should the attempts to achieve this objective fail, there is a potential threat to financial stability both in Italy and in neighboring countries. It may also become very difficult, if not impossible, to achieve and maintain the amount of credibility which is required to stay within the narrow band of the European Monetary System. In spite of well known theoretical ambiguities about the effects of the budget on the exchange rate, it is clear that, in the present Italian situation, a major fiscal correction would strengthen cohesion within the EMS by enhancing confidence and eliminating any residual fear of future monetization.[3]

Secondly, the very experience of Italy and several other countries in the last two decades shows how difficult it is to conjugate discretion and responsibility in budgetary matters and induces me to strongly favor proposals aimed at substantially reducing budgetary discretion.[4] I will <u>not</u> deal with this issue here except to say that institutional changes could be undertaken at the national level, much in the same way as it has been done in the U.S. where most states have adopted some kind of fiscal rule (typically precluding the issue of debt to cover current expenditures), but have not been required to do so by the central government. The EEC may perhaps take the lead in this area and try to coordinate and "harmonize" the rules among different countries, as it does in many other areas. This is altogether different from the proposal, to which I shall now turn, of transferring fiscal powers to the Community and conditioning to it the achievement of further progress in the direction of the monetary union.

---

[3]See Galli and Masera (1990) for a precise argument showing conditions under which these effects dominate the familiar Mundell-Fleming-Dornbusch effect with capital mobility in the short as well as in the long run.

[4]The formation of high public debts may be seen as a case of "government failure," which may be due to fiscal illusion (as argued by Buchanan et al., 1987), but may also be accounted for in models of rational agents (see, for example, Tabellini and Alesina, 1988). There is hence an issue of how to correct for the resulting intertemporal inefficiency while at the same time allowing for some degree of discretion to respond to exceptional or unexpected circumstances.

3. THE CONTROVERSY

There are several aspects to the general question of how much fiscal union is necessary for the monetary union. A useful distinction is between issues relating to fiscal discipline and issues relating to fiscal coordination. At the political level, much of the controversy concerns the first set of issues and whether a monetary union is conceivable when some countries have very large public sector debts and may run into financial difficulties. Coordination issues dominate instead the scientific literature: the focus is not on public debts, but on fiscal policy as a tool for macroeconomic stabilization.

In this discussion I will start with fiscal discipline and defer coordination issues until section 7.

Emphasis on fiscal discipline is mainly justified by two preoccupations. They concern monetary policy and distributive functions respectively, and can be formulated in the following terms:

(a) divergent fiscal policies may lead to conflicting views about the appropriate stance of the union's monetary policy because the financially weak countries may be inclined to advocate a permissive monetary policy in order to ease the financing of the deficit and/or reduce the burden of their debt;

(b) conflicts may also arise, and perhaps more disruptively, on issues related to the distribution of credit and real resources among member countries; there may be a fear that the role and functions attributed to the ECB might *de facto* oblige the stronger countries to support or even bail out members who run into serious financial difficulties.

Although there is some overlap between these two points, it is useful to treat them separately: the first one relates to the overall stance of the union (level of interest rates, total size2pf the ECB assets, etc.) while in the second one the emphasis is on distributive issues (interest rate differentials between countries, composition of ECB assets, etc.). Both impinge on the viability of the union in the sense that serious economic tensions could lead to political disagreement and, in the worst scenario, to a dissolution of the union itself.

Opinions appear to be divided between those who believe that discipline should be imposed through Community rules and those who stress the role of markets and the fact that, in a union, fiscal authorities are subject to a more stringent set of incentives.

According to the Delors Report (par.30),

- market perceptions do not necessarily provide strong and compelling signals;
- access to a large capital market may for some time even facilitate the financing of economic imbalances;
- rather than leading to a gradual adaptation, market views about the creditworthiness of official borrowers may change abruptly and result in the closure of access to market financing.

Assessing these arguments is rather difficult. On the one hand, it is hard to draw on the past experience of sovereign nations to imagine what would happen after a major shift in regime. On the other hand, there is no conclusive argument about the extent to which the experience of federal states is relevant to the European union.

Clearly, the amount of discipline that markets have been able to impose so far on sovereign nations is to be considered insufficient: Otherwise the issues would not arise. The question is, therefore what changes once a monetary union is in place. Two points can be mentioned:

- liberalization of capital movements and of the domestic financial system;
- elimination of the possibility, for individual countries, to resort to devaluations and to the monetization of the public sector deficit.

The first point (which does not coincide, but is an essential part of the program for the monetary union) is obviously relevant; any form of financial repression reduces the possibility that views about the creditworthiness of the borrowers will be reflected in yield differentials in the markets. Governments have often resorted to financial repression precisely in order to avoid the more painful (at least in the short run) route of reducing primary deficits. There is, however, at least one counterexample: The United States in the eighties.

The second point is less obvious. Inability to monetize, together with the fixity of the exchange rate, implies that interest rates will have to be more responsive to market sentiment. It is not clear, however, whether the sanction of high interest rates is more compelling than the sanctions that markets inflict today, through speculative attacks in the foreign exchange markets. Probably governments would have less room to cushion the effects of a loss of confidence;

moreover, the source of the problem would be clearer in the first than in the second case.

In the experience of federal states, yield differentials on the debts of different regions do show up, when the markets are reasonably convinced that the central government will not intervene. A good example is Canada (see on this, Bishop et al., 1989): In the provincial bond market, there is a yield spread of up to 50 or 60 basis points between the stronger (fiscally and economically) provinces and the weaker provinces. It is not clear, however, how much fiscal discipline these spreads have induced. It is even more difficult to tell whether spreads of this size could induce discipline in the large, politically independent nations of Europe.

Another argument pointing in the direction of greater discipline is suggested by the game theoretic research on externalities. The individual country does not value the negative externality on foreign inflation stemming from an appreciation of its currency: It has hence a tendency to overexpand fiscal policy and appreciate the exchange rate in order to sustain the level of activity while at the same time curbing inflation at the expense of the neighbors. This resembles what the U.S. did at the beginning of the last decade. Presumably, in the long run, the gains from this policy tend to diminish as a depreciation is required to balance the current account, inclusive of interest payments; this process may, however, take time (as the U.S. case proves) and in the meantime large debts are accumulated. In a monetary union this source of "fiscal indiscipline" is eliminated; there may, on the contrary, be a tendency for fiscal policy to be underexpansionary if its effects on foreign output are sufficiently large (see van de Ploeg, 1989).

Overall both arguments (market mechanism and externalities) suggest that problems of fiscal indiscipline are less likely to arise in a monetary union.

It cannot, however, be concluded that such problems would be completely eliminated. For this reason I share the preoccupations expressed by the Delors Report. A possible solution is to impose fiscal rules and endow the Community with the authority to control national budgets. In principle this eliminates the problem at the root, but, as we have seen, encounters political opposition and may easily be recognized as being extremely demanding on both member countries and the Community; the former would be asked to give up a conspicuous part of their sovereignity, while the Community would be faced with the very complex problems of devising the rules and enforcing them on otherwise sovereign nations.

Another solution is to design monetary rules in such a way as to prevent fiscal problems from interfering with the conduct of monetary policy. I will argue that there is some degree of substitutability between monetary and fiscal rules.

4. BUDGET DEFICITS AND THE UNION'S MONETARY POLICY

In this connection, as mentioned at the beginning of the previous section, the first problem to be tackled concerns the stance of the union's monetary policy; the preoccupation is that financially weak countries may advocate a permissive monetary policy in order to reduce the burden of their debts.

In principle, there is little difference between this and the general problem of the relations between monetary and fiscal authorities in a sovereign nation. The issues concern: How much autonomy should be given to the monetary authorities, to which body (Ministry of Finance, Government, Parliament, etc.) should they be accountable, how should their officials be appointed, how should the final objectives and operating targets of monetary policy be defined.

Some answers to these questions can be found in the Delors Report. As recalled above, the final objective (price stability) should be defined at the outset in the statute of the ECB. It is also stated that the Council of the ECB (composed of the Governors of the central banks and the members of the Board, the latter to be appointed by the European Council) should be independent of instructions from national governments and Community authorities; to ensure independence, the Report calls for "appropriate security of tenure" for the members of the Council. As to accountability, the Report proposes that the ECB report only to the European Parliament and to the European Council. In addition, "supervision of the administration of the System would be carried out independently of the Community bodies, for instance by a supervisory council or by a committee of independent auditors."

This is clearly a very general framework, which needs to be worked out in greater detail; several problems are still open, relating in particular to accountability (e.g., does the European Parliament have sufficient powers for the proposed task?). In this respect, I would like to make two remarks. The first is that due attention should be given to the fact that, in contrast with most federations, the critical issue is independence from regional (i.e. national) rather than central (i.e. Community) authorities. This has implications for the architecture of the federative structure of the ECB advocated by the Delors Report. In particular, it will be necessary to carefully design the relations between the central body (the Board) and the Council in which national central banks are represented. Voting schemes, definition of the issues to be submitted to the Council, frequency of meetings, etc. should be such as to give the Board the bulk of the responsibility for the final conduct of monetary policy.

The second remark is that, with a correct institutional design, there are reasons, based on recent experience, to foresee a high degree of cohesion around the basic principle of price stability, despite divergent fiscal positions of individual countries. European countries have been vaccinated by the painful experiences of high inflation in the seventies and disinflation in the eighties. Even in countries with high budget deficits, central banks have found a wide consensus on a strong commitment toward price stability. The success of the European Monetary System is largely due to this consensus; it has shown that a significant degree of monetary convergence can be achieved and maintained for a rather long period of time even with diverging fundamentals.

In addition, the very perspective of the monetary union is likely to bring about a greater convergence than has been experienced so far. Here again there is something to learn from the EMS; in spite of the considerable margins of flexibility allowed by the system, there is evidence that it has had a major impact on agents' expectations about the future growth of nominal variables (see Giavazzi and Giovannini, 1988). On this account, high inflation countries have gained a lot; low inflation countries have not lost. I would also argue, although based more on judgement than hard evidence, that - unfortunately with the exception of my own country - the EMS has exerted a disciplinary influence on fiscal policies too.

The monetary union is a much more radical change compared with current conditions than the EMS was compared with the uncoordinated, but managed floats of the 1970s. I would expect it to exert a much greater effect than the EMS on the expectations and actual behavior of both private agents and fiscal authorities.

5. THE DISTRIBUTIVE PROBLEM

I now turn to the second preoccupation that determines a request for institutionalized fiscal discipline. This is an essentially distributive issue which, I believe, requires further analysis. In short, the question is whether, in a monetary union, there would be a tendency or even an implicit obligation for the strong members to support the fiscally weak ones, especially when acute financing difficulties or outright debt crises arose.

It should be noted at the outset that the issue of public debt crises is likely to become more important once the union is in place, since, as argued in section 3, losses of confidence, which, with adjustable parities, usually show up in the market for foreign exchange, would, in a union, mainly affect the market for government paper. By advocating the exclusion of the fiscal authorities from direct access to central bank credit (par.30), the Delors Clommittee has shown awareness of the possible distributive implications of a monetary union, although it did not make it explicit, nor did it go into certain central banking technicalities that I will touch upon below.

Let me also note that the relations between the monetary and distributive functions of transnational monetary arrangements have always been an issue of key importance, one that has often aroused considerable confusion. It may suffice to recall the Bretton Woods debates about Keynes' Bancor project. In principle, its function was mainly that of creating international liquidity. Keynes proposed that liquidity be created through extensions of credit to countries with a balance-of-payment deficit, his purpose being to avoid the deflationary tendencies of the 1930s, which he attributed essentially to the fact that adjustment was a necessity for deficit countries and only an option for surplus countries. I agree with D.Cohen (1989) that the Keynes plan was not only inflationary: "It was unworkable" because, its very mechanism meant that surplus countries were de facto obliged to finance deficit countries almost indefinitely.

It is essential that traps of this sort be avoided in the design of the European monetary union. Here again, this can be done either by imposing fiscal rules or by defining a set of monetary rules which prevent the central monetary authority from becoming involved in the problems of individual countries.

6. THE FUNCTIONS OF THE ECB

To show the relationship between the distributive issue and the operations of a European central bank, it is useful to distinguish between three possible functions of any transnational monetary arrangement:

1. Creation of liquidity
2. Intermediation of credit
3. Tranfer of resources.

These functions are clearly distinct in principle; they may be hard to distinguish in practice. Often it is not sufficient to know the accounting nature of a particular operation to classify it into one of these three categories; other information is necesesary. Consider for instance a world composed of two identical countries, using a common fiat currency, issued by a transnational institution; if an operation is done to allocate a certain amount of currency to only one of the two countries (say country A), there is clearly a transfer of resources because country A acquires purchasing power over goods and services produced by country B. If, instead, the same operation is also done with country B the transfer effect vanishes and the only net outcome is an increase in the quantity of world money. Likewise, the purchase of a government's bonds by an international institution may be a credit, a transfer or a creation of liquidity, depending on which other operations are done with other governments as well as on the criteria adopted for the redistribution of the interest income accruing on the bonds. Their economic effects also depend, in a sense that I will clarify below, on market perceptions about the substitutability between bonds issued by different governments.

While it is clear that the central European authority should perform function 1 and not function 3, it is less clear whether or to what extent it should perform function 2.

To gain an understanding of this problem, it is useful to go through an exercise that can be labelled accounting engineering, i.e. thinking, in terms of the budget of the central European institution, about the operations and the constraints which would define its activity.

To fix ideas, imagine a situation in which, at the end of the process foreseen by the Delors Committee and with a common currency (say, the ECU), the ECB has, on the liabilities side, the entire monetary base of the Community plus an initial capital conferred by member countries; on the assets side, suppose, for the moment, that the ECB has essentially national government bonds. The profits (interest revenue minus operating costs) would be paid out to member countries according to their share of the capital (quotas, in IMF jargon). To keep things simple, let us neglect, for the moment, the relations between the central monetary authority and the national branches of the system.

To such a simplified system a number of rather general propositions apply.

(a) Transfers of real resources between countries depend, to a first approximation, on the distribution of the quotas (and hence of the profits) of the ECB and not on the distribution of its assets. The revenues of the ECB would essentially be the Community seigniorage, defined as the ECU monetary base times a nominal interest rate. To have an idea of the order of magnitude, note that, in 1988, the monetary base was 9.3 percent of Community GDP (see the table below), while the average long-term interest rate was 9.9 percent: multiplying these two numbers yields a value (.92 percent of GDP) which is not very distant from that of the entire budget of Community (in the future the relevant number may become smaller as certain countries reduce reserve ratios - see, on this, Thygesen and Gros, 1989).

(b) Neutrality in the distribution of resources mainly requires that quotas be distributed in the same proportions as holdings of ECU monetary base by residents of member countries. On the stated assumption that the entire seigniorage levied on residents of the Community accrues to the ECB, with this scheme countries would generally neither lose nor gain from the system.[5] If, instead, some sort of GDP

---

[5]Minor redistributions, relative to the present situation, would occur

criterion was used, there would be a redistribution in favor of countries with a high income velocity of the monetary base. As of today, the UK, which has a high income velocity, would get 17 instead of 6 percent of total Community seigniorage (see Table): since the latter is a little less than 6 percent of British GDP, with this criterion, the UK would receive a transfer of about 0.6 percent of its GDP every year. Spain would lose almost 1.1 percent. Differences in income velocities will probably shrink in the future, to the extent that they largely reflect differences in reserve ratios; they may, however, remain significant, as is often the case between regions of the same country.

(c) Purchases of bonds by the ECB give rise to credit relations, besides creating liquidity, only if their distribution among countries differs from that of the quotas. The share of a particular country's bonds in ECB total assets is not relevant; what matters is the difference between this share and that of capital. This point is easily understood by noting that, if the two shares are equal, the country is effectively paying no interest on its bonds placed in the ECB's portfolio.

These points are of critical importance and their implications should be discussed at an early stage of the construction of the new system. More or less disguised redistributions are much more likely to occur as a consequence of a wrong design of the rules governing the balance sheet and the profit and loss account of the ECB than because of lack of fiscal rules. On the other hand, it is not a simple matter to define what the correct design should be. Difficulties concern the operational implementation of distributive neutrality and the desirable limits to credit operations. As to the first, hair-splitting implementation of the monetary base criterion proposed above is almost impossible. Except for reserve currencies, today we have a reasonably good measure of the monetary base held by residents because this aggregate has a precise counterpart in the liabilities of the central bank. But, with a common currency or with a considerable amount of currency substitution (as would occur with irrevocably fixed parities),

---

to the extent that currencies are held outside the issuing country.

MONETARY BASE AND GDP IN THE EUROPEAN COMMUNITY
(1988; Percent)

Country	Monetary base/GDP	Share of GDP	Share of Monetary Base
Belgium	7.5	3.2	2.6
Denmark	3.7	2.3	0.9
France	5.8	20.0	12.5
Germany	9.9	25.3	26.9
Greece	14.9	1.1	1.8
Ireland	10.1	0.7	0.7
Italy	14.6	17.5	27.4
Netherlands	8.1	4.8	4.2
Portugal	13.5	0.9	1.3
Spain	20.4	7.2	15.7
U.K.	3.3	17.0	6.0
Total	9.3	100	100

Shares are computed at current exchange rates.

Source: Monetary base: IFS, line 14 (annual averages)
GDP: IFS, line 99b.

there would no longer be such a measure and statistical approximations would have to be used. It is to be hoped that a reasonable political agreement may be found on this point. It should be noted in passing that no difficulties should be raised by those who are showing sympathy towards the British plan for a market route to the union, based on currency competition; according to this plan, the whole seigniorage of the Community would accrue every year to the single country whose currency wins the market contest.

The other issue is whether, or to what extent, the ECB should extend credit to individual countries. Some limits (maximum amount of lending, time within which a country's share should go back to its quota) should certainly be fixed, at the very least to avoid large and continuous overshoots of the quotas, which would in practice amount to transfers. The question is how tight these limits should be; an extreme proposal is to impose a rule which fixes the composition of the ECB portfolio and hence of its open market operations; if the mix is right, according to point 2 above, the ECB would be precluded from extending credit; its functions would be strictly limited to the creation of outside ECUs. Without having a fully worked out solution to this problem, I am inclined to favor a rather strict rule of this kind. The main advantage is that it would eliminate any scope for pressure by fiscal authorities of individual countries aimed at finding support for their debts.[6] In addition, together with a clear provision that would exclude the possibility of a bail out by any Community body, such a rule would greatly reinforce market discipline. It would also be much easier to implement and enforce than budgetary rules.

There are difficulties, however. Some are basically technical and probably not very hard to solve: for instance, what should be done when the ECB incurs a loss due to a fall in the market value of the debt of an individual country? How should the loss be distributed among members?

A more substantial problem is that a strict rule would prevent the ECB from doing most of the things which effectively keep central bankers busy nowadays: keeping orderly conditions on the money markets, guaranteeing the smooth functioning of the payments system, lending of last resort to the government and commercial banks.

Can we do away with these functions? Or should they be attributed to the national authorities? If the second is the right answer, then the question becomes whether these functions can be performed through sterilized interventions, i.e., operations which do not impinge on the overall monetary base of the Community. For instance, national central banks could intervene to stabilize a particular market or to provide liquidity to a bank operating in the domestic clearing system by using deposits with commercial banks or other assets in their portfolio. With the government, they could operate much like an investment bank helping it to place its debentures on the market at the most favorable conditions. Quite clearly these would be major changes compared with present practices. The question is also left open of how the activities of national central banks would be financed.

Let me finally deal with two objections that may be raised to the proposal of adopting rather strict rules on the composition of the ECB assets. The first one is that they are irrelevant because bonds issued

---

[6] On this point, see also Kenen (196); Casella and Feinstein (1988); Branson (1989).

by different countries are likely to be very close or even perfect substitutes. If this was the case, a shift in the composition of the ECB assets would be completely offset by a shift of opposite sign in the composition of private portfolios, thus leaving interest rates on each country's bonds unaffected; function 2 (intermediation of credit) would still be performed by the ECB, but it would have no real or monetary consequences. The question is how seriously one should take the assumption of perfect substitutability. Clearly distributional issues are likely to arise when a country runs into financial difficulties, i.e. when the assumption of perfect substitution is violated because markets perceive different debtors' risks. More generally, if perfect substitution was really the rule, all loans extended at market rates by international organizations (or any other large institution or individual) would be a matter of irrelevance: in practice I believe that such activities are often very relevant, be it because of capital markets segmentations, imperfect substitutability, asymmetric information, signalling effects, etc.

My conclusion is that the consideration of substitution effects may reduce somewhat the preoccupations for the distributional aspects of the ECB activities, but by no means eliminates them.

The second objection is that the problem would more simply be solved by requiring the ECB to hold liabilities issued by private agents (mainly banks) rather than by national governments. Note that this is not a proposal of the Delors Report, which, in par.32, states: "While complying with the provision not to lend to public-sector authorities, the System could buy and sell government securities on the market as a means of conducting monetary policy." The proposal is, however, in the spirit, if not in the wording, of the Delors Report because it would greatly emphasize the distinction between monetary and fiscal authorities; on this ground, I think it deserves favorable attention. It would not, however, eliminate the problem of the distribution of ECB credit among countries, at least until there will be, as there is today, a high degree of coincidence between the geographical distribution of the ownership of banks and national boundaries. In addition, national governments would have an indirect interest in a generous financing policy of the ECB towards domestic banks, as long as the latter will remain among the major holders of their debts.

Undoubtedly, these problems will lose much of their relevance as Europe proceeds along the road of unification, a sense of supernational solidarity prevails and national boundaries become little more than geographic expressions. There is still, however, in this regard a rather long way to go.

7. COORDINATION OF FISCAL POLICIES

The discussion has so far dealt with the issue of whether a sound common monetary policy can be pursued despite individual countries possibly having different degrees of fiscal discipline. It has been argued that this should be feasible; the key prerequisite is not fiscal rules, but a strong monetary constitution endowing the ECB with a sufficient degree of independence from national governments.

A different issue is whether and to what extent fiscal policy should be coordinated at the Community level; even if fiscal responsibility was prevailing in all countries and monetary authorities were provided with the greatest degree of autonomy, it could be argued that fiscal policy should not be left entirely to the discretion of national governments. Basically three arguments have been put forward in support of this view (see Lamfalussy (1989) and Thygesen (1989)):

(a) undue appropriation of Community saving by one country. A high budget deficit in one country puts pressure on the overall level of interest rates, crowds out productive investment and diverts some Community saving to that country.

(b) Greater externalities. Monetary union is a part of a larger program of economic integration and would itself contribute to it. As countries become more integrated, the external effects of domestic policies acquire greater relevance. Since individual countries do not take account of such externalities, the overall outcome may be significantly inferior to the one that could be achieved with coordination.

(c) Policy coordination with third countries. Without some fiscal power at the Community level, the EMU would lack an important tool to negotiate with third countries and coordinate macroeconomic policies. On this account, an excessive burden would fall on monetary policy.

Overall it seems to me that argument (a) is unconvincing, while (b) and (c) are not compelling arguments for endowing the Community with powers on national budgets.

The first argument is unconvincing because there is no obligation for residents of the Community to finance the budget deficit of the expanding country. In the monetary union, individual governments, as well as firms and households, are part of a single, largely competitive credit market in which lenders can choose the most appropriate destination of their savings; if safe bonds issued by the government of country A are more attractive than, say, productive capital of country B, residents of country A will be well advised to purchase them. This behavior will maximize private returns; it will also generally maximize social welfare of country B. Undue appropriation of foreign savings would only be possible if country A encountered refinancing problems and was able to tax foreign residents through implicit bail-out obligations, which, as argued before, should not be a feature of the EMU.

It should also be considered that the inflow of saving to the expanding country is not necessarily larger with a monetary union than with, say, managed exchange rates. Such inflows are the counterpart of current account deficits; a budget expansion may well be associated with a larger current account deficit if, in addition to an increase in domestic income, it causes an appreciation of the real exchange rate.

As to argument (b), the issue is how much larger are the relevant externalities and, more importantly, can the resulting sub-optimalities be overcome through voluntary cooperation. As far as I know, no assessment has been made of the first point (increased relevance of externalities). One can, however, argue that the mobility of goods, labor and capital throughout Europe will not be much larger and may, perhaps, turn out to be smaller than that prevailing today between, say, Canada and the U.S. or among the Benelux countries; in neither case has there been a request for a transnational fiscal authority. At the very least it can be affirmed that the request is no more compelling in the case of the European Community.

On the second point (voluntary cooperation), suppose all member countries recognize that, as a result of uncoordinated decisions, aggregate fiscal policy is too restrictive and unemployment too high; it is hard to imagine that this problem cannot be solved through regular consultations. A more likely and serious situation arises when countries do not share the same assessment, either because they believe in different models of the economy or because they have different macroeconomic utility functions; in this case, however, there is no clear argument for cooperation based on welfare considerations.

Argument (c) has probably more validity. Clearly, without some authority on fiscal matters, the EC will be in a weaker position than otherwise in international relations. No single Community authority will be able to make commitments with the U.S., Japan or any other country on an important aspect of macroeconomic policy, without previous consultations with national governments. While this is true, it should also be noted that Europe will remain in a weak position in many other areas (environment, defence, etc.) simply because it is not a political union; on the other hand, its authority in international relations will be enhanced because it will at least have a common monetary policy.

Whatever the intrinsic merits of the last two arguments, it should be noted that they have a common logical premise in the belief that some fiscal activism is needed for the purpose of macroeconomic stabilization; they are clearly incompatible with requests for rigid forms of fiscal discipline, such as continuously balanced budgets.

If some fiscal activism is deemed necessary, the question arises of what budgets should be used to achieve the desired fiscal stance for the Community as a whole. The Delors Report suggests that the Community should have the authority to flex national budgetary policies, because the Community budget is too small to have a macroeconomic impact. This is a very difficult route and - I think - not an indispensable one.

The budget of the Community, now around 1 percent of EC GDP, will not exceed 3 or 4 percent in the foreseeable future. This size is small relative to that of most federations; clearly the <u>masse de manouvre</u> on the expenditure side will remain very limited. However, on the revenues side, where it is probably more appropriate to intervene for stabilization purposes (because of greater reversibility), it is certainly not impossible to think of changes in the order of two or more percentage points of GDP. What matters here is not so much size, but flexibility. Since changes in expenditures of this order of magnitude are out of the question, the issue is whether a tax cut may credibly be transitory: otherwise Community borrowing would quickly grow out of proportion. At present the Community budget is essentially constrained to be continuously balanced. If some activism is called for, it seems to me that the best route is to relax this constraint somewhat, for instance by requiring that the budget be balanced on average over cycles of, say, five years. In most normal circumstances, this should be sufficient to allow the Community to have an impact on the overall fiscal stance in Europe. In exceptional circumstances (say, a major depression) there is no reason to exclude the possibility of concerted actions by national governments.

The main conclusion of this section is that the arguments for a transfer of powers to the Community in the budgetary field are not decisive; in addition, those who advocate such a transfer as a way of improving the efficiency of macroeconomic policies should recognize that allowing the Community to run temporary deficits or surpluses in its own budget is both more natural and less contentious than endowing it with authority on national budgets.

8. CONCLUSION

This paper has dealt with the question of how much fiscal discipline and coordination are necessary for the viability of a monetary union. The basic suggestion is that there are no compelling arguments pointing to the fact that a common monetary policy also requires a common fiscal policy nor a major shift in decision-making power from national to Community authorities. It is much more important that a strong monetary constitution be adopted based on two principles, both requiring a clear separation between monetary and fiscal policy: price stability and distributive neutrality. The Delors Report is very explicit and states some of the institutional consequences of the former, in terms of autonomy and accountability of the ECB. The latter (distributive neutrality) should be made more explicit. In section 6 above I have tried to sketch some of its implications for the functions and operations of the ECB. In essence, they should be such as to prevent it from being involved in any way in the financial position of member states; financial markets must be convinced that neither the central bank nor any other Community institution implicitly guarantee the obligations of national governments. At the technical level, the remaining challenge is to design a well balanced system whereby the central authority controls the aggregate supply of base money, while national authorities perform the remaining central banking operations, with sterilized interventions.

I have also argued that, to the extent that the contention concerns the coordination of fiscal and monetary policies rather than the monetary implications of fiscal discipline (or lack of it), the solution should and can be found in a more flexible use of the Community budget, rather than in Community control over national budgets.

Last but not least, I have stressed that a major fiscal correction in some European countries (among which Italy) is necessary to achieve greater financial and exchange rate stability in the transition towards a monetary union. To this end and to avoid repeating past mistakes in the future, it may be appropriate to design rules which substantially reduce governments' discretion in the budgetary field. This could best be done at the national level, with the EC taking the lead to promote the adoption of such rules and, possibly, "harmonize" them across countries. This is, of course, a different proposal from that of transferring fiscal powers to Community and conditioning to it the formation of a monetary union.

REFERENCES

Bishop, G. et al. (1989), "1992 and Beyond. Market Discipline Can Work in the EC Monetary Union," Salomon Brothers, November.

Branson, W. (1989), "Trade Balances, Capital Mobility, and Fiscal Policy in the EC," Paper for the Conference "Managing Change in the EMS," Madrid, 11-12 May, 1989.

Buchanan, J., Rowley, C., Tollison, R. (1987), "Deficits," Oxford, Blackwell.

Casella, A., Feinstein, J. (1988), "Managing a Common Currency," NBER Working Paper No.2740, October.

Cohen, D. (1989), "Costs and Benefits of a European Currency," in M. De Cecco and A.Giovannini (eds.), "A European Central Bank? Perspectives on Monetary Unification after Ten Years of the EMS," Cambridge, C.U.P., pp.195-208.

Committee for the Study of Economic and Monetary Union (1989), "Report on Economic and Monetary Union in the European Community" (Delors Report), Luxembourg, Office for Official Publications of the European Communities.

Galli, G., Masera, R.S. (1990), "Fiscal Responsibility, Monetary Policy and the Exchange Rate," in and L.McKenzie and S.Zamagni (eds.), *Value and Capital, Fifty Years Later*, Proceedings of a conference held by the International Economic Association at Bologna (Italy), London, Macmillan.

Giavazzi, F., Giovannini, A. (1988),"Limiting Exchange Rate Flexibility: The European Monetary System," Cambridge (Mass.), MIT Press.

Goodhart, C. (1989), "The Delors Report: Was Lawson's Reaction Justifiable?," LSE Financial Markets Group, Special Paper No.15.

HM Treasury (1989), "An Evolutionary Approach to Economic and Monetary Union," London.

Kenen, P.B. (1969), "The Theory of Optimal Currency Areas: An Eclectic View," in R.A. Mundell and A.K.Swoboda (eds.), "Monetary Problems of the International Economy," Chicago, University of Chicago Press, pp.41-60.

Lamfalussy, A. (1989), "Macro-coordination of Fiscal Policies in an Economic and Monetary Union in Europe," in "Report on Economic and Monetary Union in the European Community" (Delors Report), Luxembourg, Office for Official Publications of the European Communities.

Padoa-Schioppa, T. (1988), "The European Monetary System: A Long-Term View," in F.Giavazzi, S.Micossi and M.Miller (eds.), "The European Monetary System," Proceedings of a Conference Organized by the Banca d'Italia, STEP and CEPR, Cambridge, C.U.P.

Tabellini, G., Alesina, A. (1988), "Voting on the Budget Deficit," UCLA Working Paper No.539, December.

Thygesen, N. (1989), "Have We Come Closer to Economic and Monetary Union?," Talk at the Royal Institute of International Affairs, Chatham House, July 5th, 1989.

Thygesen, N., Gros, D. (1989), "Concrete Steps Towards Monetary Union," Paper for the "CEPS Sixth Annual Conference 1989," Brussels, November 29-December 1st.

Van der Ploeg, F. (1989), "Fiscal Aspects of Monetary Integration in Europe," Paper for the "Conference on European Economic Integration: Towards 1992," NBER, August 3-4, 1989.

TOWARDS A EUROPEAN CENTRAL BANK: FISCAL COMPATIBILITY AND MONETARY CONSTITUTION

by: Tommaso Padoa-Schioppa

Discussant: Vito Tanzi

In his very interesting and useful paper, Dr.Padoa-Schioppa addresses the question of how much fiscal discipline and coordination among the budgets of the members of the European Community (EC) are desirable or even necessary for the viability of a full-fledged monetary union. He refers to the Delors Report that argued that quite a lot of fiscal discipline and coordination would be necessary. The prescriptions of that Report are quite demanding for member states and the Community. Establishment of fiscal rules are very difficult, both technically and politically.

Although Dr.Padoa-Schioppa clearly appreciates that "much greater fiscal discipline than we have seen so far in many European countries is desirable both to proceed toward the (monetary) union and for other reasons," he concludes that "some transfer of powers to the Community in the budgetary field... is not an absolute precondition for the union." He thus downplays the importance of fiscal rules while highlighting the importance of insuring independence from national pressures for the European Central Bank (ECB). I fully agree with his conclusion about the need for full independence of the ECB. Such independence is clearly a necessary condition if the ECB is given the task of insuring price stability. The issue I wish to address in this comment is whether it is also a sufficient condition. I will focus on this issue since this is the only part of the paper in which I felt that I was in some disagreement with the author. However, the disagreement may be one of degree rather than of substance.

Given the changes already set in motion in the European Community for 1992 and adding to these changes the creation of a full-fledged monetary union would mean that the EC countries would become parts of an economic entity characterized by a common monetary policy, irrevocably fixed exchange rates, and free movements of capital, goods, and, to a large extent, people. Seen from the rest of the world, the EC would thus become indistinguishable from a single economic entity. Or, putting it more strongly, it would acquire, in an economic sense, the same characteristics as a federation such as, for example, the United States of America. The establishment of a European Monetary Union would constitute a major political, and not just economic, step toward a United States of Europe.

The countries of the European Community would lose the capacity to control their exchange rates, to pursue independent monetary policies, and, to a large extent, to pursue independent tax policies. This is the situation of, say, California or Texas within the United States. Even though these states can levy local taxes, these cannot diverge significantly from those of other states. The taxes that really count are those imposed by the Federal government. And, of course, these states cannot pursue an independent monetary or exchange rate policy. In a typical federation the central government receives and spends well over two-thirds of all tax revenue. This spending is necessary because there are major needs associated with stabilization, redistribution, and the generation of certain public goods that cannot be satisfied, or at least cannot be satisfied adequately, by the independent actions of the states or the provinces that make up the federation.

Stabilization policy cannot be pursued by the individual states because (a) independent monetary policy is no longer possible and (b) because of the large externalities that characterize fiscal policy. In other words, much of the expansionary impact of, say, a tax cut or an expenditure increase by a member country (or a member state) would benefit other countries. This, again, is the situation of California or Texas. These states do not even attempt to pursue countercyclical policies but leave these policies to the U.S. federal government.

With increased integration of the member states and with increased population mobility (workers, students, pensioners, welfare recipients, etc.), redistributive policy would also have major externalities. It is no accident that in federations this function is largely left to the central government. But the Community in its present and foreseeable role will only have very limited resources. Therefore, its role in income redistribution and income maintenance would have to be very limited.

It is true that at this time redistributive and countercyclical policies are much less fashionable than, say, one or two decades ago. But this may be just a phase. The pendulum may very well swing once again. Bring in a major recession and you will get again strong demands for stabilization policies and for income maintenance and redistributive policies. Furthermore, the role of the Community in dealing with Community-wide public goods or public "bads" (pollution, etc.) is likely to rise, demanding once again a greater involvement by a central fiscal policy. In conclusion, I see lots of difficulties in an economic unit where a full-fledged monetary union has been created without an accompanying and much more powerful central fiscal authority than the existing or contemplated one. Just think of the United States without the Federal government. After all, historically, economies always had fiscal authorities long before the need for a monetary authority was felt.

The discussion so far has ignored the current fiscal stance of the member countries. If all the countries of the Community entered the monetary union with identical fiscal stances (say, similar fiscal deficits and a similar debt to GDP ratios), they could be expected, hopefully, to follow similar fiscal policies because of their inability to rely on the central bank to help finance their deficit. However, the fiscal situation is currently widely divergent within the Community. For example, in 1989 interest payments on public debt as a percentage of GDP ranged from about 1 percent in Luxembourg to a high of almost 11 percent in Belgium. Other relevant statistics - such as net government borrowing as a proportion of GDP and gross public debt as a percentage of GDP - show equally wide ranges. Given this situation, would the internal political process bring the needed adjustment of fiscal policies within the EC countries to allow them to live in harmony with the monetary union? I doubt it. It should be recalled that the needed fiscal adjustment would have to take place in a situation where some important tax tools would no longer be available because of the harmonization of some rates and the difficulty of taxing capital incomes with higher rates than other countries within the Community.

TOWARDS A EUROPEAN CENTRAL BANK: FISCAL COMPATIBILITY AND MONETARY CONSTITUTION

by: Tommaso Padoa Schioppa

Discussant: Alberto Giovannini

1. Introduction

The paper by Tommaso Padoa Schioppa provides a balanced assessment of the fiscal aspects of the project of monetary union in Europe, with special reference to the discussion of this problem in the Delors report. In my comments I first offer as a background a brief catalog of the concerns about the effects of diverging fiscal stances among European countries and their influences on monetary policy. Equipped with this analysis I present my interpretation and comments on Padoa Schioppa's position.

2. The Nature of the Interaction between Monetary and Fiscal Policy

The interactions between monetary and fiscal policy is either indirect - through the interest rate or the exchange rate - or direct, through the financing of budget deficits. Fiscal expansions can affect interest rates. The conditions for an increase in budget deficits (primary deficits) to increase interest rate are twofold:

- the public does not discount future taxes that are inevitably associated with higher current deficits at the same rate as the government discounts its own cash flows (in other words, the public is either short-sighted or financial markets are imperfect);
- the country is large enough to affect the world rate of interest, or its own capital markets are imperfectly integrated with the rest of the world.

An increase in primary deficits may or may not lead to an appreciation of the real exchange rate, depending on the source of the primary deficit (higher spending or lower taxes, and the attendant effects on the demand for domestic versus foreign goods), and on the wealth effects of future taxes alluded to the above.

These effects of fiscal expansions on important macro variables might exert pressures for offsetting moves by the monetary authority. But what should these offsetting moves be? Some would argue that the phenomena described above would be signs of "overheating" of the economy, and require an offsetting monetary contraction. Others would argue the opposite, that high interest rates can be readjusted by monetary expansions, and that exchange-rate appreciations are always sterilized by higher-than-expected money growth. In countries where the debt level is high, higher real interest rates increase the cost of the debt, and the total deficit as well. The pressure on the monetary authority to lower interest rates is in these cases doubled.

Another indirect pressure on central banks to react to government policies is associated with the role of central banks as lenders of last resort. Fiscal deficits have to be financed in (presumably domestic) financial markets. If these deficits are excessive, the pressure on domestic money markets can be threatening to their stability. The central bank might be asked to inject extra liquidity on these markets to ensure their smooth functioning.

Finally fiscal policy can have direct effects on monetary policy in all those countries where the government can easily, without resistance, finance deficits by asking the central bank to monetize them.

3. Inflationary Bias of Government Deficits

Direct financing of government deficits clearly has an inflationary effect on the economy, since it amounts to increases in the stock of money. By contrast, monetary policies aimed at offsetting the effects of budget deficits on interest rates and exchange rates might be either inflationary or deflationary. In the case where the central bank responds to fiscal deficits with a monetary contraction, the rate of inflation in equilibrium (and in the long run) is not likely to go up. In the case where the central bank responds to fiscal deficits with monetary expansions, the effect is inflation.

An additional complication is that the public may discount, in its own pricing decisions (price-setting by firms, wage contracts between unions and employers), these reactions of the central bank to budget deficits. In countries where the government has a history of deficits, and where the experience is accommodation of the deficits by the central bank (that is, monetary expansions in response of budget deficits), the public has higher expectations of inflation than otherwise. If the central bank does not fulfill these expectations by actually expanding in response to deficits, a recession occurs. The central bank is, in this case, almost forced to accommodate the government deficits.

4. Should Budgetary Discipline be Part of the Statute of the European Central Bank?

Padoa Schioppa's paper concludes that the answer to this question should be no. I concur. The above discussion has shown that there appear to be no compelling reasons to include budgetary discipline in the statute of the European central bank. It is, however, very important to make sure that the public has full confidence on the independence of the new institution from influences from national fiscal authorities. This can only be achieved by ruling that the European central bank will never be asked to finance budget deficits, and will never be asked to "bail out" national governments.

The observations in the previous paragraph apply to the changes in the Treaty of Rome that will be forthcoming with the intergovernmental conference. They do not imply that some convergence of budgetary performance, and in particular a containment of the deficits-debt spiral in countries such as Italy and Belgium, is an important condition for macroeconomic stability, and one that should be sought out during this period of transition to the monetary union.

3 CAN RESTRICTIONS ON BANKING REPLACE FISCAL ADJUSTMENT? SEIGNIORAGE, RESERVE REQUIREMENTS, AND MANDATORY INVESTMENT

Allan Drazen

The integration of European markets in 1992 requires integration on several levels if it is to achieve all of the beneficial effects which have been promised. On the level of macroeconomic policy, monetary integration, meaning fixed exchange rates and the possible move to a single European currency, requires convergence of monetary policy across countries. There must be convergence of inflation rates, which, given the predominant role of West Germany in the EMS, means that countries will need to follow low inflation policies.

Economic integration will require a certain degree of fiscal convergence as well. With generally unrestricted movement of both capital and labor across countries, it will be impossible for a country to levy significantly higher tax rates on income than its neighbors. Nor will a country be able to run a significant budget deficit if its neighbors have balanced budgets. With limited flexibility on tax and seigniorage revenues and on debt issuance, countries which have heavy levels of debt service will find their desired level of expenditure constrained. A crucial policy issue in the transition to 1992 is therefore how to control the growth of government debt in the period leading up to full integration.

A second transitional issue for macroeconomic policy is the extent to which rates of monetary growth and inflation are to be reduced prior to 1992. In practice this is often a question of whether to join the EMS and accept the discipline of low inflation before fuller economic integration. Most European countries have chosen this route, with previously high inflation countries finding it necessary to sharply reduce their rates of monetary growth. As is well known, a policy of lower monetary growth rates may come into conflict with the desire to control the growth of debt if a country relies heavily on seigniorage to finance government spending. The fall in seigniorage revenues must either be replaced by some other revenue source, be offset by a cut in government expenditure, or lead to growth in government debt. If adjusting regular tax revenues or government spending in the short-run is difficult, the move to a low inflation path thus induces rapid growth in government debt. This leads to the well known "Unpleasant Monetarist Arithmetic" problem of Sargent and Wallace (1981). Eventually, intertemporal solvency means that the deficit inclusive of debt service must be eliminated. If the loss of seigniorage revenue leads to ever-increasing debt service, the eventual fiscal adjustment will be all the more difficult.

Policymakers are well aware of the adverse future effects of debt accumulation. Therefore, when the move to a lower inflation path precedes the fiscal adjustments necessary to make the inflation path long-run feasible, policymakers look for alternative ways to control the growth of the debt. The purpose of this paper is to consider monetary policies that have been used in conjunction with capital controls towards this end. These include the use of high reserve requirements on banks and the forced absorption of government debt by financial intermediaries. If domestic residents are constrained from holding foreign assets, these policies serve to reduce the growth of government indebtedness and debt service. I will argue however that such policies designed to improve the government's fiscal position in the short run may do so at the expense of ultimately worsening it in the long run. Hence, these policies exhibit a <u>perverse</u> aspect similar to what Sargent and Wallace stressed about reducing the rate of growth of the money supply as an anti-inflationary policy. They argued that in the absence of fiscal adjustment, a low-money-growth policy will increase inflation eventually (and may in fact do so immediately). Policies meant to escape the Sargent-Wallace problem may have a similar "unpleasant" characteristic.

The plan of the paper is as follows. In the next section I consider the government budget constraint as the key accounting relation and briefly review the Sargent and Wallace result. In section two I outline alternative monetary policies to control the growth of the debt and thus "get around" the Sargent-Wallace problem, and present some empirical evidence on their prevalence. In the third section I discuss why these alternative strategies may have perverse effects. The final section contains conclusions.

1. THE GOVERNMENT BUDGET CONSTRAINT AND THE SARGENT-WALLACE PROBLEM

The key relation of course is the government budget constraint. The excess of government expenditure plus debt service (outlays) over regular tax and seigniorage revenues must be covered by issuing debt. Letting b be (real) government debt, r the real interest rate, g government expenditures, τ regular taxes, μ the rate of monetary growth, and m real money holdings, we have

$$\dot{b}_t = r_t b_t + g_t - \tau_t - \mu_t m_t \ . \tag{1}$$

Suppose that at time t_0 there is a reduction in μ resulting, for example, from meeting the constraints imposed by a fixed exchange rate system. To study the implications of the reduction in μ suppose that previously seigniorage revenues equalled $r_0 b_0 + g_0 - \tau_0$, so that debt was constant. If the reduction in μ induces a fall in seigniorage revenues μm (the standard presumption), this fall must lead to either an increase in some other form of taxes, or to a cut in government outlays if debt is to remain unchanged. Making such changes are of course easier said than done. Countries which rely on seigniorage do so because of difficulties in raising other sorts of taxes and in cutting government expenditures. If the primary deficit could be easily cut in response to a loss of seigniorage revenue, it would not be used as a main revenue source to begin with. Thus, in discussing possible responses to a fall in the rate of monetary growth, I assume that g and τ remain fixed.

If government spending and regular taxes are constant, the by now standard approach to the fiscal effect of a fall in μ is the Sargent-Wallace "Unpleasant Monetarist Arithmetic" (1981) approach. With the interest rate exogenous and a standard money demand function, the fall in seigniorage revenues resulting from a fall in μ implies an increased deficit and growing debt. More specifically, government debt will grow at a rate faster than the rate of interest, so that the current deficit policy means that its present discounted value is unbounded. The infeasibility of debt growing without bound implies that eventually policy must be changed.

Sargent and Wallace consider a closed economy where government spending g and regular taxes τ cannot be adjusted even in the long run, so the eventual policy change is an increase in the rate of monetary growth μ. μ is increased by enough so that seigniorage exactly covers the deficit inclusive of debt service. Since debt service is higher at the date of the policy change than at t_0, the new rate of monetary growth must be higher than it was at t_0. Hence the policy of reducing the rate of monetary growth is not simply temporary by necessity, but actually leads to higher steady state monetary growth and inflation. With a forward-looking money demand function, the inflationary effects are felt before the date of the policy switch. Sargent and Wallace present a "spectacular" result that inflation may actually increase immediately at t_0 when the rate of monetary growth is reduced. In Drazen (1985b), it is shown in a standard Sidrauski money growth model that this will arise if the interest-elasticity of money demand is equal to or greater than one.

If the policy switch towards feasibility is in fact a cut in the primary deficit, the reduction in the rate of monetary growth can in fact be permanent and the inflationary consequences are not so straightforward. Drazen and Helpman (1990) consider the effects of alternative future policy switches (also in a closed economy model) and show that an expected cut in g in the future will lead to a <u>reduction</u> in inflation, while an expected future increase in non-distortionary taxes to restore feasibility will leave the time path of inflation unchanged. In all cases, however, postponing the fiscal adjustment means that the ultimate change must be larger than it would have been were it undertaken at t_0.

More relevant to the constraints imposed by monetary integration is Drazen and Helpman (1987), who consider the attempt to follow a fixed exchange rate regime when a fiscal deficit implies growing debt. With low-inflation policies being followed other countries in the fixed-rate system, the Sargent-Wallace problem is present. The loss of seigniorage implies that either the primary deficit must eventually be cut or fixed exchange rates must be abandoned.

2. THE USE OF CONSTRAINTS ON BANKS TO CONTROL GROWTH OF GOVERNMENT DEBT

The Sargent-Wallace approach suggests the desirability of finding ways to respond to the constraint of a low rate of monetary growth which entail neither growth of debt nor difficult large short-run changes in taxes or expenditures. Policymakers of course were well aware of the desirability of such alternative responses well before the original Sargent and Wallace article. In fact, countries have used monetary policy in a broader sense than open-market operations in an attempt to control the growth of government debt. The simplest and most common way in which monetary regulation is used to improve the fiscal position is via constraints on asset holding by financial intermediaries. These constraints either increase the demand for money or the demand for government debt in an intermediary's portfolio. As we shall see, these turn out to be basically equivalent.

To put this in perspective, one can return to the government budget constraint. When $g - \tau$ is fixed, the Sargent-Wallace approach is to argue that a reduction in μ implies a reduction in μm, so that $\dot{b}$ must rise. Alternative responses to reductions in μ may be thought of as either using monetary controls to increase m, so that seigniorage does not fall, or reducing the effective interest rate r so that the fall in seigniorage is offset by a fall in interest costs.

The first alternative is the use of government controls on bank's portfolios to increase the demand for money and thus increase seigniorage. The specific mechanism is the use of high reserve requirements to increase the demand for reserve by banks. The importance of reserve requirements in generating seigniorage revenues becomes apparent when we look at countries such as Greece, Italy, Portugal, or Spain which have relied heavily on seigniorage to finance government expenditures. What is initially striking about these countries is that they have not only high inflation rates relative to their northern neighbors, but relatively high ratios of the monetary base to GDP as well (see Table 1).

Looking at the components of the monetary base, one sees that high money-to-GDP ratios in the southern countries are due not to high currency to GDP ratios, but to high bank reserves (relative to GDP), which are an order of magnitude higher. The last two columns of the table explain why this is so. High bank reserves are not so much a reflection of much larger banking sectors (as evidenced by bank deposits as a percentage of GDP not being significantly higher in the southern countries) but of a high reserve to deposit ratio. The ratio of bank reserves to deposits is several times as high in Greece, Italy, Portugal, and Spain as it is elsewhere in Europe.

The high demand for reserves by financial intermediaries reflects high reserve requirements, rather than holding of excess reserves. Table 2 indicates the sharp differences in reserve requirements across countries, which correlates highly with reserve holdings.

The importance of increased reserve requirements as a <u>response</u> to reductions in the rate of monetary growth may be found in the <u>time paths</u> of reserve requirements in the four southern countries. As Giavazzi (1988) reports, these countries raised their reserve requirements simultaneously with the adoption of policies to lower average rates of monetary growth. Marginal reserve requirements were raised from $15^3/_4$ to 25 percent in Italy after 1979; in Spain reserve requirements went from below 10% to over 25% between 1982 and 1983: in Greece they went from 12 to almost 30 percent in the early 1980's.[1]

A closely related strategy is to force domestic financial (and perhaps non-financial) institutions to absorb government debt. This may be at below market rates, or, at the market rate which is lower than it otherwise would have been due to induced demand for government debt. The easiest way to achieve this goal is to place a "secondary" reserve requirement on banks for the holding of government interest-bearing obligations. If achieved in this way, this policy of forced absorption of government debt is almost identical to the previous one. As in the case of reserve requirements to increase the demand for the monetary base, the bank is forced to hold low-interest bearing assets of a particular kind. The effect on the budget constraints and the balance sheets of both the government and the financial intermediary are the same, except for the "labelling" of the items.

---

[1]It is not entirely clear whether it will be impossible to use high reserve requirements to generate seigniorage after capital market liberalization is in place in Europe. Current banking directives require bank capital requirements to be uniform across countries, but will apparently allow countries to set liquidity requirements as they choose for banks operating within their borders. Though Italy for example could in principle continue to maintain high reserve requirements for banks (domestic or foreign) operaiting within its borders, could it do so in practice? Since retail banking appears to be unprofitable across national boundaries, it is by no means clear that competition in banking will necessarily eliminate differential reserve requirements.

TABLE 1

THE IMPORTANCE AND SOURCES OF SEIGNIORAGE REVENUES

	Seigniorage (% of tax revenues) 1979-86	Monetary Base (% GDP 1986) Total	Currency	Bank Reserves	Bank Deposits % GDP 1986	Reserve to Deposit ratio
Greece	9.1	22.6	9.8	12.8	48.6	.265
Italy	6.2	18.6	6.8	11.8	66.6	.177
Portugal	11.9	20.5	9.5	11.0	38.6	.286
Spain	5.9	19.3	7.5	11.8	60.2	.196
Belgium	0.4	8.2	7.8	0.4	33.4	.012
France	1.3	5.9	4.5	1.4	38.5	.038
Germany	0.8	9.9	5.8	4.1	53.2	.078
United Kingdom	0.5	4.6	3.6	1.0	45.7	.021

Notes: This table is drawn from Drazen (1989) based on several tables in Giavazzi (1988).

Seigniorage is the change in the monetary base, line 14 from International Financial Statistics of the International Monetary Fund. The definition of seigniorage is as in Fischer (1982), not the more general notion of total revenue from money creation suggested in Drazen (1985a).

Tax revenues are from Revenue Statistics of OECD Member Countries. They include personal and corporate income taxes, employers' and employees' social security contributions, and property, consumption, and excise taxes.

Currency is line 14a from IFS.
Bank reserves is line 20 from IFS.
Bank Deposits are demand, time and savings, and foreign currency deposits, lines 25 and 26 from IFS.

TABLE 2

RESERVE REQUIREMENTS FOR COMMERCIAL BANKS, 1988
(required reserves as a percent of demand deposits)

Greece	7.5	
Italy	25	(marginal rate)
Portugal	15	
Spain	18	
Belgium	0	
France	5	
Germany	6-12	
United Kingdom	0.5	

These figures are taken Giavazzi (1988).

Such a policy has been used, for example, in both Greece (see Welch [1981]) and Italy. In Italy portfolio constraints mandating compulsory investment in government securities (and those of special credit institutions associated with the government) have been imposed in addition to regular reserve requirements on both banks and savings and loan associations (Casse di Risparmio).[2] Such portfolio constraints have been in effect with minor interruptions from 1973 until 1986, though they were relatively loose starting in the early 1980's. When first imposed in 1973 the constraints were in terms of a required increase in holding of government securities by banks, but they were soon converted to a marginal reserve requirement, linking required increases in the holding of securities to increases in deposits.

The importance of these restrictions not only on balance sheets, but also in providing a market for government securities may be seen by comparing figures for the mid-1950's and for 1974. (All figures from Bank of Italy Annual Reports.) The proportion of deposits invested in long-term, fixed-interest securities rose from 12.65% in 1951-55 to 31.22% in 1974 when the restrictions were in force. This trend is seen

[2] I am indebted to Lorenzo Savarelli for providing me information on compulsory investment requirements.

as due primarily to holding of securities issued by special credit institutions. (These are state-owned credit institutions which float securities to raise fund to provide investment funds for specific sectors or regions.) The ratio of such obligations to total deposits rose from 3.76% in 1951-55 to 18.13% in 1974. Especially telling is the holding of long-term securities of special credit institutions by financial institutions subject to mandatory investment restrictions as a percentage of the loans made by these institutions. This rose from 12 percent in the 1950's to 47 percent in 1974. The bank market for these securities is crucial for the ability of special credit institutions to float their debt. The rationale for this policy is exactly that: to enable these institutions to market their debt at "reasonable" interest rates.[3]

These constraints on banks require constraints on individual holding of foreign assets so that domestic bank deposits are still held. Such constraints may have direct effects in increasing the demand for money. For example, restrictions on use of foreign currency in transactions (well known in high inflation economies, such as Israel), increase the demand for domestic currency. Hercowitz and Sadka (1987) consider the welfare implications of such restrictions. I will not pursue the long-run implications of these direct effects here.

3. SHORT- AND LONG-RUN EFFECTS OF PORTFOLIO CONSTRAINTS

In the short-run the two policies outlined above reduce the growth of government debt and the cost of servicing the debt, as equation (1) makes clear. Hence they have a short-run fiscal benefit.

What about their long-run effects? Slower growth of government debt suggests less crowding out and a smaller negative effect on the future tax base, in short, a definite fiscal improvement relative to the case of not using portfolio constraints. In fact, the opposite may be the case. The reason is that portfolio constraint policies reduce the

---

[3] An interesting aspect of the role of these restrictions in keeping down interest rates can be found in their evolution over time. Originally the restrictions were formulated entirely in terms of par value of the debt; this was changed when it was found that banks reduced their bite by buying securities on the secondary market when interest rates were high and hence prices were low. Though reducing the effective restriction, such a reaction has the side effect of lowering interest rates when they are cyclically high.

return to saving if foreign assets cannot be substituted for domestic ones. Hence saving is depressed. If the fall in saving exceeds the fall in government debt, net invesment will fall.

To consider this more formally, let's begin with a national income accounting relation. Denoting labor income by y, capital by k, and private consumption by g, we have

$$\dot{k} = y + rk - c - g. \qquad (2)$$

If a large part of saving is done via in banks, portfolio restrictions can have two important effects on capital accumulation. First, the interest rate paid to depositors is affected, implying possible significant effects on saving and consumption. Second portfolio restrictions can induce a direct reduction in investment and the capital stock.

To understand these two effects, let us begin with the reference case where individuals have infinite horizons and the eventual closing of the deficit is achieved via an increase in nondistortionary taxes. In the absence of portfolio constraints, increases in government debt induce just enough saving to pay off the higher debt. We have a case of Ricardian equivalence, with consumption being unaffected by the growth in government debt. Hence, by (2), capital accumulation is also unaffected. There is no crowding out.

Now consider the same situation where a positive deficit will eventually be closed by increasing non-distortionary taxes, but where portfolio constraints are temporarily imposed to lower the rate of growth of government debt. First of all the portfolio constraints imply a temporary fall in the rate of return to holding deposits, meaning a relative price change. By a consumption tilting argument, this may induce an increase in current consumption.[4] Equation (2) then implies that capital accumulation will be lower than in the previous case, that is, than in the absence of portfolio constraints. Hence, though government debt is growing <u>less</u> fast than in the previous case, there is <u>more</u> crowding out.

---

[4]"May" because the change in the interest rate has wealth effects in addition to relative price effects. If this latter (i.e. substitution) effect dominates, consumption will rise in response to lower interest rates.

There is a further possible depressing effect on capital accumulation. Once again suppose that investment is largely mediated through banks. The portfolio readjustment which occurs as regulations are put on (as in the case of Italy in 1973) means that banks may have to reduce the quantity of loans on the asset side of their balance sheets. If some of these loans are not marketable and can't simply be sold to another holder, some investment projects would have to be liquidated. This would imply that there would be a direct depressing effect on investment. (As discussed in Drazen [1989], this effect can be mitigated by accomodating monetary policy at the time that the portfolio constraints are imposed. For example, if the central bank increased their lending of reserves to banks at the same time that portfolio constraints were first imposed, the necessary portfolio readjustment would not require liquidation of loans.)

These considerations lead to a perverse fiscal effect of these policies beyond that stressed by Sargent and Wallace. A reduction in seigniorage (an increase in d for a <u>given</u> tax system) inducing growth of government debt has a further long-run fiscal effect in addition to the increase in debt service stressed by Sargent and Wallace, stemming from the possible crowding out of investment. To the extent that the future capital stock is lower than it otherwise would be, future output and hence the future tax base is lower as well. More formally, a fall in μm induces an increase in d and hence increased $\dot{b}$. For a fixed interest rate r capital accumulation is crowded out. To the extent that taxes τ depend on k, there is a doubly perverse effect of a policy that increases d today. Not only will the growth in debt mean that the adjustment in d will have to be larger the longer it is postponed; the fall in the tax base means that the same increase in total taxes will require higher rates than would otherwise have been the case.

The second policy, using portfolio constraints to create a demand for government debt, has similar effects. As indicated above, one may view this policy as reducing the interest rate relative to what it otherwise would be. Once again, we may get a consumption tilting effect, with current saving and capital accumulation falling. (Of course, to the extent that government debt is used to finance investment, as in the case of debt of special credit institutions in

Italy, the depressing effect on capital accumulation is lessened.) The possible perverse effects of reserve requirements may be thought of in terms of tax effects. Reserve requirements act like a tax on deposits, reducing the net return available to savers.

For these perverse effects to be relevant, there must be a lack of asset substitutability. In Drazen (1989) it was argued that for the high reserve requirement policy to be counterproductive the imposition of high reserve requirements must not cause depositors to switch their funds to alternative assets which finance new investment. One would think that depositors would switch to assets with similar risk and liquidity characteristics (which may be provided by institutions subject to similar controls), or perhaps to cash. In this case it is likely that the net effect will be to depress capital accumulation. On the other hand they may switch to liquid short-term government debt, where the increased demand for debt allows the government to market it at lower rates. The high reserve requirement policy would then have a favorable impact on the fiscal position, even though investment falls. One also sees why capital controls preventing domestic residents from easily switching into foreign assets are crucial.

4. CONCLUSIONS

To summarize, restrictions on banks' portfolios aimed at generating increased demand for money or at creating a market for government debt have the effect of reducing the rate of return to certain types of saving. If intermediaries subject to such controls are empirically important in the process of channelling saving to investment, aggreagate saving may be significantly affected. The implied crowding out has a long-run fiscal effect which works against the short-run fiscal improvement such policies are meant to induce. Hence, they should be seen as trading off the future for the benefit of the present. Even if these monetary policies were feasible after financial integration takes hold (see footnote 1) it is not clear that they are optimal.

The more general moral of this paper is identical to that of the original Sargent and Wallace (1981) or Drazen and Helpman papers. If monetary integration implies loss of seigniorage, there can be no escape from the hard choice of fiscal adjustment. Attempts to avoid cutting the primary deficit by means of constraints on the banking system which generate revenue can be short-term remedies at best and counterproductive at worst. The integration of European markets in 1992 requires not only monetary harmonization, but a good degree of fiscal harmonization as well.

REFERENCES

Bank of Italy, Annual Reports, 1974-80.

Drazen, Allan, "A General Measure of Inflation Tax Revenues," *Economics Letters* 17, 1985, 327-330. (a)

———, "Tight Money and Inflaton: Further Results," *Journal of Monetary Economics* 15, 1985, 113-20. (b)

———, "Monetary Policy, Capital Controls, and Seigniorage in an Open Economy," in R. Dornbusch and M. Draghi, eds., *A European Central Bank?*, Cambridge: Cambridge University Press, 1989.

——— and Elhanan Helpman, "Stabilization with Exchange Rate Management," *Quarterly Journal of Economics* 50, 1987,

——— and ———, "Inflationary Consequences of Anticipated Macroeconomic Policy," *Review of Economic Studies* 57, 1990.

Fischer, Stanley, "Seigniorage and the Case for a National Money," *Journal of Political Economy* 90, April 1982, 295-313.

Giavazzi, Francesco, "The Exchange-Rate Question in Europe," working paper, Universita' di Bologna, February 1988.

Hercowitz, Zvi and Efraim Sadka, "On Optimal Currency Substitution Policy and Public Finance," in A. Razin and E. Sadka, *Economic Policy in Theory and Practice*, London: Macmillan, 1987.

Welch, Jane, editor, *The Regulation of Banks in the Member States of the EEC*, The Hague: Martinus Nijhoff, 1981.

CAN RESTRICTIONS ON BANKING REPLACE FISCAL ADJUSTMENT? SEIGNIORAGE, RESERVE REQUIREMENTS, AND MANDATORY INVESTMENT

by: Allan Drazen

Discussant: Zvi Hercowitz

The discussion in the paper is motivated by the forthcoming European monetary unification, and its implications regarding the coordination of monetary policy. In particular, the issue addressed is the ability of the individual countries to raise revenue by the issue of money. Countries which currently use "seigniorage" more heavily will have to reduce their rates of monetary expansion to a uniform level. If fiscal adjustment, i.e., budget cuts or raising taxes, is not feasible in these countries, say for political reasons, lowering seigniorage implies increasing the rate of increase of the public debt. Drazen addresses these issues in the context of the "Unpleasant Monetarist Arithmetic" problem of Sargent and Wallace (1981). The "unpleasant" nature of the problem is that, in a closed economy context, the policy of currently switching from money to debt issue may lead to a current higher inflation rate, rather than to a lower one.

Drazen discusses proposed solutions to this problem, and then the drawbacks of these proposed solutions. Hence, it is a paper which contains its own discussion. In these comments I will try to put Drazen's own comments into some perspective.

First, given economic integration, inflation rates should be the same, and hence the Sargent and Wallace result should be reflected in the foreign reserves position of the central bank rather than in the price level. In other words, the open economy aspects of the "unpleasant arithmetic" were not addressed.

Given the postulated inability of the government to adjust the deficit, Drazen analyzes other possibilities to deal with the necessity of lowering the level of seigniorage. He discusses the use of controls on banks' portfolios as a possible way of avoiding the unpleasant results. Basically, the idea is simple. Seigniorage equals the product of the rate of monetary expansion and the real balances of high powered money. Monetary coordination implies a reduction in the former, which leads, by assumption, to a lower level of the product. Now, by imposing controls, the government may induce the private sector to hold more money balances, and in this way the level of seigniorage may be held constant in spite of the lower monetary growth rate.

One of these controls is to increase the reserve requirements imposed on the commercial banks. This is a policy which leads directly to increaing the demand for high powered money. Another related policy discussed by Drazen is to force financial institutions to absorb government debt at rates below the market rates.

In terms of the framework used by Drazen, the problem with these policies is that they are in fact ways of taxing financial intermediation. Hence they contradict the assumption that taxes are fixed. In any event, the main point here is that taxes on financial intermediation reduce the return on savings, and hence they distort the intertemporal allocation of consumption and the intratemporal consumption-leisure choice. The consequence is a reduction of capital accumulation and work effort, which reduces the future tax base even further. The need for fiscal adjustment would then be more acute in the future.

The conclusion of the paper can be described simply as "there is no free lunch." If the government is required to reduce seigniorage, it must either increase other taxes or reduce other expenditures.

4 CREDIBILITY AND CONSISTENT CENTRAL BANK POLICY: AN INSIDER VIEW

Horst Bockelmann

Allow me to start off with a general observation. Economists in central banks who are involved in formulating policy and academics who are engaged in studying questions of monetary theory and monetary policy to a large extent occupy the same ground. That, however, is not to say that their relationship is a cosy, neighborly one. They rarely succeed in joining forces or in making the best use of each other's comparative advantage. Difficulties between them seem to stem mainly from a dichotomy which may also exist in other fields of economic analysis but is perhaps nowhere more acute than here. On the one hand, monetary policy is an important part of macroeconomic policy and cannot be properly analyzed without recourse to macroeconomic theory. This implies the use of stylized facts and abstract models. On the other hand, there is a great deal of institutional detail, differing to some extent from country to country, that has to be taken into account for the actual conduct of monetary policy. Clearly, not all of it is also relevant for economic analysis. The important question is where does the dividing line run between institutional detail that is relevant and that which can be ignored without detriment to the proper analysis of specific monetary policy issues.

From the central banks' perspective much of the literature on the subject is of little help to them because it ignores essential institutional elements. They realize, of course, that theorists work under severe constraints in terms of what they can include in their models if they are to be kept manageable. That, however, cannot lead to a different judgement on the usefulness ("Let us assume that the can is open."). Perhaps it is indeed in many cases impossible to bridge this gulf.

The relatively recent literature on credibility and consistency over time[1] clearly represents an attempt to break out of the straightjacket of mechanistic models and to venture into the realm of

---

[1]See selected references at the end.

market psychology. Central bankers, however, may feel a little like Moliere's "bourgeois gentilhomme" who is told that, without being aware of it, he has been speaking prose all the time. It is not my role here to evaluate the contribution made by the literature on credibility, nor do I want to impose a narrowly utilitarian standard on the academic work carried out in this field, its direct or indirect contribution to the effectiveness of monetary policy. Economics evolves according to its own rules, and new approaches may well bear fruit in quite unexpected ways later on.

Central bankers speak of credibility problems in a very simple sense: the confidence a policy-making institution commands in terms of matching its deeds to its words. Perhaps that is already too narrow: credibility could also be established by a central bank which does not talk at all but only acts; its credibility would rest on its adherence to the revealed principles and objectives which it has followed and pursued over a long period. This, however, is not a very significant qualification. Central banks have generally been much more vocal in recent years than they used to be. Governors and Board members make frequent speeches and give interviews. Central banks publish bulletins and reports which are explicit on policy intentions and objectives. It benefits credibility if all agents of an institution speak with one voice on basic issues. Ultimately credibility stands and falls with what the central bank does, compared with what it says or otherwise leads people to expect. It is also important to emphasize the time dimension: credibility is not established overnight, it takes years or even decades to build up. On the other hand, it can be lost very quickly. Some central banks have vivid memories of occasions when they damaged their credibility; they remember well how long it took to restore it, at costs so real as to be almost quantifiable. This illustrates what may already be obvious from the context in which the term is used, that credibility is an asset, a catalyst which has a strong influence on the cost/benefit ratio of monetary policy.

Let me try to be more systematic. I shall deal first with the political environment in which the central bank operates and how that may affect its credibility. Then I shall move on to the different strategies which a central bank can adopt and discuss how they may help to enhance credibility. I shall conclude with a discussion of how credibility in turn influences the effectiveness of monetary policy.

The question of the central bank's legal or de facto position as a policy-making body should not be confused with that of the role of monetary policy in overall economic policy. At first glance it might appear that to give a high degree of independence to a central bank charged with the execution of monetary policy presupposes a high degree of functional separation of monetary policy from other forms of economic policy. I do not subscribe to that view. The link between monetary and fiscal policy is very close indeed in most countries. The money supply process which monetary policy tries to influence is an interactive process involving bank lending to the private and public sectors, bank customers' decisions on the form in which to hold their claims on the banks and the net flow of non-bank payments into or out of the country. By supplying the system with central bank balances, at a price which, as the sole source, it can fix unilaterally like any monopoly, the central bank influences this process at several points, one of the more important of which is the price of bank lending to the private sector.

If public sector credit demand is high, monetary policy has a problem, because that demand is not interest-rate-sensitive in the usual sense that at a higher rate less will be borrowed. It may be interest-rate-sensitive in a different way. With a heavy domestic debt burden, interest payments on the public debt may become such an important item of expenditure, that the government is tempted to bring pressure to bear on the central bank not to raise interest rates significantly. Even without pressure of that kind, monetary policy can be rendered ineffective by a large fiscal deficit that is financed through the banking system (even though not directly by the central bank). It is true that the central bank can squeeze lending to the private sector correspondingly more, but there are limits to that. Unfortunately, the prevailing view of the money supply process where the only thing of economic significance is the creation of monetary base by the central bank is a typical case in which institutional detail is ignored to the detriment of the analysis, i.e. the role of the banks and the microeconomic determinants of bank behavior (similar problems arise for a proper understanding of the links between current-account developments and the money supply process if attention focuses exclusively on central bank intervention).

The point I am trying to make here, however, is simply that it is often impossible for monetary policy to build up credibility unless it works hand in hand with fiscal policy. The case for central bank independence, which seems to be attracting growing support, does not rest on the functional separation of monetary policy, but on the expectation that

a) credibility is particularly relevant for monetary policy, and
b) it is easier for a central bank safe from government interference to establish credibility in this field than for a government which may have one overriding short-term objective, i.e. not to lose a forthcoming election.

Institutional continuity achieved through long, secure terms of office of those in charge of the institution is one aspect. A certain single-mindedness, the absence of any temptation to buy votes, greater consideration of the longer-term implications of a particular policy course are other aspects. Independence gives a central bank a much stronger voice in formulating the <u>common</u> economic strategy. The formula used in the United States: independent within the government expresses this very well, although I would not want to make any sharp contrast between that and being independent of the government. I regard the two as quite compatible.

I am, of course, familiar with the <u>counter-arguments</u> regarding central bank independence, some of them political, others even <u>economic</u>. To take the latter first, those economists who are in favor of monetary rules and against discretion in monetary policy have no use for central bank independence. I wonder, however, whether proposals for rules will ever become serious political issues. They have never moved from the classroom to the political arenas, which is not surprising considering the difficulties of providing a blueprint for how a monetary rule could be applied in practice. The <u>political</u> arguments against central bank independence concentrate on the lack of democratic control (independence of parliament is hardly less crucial than independence of government). It would appear, however, that a number of instances can be cited, in any democracy, in which it has proved expedient to give, through legislation, discretionary power to non-elected officials. Central bank independence may well be the exception to the rule, but nobody suggests that there should be no exceptions, the question is rather whether the benefits justify the exception. This takes the argument right back into the field of economics and the credibility benefits which independence may give.

Let me now turn to the strategies of monetary policy and how they relate to credibility. I use the term strategy here in a very broad sense, to cover final goals, intermediate targets and the use of instruments. I can say at once that final goals are all-important and instruments almost entirely unimportant for credibility. The interesting and contentious area from the point of view of credibility is that of intermediate targets. It should be immediately obvious that sticking to the final goals lies at the core of the process of establishing credibility. If the public observes any wavering in this respect credibility will suffer. This can be said almost without reference to what the final goals are.

Looking a little further, it does matter, however, what the final goals are, if only because not all final goals are equally attainable through appropriate monetary policies. A central bank committed to the final goals of full employment would have difficulty establishing credibility because there simply is no monetary policy which can ensure continuous full employment (the famous statement by Mr.Callaghan[2] still holds good - and he was not referring just to monetary policy but to any combination of the policies available). I would not be quite so emphatic with regard to the final goal of high growth, although the consensus seems to be that while monetary policy may be able to restrict growth, its capacity to stimulate it is rather limited. It is no accident, then, that credibility is most closely associated with the final goal of price stability, because that is the goal for which monetary policy can be held responsible more than any other. As I mentioned earlier in the context of the political position of the central bank, I do not believe that monetary policy can be successful in

---

[2]At the Labour Party Conference in Blackpool on 28th September 1976: "We used to think that you could spend your way out of a recession and increase employment by cutting taxes and boosting Government spending. I tell you in all candor that that option no longer exists, and that insofar as it ever did exist, it only worked on each occasion since the war by injecting a bigger dose of inflation into the economy, followed by a higher level of unemployment as the next step. Higher inflation followed by higher unemployment. We have just escaped from the highest rate of inflation this country has known; we have not yet escaped from the consequences: high unemployment."

isolation, it needs the support of other policies, but it still has a crucial role to play if price stability is to be achieved and maintained.

I have not mentioned a goal which is also often included among the final goals: external equilibrium. It needs closer definition, because neither exchange rate targets nor current-account or basic balance positions qualify as final goals per se. Maintaining external creditworthiness would come closer to ranking among final goals but most countries have such a wide safety margin on that score that there is hardly a need to acquire credibility. In any event, a good record on price stability would go a long way towards also attaining that final goal.

I can be brief on the instruments of monetary policy because the public simply does not care what instruments are employed for achieving intermediate targets, as long as they are achieved. The same cannot be said of intermediate targets, they are not without significance if only the final goals are achieved. There is the time dimension involved. Great efforts have been made to enhance the credibility of monetary policy by announcing intermediate targets and by letting the public follow the conduct of policy more closely, in the hope that this may provide a short-cut to influencing expectations. The prime example is the attempt to speed up the process of bringing inflationary expectations down by adopting monetary targets. Disinflation is a slow process under the best of circumstances because of the need to drive the cost-push out of the system (the shock treatment of a monetary reform is a different matter, but it must be resorted to only in extreme circumstances, not least because success is by no means certain). Bringing down inflationary expectations simply on the strength of the actual record on price stability will therefore take a long time. A monetary target which has been announced and which is seen to be adhered to can no doubt help restore credibility more quickly.

This is not the place to go into the central banks' experience in this respect at any great length. Some central banks based their adoption of monetary targets on strong assumptions regarding the stability of money demand functions over time, assumptions which later proved unjustified. In some countries the process of financial innovation created statistical problems with monetary aggregates. A general problem was whether central banks had sufficient confidence in their monetary targets to adjust their policies accordingly at times when other indicators were pointing in other directions. An even more basic difficulty arose from the lack of precision with which central banks can control monetary developments in the best of circumstances. This was particularly relevant in cases where targets had been formulated as averages over a year, which meant that an early aberration had such strong impact on the result as to make a later correction virtually impossible.

From a credibility point of view it mattered very much how central banks took an overshooting into account when setting the next target. In fact they had little choice but to start from the new base, but it took some explaining to justify this. Even those central banks which have continued to target monetary aggregates have made adjustments over time, either in the aggregates targeted or in the way the target has been formulated. I believe that notwithstanding all these difficulties monetary targets have played a useful role in enhancing the credibility of monetary policy, particularly during the period when everybody believed that we were all on a one-way street to higher and higher inflation rates. Monetary targets certainly became less important once it had been demonstrated that inflation could indeed be tackled. But as long as one is convinced that money matters, and the very existence of central banks rests on this belief, it is good discipline for a central bank to say what growth rate of money it considers appropriate in a given economic situation.

Another type of intermediate target that has played a great role in efforts to enhance the credibility of monetary policy, particularly in smaller countries, has been a nominal exchange rate target. Austria and the Netherlands have kept their currencies virtually at par with the D-Mark with the intention of "borrowing" credibility from the Bundesbank and have in this way acquired credibilty for themselves. Other small countries are wondering whether they should not also stay always in the upper band. Sweden has been targeting a nominal effective exchange rate based on a trade-related basket of currencies. Sticking to the intermediate target is given the highest policy priority in the cases mentioned; membership of the EMS exchange rate mechanism differs only in degree. Once markets no longer believe in both the determination and the ability of a central bank to adhere to its exchange rate target, the costs of doing so rise.

This brings me to my last point, the way in which credibility affects the effectiveness of monetary policy. Credibility, as I have already suggested several times, has to do with market expectations about the future behavior of central banks. Why do these expectations matter? The credibility of the central bank depends on it achieving a high degree of price stability. The existence or the absence of credibility can therefore be translated into expectations as to future movements of the price level, in other words inflationary expectations. As long as people expect inflation to stay high or to rise, they demand or offer an inflation premium whenever they enter into a contract involving the payment of a nominal magnitude in the future (interest, wages, etc.). Depending on the difference between the expected and the actual inflation rate, they experience windfall gains or losses. In addition to the inflation premium they will demand a risk premium to offset the uncertainty. Persistent inflationary expectations are thus one of the major obstacles to reducing inflation. If credibility helps to reduce inflationary expectations, it improves the chances for reducing inflation. Credibility thus has a self-fulfilling quality. What has been deduced here step by step about credibility with respect to price stability is immediately obvious if one talks about credibility in terms of stabilizing a certain price, such as a bilateral exchange rate. Nothing stabilizes a price as effectively as the widely held expectation that it will not change under any circumstances. But once that expectation has proved false, it takes a long time to restore belief. That is the long and the short of credibility.

REFERENCES

Alesina, A., "Alternative Monetary Regimes: a Review Essay," *Journal of Monetary Economics*, Vol.21, 1988, 175-183.

Barro, R., "Recent Developments in the Theory of Rules versus Discretion," *The Economic Journal*, Vol.96 Supplement, No.381, 23-37.

Barro, R. and Gordon, D., "Rules, Discretion and Reputation in a Model of Monetary Policy," *Journal of Monetary Economics*, Vol.12, No.1, 101-121.

Carlson, J., "Rules versus Discretion: Making a Monetary Rule Operational," *Federal Reserve Bank of Cleveland Economic Review*, Vol.24, No.3, 1988 quarter 3, 2-13.

Chari, V., "Time Consistency and Optimal Policy Design," *Federal Reserve Bank of Minneapolis Quarterly Review*, Fall 1988, 17-31.

Cukierman, A., "Central Bank Behavior and Credibility: Some Recent Theoretical Developments," *Federal Reserve Bank of St.Louis Review*, Vol.68, No.5, May 1986, 5-17.

Cukierman, A. and Meltzer, A., "A Theory of Ambiguity, Credibility, and Inflation under Discretion and Asymmetric Information," *Econometrica*, Vol.54, No.5, September 1986, 1099-1128.

Kydland, F. and Prescott, E., "Rules Rather than Discretion: The Inconsistency of Optimal Plans," *Journal of Political Economy*, Vol.85, No.3, 1977, 473-491.

Michener, R., "Rules, Commitment, and the Search for Stable Money: A Review Essay," *Journal of Monetary Economics*, Vol.23, 1989, 151-158.

Persson, T., "Credibility of Macroeconomic Policy: An Introduction and a Broad Survey," *The European Economic Review*, Vol.32, No.2/3, March 1988, 519-532.

Silbert, A. and Weiner, S., "Maintaining Central Bank Credibility," *Federal Reserve Bank of Kansas City Economic Review*, September/October 1988, 3-15.

Stein, J., "Cheap Talk and the Fed: A Theory of Imprecise Policy Announcements," *The American Economic Review*, Vol.79, No.1, March 1989, 32-42.

CREDIBILITY AND CONSISTENT CENTRAL BANK POLICY: AN INSIDER VIEW

by: Horst Bockelmann

Discussant: Thomas Franzen

I would like to thank Horst Bockelmann for a well written and balanced paper about vital questions for monetary policy. The paper correctly highlights that fiscal and monetary policy are interdependent - that there is a functional relation between them.

This has implications for the issue of credibility. If monetary policy does not work hand in hand with fiscal policy, it is hard to establish credibility for monetary policy. Mr.Bockelmann concludes that independence, defined either as the legal or the de facto position of a central bank, is not sufficient to assure credibility.

I have drawn three other conclusions from the Bockelmann paper. They are not necessarily in conflict with the views presented in the paper, but I regard them as important and think they are worthwhile considering.

My first conclusion is that the functional dependence between monetary and fiscal policy makes legal independence for a central bank even more important. If there are serious problems in conducting fiscal policy, for some reason or another, then there can be limits on the possibilities of conducting monetary policy and also on the possibilities of achieving credibility. But let's face it - credibility is not something you either have or don't have at all. It is a matter of degree; a central bank can have more or less credibility. Consequently, it is of great importance that we create a system which gives the central bank a high degree of credibility. One important way of achieving this is to increase the legal independence of the central bank.

My second conclusion is that it is of the utmost importance to find suitable forms for achieving central bank interdependence. I would like to stress, however, that achieving independence should not be bought at the expense of democratic control.

Contrary to the viewpoint of Horst Bockelmann, I think it is important to distinguish between central bank independence in relation to the Parliament and independence in relation to the Government. In a parliamentary system there can be a situation with a minority government. In particular in such a situation - but also in the case of a majority government - one can increase the stability in monetary policy and consequently the credibility, by having a central bank which is responsible directly to the Parliament.

Let me refer to a viewpoint put forward by Michael Bruno yesterday. He said that one of the most important tasks for a central bank is to participate in the discussion about economic policy. I fully agree on this, but would also like to add that independence in relation to the Government increases the credibility of the central bank in fulfilling this task.

One reason why a system with a central bank directly responsible to the Parliament can work is that in many countries there often seems to be a broad political agreement on how to conduct monetary policy.

Horst Bockelmann seems to argue that the functional relation between fiscal and monetary policy implies the following. If an upward pressure on the interest rate arises because of a too lenient fiscal policy, then there will be a pressure on the central bank to accommodate instead of fulfilling its policy of stabilizing prices.

I do not fully agree with this conclusion. High interest rates do not necessarily affect the policy of the central bank. Instead the fiscal policy can be affected. The Minister of Finance can use the high interest rates as an argument for putting pressure on the Parliament to accept a tighter fiscal policy.

Sweden is an example of a country with a system where the central bank is directly responsible to the Parliament. The details in the system can be discussed, but I think the basic principle is a good one.

How independence is defined and the ways and means to achieve independence depends, of course, on the political tradition in a particular country. But, again, I want to stress that lack of democratic control does not necessarily follow from central bank independence.

Let me sum up the discussion so far by clarifying that I think it is important to thoroughly analyze the relationship between the central bank, the parliament and the government. I do not agree with the idea that the legal relations are of minor importance.

<u>My third conclusion</u> from Mr.Bockelmann's paper is that credibility

is highly dependent on how the targets for monetary policy are formulated. I think that one important ingredient, in the work towards achieving increased credibility and independence of central banks, is to establish norms for monetary policy.

I do not agree with the comment made yesterday that central bankers strive to make life fun by not adhering to specified targets. The truth of the matter is that many European central banks have quite a booring life, if I may say so, in fulfilling exchange rate targets and by that way curbing domestic inflation. By focusing on exchnge rate targets, the antiinflationary policy works better - or faster. With fixed exchange rate targets, excessive inflation threatens to cause unemployment.

The possibility for monetary policy to take domestic considerations into account has, however, been limited. But imperfect substitutability between domestic and foreign assets has still created some room for domestic consideration in the formulation of monetary policies.

It is frustrating for a central bank to see that the inflationary rate is too high and, at the same time, know that the possibilities of pursuing a tight monetary policy is restricted by the exchange rate target. It may then be tempting to give up the exchange rate target in order to increase the manoevrability of monetary policy, but that temptation must be resisted - an exchange rate policy must rest on long-term considerations. The policy must be credible. Otherwise there is a great risk of ending up with a continued high inflation rate and, after an initial period of appreciation, facing a depreciation of the exchange rate. Perhaps the recent development in the U.K. can be used as an illustration of this risk. Perhaps it is also an illustration of the point made by Mr.Bockelmann - it is difficult for monetary policy to be credible unless it works hand in hand with fiscal policy.

However, all countries cannot rely solely on exchange rate targets in the formulation of monetary policy. In Europe, for example, Germany has served as an anchor and has given credibility to other EMS-countries. Within the EMS there has been a decrease in the frequency of realignments. This is a sign of the gradual upgrading of the goal of price stability among all the participating countries. This gradual process forms an important platform for the establishment of an European central bank.

There is, nevertheless, a risk of getting higher inflation rates than what is presently the case, when all EC countries have to decide on a common monetary policy. I think that the monetary policy conducted by a common European central bank could be less anti inflationary than the monetary policy presently pursued by the member countries. Today the monetary policy is, to a large extent, a reflection of the anti inflationary fight in West Germany. In a common central bank the monetary policy would reflect more of an average position among the EMS countries. There is a substantial risk that this average position would imply a policy that is less oriented towards fighting inflation.

5 DISCRETION, PRECOMMITMENTS AND THE PROSPECTS FOR A EUROPEAN CENTRAL BANK - FIXED PARITIES VERSUS A COMMONLY MANAGED CURRENCY

Alex Cukierman

1. INTRODUCTION

The recent acceleration in the process of economic and monetary integration in the EEC (European Economic Community) raised the far reaching possibility that the Community may eventually have a single currency managed by one central monetary authority. Following the Single Act the European Council appointed in mid 1988 a commission headed by Jacques Delors which was entrusted with the task of proposing concrete stages leading towards economic and monetary integration. The Commission submitted its report in 1989. The report proposes to achieve full monetary union in three stages. During the first two stages all obstacles to financial integration would be removed and coordination of monetary policies would be intensified. However, each central bank would continue to manage the national currency separately. In stage one "Realignments of exchange rates would still be possible" (Delors Report (1989) article 52), but an effort will be made to use other adjustment mechanisms. A similar fixed parities system with separately managed currencies is envisaged for stage two as well except that in this stage exchange rate realignments would be made only under "exceptional circumstances" (Op. Cit. article 57). The final stage would irrevocably lock exchange rates, transfer monetary management to a single European Central Bank and eventually replace all national currencies with a single Community Currency.

The last decade witnessed important developments in the positive theory of monetary policy. The early work of Kydland and Prescott (1977) drew attention to the fact that when monetary policymakers try to achieve a real objective like employment the optimal policy is dynamically inconsistent. Dynamic inconsistency arises when the optimal policy plan made prior to the conclusion of nominal wage settlements is no longer optimal for the policymaker after the conclusion of these settlements. The problem is not limited to the employment objective.

It arises whenever monetary policy is geared to achieve some real objectives like seignorage revenues (Calvo (1978)) or external balance (Cukierman and Liviatan (1990)) and the public is temporarily locked into nominal contracts or nominal assets. Since the public is normally aware of the dynamic inconsistency of monetary policy promises are not credible. Instead the public bases its current decisions on what it knows about the optimal discretionary response of policy _after_ it locks itself into nominal contracts or assets. This leads to a suboptimally high rate of inflation in comparison to a situation in which the monetary authority _precommits_ its policy prior to the conclusion of nominal contracts or the taking of positions in nominal assets by the public. The EMS can be viewed as an institutional device to attain a certain degree of precommitment of national monetary policies[1].

This paper evaluates the case for and against achieving a European Monetary Union without passing through a prolonged period of fixed but adjustable pegs in light of the new literature on credibility and endogenous policymaking. A main thesis of the paper is that monetary institutions should be judged by the policy outcomes that they induce. In particular, for the same distribution of shocks, monetary policy will respond differently under a system of fixed but adjustable pegs than under a commonly managed central bank whose Board of Directors makes decisions by majority rule. Basic policy conflicts will not be eliminated by the creation of a commonly managed currency. However, their resolution will differ under the two systems.

My presumption is that, under either type of institution, a system of partial precommitments of monetary policy will be in place but that they would be abandoned in the presence of sufficiently large shocks to the real economy. The difference between the two systems arises first because divergent monetary policies are not possible with a centrally managed currency and secondly because the commitment to price stability is abandoned under different sets of circumstances in the two systems.

Section 5 offers a somewhat limited but precise comparison between a system of adjustable pegs of the type proposed for stages one and two and a commonly managed currency of the type envisaged for stage three.

---

[1]Because of the Bundesbank's strong aversion to inflation and high degree of independence, the German Mark has recently functioned as a nominal anchor for many Community currencies (Giavazzi and Giovannini

The main results are: 1) A single country under a system of adjustable pegs is much more likely to renege on the commitment to price stability than the central bank of a commonly managed currency. 2) But the average rate of inflation under a commonly managed currency is not necessarily lower than under a system of adjustable pegs, given the degree of independence from fiscal authorities. 3) The central bank of a commonly managed currency is less likely to renege on the commitment to price stability the lower (algebraically) is the contemporaneous correlation between the shocks which affect the different countries. Result number 1 and additional considerations (discussed in section 6) lead me to conclude that stage two is not only unnecessary but actually detrimental for mobilizing the political and public support required for ultimately reaching full monetary unification.

In view of the slim political prospects for quick achievement of a commonly managed currency (Pöhl (1989)) a comparison between an adjustable peg system with different currencies and a commonly managed currency may seem to be a mere academic exercise. I believe, however, that it is important to engage in such exercises. First, the results of such comparisons may feed back on the political process and change the attitude of politicians towards quicker monetary unification. But even if it does not, a better understanding of the different responses of the two systems may prove useful when a European central bank is ultimately created[2].

In order to make the paper self-contained, the first three sections present a brief survey of policy outcomes under discretion in the presence of various motives for monetary expansion and demonstrate the benefits of precommitments. The employment motive is discussed in section 2 and the revenue and external balance motives are discussed in sections 3 and 4, respectively. An attempt is made to put the various models in the particular context of the EEC countries. For instance, to capture the high degree of unionization of EEC countries, the employment and external balance motives are discussed in the context of simple games between a national monetary authority and a union. Those three sections draw freely on Cukierman (1990) and Cukierman and Liviatan (1990) and contain little novel material. But they are used as building

---

[2]Various other aspects of a prospective monetary unification in Europe are discussed in De Cecco and Giovannini (1989).

blocks for the comparison of an adjustable peg system with a commonly managed currency in sections 5 and 6. The reader that is familiar with the modern literature on endogenous monetary policy may go directly to section 5 after a quick glance through the previous three sections. Section 5 contains the main new analytical results and uses them in order to evaluate the desirability of "stage two" as described in the Delors Report. Section 6 introduces additional considerations bearing on this question. This is followed by concluding remarks.

2. THE EMPLOYMENT MOTIVE FOR MONETARY EXPANSION

a. Central Bank Objectives

Consider a central bank that is concerned with both price stability and high employment. More precisely, let the objective of the bank be to maximize

$$-\left[\frac{A}{2} (N^* - N)^2 + \frac{\pi^2}{2} \right], \qquad N^* - N \geq 0 \tag{1}$$

where N and N* are the actual and the desired levels of employment, π is the rate of inflation, and A is a positive parameter that reflects the relative concern of the central bank for high employment and price stability. The higher A the stronger the relative concern of the monetary policymaker for maintaining employment near its desired level N*.

b. The Labor Market

Most economies in the European Economic Community (EEC) are heavily unionized. To capture this element in a simple manner, I consider the case of a single union encompassing the entire labor force facing a competitive demand for labor. The union possesses market power and is able to enforce a real wage, w_u, that is higher than the market clearing real wage w^*[3]. At the beginning of each period a nominal wage contract

[3]w_u can be derived from a union objective function that depends on the real wage and employment. Details appear in Cukierman and Liviatan (1990). The case of many unions with overlapping nominal wage contracts is discussed in section (2.3) of Cukierman (1988). Other models in which monetary policy interacts with a union appear in Horn and Persson (1988) and Tabellini (1988).

is concluded between the union and employers. The nominal wage, W, is set so as to achieve the union's desired real wage, w_u, given what the union believes about the rate of inflation that will prevail during the period of the contract. This rate depends in turn on the actions taken by the central bank during the period after the union and employers have committed to a given nominal wage[4]. A period is defined by the length of the nominal contract.

If the union has its way, the real wage, w_u, is higher than the real wage, w^*, that would be obtained under competition and the level of employment, N_u, is correspondingly lower than N^*, the employment level under competition. Figure 1 illustrates this outcome. Note that at the real wage, w_u, imposed by the union, there is an excess supply of labor of size $N^s - N_u$. In order to prevent this excess supply from pushing the real wage below w_u, the union limits the effective supply of labor at contracting time to N_u. Since the contract is made in nominal terms and the union is interested in securing the real wage, w_u, it sets the (nominal) contract wage, W_c, so as to achieve w_u given what it believes the central bank policy will be during the period. This is the content of equation (2) in which P_{-1} is the actual price level at contracting time and π^e is the rate of inflation expected to occur between the previous and the current period.

$$W_c = w_u P_{-1} (1 + \pi^e) . \qquad (2)$$

If the union guess materializes, the actual real wage is indeed w_u and employment is at N_u. This outcome is, however, not optimal from the point of view of the central bank, whose desired level of employment is the competitive level, N^*. (See the bank's objective function in equation (1)). This objective function implies that, although it dislikes inflation, the central bank is willing to tolerate some inflation if it can thereby increase employment above N_u. Does it have this ability? The answer depends on the reaction of the union to a decrease in the real wage rate that is due to inflation.

---

[4]If the central bank is not totally independent, those actions reflect some combination of the policy preferences of the central bank and of other more politically oriented branches of government like the Treasury.

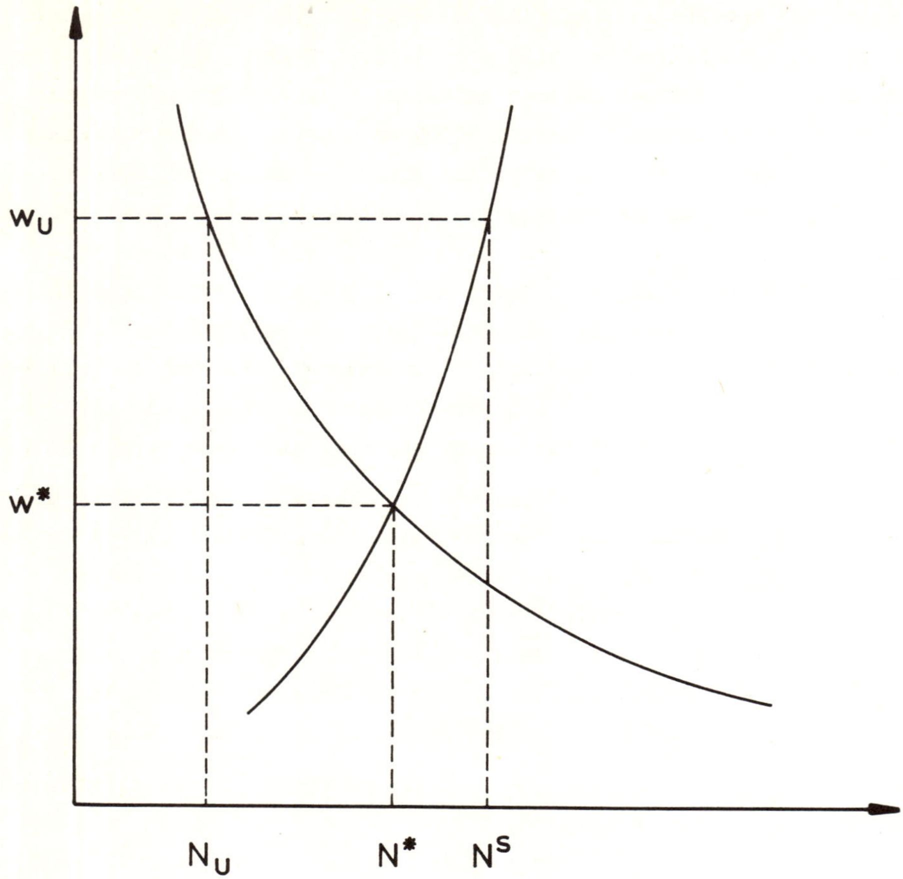

Figure 1: Labor Market Equilibrium .

c. Origin of the Phillips Curve

Suppose the monetary authority succeeds in reducing the real wage rate below w_u. Since the lower real wage rate is due to the actions of a third party, the union leadership cannot claim breach of agreement on the part of employers. It therefore takes the lower real wage as given and, being concerned about the welfare of its members, lets them do what is best for them given this real wage. But the best level of employment for each individual at a given wage rate is given by his supply curve. Hence, given that the real wage rate has decreased not because of breach of contract by employers, the best ex-post strategy for the union is to let its members supply their labor along the supply curve (see Figure 1). As long as $w_u > w^*$, this implies that employment is demand determined since, in this range, demand constitutes the short end of the market. Since the central bank knows that this will be the ex-post response of union members, it is tempted to use monetary policy in order to boost employment up towards N* and monetary policy has an inflationary bias[5]. The potential gains in employment are proportional to the difference between w_u and the actual real wage during the period. This difference is (using equation (2))

$$w_u - w = w_u\left[1 - \frac{1 + \pi^e}{1 + \pi}\right]. \tag{3}$$

Given π^e, the higher π, the larger the difference $w_u - w$ and the higher the gains in employment. This is basically a short run Phillips type relation between the deviation of employment from its natural level (which is N_u) and unanticipated inflation. Using linear approximations this structural relation may be written

$$N - N_u = a(\pi - \pi^e), \quad a > 0 \tag{4}$$

where the size of a is directly related to the sensitivity of the demand for labor with respect to the real wage rate.

[5]More details, as well as an analysis of the case of a partially unionized economy, appear in Chapter 2, section 6 of Cukierman (1990).

d. The Central Bank's Reaction Function

Since π^e has been embodied in the contract nominal wage rate, the central bank takes it as given when choosing π during the period. The optimal choice (for the central bank) of π as a function of π^e is[6]

$$\pi = \frac{aA}{1 - a^2 A} \left[N^* - N_u + a\pi^e \right] \equiv \phi(\pi^e) . \tag{5}$$

Since desired employment is larger than natural employment, the central bank picks a positive rate of inflation even when expected inflation, π^e, is zero. I assume for simplicity that the rate of inflation is equal to the rate of monetary growth[7]. Hence, π and π^e can also be viewed as the actual and the expected rates of monetary expansion respectively and will, at times, be referred to as such. Equation (5) can be viewed as the reaction function of the monetary authority. It determines the best choice of monetary expansion after contractual relations have been locked in. This reaction function is represented by the curve labeled $\phi(\cdot)$ in Figure 2.

e. Union's Expectations and the Discretionary Equilibrium

We turn next to the formation of expectations. There is no uncertainty of any kind. In particular, the union is perfectly informed about the objectives of the central bank. It can therefore calculate, using equation (5), the rate of monetary growth that will be picked by the central bank at each level of expectation, π^e. Any expectation that does not reproduce itself through equation (5) is not rational from the union's point of view, since it implies that it believes inflation will be π^e in spite of the fact that it knows that with such an expectation the central bank's best response is a rate of monetary growth which differs from π^e. Hence, under certainty, a rational expectations

[6]This reaction function is obtained by substituting (4) into (1) and by maximizing with respect to π. More details appear in Chapter 2 of Cukierman (1990).

[7]This abstracts from possible short run deviations between those two rates as well as of real shocks. Allowing for such elements would not change the qualitative conclusions but would complicate the analysis.

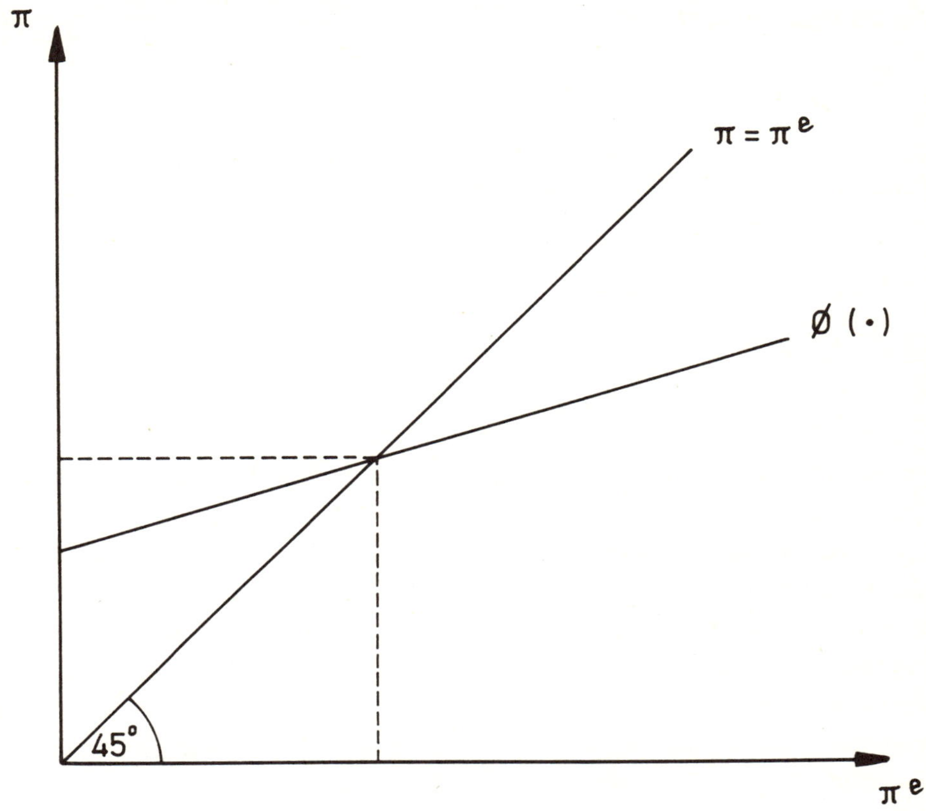

Figure 2: The Inflationary Bias of Monetary Policy.

equilibrium implies

$$\pi^e = \pi \, . \tag{6}$$

Combining (5) and (6) the equilibrium rate of monetary expansion is

$$\pi_d = A\alpha\left[N^* - N_u \right]. \tag{7}$$

Since desired employment, N*, is larger than the natural rate, N_u, the equilibrium rate of monetary expansion is positive. This equilibrium is represented by the point of intersection of the reaction function $\phi(\cdot)$ in Figure 2 with the 45° degree line along which actual and expected inflation are equal.

Since actual and expected inflations are equal, the central bank has no effect on employment, which remains at its natural level. But the rate of inflation is positive. Given the central bank's objective function in equation (1), this outcome is obviously dominated by one in which employment is still at the natural rate, but both actual and expected inflations are zero. Hence, prior to the determination of the expectations the policymaker's best strategy is to pick a zero rate of inflation. However, once expectations have been embodied in nominal contracts, the policymaker takes them as given. As a result, her incentives change, and she is motivated to pick a positive rate of inflation. The union, being aware in advance of this change in the structure of incentives, anticipates that the rate of inflation will be π_d, since this is the only rate that, if expected, induces the policymaker to reproduce it.

The upshot is that when the level of employment desired by the central bank is higher than the natural level, monetary policy has an inflationary bias. This bias is directly traceable to the fact that monetary policy is chosen after expectations and actions based on these expectations have been determined. This is one of the best-known examples of dynamic inconsistency[8]. Dynamic inconsistency arises when

[8]A barebone form of this example was initially introduced by Kydland and Prescott (1977) and developed further by Barro and Gordon (1983). The more explicit presentation used here is adapted from Chapter 2 of Cukierman (1990).

the plan currently made for some future period by one of the players in a dynamic game is no longer optimal from his point of view when that period arrives. In the present simple context there is dynamic inconsistency because the best choice of monetary growth for a period is different before and after wage contracts have been set. Prior to the conclusion of contracts, the best choice for the period's inflation is zero. But once within the period, the best choice involves a positive rate of monetary expansion.

The equilibrium described here is sometimes referred to as "discretionary" because the policymaker retains the discretion to alter monetary policy at any moment in time. Prior to the setting of expectations, the policymaker may try to claim that she is contemplating a zero rate of inflation for the period. However, the union will ignore such claims since it knows that, no matter what she says, the policymaker has an incentive to inflate at a positive rate once expectations have been set.

The features of the discretionary solution for monetary growth in equation (7) are of particular interest. The equilibrium rate of monetary expansion is larger the higher the relative concern of the policymaker for employment (the higher A) and the larger the short-run effect of unanticipated money on output (the larger α). Thus, other things remaining the same, a higher concern by the central bank for employment induces a higher rate of inflation in spite of the fact that the higher inflation has no effect on employment. In addition, for given A and α, the inflationary bias is larger the larger the discrepancy between the natural and the desired levels of employment (the larger $N^* - N_n$). Hence, ceteris paribus, an economy with more union power (in the sense that $w_u - w^*$ is larger) will experience a larger discretionary rate of inflation.

f. Precommitment as a Device to Eliminate the Inflationary Bias

The fact that the discretionary equilibrium results in a suboptimally high inflationary bias leads to the following natural question. How can the institutional framework within which monetary policy operates be reformed so as to eliminate the bias? One answer is that the central bank should irrevocably commit its policy for the period prior to the setting of the wage contract. Under this institutional setup, pronouncements made by the central bank about future policy are fully believed since the union knows that the bank is precommitted to fulfill the announced policy. As a result, any announcement of policy is credible. By giving up the discretion to alter policy after nominal wages have been set, the bank gains the ability to affect those wages by simply announcing its intentions.

In contrast to the discretionary regime, the policymaker now takes into consideration that any choice of monetary growth has an immediate and full impact on expected monetary growth. As a consequence, with a precommitment the policymaker chooses a zero rate of monetary expansion[9]. The attachment of the Bundesbank to quantitative stock targets for M3 and the resolution of other EEC countries to maintain fixed parities between their respective currencies are some of the devices currently used to produce a credible precommitment of national monetary policies. As a matter of fact, the combination of fixed parities in conjunction with the strong aversion of the Bundesbank to inflation creates a system in which German monetary policy provides a nominal anchor to other EEC countries (Giavazzi and Giovannini (1989)).

An important consequence of the analysis in this section, to which I return later, is that the behavior of nominal wages depends on what the union believes about the degree of precommitment of the national monetary authority.

g. Extensions

Provided the supply of labor is relatively insensitive to the real wage rate, the inflationary bias of monetary policy carries over to economies with partial unionization (Cukierman (1990) Chapter 2, section 6).

The discretionary equilibrium described above implies that the central bank's attempt to stimulate employment fails. However, when there are changes over time in the preferences of policymakers (A changes) and the central bank has better information than the union about those changes, monetary policy affects employment (Cukierman and Meltzer (1986)). Similar effects may arise when, due to real shocks, $N^* - N_u$ changes over time and the central bank has better information about

---

[9]Further elaborations appear in Chapter 2 of Cukierman (1990).

those changes. However, in both cases an inflationary bias remains.

3. THE REVENUE MOTIVE FOR MONETARY EXPANSION[10]

a. Introduction

Policymakers may be tempted to use monetary policy in order to achieve other real objectives besides employment. The most prominent are the revenue motive and the balance of payments motive. The first motive is more important in countries that finance a relatively large fraction of government expenditures by means of seignorage or in countries that have accumulated a relatively large nominal debt. Seignorage as a percentage of total government revenues (including seignorage) for some EEC countries is shown in Table 1.

TABLE 1

Seignorage as a Percentage of Government's Revenues Including Seignorage 1971 - 1982 in the EEC Countries

Country	Seignorage	Country	Seignorage
Belgium	1.9	Ireland	5.8
Denmark	0.8	Netherlands	1.1
France	2.1	Portugal	16.6
Greece	14.6	Spain	9.1
Italy	12.5	West Germany	2.5
		U.K.	1.8

Source: Table 1 of Cukierman, Edwards, Tabellini (1989).

It is apparent from the table that the revenue motive for inflation is likely to be relatively larger in Italy, Portugal, Spain and Greece.

Seignorage is an obvious motive for inflation. However, the fact that all countries in Table 1 had positive seignorage revenues does not necessarily imply that this was the prime motive for inflation. The accruance of seignorage revenues may be the byproduct of government's attempt to attain other objectives like high employment (section 2) or balance of payments adjustment (section 4)[11].

---

[10]This section draws on Cukierman and Liviatan (1990) and on Chapter 3 of Cukierman (1990).

[11]However, it is likely that the revenue motive is relatively more important in countries with a larger share of seignorage within total government revenue.

This section considers some implications of the revenue motive. In particular, it demonstrates that in the absence of precommitments the rate of inflation will be too high even if the only motive for monetary expansion is to finance the government budget.

b. Seignorage and the Hyperinflation Puzzle

Seignorage revenues are defined as the amount of real resources bought by the government by means of new base money injections. Denoting by M and P the stock of base money and the price level respectively, seignorage revenues are given by

$$S \equiv \frac{\dot{M}}{P} = \frac{\dot{M}}{M}\frac{M}{P} = \mu L(\pi^e) \tag{8}$$

where μ is the rate of monetary growth, $L(\cdot)$ is the demand for real base money balances and π^e is the expected rate of inflation. The last equality in equation (8) follows from the money market equilibrium condition. By analogy to public finance, μ is usually referred to as the tax rate and $L(\cdot)$ as the tax base.

It is well known that, past a sufficiently high rate of inflation, further increases in the rate of monetary expansion decrease seignorage revenues at least in the steady state. This is due to the fact that a permanent rise in the tax rate, once understood, raises inflationary expectations. At sufficiently high rates of inflation the increase in inflationary expectations reduces the tax base, $L(\cdot)$, by more than the increase in μ. As a consequence, seignorage revenues drop. It is obviously important to know in particular instances at what point seignorage revenues stop going up with further accelerations in the rate of monetary growth and start going down. An answer to this question for eight episodes of hyperinflation in Europe was given in Cagan's (1956) classic study of hyperinflation for steady state situations. The steady state is characterized by the condition that actual and expected inflation are equal. The money market equilibrium condition implies that in the absence of real growth actual inflation is equal to the rate of monetary growth. Hence, in a no growth steady state

$$\pi^e = \pi = \mu . \tag{9}$$

Combining (8) and (9) steady state seignorage revenues may be written

$$S = \mu L(\mu) \ . \tag{8a}$$

Maximal steady state seignorage revenues are achieved when the rate of monetary expansion is set at the level for which the elasticity of real money demand with respect to its argument is equal to unity in absolute value.

Cagan posited a semi logarithmic money demand function of the form

$$L(\pi^e) = \exp[- a\pi^e] \tag{10}$$

and estimated the coefficient a for each of the countries in his sample. Noting that $- a\pi^e$ is the elasticity of money demand with respect to expected inflation and using equation (10) in equation (8a), steady state seignorage revenues are maximized when

$$a\mu = 1 \quad \text{or} \quad \mu = \frac{1}{a} \ . \tag{11}$$

Cagan's money demand function implies that seignorage revenues initially rise with monetary expansion, reach a maximum at $\mu = 1/a$ and then gradually decrease. Cagan's estimates of a imply that, in most of the hyperinflations he examined, the rates of monetary expansion actually observed were higher than $1/a$, implying that governments could increase their seignorage revenues by lowering their rates of monetary expansion, but failed to do so.

This behavior of central bankers or of the governmental authorities that made them expand the money supply at such high rates does not seem rational. By slowing down the rate of monetary expansion they could have decreased inflation and increased seignorage revenues. Yet they failed to do so. The following subsection provides an explanation for this phenomenon, which is based on a dynamic inconsistency of monetary policy in the context of the revenue motive. This type of dynamic inconsistency was first analyzed by Calvo (1978) and later on by Barro (1983).

c. <u>A Seignorage Related Dynamic Inconsistency of Monetary Policy under Discretion</u>

Consider a government whose objectives are positively related to the amount of seignorage revenues it gets and negatively related to both actual and expected inflation. Equation (12) presents a formalization of such an objective function

$$\delta S - \phi(\pi, \pi^e), \quad \delta > 0, \quad \phi_\pi > 0, \quad \phi_{\pi^e} > 0 \ . \tag{12}$$

The use of the term "government" rather than "central bank" is deliberate since, when the extraction of seignorage is the main motive for inflation, decisions about the money supply are normally made by the executive branch of government rather than by the central bank. To reflect this tendency we use the term "policymaker" or "government" to denote the institution that makes decisions about the supply of base money.

The postulated negative effect of π^e on government's objectives is due, among other things, to the fact that with higher inflationary expectations there is a welfare cost associated with decreased money holdings by the public. This is the familiar "shoe leather" cost of perfectly anticipated inflation. The negative effect of actual inflation proxies for, among other things, the loss of regular tax revenues triggered by higher inflation in the absence of tax structure indexing, as well as for other undesired redistributions. δ is a parameter that measures the relative importance attributed by government to seignorage revenues and to avoiding the costs of inflation. Substituting equation (8) into equation (12), government's problem is to choose μ so as to maximize

$$\delta\mu L(\pi^e) - \phi(\pi, \pi^e) \ . \tag{12a}$$

The dynamic inconsistency of monetary policy arises because the incentives of government to inflate change before and after the public has chosen the level of real money balances. Before the public commits itself to a given level of real balances, government takes into consideration the downward effect that a higher rate of inflation has on real money balances and therefore on the tax base. But, after this choice has been made, government takes the level of real money balances as given and reoptimizes. To make this effect more precise, suppose that expectations and therefore real money balances, are chosen at the beginning of the period for the period. Subsequently, during the period, government picks μ, taking expectations, π^e, as given. Since $L(\pi^e)$ is given, the money market equilibrium condition implies that $\mu = \pi^e$ [12]. Hence, government's problem after expectations have been set is

$$\max_{\mu} \ \delta\mu L(\pi^e) - \phi(\mu, \pi^e) \tag{12b}$$

with corresponding first order condition

$$\delta L(\pi^e) - \phi_\pi(\mu, \pi^e) = 0 \tag{13}$$

This equation provides an implicit solution for μ as a function of π^e, which is government's expost reaction function. When it set the expected rate of inflation at the beginning of the period, the public knows that after it commits to a certain level of real balances money growth and inflation will be determined by equation (13). Since there is no uncertainty, any expectation that does not induce government to pick $\mu = \pi = \pi^e$ is not rational. Hence, in a rational expectations equilibrium this equality must hold. Combining it with government's reaction function in equation (13) and rearranging, we obtain

$$\eta \equiv \frac{L'(\mu)}{L(\mu)} \mu = \frac{\delta}{\phi_\pi(\mu, \mu)} \mu L'(\mu) \tag{14}$$

where the left-hand side is the elasticity, η, of money demand with respect to expected inflation and $L'(\cdot)$ is the derivative of real money demand with respect to its argument.

---

[12] Money market equilibrium implies $M/P = L(\pi^e)$. Since the right hand side is given once expectations have been set, any increase in money supply must be matched one to one by an increase in the price level.

Examination of this equation reveals that if $\delta/\phi_{\pi}(\cdot)$ is sufficiently large government will choose to operate in a range of inflation in which the elasticity η is larger than one in absolute value[13]. This implies that, if government values seignorage revenues a lot in comparison to its marginal valuation of the costs of inflation, rates of monetary expansion and of inflation may be in a range in which steady state seignorage revenue could be increased by lowering the rate of monetary expansion.

Why does government operate in this range in spite of its obvious inefficiency in terms of its own objectives? The answer is that in the absence of precommitments, government follows the best course once expectations have been set, and the public, knowing that, expects such behavior in advance and picks its money balances in accordance. The inability to precommit monetary policy prior to the choice of real balances induces an inefficient equilibrium in terms of government's own objectives.

d. Precommitments and Seignorage

The inefficient equilibrium occurs because during the period government optimizes for a given real money demand. However, prior to the choice of money demand by the public, government takes the effect of its action on expectations and money demand into consideration. If government can precommit its action for the period already at this stage, it will never choose to operate in the inefficient range. The following discussion establishes this result.

In the presence of precommitments, government announces the rate of inflation for the period prior to the choice of money balances by the public and actually delivers this rate during the period. Since government's ability to precommit is common knowledge the announcement is credible. It therefore affects the choice of real money balances by the public so that government's decision problem in (12) now becomes

$$\max_{\mu} \; [\delta\mu L(\mu) - \phi(\mu, \mu)] \; . \qquad (15)$$

The crucial difference between this expression and the one obtained in

---

13 A specific example in which this is the case appears in Chapter 3 of Cukierman (1990).

the absence of precommitments is that now government possesses the ability to influence the public's expectations. Essentially, by giving away its discretion to change policy within the period, government gains an additional exante policy instrument. The first order condition necessary for the maximization of (15) is

$$\delta \frac{\partial}{\partial\mu} [\mu L(\mu)] = \phi_\pi + \phi_\pi e \ . \tag{16}$$

Since the right hand side of (16) is positive (by equation (12)) it follows that government operates in the range of monetary expansion for which seignorage revenues increase in μ. Hence, advance precommitments by government resolve the dynamic inconsistency associated with the revenue motive under discretion. Note, however, that the revenue motive induces some inflation even with precommitments. This contrasts with the policy outcome under precommitments when the only motive for inflation is employment. As we saw in section 2, precommitments lead in this case to full price stability. The reason for the difference is that inflation does not produce any benefits for governmental objectives when employment is the objective. But it does benefit government objectives when financing of the budget is the real objective aimed at by monetary expansion.

It is likely that in the EEC countries δ is such that policy operates in the range of monetary expansion in which seignorage revenues increase with μ even in the absence of precommitments. However, the advantage of a precommitment is that it enables government to raise a given amount of seignorage with lower inflation. The reason is that, since inflation is lower under commitments than under discretion, the tax base is higher. This compensates for the lower seignorage tax rate.

e. Extensions: Nominal Debt and Asymmetric Information

The presence of nominal debt whose real value can be reduced by unanticipated inflation reinforces the incentive of government to inflate under discretion. But, in the presence of credible precommitments the existence of debt does not alter the behavior of government in comparison to the case in which there is no debt.

Under discretion, the public knows in advance that once it commits to a certain portfolio of government debt the government will try to inflate part of it away. It therefore requires an appropriate premium that takes the form of a higher nominal interest rate. As a result, the real rate remains unaffected but nominal rates are higher.

By contrast, in the presence of credible precommitments the outstanding quantity of bonds has no effect on the propensity of government to inflate. The intuitive reason is that when it has to precommit to a certain rate of inflation government takes into consideration that any inflation induced decrease in the value of the debt is fully compensated by an appropriate increase in the nominal rate of interest. Hence, there is no net revenue gain from decreases in the value of the debt at the margin. But when government retains the discretion to choose monetary growth within the period, the size of the debt affects its choice of monetary growth, since it optimizes taking the nominal interest rate as given. A more explicit discussion of those intuitive results appears in Chapter 3 of Cukierman (1990). A discussion of the effects of debt on government policy within an explicit public finance framework appears in section 4, Chapter 6 of Persson and Tabellini (1989).

In the presence of asymmetric information about the relative importance given by government to seignorage revenues and to the costs of inflation (the parameter δ in equation (12)) the public gradually learns from changes in the rate of inflation about changes in the preferences of government. When government cares about both the future and the present, this learning process alleviates the seignorage related dynamic inconsistency of monetary policy under discretion. Furthermore, it goes a long way towards explaining the seeming puzzle that steady state seignorage revenues could have been increased during some hyperinflationary episodes (like in post World War I Germany) by reducing the rate of monetary expansion. As a matter of fact, a closer look at the post World War I German experience indicates that even during the last stages of the hyperinflation, monetary growth and seignorage were positively correlated. There is also evidence that there were substantial lags in the adjustment of inflationary expectations and in the public's understanding of the underlying changes in government's priorities. All this evidence is consistent with the view that for most of the hyperinflation German authorities experienced a series of strong increases in the parameter δ which were uncovered by the public only with some lag. In the interim, the government was able to temporarily increase seignorage revenues by increasing the rate of monetary expansion. A detailed discussion of those issues and of the underlying evidence appears in Cukierman (1988).

4. THE MERCANTILISTIC OR BALANCE OF PAYMENTS MOTIVE FOR DEVALUATIONS[14]

a. Introduction

Policymakers of countries with persistent deficits in the current account of the balance of payments may be tempted to reduce such deficits by devaluing the currency. This policy is effective if it also results in a real devaluation of the currency. However, the central bank or whoever else decides on monetary policy directly controls only the nominal rate of exchange. The real rate of exchange is also affected by the actions of individuals in the private sector and by the makers of fiscal policy.

A nominal devaluation may reduce a balance of payments deficit or increase a surplus in it through several channels. First, in the presence of nominal wage contracts and unions that set the real wage above its market clearing level, a nominal devaluation -- by reducing the real wage rate -- stimulates employment and output[15]. This increases the amount of resources available for exports or for import substitutes and decreases the current account deficit. The increase in output also increases income and therefore domestic consumption. The effect of this change taken alone is to increase the current account deficit. However, if the marginal propensity to consume is smaller than one, the first effect dominates and the net effect of the nominal devaluation is still to reduce the current account deficit. Second, a nominal devaluation also reduces the public's consumption by reducing the real value of nominally denominated government obligations held by the public. This decrease in domestic absorption also contributes to reducing the current account deficit.

There are a number of episodes in which the governments or central banks of countries with current account deficits devalued, causing an

---

[14]This section draws on Cukierman and Liviatan (1990) and on Chapter 4 of Cukierman (1990).

[15]The precise transmission mechanism is discussed in section 2.

upward bulge in the rate of inflation, without any apparent improvement in the balance of payments. This phenomenon, although not restricted to such countries, seems to be more prevalent in countries with high degrees of unionization. A dramatic example is Israel during 1984 and early 1985 just prior to the successful July 1985 stabilization program. During the second half of 1984, the government and the Histadruth (the general labor union) reached an agreement known as a "package deal", one component of which was the temporary freezing of nominal wages. In return, the government promised to refrain from raising taxes and reducing subsidies for the period of the deal. Although freezing of the exchange rate was not part of the deal there was an understanding that the rate of exchange would not be actively used as an instrument of external balance. But in late 1984, due to increasing concern over the growing current account deficit, government devalued. This led to an acceleration in the rate of inflation without much effect on the current account deficit. There were subsequent attempts to reduce inflation through package deals. But the labor union demanded such high nominal wage increases in return for its willingness to agree to additional freezes that government was forced to devalue just to prevent a deterioration in the balance of payments. There ensued a spiral of broken package deal, devaluations and nominal wage increases with no apparent improvement in the balance of payments. This process came to an end with the successful July 1985 stabilization[16].

Greece, with its persistent postwar current account deficits and relatively high degree of unionization is another example of a case in which discretionary devaluations designed to reduce the deficit resulted in persistent inflation.

The main message of this section is that such outcomes are to be expected under discretion. Basically, dynamic inconsistency problems similar to those encountered in previous sections explain why nominal devaluations do not improve the current account's position and only cause inflation. The basic idea is that under discretion the public knows in advance that policymakers are willing to tolerate devaluations and inflation in order to improve the balance of payments. Since policymakers are not bound by any commitments, individuals know that

[16]A detailed account of the Israeli stabilization and of its aftermath can be found in Bruno and Piterman (1988) and in Cukierman (1988).

once nominal wage and financial assets contracts have been concluded government and the central bank will have an incentive to devalue. They, therefore, ask and obtain higher nominal wage rates and interest rates. After the conclusion of those contracts, government indeed devalues at the expected rate. However, relative to a situation without a devaluation and no expectation of a devaluation, such action has no effect on the current account, since the prior actions of the public have neutralized such an effect. This mechanism is briefly sketched in the next subsection. A detailed analysis is in Chapter 4 of Cukierman (1990).

b. A Simple Game between the Central Bank and a Union in the Presence of a Balance of Payments Motive under Discretion

All the labor force in the economy is organized in one union that has, as in Chapter 2, the power to determine the real wage rate. The union's objectives are such that its most preferred real wage is higher than the real wage under a competitive labor market. But the union does not set the real wage. Instead it sets (as in section 2), at the beginning of each contract period, the nominal wage for the period. This choice is based on the union's (rational) expectation of the price level during the contract's period and the real wage aimed at. Since this real wage is above the competitive wage, there is an excess supply of labor at the union's preferred real wage. Hence, given the contract nominal wage, an increase in the price level stimulates employment through the mechanism described in Chapter 2. This creates a positive relationship between the price level and output during the period of the contract. Since the marginal propensity to absorb current output is smaller than one, an increase in output triggers a smaller increase in absorption- releasing resources for external uses and decreasing the deficit in the current account of the balance of payments. This effect may be reenforced by a decrease in consumption triggered by the decrease in the real value of monetary assets due to the increase in the price level. The upshot is that, after the union has committed itself to a certain nominal wage and positions in monetary assets taken, the policymaker faces a temporary tradeoff between inflation and the current account deficit.

The monetary authority has the discretion to pick the exchange rate, after the contract nominal wage rate has been determined. In a small open economy this determines the price level, provided the domestic monetary aggregates are adjusted so as to back up the exchange rate chosen by the policymaker. Since the central bank dislikes both inflation and the current account deficit it picks a rate of devaluation and therefore a rate of inflation that minimizes the combined costs of these two "bads". This rate is usually positive and finite. In doing that, it takes the contract nominal wage rate and the magnitudes of the government's budget and of tax collections (both of which are set by the fiscal authority) as given. Provided the marginal costs, to the policymaker, of either inflation or of a current account deficit (or of both) increase with the values of those two "bads", the rate of devaluation it chooses is larger, the larger is the current account deficit.

The union knows the objective function of the monetary authority as well as the magnitudes of the variables chosen by the fiscal authority. It can therefore calculate the rate of inflation that will be produced by the monetary authority during the period of the contract. Given this (rational) forecast it sets the nominal wage at a level that achieves its most preferred real wage, taking the expected response of the monetary authority during the contract period into account. As a result, the authority's attempt to improve the current account by stimulating output through a devaluation fails since the union manages to obtain the real wage it desires. Moreover, since the union sets the nominal wage rate on the basis of a rationally expected inflation, the policymaker has to inflate at this rate just in order to prevent a deterioration in the current account. Thus, the ultimate equilibrium is characterized by positive inflation and no ability, on the part of the monetary authority, to improve the current account position.

c. The Fiscal Stance and the Current Account Motive under Discretion

An important implication of the model is that the larger government expenditures and the lower taxes, the stronger the incentive of the monetary policymaker to devalue. Since this is known by the union and everybody else at contracting time, higher nominal wages are demanded and obtained and the economy settles into an equilibrium with higher devaluations. Thus, higher budgetary deficits lead to higher inflation by increasing the incentive of monetary policymakers to devalue in order to improve the current account balance[17]. This occurs in spite of the fact that the current account is not affected by monetary policy in equilibrium. In a well known article, Sargent and Wallace (1981) argue that deficits and inflation should be positively correlated in the long run. Sargent's mechanism works through government's intertemporal budget constraint in a framework in which government policy is exogenous. By contrast, the mechanism discussed here works immediately through the endogenous response of policymakers to current account deficits. An important implication of the mechanism described here is that fiscal restraint, by improving the current account, reduces the inflationary bias of monetary policy.

d. Precommitments in Theory and Practice

The equilibrium described in the previous subsections is obviously inefficient since government's discretionary attempt to alter the current account balance fails and only produces higher inflation. Again, this is a direct consequence of dynamic inconsistency, since prior to the closing of contracts government has no incentive to devalue.

This inefficient outcome can be avoided by precommitting monetary policy prior to the finalization of contracts. One way to implement the precommitment is to credibly peg the exchange rate. The reason is that, in the presence of a credible peg, unions rationally expect no inflation and have no reason to ask for nominal wage increases provided the current nominal wage is, to start with, at the level that produces the real wage desired by them.

Policymakers of highly open economies with persistent current account deficits and widespread unionization normally have a strong incentive to devalue. But this does not imply that all countries with such features will have a balance of payments induced inflation bias. Austria, for example, in spite of having all those characteristics, enjoys a high degree of price stability. The reason is that it pegs its currency to the Mark and adjusts its monetary policy so as to maintain this peg. Since this policy has been consistently followed for many years, it is widely know and believed by unions and the public. This

[17]As far as I know, this mechanism was first noted in Cukierman and Liviatan (1990).

keeps nominal wages and interest rates low, making it unnecessary to devalue just in order to deep the current account at its natural level. Austrian policymakers have, in effect, credibly precommitted to peg their currency to the German Mark and to subjugate their monetary policy to this rule.

e. Concluding Reflections

The current account motive is normally not in evidence in countries with large current account surpluses like West Germany and Japan. However, periodic episodes of exogenously caused deficits in the West German current account balance are consistent with the view that German policymakers are sensitive to such deficits and may even dislike states in which current account surpluses are too low. This means that German policymakers may have a mercantilistic bias. The fact that they allowed inflation to accelerate during the second oil shock when the current account surplus was severely reduced and even turned into a deficit supports this view.

Use of the exchange rate as an anchor for stable prices works in the long run only if stock are adjusted so as to support the exchange rate peg. A drawback of using the exchange rate as a nominal anchor is that it may tempt policymakers to tolerate the development of substantial divergences between the actual supply of money and the supply necessary to sustain the exchange rate at its predetermined peg over the long run. Such divergences can be allowed to develop without necessitating immediate parity adjustments because direct interventions in foreign exchange markets affect the exchange rate more quickly than changes in net domestic credit. However, the impact of persistent increases in net domestic credit on the exchange rate cannot be offset by unsterilized interventions forever. An adjustment of the peg must eventually take place. But because of the different speeds with which foreign exchange operations and net domestic credit changes affect the exchange rate policymakers have some discretion with respect to the timing of the adjustment.

5. A SYSTEMATIC COMPARISON OF POLICY OUTCOMES UNDER A FIXED PARITIES SYSTEM WITH OUTCOMES UNDER A COMMONLY MANAGED CURRENCY SYSTEM

a. Introduction

The Report on Economic and Monetary Union in the European Community (1988), known as the "Delors Report", envisages the attainment of monetary union in three stages. In stage two

> "Exchange rate realignments would not be excluded as an instrument of adjustment, but there would be an understanding that they would be made only in exceptional circumstances". (Op. Cit. article 57)

In the third and last stage of the union the report suggests that the change over to a single currency will be preceded by the

> "...irrevocable locking of exchange rates..." and concurrently "...the responsibility for the formulation and implementation of monetary policy in the community would be transferred to the European System of Central Banks (ESCB)". (Op. Cit. article 60)

An important question is whether stage two is a necessary or even useful step in the transition to the full monetary unification envisaged in stage three. This section offers a somewhat limited[18], but precise, comparison of a fixed parities system of the type envisaged for stage two with a single currency system. The comparison implies that stage two may, for some configurations of shocks, have deleterious effects on the credibility of the system making it more difficult politically to reach a stage of complete monetary unification later on. It also clarifies some of the likely differences in the choice of monetary policy within a system like the current European Monetary System (EMS) in comparison to the monetary policy chosen by a single central bank whose board is composed of representatives from the various member countries.

The existing version of the EMS handles the inflationary temptations described in previous sections by making it costly for monetary policymakers of individual EEC countries to change parities. This cost checks the temptation to inflate as long as the potential benefits from monetary expansion to an individual government are smaller than the

---

[18]It is argued in subsection e below that the type of analysis performed here for the employment motive can be extended to cases in which other motives for monetary expension, like the revenue and the balance of payments motives, operate.

political and other perceived costs of parity adjustments. But when country specific shocks make the potential benefits larger than this cost, monetary policy in the concerned country is likely to deviate from the community norm and sooner or later a parity change follows. Hence, the current EMS can be described (using the terminology of sections 2-4) as a system of limited precommitments. When shocks fall within certain bounds, policymakers stick to the precommitment[19]. But they revert to discretion at the level of the individual country when shocks fall outside those bounds. Stage two of the monetary unification process is similar in conception except possibly for the fact that the political costs of a parity adjustment may be higher. But parity adjustments are still possible and have a positive probability in general. This fact cannot escape the attention of price and wage setters in the different economies. Realizing that parities can be changed, union leaders of countries that shall be hit by shocks which increase the temptation to inflate will demand higher wage increases. Similarly holders of interest bearing monetary assets will demand a higher nominal premium and speculators may attack the currency of the country in question.

The collapse of the Bretton Wood system in the early seventies is a vivid reminder of the fact that in the face of sufficiently large and diverse shocks parities are normally adjusted. The upshot is that in the presence of separately managed currencies sufficiently large shocks may increase the preoccupation of domestic policymakers with employment, seignorage or the balance of payments by enough to switch back to discretion.

This may also be true with a commonly managed currency. A monetary union, as of itself, does not assure that precommitments will prevail over discretion nor that precommitments will be always adhered to. But, as this section shows, for the same degree of precommitment (to be defined more precisely) the common monetary authority is less likely to switch back to discretion than an individual country in a multiple currencies system. At first blush, this would also seem to imply that the common monetary authority will produce on average a lower rate of

---

[19]Because of the stronger aversion of the Bundesbank to inflation, this results in other community members emulating German monetary policy (Giavazzi and Giovannini (1989)). In this range of shocks the Bundesbank provides an externality to other EEC countries by playing the role of Rogoff (1985) conservative central banker.

inflation than the community average inflation produced under a system of multiple currencies with fixed but not irrevocably fixed exchange rates. However, this is not always the case. As explained in subsection d below, this depends on the distribution of real shocks.

For briefness I shall, in what follows, refer to a system with one centrally administered money supply as a Commonly Managed Currency System (CMCS). A system with separately managed money supplies with serious but not irrevocable commitment to fixed parities will be referred to as an Adjustable Peg with Limited Commitment (APLC). Additional results are:

1. A CMCS is more likely to break its precommitment when shocks are positively correlated across the union's members.
2. Even if the shocks affecting individual countries are large, a CMCS is likely to honour its precommitment if shocks are negatively correlated across countries.

Under an APLC there is a positive probability that a single country will deviate to discretion. Such a unilateral move is precluded by construction in a CMCS. Hence, the cohesion of a monetary union and its credibility is larger in a CMCS. As a matter of fact, in the presence of unlucky shocks, periodic changes in parities during stage two may weaken the political cohesion and resolve necessary to move into a full monetary union. Hence, there is a substantial advantage in going directly from the current EMS to a CMCS.

b. When Does an Individual Country in an APLC Break its Commitment?

Consider a single policymaker who cares about employment and dislikes inflation, that faces a domestic union. We saw in section 2 (equation (7)) that under discretion the equilibrium rate of inflation in this case is

$$\pi_d = A\alpha s \tag{7a}$$

where $s \equiv N^* - N_u$ is the difference between the level of employment preferred by the policymaker and the natural level of employment. Suppose that due to various real shocks s fluctuates randomly over time but is always positive. The policymaker precommits to a zero rate of inflation by adhering to a monetary policy that maintains a fixed parity with a country that has a zero rate of inflation. There is a fixed political cost, c, of breaking this precommitment. As long as the gains from breaking the precommitment are smaller than the advantages from reneging on it, the precommitment is maintained. But in the opposite case the policymaker breaks the commitment. Whether the national policymaker reneges and changes the peg or maintains it depends on the realization of the shock and on what the domestic union believes about monetary policy. The remainder of this section characterizes the ranges of s for which the policymaker maintains and reneges on his precommitment.

Substituting (4) into (1), we obtain the policymaker's objectives as a function of his action, π, the union's expectation, π^e, and the shock s. This is shown in equation (17).

$$W\left[\pi, \pi^e, s\right] \equiv -\left[\frac{A}{2}(s - a(\pi - \pi^e))^2 + \frac{\pi^2}{2}\right]. \tag{17}$$

For simplicity, I abstract from faulty perceptions by assuming that both the policymaker and the union learn about the realization of the shock s as soon as it occurs. Within each period the timing of events is as follows. First the shock, s, realizes and is observed by everybody. Second, based on its expectation of the subsequent action by the policymaker, a nominal wage contract is agreed upon. Finally, government decides whether to keep or to renege on its commitment[20].

Since expectations are rational and the cost of reneging, c, is common knowledge, the union can always "enter into the shoes" of the policymaker and calculate when it will pay the policymaker to renege, given the union's contract, and when it will not. Hence, in equilibrium the union always forecasts correctly the subsequent action of the policymaker. Two conditions are of particular interest in characterizing the possible equilibria. One is that when the union anticipates that the commitment will be kept, it pays government to honour the commitment. The other is that when the union expects government to renege it indeed pays government to renege. Both conditions are implied by the rationality of expectations and are given

[20]I do not identify who, within the public sector, makes this decision. To underscore this deliberate vagueness, the terms policymaker, government and central bank are used interchangeably.

in equations (18a) and (18b) respectively.

$$\text{Peg is maintained when } W\left[\pi_d(0,s),0,s\right] - W\left[0,0,s\right] < c \tag{18a}$$

$$\text{Peg is adjusted when } W\left[\pi_d(\pi_d,s),\ \pi_d,s\right] - W\left[0,\pi_d,s\right] > c \tag{18a}$$

where $\pi_d(\pi^e,s)$ is the discretionary rate of monetary expansion chosen by the policymaker when the union expects this rate to be π^e and the divergence between the natural and the desired levels of employment is s. Given the values of π^e and of s the discretionary action $\pi_d(\pi^e,s)$ is, from equation (5),

$$\pi_d(\pi^e,\ s) = \frac{aA}{1 + a^2A}[s + a\pi^e]. \tag{19}$$

Using (19) in equations (18), and rearranging, the conditions for maintaining the peg and for adjusting it (in rational expectations equilibria) are respectively:

$$s^2 < \frac{2c}{(aA)^2}\ (1 + a^2A) \equiv S_H^2 \tag{20a}$$

$$s^2 > \frac{2c}{(aA)^2}\ \frac{1}{1 + a^2A} \equiv S_L^2\ . \tag{20b}$$

Since a^2A is positive S_H^2 is larger than S_L^2. Hence, if s falls in the open range $(S_L,\ S_H)$, both reneging as well as maintenance of the fixed peg qualify as possible self fulfilling equilibria. However, since the status quo involves a fixed peg, it seems reasonable that when both types of equilibria are possible the fixed peg one will prevail. In addition whenever either type of equilibrium may arise, it is possible to eliminate the discretionary one by appealing to the Cho-Kreps (1987) intuitive criterion. Whenever s falls in the multiple equilibrium range, the government can approach the union prior to the settlement of the wage contract and argue as follows: I am going to maintain the fixed peg as promised. You should believe me and settle on a wage contract that is based on this premise, for if you do, I have (as you can verify) no incentive to adjust the peg. In view of those arguments the remainder of the discussion is based on the presumption that whenever $S_L < s < S_H$ the commitment to a fixed peg is honoured and the union knows that. I further assume that when indifferent between maintaining and reneging on the fixed parity, the government sticks to its precommitment and maintains the peg. The upshot is that

$$\text{Precommitment to peg is honoured if} \quad s \leq S_H \tag{21a}$$

$$\text{Precommitment to peg is broken if} \quad s > S_H \, . \tag{21b}$$

Basically, when the divergence between actual and desired employment (s) becomes larger than the threshold, S_H, the benefits to government from stimulating employment become large enough to justify the costs of a devaluation taking as given that the union anticipates such behavior. For reasons elaborated upon in section 2, this outcome arises in spite of the fact that the divergence between actual and desired employment stays at s in the resulting equilibrium[21]. Faced with a forward looking and intelligent union and adverse shocks, government has to devalue just to prevent this divergence from getting any bigger.

c. <u>Policy Outcomes under a Commonly Managed Currency System (CMCS)</u>

Consider now a CMCS in which the commitment to price stability is abandoned only if there is a majority on the board of the common central bank for such action. Suppose further that all countries in the system are represented on the board and that each representative votes for or against reneging on the commitment, taking only the objectives of his own government into consideration. The commitment to price stability is the status quo and it is abandoned only if there is a majority in favor of discretion. To maintain comparability with the previous case, I assume that the costs of reneging at the individual country level are the same as under the APLC system. This seems as a reasonable description of the possible modus operandi of a ESCB in stage three of

---

[21] In the presence of asymmetric information and gradual learning by the union about government's perception of s (along the lines of Cukierman and Meltzer (1986)) the policymaker can temporarily reduce the divergence between natural and desired employment.

the union as conceived in article 60 of the Delors Report. With differences in the parameters a, A and c across counties, the discretionary rates of inflation of different countries generally differ. For simplicity, I abstract from those differences by assuming that those parameters are identical across countries. Under those circumstances the discretionary rate of inflation preferred by the policymaker of a country that sustained a shock s and whose union contracts for nominal wages on the basis of expectation π^e is given by equation (19).

Even with identical parameters, the discretionary rates of inflation preferred by the different governments differ since the realizations of the shocks, s, differ across countries. In spite of this conflict of interest, the actual and the expected rates of inflation are uniform across countries in a CMCS. The reason is that whether it is decided to stick to, or to abandon, the commitment to price stability this decision binds all countries in the community. Since unions in the individual countries are aware of this fact, their inflationary expectations converge. This brings about uniformity in nominal wage settlements throughout the community in comparison to an APLC.

Since the realizations of s differ across countries, equation (19) implies that, given the common value of π^e and given a majority decision to abandon the commitment to price stability, there will be disagreements about the discretionary rate of monetary growth to follow. In particular, if i and j are two countries in the community such that $s_i > s_j$, policymakers in country i will desire a larger discretionary rate than policymakers in country j.

Let n be the number of countries and let $\underline{s} = (s_1, s_2, \ldots s_n)$ be the current realization of shocks in the n countries. Suppose, without loss of generality that

$$s_1 \le s_2 \le \ldots \le s_n \ . \tag{22}$$

If n is odd the median of the vector $\underline{s}$ coincides with s_m where $m \equiv \text{int}[n/2 + 1]$[22]. If n is even there is a median range that is characterized by the closed interval $[s_{m-1}, s_m]$. From equation (19) the discretionary

[22]int [x] denotes the largest integer contained in x.

rates preferred by different countries have the same ranking as the shocks, s_i.

<u>Assumption 1</u>: (Decisiveness of the Median over the Discretionary Rate). If the majority within the commonly managed central bank is for abandoning the commitment to price stability, the precise rate of monetary growth that is chosen coincides with the discretionary rate preferred by country m.

Country s_m (meaning "the policymakers of the country that sustained the shock s_m") votes for maintaining the commitment to price stability when $\pi^e = 0$ if

$$W\left[\pi_d(0,\ s_m),\ 0,\ s_m\right] - W\left[0,\ 0,\ s_m\right] < c\ . \tag{23}$$

Using equation (19) in equation (23) and rearranging, this is equivalent to the condition

$$s_m < S_H\ . \tag{23a}$$

Condition (23) (or its alternate form in equation (23a)) states that country s_m votes for maintaining the commitment (when unions throughout the community believe the commitment will be honoured) provided the benefit from the switch to the discretionary rate $\pi_d(0,\ s_m)$ is smaller than its political cost, c. By assumption 1, in case the central bank council decides to renege, $\pi_d(0,\ s_m)$ will be the discretionary rate chosen. Hence, country $i \neq m$ votes against reneging if

$$W\left[\pi_d(0,\ s_m),\ 0,\ s_i\right] - W\left[0,\ 0,\ s_i\right] < c \tag{24}$$

which is equivalent to the condition

$$2(1 + aA)\ s_i s_m - (1 + a^2 A) s_m^2 < \frac{2c}{(aA)^2}\ (1 + aA)^2\ . \tag{24a}$$

Condition (23a) implies that condition (24a) is satisfied for all countries with $s_i \leq s_m$. Hence, when the country at the median of the discretionary rates opposes reneging, given $\pi^e = 0$, there is a majority against reneging at the central bank council and the expectation $\pi^e = 0$ is self fulfilling. This leads to the following proposition:

Proposition 1: When the median country, m, is decisive over the discretionary rate, and unions expect the common central bank to honour its commitment, this expectation is self fulfilling if country m is better off when the commitment is honoured. This is the case, in turn, if condition (23a) is satisfied.

Similar considerations, which are elaborated in part 1 of the appendix, lead to the following proposition:

Proposition 2: Provided the median country, m is decisive over the discretionary rate, and unions expect the common central bank to renege on its commitment, this expectation is self fulfilling if country m is better off when the CMCS reneges on its commitment. This is the case, in turn, when

$$s_m > S_L . \tag{25}$$

Since $S_H > S_L$ there are both self-fulfilling reneging and non reneging equilibria when $S_H > s_m > S_L$. However, the reneging equilibria in this range can be eliminated by appealing again to the Cho-Kreps (1987) intuitive criterion. The central bank council can argue that if unions believe the commitment will be maintained there indeed will be a majority at the council to maintain it. I also assume that when country m is indifferent between honoring and not honoring the commitment (for $\pi^e = 0$), the status quo prevails. This leads to the following proposition:

Proposition 3: When the median country, m, is decisive over the discretionary rate, the community central bank maintains its commitment when $s_m \leq S_H$ and reneges on its commitment when $s_m > S_H$.

d. Comparison between a Commonly Managed Currency System (CMCS) and an Adjustable Peg with Limited Precommitments (APLC)

Let R_p and R_c be, respectively, the event that a single country in the community reneges on its commitment under an APLC and the event that the CMCS reneges on its commitment. In view of equations (21) and proposition 3, the precise definition of those events is

$$R_p \equiv \{s > S_H \text{ for at least one country}\} \quad (26a)$$

$$R_c \equiv \{s_m > S_H\} \, . \quad (26b)$$

Since s_m is the median of s across countries, the event R_c is also equivalent to the event that $s_i > S_H$ for at least half of the countries in the community. R_c is a proper subset of R_p since the realization of R_c always implies that R_p realizes, but the reverse is not always true. Hence the probability that a single country in an APLC reneges is larger than the probability that the central bank of a CMCS reneges. This leads to the following proposition:

Proposition 4: Under an APLC, the probability that a single country will renege on its commitment and follow policies that necessitate an adjustment of the peg is larger than the probability that a CMCS will renege.

Note that this result is obtained even under the conservative assumption that the degree of independence of the central bank in a CMCS is the same as the degree of independence of each individual central bank from its national fiscal authority under the current APLC system. It is likely, however, that the centralization of monetary authority within one European central bank will make this bank more independent than its national counterparts for most countries in the community. Central banks are normally thought to be relatively more concerned about price stability than fiscal authorities[23]. In terms of the model this implies that A is lower in a CMCS than in an APLC system. It is demonstrated in part 2 of the appendix that when A is lower S_H is higher making the probability of broken commitments under a CMCS even lower.

[23]See Alesina and Tabellini (1987).

Since the APLC and the CMCS correspond respectively to stage two and to the final phase of stage three of the Delors Report, it is likely that if stage two is implemented there will be parity adjustments during this stage. In particular, if some countries would experience substantially larger values of s than others it is very likely that peg adjustments would occur. The deleterious effect of such developments on the credibility of the process leading towards monetary unification cannot be overemphasized. Since stage two is presented as a move towards more cohesion realignments during this stage risk being taken, by politicians and the public, as a sign that the movement toward monetary unification is impractical. It actually may undermine the political resolve to move towards stage three. Such a backlash is likely to be more serious the more stage two is construed as a significant move towards monetary unification in comparison to the current EMS. It seems therefore that the benefits of stage two are limited and the risks it carries quite substantial.

Frequent realignments during stage two, done by one or two countries at a time may be highly detrimental. As a matter of fact, even if the probability that $s > S_H$ for a single country is relatively low, the probability that one or two countries in the community will realign their currencies may be quite substantial. To see what is involved, consider the particular case in which the shocks s have identical and independent (across countries) distributions. Let q be the probability that $s \leq S_H$ in a <u>given</u> country. Hence, q is the probability that a given country maintains the commitment and 1 - q is the probability that it reneges on it. The probability that at least one country reneges and adjusts its parity is 1 minus the probability that all twelve countries in the community experience shocks that are lower than S_H. Hence,

$$\text{Probability that at least one country adjusts parity} = 1 - q^{12} .$$

Simple combinatorial considerations imply that the probability that at least two countries adjust their parities is

$$1 - q^{12} - 12(1 - q)\, q^{11} .$$

For q = 0.9, the first probability is almost 0.72 and the probability that at least two countries go through a realignment is about a third. Such probabilities appear to be dangerously high for a system that is designed to pave the way towards a common central bank.

It would seem at first blush that a corollary to proposition 4 is that the expected value of the community average rate of inflation should be lower under a CMCS than under an APLC. It turns out, however, that this conjecture is not true in general. The following discussion clarifies the reasons for the ambiguity. For simplicity, I focus on the case in which the distribution of s_i is the same across countries.

Let the average rate of inflation in the community under an APLC be

$$\pi = \sum_{i=1}^{n} f_i \pi_i \ , \qquad \sum_{i=1}^{n} f_i = 1 \tag{27}$$

where f_i $(i = 1,\ldots,n)$ is a positive weight that measures the relative size of country i. Let

$$R_{pi} \equiv \left\{ s_i > S_H \text{ in country } i \right\} . \tag{28}$$

R_{pi} is the event; "country i reneges on its commitment". When this occurs, country i inflates at the discretionary rate which is given by equation (7a). Let $P(R_{pi})$ be the (common across countries) probability of the event R_{pi}. The community average rate of inflation under an APLC is therefore

$$\pi_p = \sum_{i=1}^{n} f_i \left[(1 - P(R_{pi})) \ .0 + P(R_{pi}) a \ A \ s_i \right] . \tag{29}$$

The expected value of this expression is

$$E\pi_p = P(R_{pi}) a \ A \ \mu_s \tag{29a}$$

where μ_s is the expected value of s_i.

Consider now the community wide rate of inflation under a CMCS. The community central bank reneges only when event R_c in equation (26b) occurs and inflates, in this case, at rate

$$\alpha \; A \; s_m \; . \tag{30}$$

Hence, under a CMCS, the community wide rate of inflation, π_c, is either 0 or α A s_m. Consequently, the expected value of π_c is

$$E\pi_c = \left[1 - P(R_c)\right] .0 + P(R_c)\alpha \; A \; E \; s_m \tag{31}$$

where $P(R_c)$ is the probability of the event R_c. Since s_m is drawn from a distribution whose expected value is μ_s, it follows that

$$E\pi_c = P(R_c)\alpha \; A \; \mu_s . \tag{31a}$$

Hence, $E\pi_c$ is lower or higher than $E\pi_p$ depending on whether $P(R_c)$ is lower or higher than $P(R_{pi})$. If the probability that at least m countries decide to renege on the commitment is smaller than the probability that a <u>particular</u> country decides to renege $E\pi_c$ is lower than $E\pi_p$[24]. This is the case, in turn, if the probability that s is larger than the threshold S_H in a given country is larger than the probability that s is larger than S_H in at least m countries. But this may or may not be the case. The reason is that there are two opposing effects. On one hand, the requirement that if $s_i > S_H$ there are at least m - 1 countries in which $s_i > S_H$ too is more stringent than just requiring $s_i > S_H$. This tends to make $P(R_c)$ smaller than $P(R_{pi})$. On the other hand, there are many ways in which the event R_c can realize and this works in the opposite direction. An example may help clarify the elements that are involved. Suppose n = 3 and let

$$P(R_{pi}) \equiv p \; . \tag{32}$$

For n = 3, the event R_c is

$$R_c = R_{p1} \cap R_{p2} \cap \bar{R}_{p3} \cup R_{p1} \cap \bar{R}_{p2} \cap R_{p3} \cup \bar{R}_{p1} \cap R_{p2} \cap R_{p3} \cup R_{p1} \cap R_{p2} \cap R_{p3} \tag{33}$$

[24]Note that the probability that a <u>particular</u> country reneges is not identical to the probability that <u>a</u> country in the community reneges. The second probability is always larger.

where $\bar{R}_{pi}$ is the complement of R_{pi}. That is $\bar{R}_{pi}$ is the event: "Country i in a system of APLC does not renege". If the distribution of shocks is independent across countries

$$P(R_c) = 3p^2(1-p) + p^3 . \tag{34}$$

Hence, $P(R_c) < P(R_{pi})$ if and only if

$$3p^2(1-p) + p^3 < p \iff Q(p) \equiv 2p^2 - 3p + 1 > 0 . \tag{35}$$

Simple algebra establishes that $Q(p)$ is larger than, equal to, or smaller than zero depending on whether p is smaller than, equal to, or larger than 0.5. Hence, for the case of three countries, if the probability that $s_i > S_H$ is smaller than 0.5, a CMCS produces a lower mean inflation than an APLC. The reverse is true for $p > 0.5$. I conjecture that the feature of this example that is generalizable to any number of countries is that for sufficiently low values of p expected inflation in the community is lower under a CMCS than under an APLC. In any case, it is possible to repeat the same exercise for the actual number of countries in the community, which is twelve. This is a well defined algebraic problem that has a well defined solution. But I have not attempted to do that. A fuller analysis will also need to take into consideration the possibility that the distributions of the shocks, s_i are not independent across countries.

Before closing this subsection, note that with a CMCS the likelihood that at least m countries will simultaneously desire to renege is larger when there is a positive cross countries correlation between the shocks[25]. Hence, the larger the correlation of the shocks, s_i, across countries, the more likely it is that a CMCS will abandon the commitment to price stability. Conversely, if shocks are negatively correlated across countries, the likelihood that a CMCS reneges is smaller than under statistical independence of the shocks. This is summarized in the following proposition:

[25]Larger by comparison to the benchmark of shocks that are independent across countries.

Proposition 5: The larger, algebraically, is the degree of cross country correlation among the real shocks, s_i, the more likely is a CMCS to renege on the commitment to price stability.

e. Comparison between a CMCS and an APLC in the Presence of Additional Motives for Monetary Expansion

To this point the analysis in this section was based on the implicit assumption that policymakers inflate only because of the employment motive. However, a similar analysis can be performed in the presence of systematic or random differences in the potency of the revenue and the balance of payments motives across countries. Cross country differences in the level of government debt and in the parameter δ across countries will lead to differences in the adherence of different countries to the price stability commitment. Countries that have a relatively high valuation of seignorage revenues ($\delta/\phi_\pi(\cdot)$ in equation (14) is high) and larger debts, will normally desire to abandon commitments more frequently than countries with lower valuations. Italy, Spain, Portugal and Greece are probably in the first group. Analogously, countries that experience larger current account deficits will also desire to abandon commitments more frequently. A comparison of monetary policy outcomes under a CMCS with policy outcomes under an APLC in the presence of those additional motives may proceed along similar lines and is likely to produce similar qualitative conclusions. In particular, proposition 4 is likely to generalize implying that the strains on an APLC of the type proposed for stage two in the Delors Report will be more severe the higher and the more divergent the shocks that affect the different countries.

f. A Remark on Asymmetric Information

For simplicity, I have assumed that the public and policymakers get the information on which policymakers base their actions simultaneously. In practice, policymakers have some relevant temporary information advantage about various variables like their own fiscal needs, the degree to which they intend to lean on seignorage, the current account and short run forecasts of employment and unemployment. They certainly have an information advantage about their own forecasts. Since policy is normally based on such forecasts, this advantage is relevant.

The presence of an information advantage on the part of policymakers enables them to temporarily move employment and the current account in desired directions. It therefore alters the intensity of their temptation to renege on the commitment to price stability. An analysis of the behavior of an employment motivated policymaker under discretion and asymmetric information appears in Cukierman and Meltzer (1986).

6. IS STAGE TWO USEFUL? ADDITIONAL CONSIDERATIONS

This section evaluates the case for and against the elimination of stage two by going directly from the current EMS to a commonly managed currency.

a. The Case Against Stage Two

1. The analysis of the previous section suggests that the natural tendency of monetary policies to diverge under an APLC and large shocks in some countries is dangerous for the development of the political consensus needed for continuation towards a full monetary union. A corollary is that full monetary union has better chances of being implemented in periods with relatively small shocks.

2. A drawback of the different currencies management inherent in an APLC system is the negative externality due to the common resource problem. With fixed parities, each monetary authority affects the rate of inflation of the entire community. But national central banks or governments do not internalize the costs of the inflation they impose on other members of the community (Aizenman (1989)). On the other hand, the political costs of changing parities can alleviate this problem by internalizing some of the externality for countries that are tempted to produce above average monetary growth. However, there is no guarantee that the distribution of those costs across countries corresponds to the one that would produce the correct incentive structure.

3. The actual and planned increases in capital and labor mobility throughout the community also strengthen the case for going directly to a common currency because of the usual optimal currency area argument (Mundell (1961), McKinnon (1963)). With higher mobility, adjustments to divergent real shocks can be more easily achieved by factor flows freeing monetary policymakers from the task of trying (many times in vain) to achieve those adjustments. A larger free trade area also

increases diversification within the area, facilitating adjustment without parity changes (Kenen (1969)).

4. During 1990, restrictions on capital flows between the EEC countries will be lifted. Under the existing EMS or some tighter version of an APLC, national monetary authorities will have to avail themselves with sufficient reserves to prevent speculative attacks on the fixed parities system. They also may have to periodically coordinate swap arrangements. This elaborate machinery is totally unnecessary in a single currency system since such attacks are not possible in such a system. Moreover, speculative attacks, which are quite possible under the institutional structure planned for stage two, are likely to bring about the reenactment of capital controls in some countries[26]. Hence, a lengthy period with a "stage two" monetary system may retard progress towards the free flows of capital.

5. The nominal exchange rate between two currencies is fundamentally the relative price of those currencies. It is therefore affected by the relative supplies of the currencies. Under an APLC, those supplies are determined by the national central banks. This characterization of exchange rates determinants implies that sterilized interventions in foreign exchange markets have no effect on the exchange rate. In particular, if the national central bank sells foreign exchange, absorbing some domestic currency, but then sterilizes the effect on the money supply by increasing Net Domestic Credit (NDC), there should be no effect on the exchange rate. This characterization is appropriate in the long run. However, in the short and intermediate runs, such a sterilized intervention in the foreign exchange market prevents the foreign exchange from rising. The reason is that the new money created through the expansion of NDC, does not immediately find its way back to the foreign exchange market. In other words, sterilized interventions normally have temporary effects on the rate of exchange. The lag between an expansion of NDC (and the effect of the new domestic money that is thereby created) on the exchange rate increases the temptation of national central bankers to expand NDC in order to achieve various real objectives while temporarily maintaining the exchange rate at its

[26]Under existing provisions, a country will be allowed to temporarily reenact controls on flows of capital even after 1990.

peg by selling foreign exchange to the public[27]. This temptation is stronger the larger the rate of time preference of policymakers and the longer the lags between the creation of NDC and the full impact of the new money on the foreign exchange market. Such temptations put additional strains on the APLC system envisaged for stage two. By contrast, in a CMCS those intra community temptations are nonexistent since the policymaking institutions do not allow their manifestation by construction.

6. An immediate switch to a CMCS will bring about the savings in real resources used up in the process of intra EEC currency exchange early on. As far as I know, there is no systematic investigation of the magnitude of those costs. A back of the envelope calculation suggests they may be as large as one percent of the community GDP[28].

7. A single European currency increases the likelihood that this

---

[27]This mechanism was in evidence in Israel in the post 1985 stabilization.

[28]This statement is based on assumptions regarding the spread between buying and selling rates in foreign exchange transactions multiplied by a "guesstimate" of total foreign exchange transactions within the EEC countries. The November 1989 issue of the Bank of England Quarterly Bulletin (p. 531) reports that the daily foreign exchange trading in London was roughly 187 billion dollars in April 1989. This figure was converted into yearly terms by assuming 240 trading days per year. It was further assumed that the average spread between buying and selling rates is 0.1136 of a percent. This figure was arrived at by assuming that for 86% of transactions the spread is 0.01 of a percent, that it is 0.5 of a percent for 7% of transactions and one percent for the remaining 7% of transactions. The breakdown of total net turnover in London in April 89 into interbank and non interbank (86% and 14%) was obtained from the BIS. It was assumed that the same breakdown applies to all countries in the community and that half of the non interbank volume (7%) is with corporations, which pay the average rate of half a percent, and the other 7% of turnover are with households, who pay the average rate of one percent. This is the information and the assumptions underlying the average spread of 0.1136 of a percent.

Only 40% of the total London turnover in the April 89 survey is directly between two EEC currencies. In spite of the fact that some transactions between two EEC currencies are made via a roundtrip through the dollar, the calculation assumes, to be conservative, that only 40% of the April 89 London volume represents transactions between EEC currencies. Finally, the statement in the text relies on the presumption that the 40% of London volume does not represent more than half of the total foreign exchange transactions between EEC currencies in the entire community. Andrew Crockett, Peter Kenen and Richard Levich were instrumental in narrowing down the range of uncertainty regarding some of the assumptions. They obviously are not responsible currency will become a key currency. As a result, a European central bank may share in some of the seignorage currently obtained by the Fed due to increases in the demand for $ because of its function as a key currency. The resulting seignorage revenues may be used to partially compensate the fiscal authorities within the EEC for giving up the ability to raise seignorage revenues domestically.

8. In the presence of national monies governments can redistribute domestic resources through inflation without making explicit legislative decisions. Some may view the removal of this option under a CMCS as a drawback. I view it as an advantage since it makes the transfer policy of government more explicit, increasing the accountability of government to its constituency.

b. <u>The Case for Stage Two</u>

The list of arguments in favor of having a "stage two" is extremely short.

1. The process of economic and monetary unification may bring with it some completely unexpected (in the Knightian sense) structural changes. One can argue that it may be easier to readjust institutions, after the realization of those changes, before the substantial institutional restructuring needed for a CMCS is made. On the other hand, the ultimate test of an institutional structure is its performance in the face of various shocks. Without actually trying some version of a CMCS in the face of various changes it may be difficult to evaluate its advantages and disadvantages. Put differently, a period of trial and error with some version of a CMCS may be needed in any case.

2. Adoption of a CMCS means that individual governments have to give up this form of taxation. From the point of view of individual governments, seignorage is a quickly available form of taxation. In an uncertain world the flexibility and immediacy of seignorage is an asset for government. This is true even for fiscal authorities that rely relatively little on seignorage on average. In other words, the advantage of seignorage is that it facilitates the creation of deficits when the necessity to do so arises.

On the other hand, seignorage is not the only way to finance deficits, since governments can also issue debt. Removal of the

---

for the quality of the estimates.

seignorage option reduces the ability of fiscal authorities to create deficits by a lot when they face narrow capital markets. An example is Bolivia. However, this is not the case for the EEC countries although there are some differences in borrowing abilities among the countries in the community. Furthermore, the liberalization of capital flows will make it easier for governments to tap funds from the wider market. In addition establishment of a single currency eliminates exchange risks. Both elements are likely to make it easier to borrow on the community wide market. The upshot is that some of the loss in the ability to finance deficits through seignorage will be compensated by more elastic supplies of funds to national fiscal authorities.

c. Relative Fiscal Cohesion and Discipline under an APLC and a CMCS

The institutional organ for a CMCS is a European Central Bank (ECB). There is, at present, substantial uncertainty about the precise organizational structure and degree of independence that a ECB, if it ever came into existence, might have[29]. However, there seems to be a large consensus that a ECB would be more independent from the national fiscal authorities than the central banks of most EEC countries[30]. In particular, the ECB will not be required to finance the deficits of individual governments. On the other hand, under an APLC of the type envisaged for stage two, the current degrees of independence are likely to prevail or to increase a little. Hence, an APLC will have to be reinforced by various devices to prevent national fiscal policies from drifting too far apart from each other. Such safeguards are largely unnecessary in the presence of a fairly independent ECB since the temptation to create divergent deficits will be checked automatically through capital markets. Countries that borrow a lot will face higher real rates. This will provide automatic incentives for convergent fiscal policies. The higher average degree of independence of a ECB is also likely to reduce the average tendency to create deficits in the community[31].

---

[29]Alternative points of view appear in Sylla (1988) and Bouvier (1988).

[30]The notable exception is the Bundesbank.

[31]There is some evidence that fiscal discipline is stronger in countries with more independent central banks (Parkin (1987)). See also Alesina and Tabellini (1987) for a theoretical analysis.

d. Political Considerations

The case for switching to a commonly managed currency without going through an additional period of adjustable pegs seems strong. The main drawback seems to be political rather than economic. Countries that rely relatively heavily on seignorage and/or have large outstanding public debts may block the process of monetary unification because of their heavier reliance on seignorage. There are, I believe, two possible solutions to this conflict of interest. One is to convince them to join a CMCS by providing them privileged access to the seignorage revenues of the ECB for a number of years to be negotiated. The other possibility is that countries with fairly uniform recent records in the use of seignorage like West Germany, France and the U.K. create a commonly managed currency of their own with provisions for the subsequent joining of additional community members. Smooth functioning of a more narrowly based but more homogenous (in terms of policy objectives) CMCS may convince those that will not join initially to join later on. The first option seems preferable but perhaps less likely politically.

7. CONCLUDING REMARKS

This paper presented a systematic comparison of policy outcomes under an adjustable peg system with outcomes under a single community wide monetary authority. The formal analysis was restricted to the case in which only the employment motive is operative and the distributions of real shocks are the same across countries. The same method of analysis can, however, be applied when additional motives are operatives or when distributions of shocks differ. Such exercises seem to be useful extensions.

I assumed for simplicity that unions are perfectly informed about the degree of precommitment of policymakers -- they know the parameter c with certainty. The analysis can be extended along the lines of Cukierman and Liviatan (1991) to the case in which unions are uncertain about c. It is likely that in this case strong policymakers with relatively high values of c will renege on commitments more often than in the case in which their identity is known with certainty.

At the more operational level, the main conclusion of this paper is that the benefits of a stage two, as proposed in the Delors Report, are not worth the risks that such a stage carries for the continuation of the process towards full monetary unification. It seems that, as long as a switch to a commonly managed currency is not politically feasible, it is better to acknowledge publicly that some version of the EMS will continue to exist. In particular, it is important to prewarn politicians and the public that under such an arrangement parity adjustments are likely to continue. Otherwise, the parity adjustments that would follow unfortunate shock realizations may be misconstrued as indicating that full monetary unification is impractical. Such a misunderstanding would be quite unfortunate since, as suggested by the analysis in section 5, policy outcomes under an adjustable peg system provide little guidance for evaluating policy outcomes under a commonly managed currency.

APPENDIX

1. PROOF OF PROPOSITION 2

Assumption 1 implies that if the central monetary authority reneges it picks the discretionary rate in equation (19) for $s = s_m$. If unions anticipate this behavior

$$\pi_d(\pi_d, s_m) = \frac{\alpha A}{1 + \alpha^2 A} [s_m + \pi_d] . \qquad \text{(A1)}$$

This implies that when the community central bank is expected to renege, both actual and expected inflation are

$$\alpha A s_m .$$

Given that $\pi^e = \alpha A s_m$, country m votes to renege if

$$W\left[\alpha A s_m, \alpha A s_m, s_m\right] - W\left[0, \alpha A s_m, s_m\right] > c \qquad \text{(A2)}$$

which, using (17) and rearranging, is equivalent to

$$(\alpha^2 A - 1) s_m^2 + 2s_m^2 > \frac{2c}{(\alpha A)^2} \qquad \text{(A2a)}$$

and to

$$s_m > S_L. \tag{A2b}$$

Under the same circumstances country i ≠ m also votes to renege if

$$W\left[\alpha A s_m, \alpha A s_m, s_i\right] - W\left[0, \alpha A s_m, s_i\right] > c . \tag{A3}$$

(A3) is equivalent to the condition

$$(\alpha^2 A - 1)\, s_m^2 + 2 s_m s_i > \frac{2c}{(\alpha A)^2} . \tag{A3a}$$

Comparison of (A2a) with (A3a) implies that if the median country has a preference for breaking the commitment, so do all the countries with $s_i \geq s_m$. Hence, when country m prefers to renege, there is a majority in favor of such a move and condition (25) in the text is satisfied.

QED

2. PROOF THAT S_H^2 IS DECREASING IN A

Differentiating the expression for S_H^2 in equation (20a) with respect to A, we obtain

$$\frac{\partial S_H^2}{\partial A} = -\frac{2c}{A^2}. \tag{A4}$$

which is unambiguously negative.

REFERENCES

J. Aizenman (1989) "Competitive Externalities and the Optimal Seignorage", Manuscript, September.

A. Alesina and G. Tabellini (1987) "Rules and Discretion with Non Coordinated Monetary and Fiscal Policy", *Economic Inquiry*, 25, October, 619 - 630.

R. Barro (1983) "Inflationary Finance under Discretion and Rules", *Canadian Journal of Economics*, 16, February, 1 - 25.

R. Barro and D. Gordon (1983) "A Positive Theory of Monetary Policy in a Natural Rate Model", *Journal of Political Economy*, 91, August, 589 - 610.

J. Bouvier (1988) "The Banque de France and the State from 1850 to the Present Day", G. Toniolo (ed.) *Central Banks' Independence in Historical Perspective*, Walter de Gruyter, Berlin, New York.

M. Bruno and S. Piterman (1988) "Israel's Stabilization: A Two Year Review", M. Bruno, G. Di Tella, R. Dornbusch and S. Fischer (eds.) *Inflation Stabilization, The Experience of Israel, Argentina, Brazil, Bolivia and Mexico*, The MIT Press, Cambridge, Massachusetts.

P. Cagan (1956) "The Monetary Dynamics of Hyperinflation", M. Friedman (ed.) *Studies in the Quantity Theory of Money*, University of Chicago Press, Chicago.

G. Calvo (1978) "On the Time Consistency of Optimal Policy in a Monetary Economy", *Econometrica*, 46, November, 1411 - 1428.

I.K. Cho and D. Kreps (1987) "Signaling Games and Stable Equilibria", *Quarterly Journal of Economics*, 102, May, 179 - 221.

A. Cukierman (1988) "The End of the High Israeli Inflation: An Experiment in Heterodox Stabilization", M. Bruno, G. Di Tella, R. Dornbusch and S. Fischer (eds.) Inflation Stabilization, *The Experience of Israel, Argentina, Brazil, Bolivia and Mexico*, The MIT Press, Cambridge, Massachusetts.

A. Cukierman (1988) "Rapid Inflation - Deliberate Policy or Miscalculation?", *Carnegie-Rochester Conference Series on Public Policy*, 29, (Money, Cycles and Exchange Rates: Essays in honor of A.H. Meltzer), Autumn, 11 - 75.

A. Cukierman (1990) *Central Bank Behavior, Credibility Accommodation and Stabilization*, Chapters 1-11, Manuscript, May (In preparation for MIT Press).

A. Cukierman, S. Edwards and G. Tabellini (1989) "Seignorage and Political Instability", Manuscript, November.

A. Cukierman and N. Liviatan (1990) "Rules, Discretion, Credibility and Reputation", *Bank of Israel Economic Review*, 65, July, 3-25.

A. Cukierman and N. Liviatan (1991) "Optimal Accommodation by Strong Policymakers under Incomplete Information", *Journal of Monetary Economics*, 27, 1, January.

A. Cukierman and A. Meltzer (1986) "A Theory of Ambiguity, Credibility and Inflation under Discretion and Asymmetric Information", *Econometrica*, 54, September, 1099 - 1128.

M. De Cecco and A. Giovannini (eds.) (1989) A European Central Bank? *Perspectives on Monetary Unification after Ten Years of the EMS*, Cambridge University Press, Cambridge, U.K.

J. Delors (1989) "Report on Economic and Monetary Union in the European Communities", in *Report on Economic and Monetary Union in the European Community and Collection of Papers*, Office for Official Publications of the European Communities, Luxembourg.

F. Giavazzi and A. Giovannini (1989) *Limiting Exchange Rate Flexibility: The European Monetary System*, The MIT Press, Cambridge, Massachusetts.

H. Horn and T. Persson (1988) "Exchange Rate Policy, Wage Formation and Credibility", *European Economic Review*, 32, October, 1621 - 1636.

P. Kenen (1969) "The Theory of Optimum Currency Areas: An Eclectic View", R. Mundell and A. Swoboda (eds.) *Monetary Problems of the International Economy*, The University of Chicago Press, Chicago and London.

F.E. Kydland, and E.C. Prescott (1977) "Rules Rather than Discretion: The Inconsistency of Optimal Plans", *Journal of Political Economy*, 85, 473-492.

R. McKinnon (1963) "Optimum Currency Areas", *American Economic Review*, 53, September, 717 -725.

R. Mundell (1961) "A Theory of Optimum Currency Areas", *American Economic Review*, 51, September, 657 - 664.

M. Parkin (1987) "Domestic Monetary Institutions and Deficits", in J. Buchanan, C. Rowley and R. Tollison (eds.) *Deficits*, Basil Blackwell, Oxford.

T. Persson and G. Tabellini (1989) *Macroeconomic Policy, Credibility and Politics*, Revised draft April, To be published by Harwood Academic Publishers.

K.O. Pöhl (1989) "The Further Development of the European Monetary System", *Report on Economic and Monetary Union in the European Communities and Collection of Papers*, Office for Official Publications of the European Communities, Luxembourg.

K. Rogoff (1985) "The Optimal Degree of Commitment to an Intermediate Monetary Target", *Quarterly Journal of Economics*, 100, December.

T. Sargent and N. Wallace (1981) "Some Unpleasant Monetarist Arithmetic", *Federal Reserve Bank of Minneapolis Quarterly Review*, 5, Fall, 1 - 17.

R. Sylla (1988) "The Autonomy of Monetary Authorities: The Case of the U.S. Federal Reserve System" G. Toniolo (ed.) *Central Banks' Independence in Historical Perspective*, Walter de Gruyter, Berlin, New York.

G. Tabellini (1988) "Centralized Wage Setting and Monetary Policy in a Reputational Equilibrium", *Journal of Money, Credit and Banking*, 20, February, 102 - 118.

DISCRETION, PRECOMMITMENTS AND THE PROSPECTS FOR A EUROPEAN CENTRAL BANK - FIXED PARITIES VERSUS A COMMONLY MANAGED CURRENCY

by: Alex Cukierman

Discussant: Hermann-Josef Dudler

It is not easy to comment on Alex Cukierman's highly interesting paper under a tight time and space constraint. The author deals with a complex topic, develops an ambitious theoretical framework, arrives at politically "loaded" policy conclusions from the Bundesbank's point of view, and - all in all - presents a text of some 60 fascinating pages. In order to simplify my comments, I shall put forward only some personal reflections. In so doing, I shall not quarrel too much with the game-theoretic methodology adopted in the paper but rather assess its usefulness in the context of the ongoing European integration debate.

The analytical framework, on which the paper is based, may be said to incocporate highly simplified "games" in the light of recent literature in the field. The empirical relevance of such rudimentary game-theoretic applications has been seriously questioned.[1] Nevertheless, I came across a number of theoretical propositions in the paper which I found quite attractive. The paper drops, from the very beginning, the empirically dubious game-theoretic notion of atomistic private agents, extends the more traditional game-theoretic analysis of inflation to seigniorage and devaluation policy issues, develops plausible criteria for assessing the relative merits of adjustable peg systems and the currency area approach to European Monetary Union, and finally helps to put key issues in the current European integration debate coherently into focus.

I share the doubts which Alex Cukierman raises with respect to the usefulness of "stage two" of the Delors plan towards European Monetary Union. This element of the Delors integration blueprint is not well defined. Moreover, it incorporates a proposed institutional feature which could jeapardize the smooth functioning of monetary policy coordination on the way to monetary union: namely the existence, side

---

[1]See the critical assessment by Keith Blackburn and Michael Christensen, "Monetary Policy and Policy Credibility: Theories and Evidence," Journal of Economic Literature, Vol.XXVII (March 1989), 1-45.

by side, of a European Central Banking System and of national Central Banks which remain in ultimate control of vital policy decisions. Such an institutional arrangement could easily lead to power struggles between competing European and national decision-makers and central bank bureaucracies and thus seriously disturb money and capital markets and retard the European integration process.

I have some doubts, however, whether I would subscribe also to the fundamental policy conclusions which Alex Cukierman derives from his model. To readers familiar with the Delors Report, the paper implicitly collapses "stage one" and "stage two" of the Delors plan and seems to suggest that a common European currency area could be introduced more or less immediately. The paper does not seriously discuss the potential virtues of "stage one" of the Delors blueprint. This phase precedes the transition to a quasi-currency union and the ultimate introduction of a common European currency. During this preparatory stage, parity changes are retained deliberately as a legitimate instrument of external adjustment and supplement tight forms of monetary policy coordination and "multilateral surveillance" of general economic policies in the initial phase of the European integration process. I see a number of reasons why "stage one" should, in fact, not be omitted, but rather be implemented carefully as a necessary testing period, during which serious obstacles to full monetary integration must gradually be overcome:

- It is not clear whether governments and public opinion in EC member countries already exhibit compatible policy preferences, especially with respect to perceived longer-run inflation/unemployment tradeoffs. The lively debate about "asymmetries" and "biases" allegedly built into the EMS exchange rate mechanism in the second half of the 1980s actually points to the existence of hidden policy disagreements among major European "players."
- European governments' and central banks' ability to credibly enter into coordinated non-accommodating financial policy commitments remains open to doubt. Taking in particular the widely differing national cultures in the field of European trade unionism into account, governments may not be able to effectively implement joint policy commitments in all cases even if they initially agree on consistent ultimate policy objectives and medium-term programs

aiming at a high degree of convergence in economic performance in the community.

- Due to differences in the structure and adaptive capacity of national industries, individual countries' ability to absorb external shocks (such as changes in oil and raw material prices, real exchange rate disturbances and increased competition from newly industrialized countries) or normal changes in tastes, consumption patterns and technology varies greatly. In particular, less developed Mediterranean regions may have to complete a process of industrial "catching-up" before they could sensibly enter a system of irrevocably fixed exchange rates or a European currency union.

Finally, Alex Cukierman's paper makes a good case why inflation-prone economies should forego the option of currency depreciation, even if significant inflation differentials initially persist in the European Community. But why should central banks in low-inflation countries accept a currency area approach in conditions under which they will run the risk of "importing" inflation permanently from inflation-prone European economies through international price arbitrage in tradeable goods? A positive answer to this question might be given, if it could be shown convincingly that a system of irrevocably pegged exchange rates or a European currency union are likely to generate economic and social welfare benefits as "externalities" which more than offset the perceived costs of higher inflation. But in order to demonstrate the existence of such a favorable tradeoff a separate ambitious paper would probably be needed.

DISCRETION, PRECOMMITMENTS AND THE PROSPECTS FOR A EUROPEAN CENTRAL BANK-FIXED PARITIES VERSUS A COMMONLY MANAGED CURRENCY

by: Alex Cukierman

Discussant: Zvi Hercowitz

In this paper Cukierman offers an analytical framework to address the proposals of the commission headed by Jacques Delors on European monetary integration. The commission recommended the achievement of full monetary union in three stages. During the first two, coordination is intensified, but each central bank is still allowed to adjust the exchange rate in "exceptional circumstances." In the final stage, exchange rates become irrevocably fixed, and the individual currencies are eventually replaced by a single European currency.

Cukierman uses an analytical framework from the new literature, to which he has contributed, where the public - or a labor union - and the government, interact in a game-theoretic manner. The way the current framework works can be described as follows. The union sets the nominal wage in anticipation of the policies to be carried out by the government. Once the nominal wage is set, the government has the motivation to inflate or devalue in order to achieve goals in the areas of employment, balance of payments, or revenues. Since the union knows about these motives in advance, the nominal wage is set so that the ex-post real wage is at the desired level. The outcome of this game is that the specific goal of the government is not achieved by inflating or devaluing, but the rate of inflation, or devaluation is permanently higher making everyone worse off. Hence, a commitment to price or exchange stability is welfare improving.

This framework of thought is both simple and elegant. It has the appeal that it captures a lot of what we observe in the real world. In the context of the problem at hand it leads to the result, stressed by Cukierman, that the stage of adjustable peg is likely to be accompanied by significantly higher exchange rate instability than that emerging from the stage of full unification. His recommendation is the direct implementation of the final stage, where monetary and exchange rate policies are set by a single central bank.

The qualifications that I would add to the results are the following. The analytical framework is fairly well suited to deal with a single economy, stressing the game played by the public and the government. However, in its analysis of the adjustable peg system, where each government determines its own policy, there is no interaction between the different countries. Each one acts separately, being completely unaffected by the policies of the others. In reality, devaluations in one country may be seen critically in another country which also has mercantilistic motivations. Hence, there may be external political pressures on individual countries to comply with the peg. These kind of considerations were not addressed in the paper.

Elhanan Helpman and Leonardo Leiderman[1]

I. INTRODUCTION

An ideal evaluation of exchange rate systems would proceed along the lines of standard welfare economics. It would compare regimes in terms of costs and benefits, and derive net welfare gains for every country. Exchange rate systems would than be ranked according to Pareto's criterion in order to see which fare best. This procedure is unlikely to lead to a unique best choice, however, because more than one regime is expected to top the list. Regimes differ in their distributional implications, some favoring one set of countries and others favoring a different set.

At this stage it would make sense to examine cooperative rules of conduct that exploit the available surplus in a way that benefits all parties. If the implementation of side payments that compensate losing countries from the adoption of a more efficient system is judged to be out of reach, one would seek a cooperative regime that has a built in mechanism for the sharing of benefits.

This selection procedure is rooted in standard economic thinking. It represents an approach that has been widely used in theory and practice. Examples include the evaluation of public utilities, the tunnel beneath the English channel, and the debate about socialism between Lange, Lerner and von Misses. It has, however, played only a limited role in discussions of exchange rate regimes. Why?

One reason is that the study of exchange rates has become part of macroeconomics when the latter evolved into as a separate field of inquiry. Initially macroeconomics addressed a new set of issues that did not fit in well with mainstream economics of the time. This gave it

---

[1]The original version of this paper was completed in December 1989. For the purpose of the current revision we have not updated the literature, as is particularly evident from section IV dealing with exchange rate bands. We will deal with exchange rate bands in more detail in a forthcoming paper. We thank the Israeli International Institute for supporting our research project on exchange rate systems.

strength, and it has become an important area. Unfortunately, macroeconomics also developed its own terminology, models, evaluation criteria, and the like, and resisted integration with mainstream economics for many years to come. The letter proved to be detrimental. These developments affected the ways in which economists have been thinking about exchange rates, postponing for many years the natural approach outlined at the beginning of this section.

Second, the study of exchange rates involves considerations of international trade, pricing policies, financial markets, international capital flows, interest rates, monetary and fiscal policy, and more. In short, exchange rates are relative prices of the utmost importance. They affect many facets of economic activity on the one hand, and they are affected by many structural features of national economies and the international system on the other. Consequently, their proper understanding requires knowledge of different areas of economics and the ability to integrate their complex interactions. This is a difficult task to the best of economists, exchange rate theorists and practitioners not withstanding.

The treatment of complex problems involves compromises in research strategies, often in the form of short cuts in the formulation of problems. In retrospect some short cuts prove to be well chosen, in the sense that their implications survive more elaborate analyses. Others, however, prove to be far fetched. The study of exchange rates is no exception.

A major compromise consists of the evaluation of exchange rate regimes by means of criteria that are only loosely related to acceptable welfare measures. Proper welfare analyses of exchange rate systems are hardly available (see, for example, the Handbook of International Economics, edited by Ronald W. Jones and Peter B. Kenen). Attention has been focused instead on the performance of exchange rate regimes in terms of the variability of output, variability of the price level, and the like. One may argue that these criteria are important, and that they are related to the ultimate measures of welfare, as indeed they are. This is a good reason to explore their behavior under alternative exchange rate systems. But to draw from such studies firm conclusions about the desirability of alternative exchange rate systems is a different matter altogether.

The degree of confidence one has in the use of these proxies as welfare measures is a matter of judgment; there exist no objective way to form an opinion on this isssue. Occasionally the pendulum of confidence tilts in a particular direction as a result of a new theoretical development or empirical finding, subsequently it changes course. This point is demonstrated by the current debate on the desired international monetary system, that reveals again lack of common ground in the desired approach and in the use of evaluation criteria. On the face of it, the current debate resembles similar debates in the fifties and sixties. There exist, however, important differences. These have to do with methodological innovations as well as with the nature of the debated proposals. Moreover, available evidence from empirical studies is now broader and more reliable than ever before.

The old debates have been documented and reviewed extensively in the literature. For this reason we focus on recent theoretical and empirical developments that shed new light on the main issues. In Section II we review the literature that uses proper welfare criteria in comparisons of exchange rate systems. This approach is still underdeveloped. So far technical reasons and other difficulties have prevented it from dealing with a number of central problems in the choice of an exchange rate systems. Consequently, simple performance measures have been used instead, such as the variabilities of output, the price level, consumption, and the real exchange rate (for early theoretical explorations along this lines see Mundell (1973) and Fischer (1977)). We report in Section III empirical evidence on the variability of real exchange rates and other macroeconomic variables under alternative systems. We elaborate on possible explanations for the major finding that real exchange rates are more volatile under flexible rates.

The next section addresses issues related to the viability of exchange rate pegs. We pay particular attention to dynamic processes that arise in the presence of expectations of a change in regime. Such expectations develop in response to monetary and fiscal policies that are inconsistent with the announced exchange rate policy. We show how the theory has been used to explain important empirical regularities and we describe empirical studies of the collapsing exchange rate pegs. In Section IV we review studies of exchange rate bands. This system has become particularly topical with the evolution of the European Monetary System. Our conclusions are presented in Section V.

II. WELFARE COMPARISONS

A number of studies have examined welfare properties of exchange rate systems by comparing utility levels across regimes (see Helpman and Razin (1979), Kareken and Wallace (1981), Helpman (1981), and Lucas (1982)). They brought out two main points. First, proper comparisons require careful formulation of the problem in order to avoid building in asymmetries that are not inherent in the systems per-se. This came out particularly forcefully in the treatment of international capital mobility. While it was common to restrict capital mobility in flexible exchange rate regimes, formulations of fixed exchange rates implicitly allowed for international capital movements through the flow of international reserves (see, for example, Mundell (1973)). Naturally, this approach biased the outcome in favor of fixed exchange rates, despite the fact that international financial integration can be part of a flexible exchange rate system. Second, these studies identified conditions under which fixed and flexible exchange rates have the same welfare implications.

The employment of explicit models with utility maximizing agents involves much more complexity than the use of simple reduced form macroeconomic models. The strength of the maximizing approach lies in its explicitness. It requires, for example, a clear statement of the economic mechanisms that drive and interline transactions. As of now, however, the weakness of this approach lies in its inability to accommodate elaborate monetary mechanisms and realistic structures of financial markets. This shortcoming is important, because the structure of financial intermediation, the monetary mechanism, and the behavior of monetary authorities are central to the understanding of exchange rate systems. This is not to say that alternative approaches fare better on these accounts. It only makes clear the point that explicitness in an approach makes these shortcomings rather visible, while in some alternative formulations the emperor seems to wear clothes when in fact he does not.

Contrary to some evaluations, the explicit approach is not a narrow brand of the new classical macroeconomics. And contrary to those evaluations (see, for example, Dornbusch and Frankel (1988)) it has been designed to deal with frictions. Moreover, one of its main tasks is to explicitly model frictions in order to evaluate the comparative advantage of exchange rate regimes to overcome them. Thus, for example, it has been found that certain forms of financial markets ensure the irrelevance of frictions that result from cash in advance constraints in the use of money in both fixed and flexible exchange rate regimes (see Helpman (1981) and Lucas (1982), and the exception reported in Ashauer and Greenwood (1984)). On the other hand, incompleteness of financial markets (that limits risk sharing opportunities) has important affects on the ranking of exchange rate systems. For example, market incompleteness of the form studied by Helpman and Razin (1982) -- that results from the need to commit to a portfolio of assets before one observes commodity prices -- was shown to favor flexible rates.

If anything, the explicit approach should be criticized for not going far enough in its designated direction. Occasionally interesting frictions have been introduced in these models, but their welfare implications have not been studied (e.g., Svensson (1985) and Grilli and Roubini (1989)). The roles of other frictions need to be studied, frictions related to informational problems, financial intermediation, agents heterogeneity, and the like. And the cash in advance monetary mechanism employed in much of this line of work should be modified to better fit reality.

III. MACROECONOMIC STABILITY

A recent interesting line of empirical research compares the statistical properties of key macroeconomic variables across fixed and floating exchange rate regimes. An attempt is made to detect whether means, variances, and other moments of output, real exchange rates, consumption, and other variables, have changed in moving from one exchange rate system to another.

The behavior of real exchange rates in a fixed and floating exchange rate system was empirically studied by Mussa (1986). He compared the experiences of sixteen of the more advanced industrial countries since 1957. For pairs of countries with similar moderate rates of inflation, Mussa has detected the following regularities. First, real exchange rates typically show much greater short term variability in a floating than in a fixed rate regime. Stockman (1983) reached a similar conclusion based on estimation of a fixed-effects variance-components model in which a measure of the variability of the real exchange rate was regressed on a fixed country effect, on a fixed year effect, and on a dummy variable that indicates the exchange rate regime. Second, the increased variability in a floating rate regime is largely accounted for by the increased variability of nominal exchange rates, with little contribution from changes in the variability of ratios of national price levels or the covariances between movements in nominal exchange rates and movements in relative prices. Third, changes in real exchange rates under floating rates exhibit relatively high persistence, similar to the persistence of nominal exchange rate movements. On the other hand, the degree of persistence of changes in ratios of national price levels does not appear to change from one regime to another.

In interpreting these empirical regularities, Mussa indicates that they provide strong evidence against models that embody the property of "nominal exchange rate neutrality." According to simple versions of these models, the behavior of real exchange rates should not be affected systematically by the nominal exchange rate regime. According to Mussa, the regularities conform with models that assume sluggishness in the adjustment of nominal price levels relative to the speed of adjustment of nominal exchange rates (in a floating rate regime). These models imply that real exchange rates would move more slowly under fixed than under flexible rates, and this implication seems to be in line with the sample information.

The paper by Baxter and Stockman (1989) investigates differences in time series behavior of major macroeconomic aggregates. They study the Bretton Woods system that broke down between 1971 and 1973, and the flexible rate regime during the 1973-1986 period. Since most of the time series they investigate are nonstationary, they filter the data in order to achieve stationarity before they compute statistics such as means and variances. They employ two common filters: (i) removal of a linear trend fitted to the log of a given variable; and (ii) computing first differences of the log of a variable. They use a sample of postwar data for 49 countries that consists of industrial production, consumption, trade flows, government consumption spending, and real exchange rates.

Their main conclusion is that there is no evidence to support the view that the cyclical behavior of real macroeconomic aggregates (as reflected in the standard deviations of the filtered variables), such as industrial production, private consumption, and real trade flows, depends systematically on the exchange rate regime. The only exception is the real exchange rate, which exhibits higher volatility under flexible than under fixed rates. These conclusions were reinforced by the results of two episodes in which countries changed their exchange rate regime at times other than the breakdown of Bretton Woods. The episodes are the switch of Ireland from a peg to sterling before 1979 to the DM (via the EMS) after 1979, and the Canadian float against the U.S. dollar from 1951-62 (that was resumed in 1970).

On the other hand, Grilli and Kaminsky (1988) argue that Mussa's (1986) finding that variances of the real exchange rates of the major countries are eight to eighty times higher during the floating than during the fixed rate period, holds only for samples of post WWII data. They investigate the time series properties of the dollar/pound real exchange rate between January 1885 and December 1986. Their chronology suggests the following exchange rate regimes for the dollar/pound rate:

1. The Gold Standard Period, January 1879 - June 1914.
2. Transition to Wartime Markets, July 1914 - November 1914.
3. Controlled Floating, December 1914 - June 1919.
4. Floating Back to the Gold Standard, July 1919 - March 1925.
5. Gold Exchange Standard, April 1925 - August 1931.
6. Abandonment of Fixed Exchange Rates, Sept. 1931 - August 1939.
7. Wartime Foreign Exchange Controls, Sept. 1939 - Sept. 1949.
8. Fixed Exchange Rates (Bretton Woods), Sept. 1949 - Feb. 1973.
9. Floating Exchange Rates, March 1973 - present.

These authors first provide a preliminary analysis of real exchange rate behavior by means of summary statistics. Second, they perform a nonparametric test of whether the observations from different exchange rate periods belong to one sample. Third, they test this hypothesis using a simple fixed-effects variance-components model also used by Stockman (1983).

Their main findings are that: (i) real exchange rates behaved differently in the postwar (WWII) than the prewar period; and (ii) large differences in the volatility of real exchange rates between fixed and flexible regimes are present only in the postwar period. In particular, the Bretton Woods period appears extremely stable when compared not only to flexible rate periods but also to other fixed rate periods. They conclude that the real exchange rate is more a function of the specific historical episodes than of the nominal exchange rate system.

In order to examine how well Israel fits into the broader evidence, we have used monthly data on the rate of inflation and the rate of depreciation of the domestic currency relative to the U.S. dollar to perform calculations similar to Mussa's. There are three exchange rate systems that we considered: a crawling peg (from July 1975 to September 1977), a float (from February 1978 to July 1985), and a quasi-fixed exchange rate that was adopted as part of the 1985 stabilization program. Our variables consist of DE, the rate of change of the exchange rate relative to the dollar (monthly average); DP, the rate of inflation; and DRE (= DE-DP), the rate of change of the real exchange rate. (To simplify matters, we abstracted from foreign inflation).

Table 1 contains the results. It shows that the variability of the real exchange rate was highest during the floating rate period. In fact, in recent years -- with disinflation and a quasi fixed exchange rate -- the variance of the rate of change of the real exchange rate equals about 50 percent of the previous variance. Similarly, under the crawling peg there was lower real exchange rate variability than under the float. These observations support the view that real exchange rates are more volatile under floating than under fixed exchange rates.

Next we examine whether increased real exchange rate volatility under the Israeli float can be attributed, as in Mussa, to increased volatility of nominal exchange rate changes. Interestingly, here our findings differ. In particular, comparing the floating rate period with the recent quasi-fixed rate period indicates that <u>both</u> inflation and nominal exchange rate variances have substantially decreased in the recent period. Specifically, the variance of inflation fluctuations in the most recent period (of a quasi-fixed exchange rate) equals about 4 percent its level in the preceding period, and the variance of nominal exchange rate fluctuations equals about 16 percent of its previous level. In addition, the covariance between movements in inflation and nominal depreciation has decreased; the correlation is 0.239 in the later period whereas it was about 0.835 in the preceding period. Similar results hold for comparisons of the crawling peg and floating rate periods. Thus, there are marked changes in the variance of inflation along with changes in the variance of the nominal exchange rate, and one cannot attribute (in a statistical sense) the fluctuations in the real exchange rate mostly to fluctuations in the nominal exchange rate. In our view, this evidence does not conform with the implications of the sticky price models discussed by Mussa. This may well be a reflection of the fact that the sluggishness in prices for which Mussa found support is not particularly relevant for high inflation economies such as Israel (recall that Mussa's sample consisted of industrial countries with relatively low inflation rates).

So far we have discussed evidence for real exchange rate volatility. What about the behavior of other macroeconomic variables? A partial answer to this question can be obtained from a recent investigation by Leiderman and Liviatan (1989), who quantitatively compared the behavior of macroeconomic variables before and after disinflation in Israel. From this comparison one learns that the shift to lower exchange rate flexibility was accompanied by a decrease in the variability of real exchange rate movements, yet no major change has been observed for the variabilities of changes in real output, employment, consumption, and the trade deficit. This result conforms remarkably well with the findings of Baxter and Stockman.

TABLE 1 - NOMINAL AND REAL EXCHANGE RATE VARIABILITY IN ISRAEL

Statistic	Crawling Peg (75:7-77:9)	Float (78:2-85:7)	Quasi Fixed (85:9-89:10)
Mean DE	1.937	8.046	0.624
Mean DP	2.396	8.429	1.493
Mean DRE	-0.459	-0.384	-0.870
Var DE	3.108	32.429	5.206
Var DP	2.992	27.413	1.148
Var DRE	3.380	10.058	5.184
Corr (DE,DP)	0.446	0.835	0.239

Note: DE is the rate of change of the nominal exchange rate for the dollar (monthly average); DP is the rate of inflation; and DRE = DE - DP. All data are monthly and taken from the data base of the Bank of Israel.

The approach underlying these quantitative comparisons has several limitations, however, some of which have been explicitly discussed by the authors. The first and most important limitation results from the fact that in these studies it is difficult to control for the contribution of other factors to the variability of the macroeconomic variables. Consequently there exists great uncertainty as to whether the observed changes in the statistical behavior of these variables can be attributed to the change in the exchange rate regime per-se. Government policies, the nature of disturbances, structural parameters, and the like may have changed during the sample period independently of the change in the exchange rate regime. This difficulty is especially evident in the case of Israel, where the shift to quasi-fixed exchange rates in 1985 was part of a broader policy switch that consisted of major changes in monetary and fiscal policy.

Can we conclude from the evidence about higher real exchange rate volatility in a floating rate regime that fixed exchange rates are preferable ? This central question has no simple answer. Naturally, there exists a relationship between welfare and uncertainty in important economic variables, but this relationship is involved, especially with regard to endogenous variables, such as the real exchange rate. Fluctuations of endogenous variables result from the interaction of market forces and fluctuations of fundamentals, as has been observed by Friedman (1953) long ago. For this reason it is essential to identify changes in fundamentals when moving from fixed to floating exchange rates in order to interpret these empirical findings. On the other hand, Friedman's argument was based on the notion that speculation is stabilizing. That is to say, the presence of potential exchange rate variability per-se cannot bring about actual exchange rate variability, because speculation is stabilizing. The last argument is incorrect, however. Recent research has demonstrated that rational bubbles and noisy traders in asset markets may generate substantial variability (e.g., Blanchard and Fischer (1989, chapter 5) and De Long et al. (1990)). The presence of these factors can induce fluctuations beyond and above fundamentals that Friedman had in mind. On the other hand, the welfare implications of these factors are yet unclear. Future research should provide better answers to these important questions.

IV. VIABILITY OF EXCHANGE RATE PEGS

Since exchange rates are relative prices of monies and governments have the power to issue money, there exist cooperative arrangements between governments that can sustain fixed exchange rates. Experience suggests, however, that even in potentially viable systems it can be difficult to secure the needed cooperation when some countries impose serious strain on the system. We will come back to this issue in the next section. Here we consider the difficulty facing a single country that attempts to peg its exchange rate without help from other countries. The following discussion applies to single currency pegs as well as to pegs to currency baskets.

A country that pegs its exchange rate can always support it with suitable monetary and fiscal policies. If it is free and willing to adjust these policies it can forever maintain its exchange rate peg. In practice, however, difficulties in maintaining fixed parities abound. They typically result from difficulties to adjust other policies. Such situations lead to the loss of reserves and increasing foreign debts. Eventually the exchange rate peg is abandoned or the parity adjusted. Occasionally other policies are altered in the framework of a stabilization program.

Several interesting features have been observed about such adjustments. First, countries suffer international reserve losses long before a collapse of the peg, with a run on reserves preceding the collapse. Second, prior to the policy change there is an increase in nominal interest rates and premia emerge in forward and black markets for foreign exchange, despite the observed constancy of the spot exchange rate (this has been termed "the Peso Problem"). Third, a one-time (jump) depreciation of the exchange rate follows policy adjustments. These regularities have been observed in a number of episodes, including the following (see Penati and Penacchi (1989)): (i) The collapse of the French franc in March 1983, when the currency was devalued by 8 percent relative to the D-mark. After the collapse the country went back to a fixed exchange rate regime. (ii) The collapse of the Italian lira on January 1976, that resulted in a depreciation of about 16 percent relative to the D-mark and a shift to a freely floating regime until the establishment of the EMS in 1979. (iii) The collapse of the Mexican peso in February 1982, that resulted in a 28 percent devaluation relative to the U.S. dollar. (iv) The collapse of the Chilean peso in June 1982. After more than three years with a fixed exchange rate of 39 pesos per dollar, Chile adopted a system of pre announced monthly exchange rate devaluations.

In what follows we discuss these issues in two parts. We begin with a description of the theory that has been developed to explain them. In the second part we describe empirical studies.

A. Theory

Theoretical explanations of these regularities have been provided in a number of studies (see Krugman (1979), Lizondo (1983), Flood and Garber (1984), Obstfeld (1986), Drazen and Helpman (1987, 1988), van Wijnbergen (1988) and Penati and Penacchi (1989)). The abrupt large loss of reserves has been originally explained by Krugman (1979), for the case in which at a known date a fixed exchange rate is replaced by a free float. His fundamental insight is explained first.

Consider a situation of free international capital mobility, and a peg to a foreign currency with a constant foreign interest rate. Before the peg is abandoned the exchange rate remains constant and its instantaneous expected rate of change equals zero. Therefore arbitrage between domestic and foreign interest bearing assets ensures that the domestic interest rate equals the foreign interest rate. With a constant domestic interest rate the demand for real balances remains constant (other factors that affect the demand for money are assumed constant).

Now, at a predetermined date the exchange rate peg is abandoned and replaced with a free float. Assume that from that moment on the money supply grows at a positive rate, at least for some time (in order to, say, finance the budget deficit). Then at the moment of policy switch the demand for real balances drops discretely, because the interest rate rises discretely as a result of the uncovered interest parity condition (that ensures the absence of arbitrage opportunities between domestic and foreign currency denominated assets). It rises from the foreign level to a level that exceeds the foreign level by the correctly forecasted rate of inflation. After the policy switch inflation results from money growth. Since the exchange rate cannot jump in an anticipated fashion at the time of the policy switch (because this would produce unbounded arbitrage opportunities between domestic and foreign assets), the lower demand for real balances is accommodated by a lower money supply. The lower money supply is attained by a run on reserves a moment before the policy switch.

The timing of the run on reserves can in fact be determined endogenously from the central bank's monetary policy. If the central bank expands domestic credit during the fixed exchange rate period, every unit of additional credit finds its way back to the central bank in exchange for foreign currency. This results from the fact that during this time interval the demand for real balances remains constant and so does the price level (due to the peg). When the value of reserves exceeds the smallest permissible level by an amount just equal to the contraction of the money supply that is required by a switch to a free float, a run on reserves takes place exactly in this amount. As a result of the run reserves drop to the minimum level, and the authorities abandon the exchange rate peg.

This story is very powerful, because it identifies a mechanism that has broader applications than the particular policy experiment. Once it is understood, one can ask, for example, how will the adjustment differ if instead of abandoning the exchange rate peg and resorting to inflationary finance the authorities were to maintain a fixed exchange rate and raise taxes instead, or cut expenditure on traded goods, or cut expenditure on nontraded goods. Drazen and Helpman (1987) have shown, for instance, that only the last alternative leads to a run on reserves while the first two do not (with taxes being lump-sum). They also showed that the anticipation of different policies for dealing with the loss of reserve problem have different implications for the trade and current account. For example, when the foreign interest rate equals the subjective discount rate, the use of taxes is preceded by a balanced current account while the use of budget cuts on traded goods is preceded by a deficit on current account. In all cases, however, real balances remain constant prior to the policy switch. The last finding is disturbing, because often one observes declines in real balances in anticipation of a policy change even when the exchange rate remains constant.

To remedy this difficulty one can introduce uncertainty about the timing of the policy switch (see Drazen and Helpman (1988)). This added feature also helps to explain (a) domestic interest rates that exceed the foreign interest rate during the peg; (b) premia on forward and black markets for foreign exchange during the peg (the Peso Problem); (c) declining real balances during the peg; and (d) discrete devaluations as part of the policy switch.

Consider a situation in which the exchange rate is pegged but the public expects a devaluation. In this case uncovered interest parity requires the domestic interest rate to exceed the foreign interest rate at least by the expected rate of devaluation (in the absence of risk aversion the interest rate differential just equals the expected rate of devaluation). These expectations are also reflected in a higher exchange rate in the forward market and a higher premium on the black market for foreign exchange (see Lizondo (1983)).

The larger the expected rate of devaluation, the larger is the interest rate differential, the higher is the exchange rate in the forward market, and the larger is the premium on the black market. A larger expected rate of devaluation may result from expectations of a larger devaluation or a larger probability of devaluation. If the probability of a devaluation rises over time or the required exchange rate adjustment rises over time, they will be reflected in rising nominal interest rates, rising exchange rates in the forward market, and rising premia on the black market, as one typically observes.

The point of departure of our preceding discussion was the presence of an expected devaluation. But one may ask what are the circumstances in which a required policy adjustment leads to a rationally expected devaluation? To begin with, the imbalance in the monetary-fiscal policy mix that leads to reserve losses can be corrected without recourse to the abandoning an exchange rate peg. Consider, for example, a situation in which the government is expected to raise taxes, cut spending on traded goods, or cut spending on nontraded goods in order to balance the budget. In such cases there is no money growth after the policy switch and therefore the exchange rate remains constant after the policy switch even if the exchange rate peg is abandoned. When the budget is balanced with lump-sum taxes or spending cuts on traded goods the expected rate of devaluation equals zero at each point in time, and indeed there is no change in the exchange rate at the policy switch date. Consequently real balances remain constant and no run on reserves takes place (see

Drazen and Helpman (1988)).

When the authorities are expected to balance the budget with an expenditure cut on nontraded goods, however, it matters whether the public expects the exchange rate peg to prevail after the policy switch (in fact it matters whether the peg prevails only a short while after the policy switch). If the exchange rate peg is expected to prevail a while after the policy switch the public expects no devaluation, and money balances remain constant until the policy switch takes place (despite the fact that the timing of a policy switch is uncertain). At the moment of the budget cut the real exchange rate depreciates as a result of a decline in the nominal price of nontraded goods and the nominal exchange rate remains constant (assuming full price flexibility). The decline in demand for real balances as a result of the real depreciation is satisfied by means of a run on reserves (see Drazen and Helpman (1988)). This run on reserves is possible only if the authorities do not abandon the peg following the budget cut.

On the other hand, if the peg is abandoned with the budget cut on nontraded goods, the decline in demand for real balances that results from the real depreciation cannot be satisfied by an asset swap. Consequently a nominal devaluation has to follow the policy switch. This leads to expectations of a devaluation prior to a policy switch with the expected rate rising over time as long as the policy switch does not take place. The observed result will be rising interest rates, rising exchange rates on forward markets, and a rising premium on the black market (see Drazen and Helpman (1988)).

Finally, the presence of timing uncertainty of a policy switch that consists of the abandoning of a peg and recourse to money-financed budget deficits, leads to expectations of a devaluation prior to the policy switch. The expected rate of devaluation rises over time because the probability of a policy switch rises (as long as this probability rises with the degree of imbalance) and because the required exchange rate adjustment is larger the more time elapses without a policy change. The latter point can be seen from the observation that the longer the authorities maintain the imbalance, the larger the accumulated government debt, and therefore the larger the budget deficit that has to be financed with an inflation tax. Consequently the more time elapses, the larger the post policy switch rate of money growth and the higher the post policy switch nominal interest rate. This implies that the demand for real balances drops more the later the policy adjustment takes place, and therefore the larger the required devaluation. The result is that real balances, the nominal interest rate, the forward rate and the black market rate, behave similarly to the case of a budget cut on nontraded goods with an abandoning of the peg.

We have thus seen that expectations of policy adjustments that rely on the abandoning of exchange rate management and either a budget cut on nontraded goods or inflationary finance lead to (a) rising nominal interest rates; (b) rising forward exchange rates; (c) rising premia on the black market; (d) declining real balances; and (e) discrete devaluations at the time of the policy switch. These are realistic features that help to explain many observed episodes (see, for example, Helpman and Leiderman (1988)).

B. Estimation and Evidence

Several studies have empirically examined exchange rate dynamics in environments in which economic agents assign a non negligible probability to the event of a change in regime. Research on speculative attacks, on collapsing exchange rate systems, and on the Peso Problem fall squarely into this category. We first discuss studies of speculative attacks and collapsing regimes. Next, we turn to studies of the impact on exchange rate dynamics and forecast errors of gradual learning about changes in the stochastic processes that drive the exchange rate.

A good example of the first area is the paper by Blanco and Garber (1986). They develop an empirical method for predicting the timing and magnitude of devaluations forced by speculative attacks on fixed exchange rate systems. The method is applied to the Mexican experience during 1973-82. After more than 20 years with a fixed exchange rate, Mexico devalued the peso in August 1976, and in February and August of 1982.

The Blanco-Garber devaluation model has the following ingredients. First, they focus on equilibrium in the money market. Domestic credit creation is exogenous, possibly reflecting needs to partially finance the government's budget deficit. Money demand takes a standard form and depends on output and the domestic interest rate. The latter is related to the foreign interest rate and to expected devaluations through the assumption of uncovered interest parity. The domestic price level satisfies a stochastic version of Purchasing Power Parity. Under a fixed exchange rate, movements in international reserves are the equilibrating factor in the money market. These features can be fit into the theoretical models of sub-section A above.

The next building block consists of the devaluation policy. When the domestic credit requirements and money market conditions impose extreme pressure on the central bank's reserves at the prevailing exchange rate, the exchange rate peg is relinquished. Namely, given a fixed exchange rate $\bar{e}$ the central bank stops intervening in the foreign exchange market when net reserves reach a critical level $\underline{R}$.

The authors provide expressions for the probability of devaluation at time t+1 based on information available at time t. Using this probability they calculate conditional and unconditional expected (forecasted) future exchange rates. When applied to the Mexican experience, the model's probabilities of devaluation reach relatively high values prior to actual devaluations, and the expected exchange rates conditional on devaluation are close to the values that prevailed in those episodes.

Among the limitations of their analysis we point out the following. First, the minimum level of reserves $\underline{R}$ is taken to be time invariant, given with certainty, and taken from outside the model. Second, the model postulates a fixed exchange rate with recurrent devaluations. It excludes by assumption a post attack free float as well as other alternatives. Finally, the government is assumed not to impose foreign exchange controls in the face of a speculative attack. Though these assumptions may fit well the Mexican case ex-post, they are rather limiting and prove less useful for other countries.

Cumby and van Wijnbergen (1989) apply a similar model and a similar methodology to the Argentine experiment with a crawling peg between December 1978 and February 1981. Their analysis contains an important extension; they allow for uncertainty about the level of reserves that will trigger abandonment of the crawling peg regime. In other words, agents cannot calculate with certainty the critical level of domestic credit that will result in a discrete devaluation. A key assumption in their work is that, to the extent that the crawling peg proves to be unsustainable, the authorities will shift to a free floating exchange rate. These changes affect the estimates of collapse probabilities.

The authors assume a uniform distribution with a finite support for the public's beliefs about the central bank's critical value of international reserves. They also assume that the upper limit is the current level of reserves and the lower limit equals minus the central bank's current gross foreign liabilities. Under these assumptions, Cumby and van Wijnbergen calculate the probability as of the end of period t that a collapse will occur at the end of period t+1, which is the probability that reserves will fall below the critical level. They find that credit expansion in the second quarter of 1980 undermined the credibility of the crawling peg. Eventually, credibility was lost almost completely, and the one-month-ahead probability of collapse rose to 77 percent immediately before the abandonment of the crawling peg.

The foregoing discussion was confined to collapsing exchange rate systems. Peso Problems may arise not only in these cases but also when economic agents gradually learn and revise their beliefs about changes in the stochastic process followed by fundamentals, without necessarily implying that there is a switch in the exchange rate regime. In a recent paper, Lewis (1989) develops and estimates a model designed to account for what appears to be a systematic under prediction by market participants of the strength of the U.S. dollar in the early 1980s. Her model shows how systematic forecast errors may arise during a period in which the market gradually learns about a change in fundamentals (using Bayesian updating). The model is applied to U.S. data so as to empirically investigate the impact upon dollar forecast errors of learning about the increase in U.S. money demand that occurred in the early 1980s. The expansion of money demand is interpreted as a one-time shift in the drift term that characterizes the stationary first-difference process of fundamentals. Lewis' learning model results in systematic under-prediction of the dollar's strength by about one-half the levels suggested by the forward exchange rate. It represents progress in attempting to account for the observed forecast errors. Contrary to the implications of the model, however, the systematic nature of the forecast errors -- as implied, for instance, by the forward rate -- does not appear to die out over time. Thus, in addition to the learning process emphasized by Lewis, anticipations of future policy changes and fluctuations in risk premiums may account for these persistent errors.

Kaminsky (1988) studied the Peso Problem for the U.S. dollar/pound exchange rate during 1976-87 (assuming rational learning by investors). In one case investors are assumed to forecast the future path of the exchange rate conditional on past observations of the exchange rate and on the Federal Reserve officials' announcements about current and future monetary policy (as published in the media). These announcements were assumed to provide only imperfect information about the exchange rate process. The assumptions of the model yield a solution for the rate of currency depreciation at time t,

$$d_t = \delta_i + \epsilon_t ,$$

where d is the rate of depreciation, δ_i is the value of the drift term in regime i, and ϵ is white noise (δ_i does not change over time). Regimes are classified by different values of δ_i. Changes in these values can be thought of as arising from shifts in the drift term of the domestic money supply process. Kaminsky provides evidence indicating that exchange rate depreciation can indeed be described by an uncorrelated shock around a drifting mean, that was negative in 1981-84 and positive in the 1970s and late 1980s. Her model is also consistent with a Peso Problem, in that investors anticipated an appreciation of only .24 percent per month during the 1981:2-1985:2 period when in fact the dollar appreciated at an average of 1.6 percent per month.

An important shortcoming of Kaminsky's and Lewis' work is that regime changes that are captured by shifts in their drift parameters are not linked to changes in fiscal and monetary policy. In principle, it would be possible to link their models to the theoretical models of collapsing exchange rate regimes. One could stipulate, for example, that δ_i is set by the authorities according to the state of, say, inflation. Thus, the higher the rate of inflation, the higher the probability that low values of δ_i will be chosen by the authorities (thus reflecting contractionary monetary policy). As it stands, however, the models contain a very simple formulation of regimes and the role of macroeconomic factors in endogenizing the choice of regime.

These issues, as well as the processes that drive fundamentals, need to be studied in more detail.

V. EXCHANGE RATE BANDS

So far we have dealt with rigid exchange rate pegs. The fact is, however, that even fixed exchange rate regimes provide some flexibility for exchange rate movements within pre specified narrow bands, the Bretton Woods system being a prime example (its band was 1%). The interest in exchange rate bands has significantly increased in recent years, because many countries have adopted exchange rate bands as an explicit policy (such as Norway, Sweden and Israel), with the most prominent example of this regime provided by the European Monetary System (EMS). There also exist proposals for an application of bands to the major currencies (see Williamson (1983) and Williamson and Miller (1988)).

The existence of bands rather than fixed parities raises a number of questions, the first being how do exchange rates behave within pre-specified bands. Do they fluctuate in the interior of a band as they would if they were freely floating? Do bands eliminate the danger of balance of payments crises of the type discussed in the previous section? How do they affect interest rates as compared to fixed parities or a free float? These questions have been recently investigated and the answers have turned out to be very interesting (see Krugman (1987), Krugman and Rotemberg (1990), Flood and Garber (1989), Froot and Obstfeld (1989), Svensson (1989) and Buiter and Grilli (1989)).

It proves useful to begin with a simple case in which the authorities choose an upper bound on the exchange rate. The meaning of the upper bound is that whenever the exchange rate reaches that ceiling, the central bank stands ready to sell foreign exchange as much as required, as long as the stock of reserves remains above a predetermined minimum level. For current purposes we assume that whenever the reserves that have been allotted to defend the exchange rate are exhausted, the exchange rate ceiling is abandoned and replaced with a free float. It should be clear at this point that alternative scenarios are also possible, such as the defense of the ceiling with fiscal instruments as described in the previous section.

The most interesting cases of exchange rate bands arise when there exist random elements that drive the exchange rate. Since empirically proportional changes in exchange rates are reasonably well approximated by a random walk process (i.e., a process whose increments are independently distributed), suppose that proportional shifts in money demand follow a continuous time random walk without drift (a Wiener process) and thereby induce fluctuations in exchange rates (the addition of a drift does not change the arguments in any substantial way). There is no domestic credit expansion and the money supply remains constant. Using a simple monetary model of exchange rate determination this specification implies that the unrestricted free floating exchange rate possesses the random walk property and the natural logarithm of the exchange rate e is linearly related to the logarithm of the proportional shocks to money demand v, as depicted by curve FF in figure 1. Hence, the larger v (the lower the demand for money) the higher the exchange rate (i.e., the weaker the domestic currency). In the absence of intervention in the foreign exchange market fluctuations in v induce fluctuations in e along FF (see Krugman and Rotemberg (1990)).

Next suppose the authorities announce a ceiling $\bar{e}$ on the exchange rate, which will be defended with existing reserves (see figure). Will now the exchange rate follow FF in response to shifts in money demand, at least for values of v below $\bar{v}$? The answer is no. For suppose v is below $\bar{v}$ but very close to it. At this point the public expects increases in v to the same extent that it expects decreases (the random walk property). In the absence of a ceiling it expects symmetrical increases and decreases in the exchange rate, so that the expected rate of devaluation equals zero and the domestic interest rate equals the foreign interest rate. In the presence of the ceiling some upward increases in the exchange rate in response to increases in v will not materialize, because the central bank will intervene in order to prevent the exchange rate from crossing the ceiling. Consequently the expected rate of devaluation is negative and the foreign interest rate exceeds the domestic interest rate. As a result of the interest rates differential the demand for real balances is lower in the presence of a ceiling. It follows that the supply of real balances has to be higher in the presence of a ceiling. Observe, however, that the nominal stock of money remains constant as long as the exchange rate ceiling has not been reached. Under these circumstances the exchange rate has to be lower in the presence of an exchange rate ceiling in order raise real balances to its equilibrium level.

In fact, the relationship between e and v is now along a lower curve, such as CC in figure 1. The larger v, the larger the deviation of the exchange rate from FF. Thus, the existence of an exchange rate ceiling reduces the exchange rate's sensitivity to velocity shocks (see Krugman and Rotemberg (1990)). This result is central to the understanding of exchange rate bands. Evidently, the behavior of an exchange rate in the interior of a band differs from a free float (the current case can be considered as a band with an unbounded lower limit).

Available reserves determine the critical value of v_c at which CC reaches the ceiling. If available reserves are small, v_c is close to $\bar{v}$, and once v_c is attained there will be a run on reserves that will wipe out the entire available stock. This will reduce the stock of nominal money balances and shift to the right the free floating curve FF (this curve is higher the higher the stock of money). Since the exchange rate cannot jump in an anticipated fashion (because it would provide unbounded arbitrage opportunities), the free floating exchange rate just after the run on reserves has to equal $\bar{e}$. Given the required stock of reserves, that determines the rightward shift of the FF curve in case of a run on reserves that depletes them to the postulated minimum, this condition determines v_c and the end point of the CC curve.

We have thus described a situation in which the exchange rate floats below a pre-specified ceiling, responding to velocity shocks less elastically than in an unrestricted float, and a run on reserves takes place the moment it hits the ceiling. As mentioned above, this situation applies when reserves are low. Figure 2 describes a situation with a large amount of foreign exchange reserves (see Krugman and Rotemberg (1990)). The corresponding CC curve lies below FF as before, except that this time it reaches a peak at the ceiling.

Suppose the initial value of v is lower than v_c. Fluctuations in v that remain below v_c lead to corresponding exchange rate fluctuations along CC. If, however, v_c is reached and the exchange rate hits the ceiling, this time there is no run on reserves. Instead the central bank defends the ceiling by selling foreign currency. The required interventions are small and deplete only gradually the stock of reserves. Each time the exchange rate hits the ceiling sales of reserves reduce nominal money balances and the FF and CC curves shift to the right. This process continues as long as the central bank has reserves. The exchange rate fluctuates on CC below the ceiling for some time, hits the ceiling, thereby inducing a shift to the right of the CC curve, and fluctuates on the new CC curve until the next time it hits the ceiling. When the entire stock of available reserves gets exhausted the central bank abandons the ceiling and changes its exchange rate policy to a free float. In this case no run on reserves precedes the abandonment of the ceiling.

An important feature of the above described exchange rate movements is the positive association between v and e. Namely, declines in money demand lead to exchange rate depreciations independently of whether the exchange rate floats freely or is restricted by a ceiling. This results from the fact that a policy that defends the ceiling with infinitesimal interventions prevents the exchange rate from following the downward slopping portion of the CC curve in figure 2 (to the right of v_c). As pointed out by Flood and Garber (1989), however, a different intervention strategy leads to very different consequences.

Thus, suppose that instead of intervening in a minimal fashion in order to defend the ceiling (as described above) the central bank uses a pre announced finite amount of reserves each time it intervenes in the foreign exchange market. In this case the downward slopping part of CC will also be followed by the exchange rate. In figure 2 intervention will take place only when v_f is reached. The finite size intervention will bring about a decline in money balances, FF and CC will shift to the right, and the new CC curve will pass through point 1 (this is how v_f is determined for a pre-determined size of the intervention). The crossing of the new CC curve with the old one at point 1 prevents an anticipated jump in the exchange rate in response to the intervention. As a result of this intervention rule one observes periods during which declines in money demand are associated with exchange rate appreciations. Such "paradoxical" co movements necessarily precede the central bank's intervention.

It follows from this discussion that in the presence of a band there does not exist a simple relation between fundamentals and the exchange rate. This complexity has a bearing on empirical tests of exchange rate theories. For example, many studies of the simple monetary approach have regressed the log of the exchange rate on the log of relative money supplies (and on other variables) and have tested for a coefficient of unity on this explanatory variable. It is evident from our discussion that this test is not suitable in the presence of a band.

We have so far discussed exchange rate ceilings. It is now straightforward to see what happens when there also exists a lower bound on the exchange rate; i.e., when there exists an exchange rate band. Figure 3 describes a band $[\underline{e},\overline{e}]$ that is defended with a large stock of reserves. Suppose that the central bank engages in minimal interventions at the limits of the band. A free floating exchange rate would fluctuate along FF while in the presence of a band it fluctuates along CC as long as v remains in $(\underline{v}_c,\overline{v}_c)$. If the exchange rate hits the lower limit (v hits $\underline{v}_c$) the central bank buys foreign currency and increases its reserves. The money supply increases and our curves shift to the left. When the exchange rate hits the upper limit the central bank sells foreign currency and depletes its reserves. The money supply declines and our curves shift to the right.

Since there exists no limit on the feasible accumulation of reserves (from the point of view of a single country), the band can be maintained as long as the upper ceiling can be defended. It cannot be defended, however, for prolonged periods of time when the exchange rate hits the ceiling very often. This happens when v has a strong positive drift. Namely, when there exists a strong secular decline in the demand for money. Or alternatively, when domestic credit grows fast.

These models contain an inherent relation between the variability of the interest rate and the width of the band. Naturally, they also contain an inherent relation between exchange rate variability and the width of the band; the wider the band the more volatile the exchange rate (for given fundamentals). Svensson (1989) has shown that interest rate variability rises with the width of the band for narrow bands and declines with wide bands. It follows that for narrow bands the widening of the band raises the volatility of both the interest rate and the exchange rate. For wide bands, however, widening the band gives rise to a trade-off, in that it raises volatility of the exchange rate but reduces volatility of the interest rate. These consideration are of major concern to central banks who determine the size of their band. As argued in section III, volatility in nominal exchange rates can result in real exchange rate volatility, which is often thought to be detrimental. Similarly, nominal interest rate volatility may affect the volatility of real interest rates, which are important relative prices. In addition, the behavior of nominal interest rates may affect the functioning of financial markets, which are in the responsibility domain of central banks.

At this stage the theory of exchange rate bands has not reached the same stage of development as the theory of collapsing exchange rate regimes. The two are, of course, related, as is evident from our discussion. We need further extensions of the band theory in order to better understand the relationship between interventions at pre-announced or uncertain limits of exchange rate movements and monetary and fiscal policy. In view of the theory of collapsing exchange rate regimes one can see immediately that it may make a major difference whether the defense of a band limit is carried out by means of foreign exchange intervention, open market operations, adjustments in government spending or taxes. Here one may distinguish short-term responses from long-term responses, where in the short term the major burden of defense is assigned to monetary policy and foreign exchange intervention while in the long-run fiscal policy carries the burden. These important issues, as well as the welfare implications of alternative policies, remain to be explored.

Many useful empirical implications of the band models have not yet been fully articulated. As pointed out by Froot and Obstfeld (1989), for example, bands imply nonlinear exchange rate equations. They also imply stationarity for the log of the exchange rate, thereby contradicting the random walk theory that has served as the null hypothesis in recent years. Thus, commonly used empirical models are miss specified when dealing with data from countries with exchange rate bands. Another example concerns volatility tests that can be used to examine band theories. As pointed out above, different band sizes have different implications for the co movement of volatility measures of interest rates and exchange rates. These implications could be tested with cross country data.

VI. CONCLUDING REMARKS

In these remarks we briefly elaborate on a number of additional important issues related to the choice of the exchange rate regime which have not been discussed in the foregoing analysis. First is the issue of hysteresis. Conventional analysis of floating exchange rates uses some version of Purchasing Power Parity whereby, assuming that foreign prices are given, domestic prices move in line with exchange rate movements. Recent evidence on domestic prices of imported goods and services in the U.S. fails to support this hypothesis (see, for example, Krugman and Baldwin (1987)). That is, prices of imported goods in the U.S. have not moved in unison with movements in dollar exchange rates and have exhibited an important degree of sluggishness. A number of authors have constructed theoretical models to explain this phenomenon (see Baldwin and Krugman (1989) and Dixit (1989)).

The main line of work has built on the notion that exporting firms face entry (exit) costs that become sunk costs after the event of entry (exit). These costs are denominated in the currency of the export market while manufacturing costs are denominated in the firms' domestic currency. The implication is that there exists a range of exchange rate movements within which an incumbent firm does not leave the export market while a new firm does not enter it. This range depends on structural features as well as on the drift and variability of the exchange rate. Hence, the process of exchange rate movements affects the degree of sluggishness in the response of supply to the export market. This is an important point that has a bearing on the ranking of alternative exchange rate arrangements that we have not discussed in detail. (Froot and Klemperer (1989) provide an alternative explanation).

Second is the issue of disinflation. Two branches of research have converged into the hypothesis that moving toward fixed exchange rates helps achieve disinflation through a more rapid and less costly transition than under alternative exchange rate systems. It has been argued that for countries such as France and Italy joining the EMS enhanced credibility, discipline, and commitment, that are necessary to generate a fast downward adjustment of inflationary expectations. And this adjustment, in turn, played a key role in generating the observed convergence in rates of inflation toward the rate prevailing in Germany. Another line of research has dealt with disinflation in high inflation countries, such as Argentina, Brazil and Israel. There the argument has been that in the presence of the required adjustments in monetary and fiscal fundamentals, fixing the exchange rate can help break existing inflationary inertia. Moreover, examples have been constructed showing that using the exchange rate as a nominal anchor may disinflate the economy with lower sacrifice ratios than using monetary targets; see Fischer (1988).

Although the argument that, during disinflation a fixed exchange rate serves as a useful anchor of nominal values, has its merits, its empirical validity has not been definitively established. Some evidence indicates that in the early to mid 80s the EMS countries performed poorer than other OECD countries, in the form of higher unemployment rates and lower growth rates of output and employment (see De Grauwe (1989)). Similarly, the relatively slow downward adjustment of actual and expected inflation in countries such as France and Italy in the 80s indicates that credibility problems may have well persisted despite the fact that both countries joined the EMS (see Collins (1989) and Giavazzi and Giovannini (1989, ch. 5)). In addition, the quantitative importance of fixing the exchange rate in producing low rates of inflation in previously high-inflation economies has not yet been determined. In order to meaningfully determine this quantitative importance it is required to provide estimates that control for the effects of other changes, such as monetary and fiscal adjustments, changes in wage indexation rules, price controls, etc., whose precise empirical specification is as yet unknown (see Helpman and Leiderman (1988)).

Third, there exists the issue of policy coordination. The choice of an exchange rate regime is important in an imperfect world where markets are incomplete, there exist informational problems, and other market failures (see section II). In such cases markets do not allocate resources efficiently. These inefficiencies are not restricted to national boundaries but also impinge on the international economy. For these reasons there exists an a-priori case for policy coordination. In addition, many exchange rate systems, such as Bretton Woods and the EMS, inherently build on a specific form of policy coordination.

The literature on policy coordination in a world of strategic behavior has shown that coordination may or may not be desirable (see Oudiz and Sachs (1984) and Rogoff (1985)). Distortions that result from competitive policies may be worse than distortions that result from market failures. These findings imply that detailed analysis of cooperative exchange rate arrangements is required in order to form an opinion about their merits and shortcomings. The success of an exchange rate regime depends not only on the form of cooperation in exchange rate arrangements but also on the form of cooperation of fiscal policies. For monetary policies, for example, the creation of a European Central Bank would be an important ingredient in a general policy package. There exists an extensive literature on these problems that we have not reviewed.

Are there new answers to the old questions? Our review shows clearly that during the many years that have passed since the publication of Friedman's (1953) defense of floating exchange rates the debate has shifted from the narrow comparison of fixed vs. floating exchange rates to debates on much richer menus of choice. This outcome has resulted from the wide recognition that neither one of these polar regimes is perfect and that the best solution lies in an intermediate system. For this reason much of the research and practical policy debate has been redirected to the identification of a good intermediate case. It is, therefore, not surprising to find that we now face many new questions and have to deal with many new issues that were not considered in earlier debates. For example, the emphasis of recent research on the response of the private sector to the possibility of a regime switch had no place in discussions of pure floats or pure fixed exchange rate regimes. In addition, the wealth of empirical evidence that has accumulated over the years sheds new light on the functioning of alternative exchange rate systems, and no practical policy debate or theoretical argument can ignore it. Although the issue of the best exchange rate regime is yet unsettled, we may safely conclude that we have learned a great deal from recent research.

REFERENCES

Aschauer, David A. and Greenwood, Jeremy, "A Further Exploration in the Theory of Exchange Rate Regimes," *Journal of Political Economy* 91, 868-875, 1983.

Baxter, Marianne and Stockman, Alan C., "Business Cycles and the Exchange-Rate Regime: Some international evidence," *Journal of Monetary Economics* 23, 377-400, 1989.

Blanchard, Olivier and Fischer, Stanley, Lectures on Macroeconomics (Cambridge, MA: The MIT Press, 1989).

Blanco, Herminio and Garber, Peter M., "Recurrent Devaluation and Speculative Attacks on the Mexican Peso," *Journal of Political Economy* 94, 148-166, 1986.

Buiter, Willem H. and Grilli, Vittorio U., "The 'Gold Standard Paradox' and its Resolution," mimeo, Yale University, 1989.

Collins, Susan M., "Inflation and the European Monetary System," in Giavazzi, Francesco and Pagani, Marco (eds.) *The European Monetary System* (Cambridge: Cambridge University Press, 1989).

Cumby, Robert E. and Van Wijnbergen, Sweder, "Financial Policy and Speculative Runs with a Crawling Peg: Argentina 1979-1981," *Journal of International Economics* 27, 111-127, 1989.

De Grauwe, Paul, "The Cost of Disinflation and the European Monetary System," Discussion Paper No. 326, CEPR, 1989.

De Long, Bradford J., Shleifer, Andrei, Summers, Lawrence H., and Waldmann, Robert J., "Nose Trader Risk in Financial Markets," *Journal of Political Economy* 98, 703-738.

Dixit, Avinash, "Hysteresis, Import Penetration, and Exchange Rate Pass-Through," *Quarterly Journal of Economics* 104, 205-228, 1989.

Dornbusch, Rudiger and Frankel, Jeffrey, "The Flexible Exchange Rate System: Experience and Alternatives," in Borner, Silvio (ed.), *International Finance and Trade in a Polycentric World* (London: Macmillan, 1988).

Drazen, Allan and Helpman, Elhanan, "Stabilization with Exchange Rate Management," *Quarterly Journal of Economics* 11, 835-855, 1987.

——— and ———, "Stabilization with Exchange Rate Management Under Uncertainty," in Helpman, Elhanan, Razin, Assaf and Sadka, Efraim (eds.) *Economic Effects of the Government Budget* (Cambridge, MA: MIT, 1988).

Fischer, Stanley, "Stability and Exchange Rate Systems in a Monetarist Model of the Balance of Payments," in Aliber, Robert Z. (ed.) *The Political Economy of Monetary Reform* (Montclair, NJ: Allanheld, Osmun and Co., 1977).

——— , "Real Balances, the Exchange Rate, and Indexation: Real Variables in disinflation," *Quarterly Journal of Economics* 103, 27-50, 1988.

Flood, Robert D. and Garber, Peter M., "Collapsing Exchange Rate Regimes: Some Linear Examples," *Journal of International Economics* 17, 1-13, 1984.

——— and ———, "The Linkage Between Speculative Attack and Target Zone Models of Exchange Rates," NBER Working Paper No. 2918, 1989.

Friedman, Milton, "The Case for Flexible Exchange Rates," in his *Essays in Positive Economics* (Chicago: University of Chicago Press, 1953).

Froot, Kenneth A. and Klemperer, Paul D., "Exchange Rate Pass-Through When Market Share Matters," *American Economic Review* 79, 637-655, 1989.

Froot, Kenneth A. and Obstfeld, Maurice, "Exchange-Rate Dynamics Under Stochastic Regime Shifts: A Unified Approach," NBER Working Paper No. 2835, 1989.

Giavazzi, Francesco and Giovannini, Alberto, *Limiting Exchange Rate Flexibility: The European Monetary System* (Cambridge, MA: The MIT Press, 1989).

Grilli, Vittorio and Kaminsky, Graciela, "Nominal Exchange Rate Regimes and The Real Exchange Rate: Evidence from the U.S. and Britain, 1885-1986," Discussion Paper No. 19, International Economics Research Center, University of Pennsylvania, 1988.

——— , and Roubini, Nouriel, "Financial Integration, Liquidity and Exchange Rates," NBER Working Paper No. 3088, 1989.

Helpman, Elhanan, "An Exploration in the Theory of Exchange Rate regimes," *Journal of Political Economy* 89, 865-890, 1981.

——— and Leiderman, Leonardo, "Stabilization in High Inflation countries: Analytical Foundations and Recent Experience," *Carnegie-Rochester Conference Series on Public Policy* 28, 9-84, 1988.

——— and Razin, Assaf, "A Consistent Comparison of Alternative Exchange Rate Regimes," *Canadian Journal of Economics* 12, 394-409, 1979.

——— and ———, "A Comparison of Exchange Rate Regimes in the Presence of Imperfect Capital Markets," *International Economic Review* 23, 365-388, 1982.

Jones, Ronald W. and Kenen, Peter B. (eds.) Handbook of International Economics, vol. II (Amsterdam: North Holland, 1985).

Kaminsky, Graciela, "The Peso Problem and the Behavior of the Dollar-Pound Exchange Rate: 1976-1987," Working paper, University of California, San Diego, 1988.

Kareken, John and Wallace, Neil, "On the Indeterminacy of Equilibrium Exchange Rates," *Quarterly Journal of Economics* 96, 207-222, 1981.

Krugman, Paul R., "A Model of Balance of Payments Crises," *Journal of Money, Credit and Banking* 11, 311-325, 1979.

——, "Trigger Strategies and Price Dynamics in Equity and Foreign Exchange Markets," NBER Working Paper No. 2459, 1987.

—— and Rotemberg, Julio, "Target zones with limited reserves," NBER Working Paper No. 3418, 1990.

—— and Baldwin, Richard, "The Persistence of the U.S. Trade Deficit," *Brookings Papers on Economic Activity* 1, 1-56, 1987.

Leiderman, Leonardo and Liviatan, Nissan, "Comparing Macroeconomic Performance Before and After Disinflation in Israel," Working paper, The World Bank, Washington, D.C., 1989.

Lewis, Karen K., "Changing Beliefs and Systematic Rational Forecast Errors with Evidence from Foreign Exchange," *American Economic Review* 79, 621-636, 1989.

Lizondo, Jose S., "Foreign Exchange Futures Prices under Fixed Exchange Rates," *Journal of International Economics* 14, 69-84, 1983.

Lucas, Robert E. Jr., "Interest Rates and Currency Prices in a Two-Country World," *Journal of Monetary Economics* 10, 335-359, 1982.

Mundell, Robert, "Uncommon Arguments for Common Currencies," in Johnson, Harry, G. and Swoboda, Alexander K. (eds.), *The Economics of Common Currencies* (Cambridge, MA: Harvard University Press, 1973).

Mussa, Michael, "Nominal Exchange Rate Regimes and the Behavior of Real Exchange Rates," in: K. Brunner and A.H. Meltzer, eds., *Real Business Cycles, Real Exchange Rates, and Actual Policies.* Carnegie-Rochester conference series on public policy (Amsterdam: North-Holland, 1986).

Obstfeld, Maurice, "Rational and Self-Fulfilling Balance of Payments Crises," *American Economic Review* 76, 72-81, 1986.

Oudiz, G. and Sachs, Jeffrey, "Macroeconomic Policy Coordination Among The Industrial Economies," *Brookings Papers on Economic Activity* 1, 1-64, 1984.

Penati, Alessandro and Penacchi, George, "Optimal Portfolio Choice and the Collapse of a Fixed Exchange Rate Regime," *Journal of International Economics* 27, 1-24, 1989.

Rogoff, Kenneth, "Can International Monetary Policy Coordination be Counterproductive?" *Journal of International Economics* 18, 199-217, 1985.

Stockman, Alan C., "Real Exchange Rates under Alternative Nominal Exchange-Rate Systems," *Journal of International Money and Finance* 2, 147-166, 1983.

Svensson, Lars E. O., "Currency Prices, Terms of Trade, and Interest Rates: A General Equilibrium Asset-Pricing Cash-in-Advance Approach," *Journal of International Economics* 18, 17-41, 1985.

———, "Target Zones and Interest Rate Variability," Institute for International Economic Studies, Seminar Paper No.457, 1989.

van Wijnbergen, Sweder, "Inflation, Balance-of-Payments Crises, and Public Sector Deficits," in Helpman, Elhanan, Razin, Assaf and Sadka, Efraim (eds.) *Economic Effects of the Government Budget* (Cambridge, MA: MIT, 1988).

Williamson, John, *The Exchange Rate System* (Washington: Institute for International Economics, 1983).

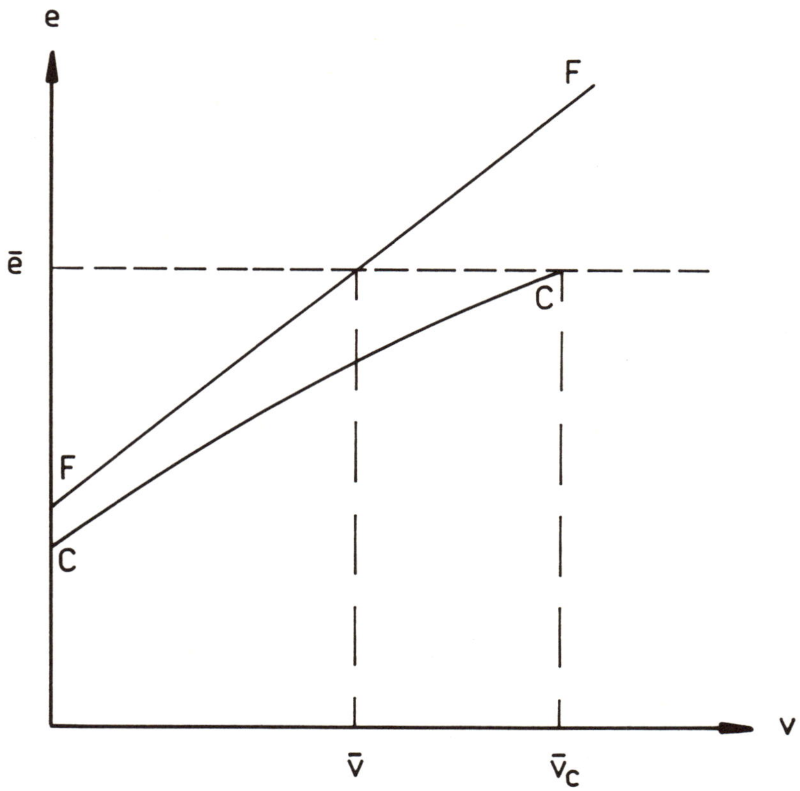

Figure 1

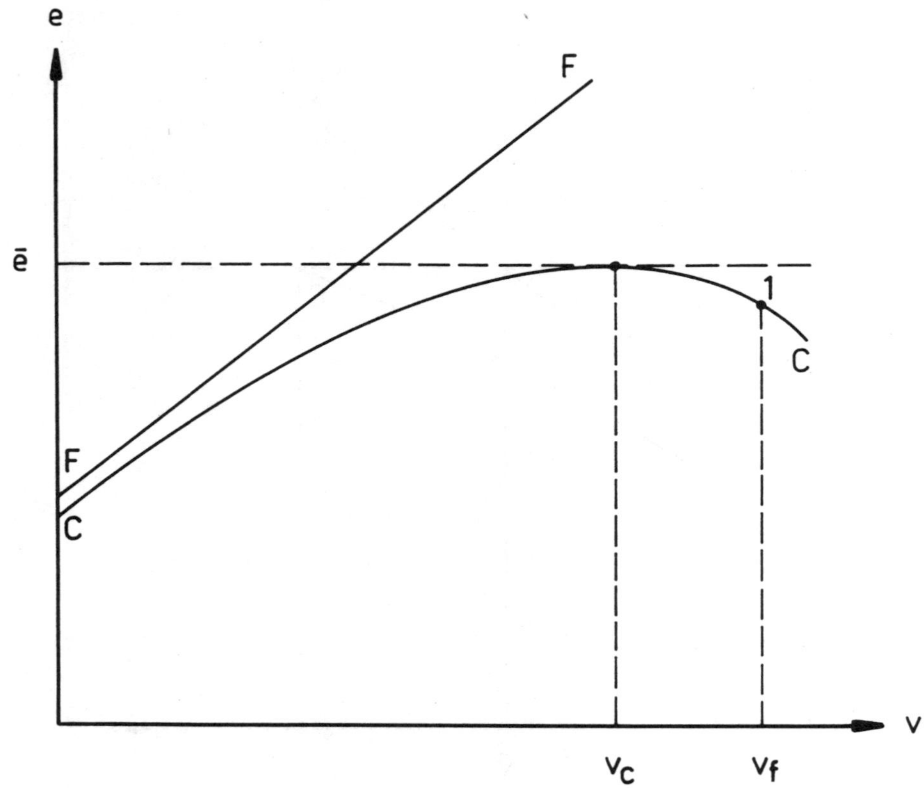

Figure 2

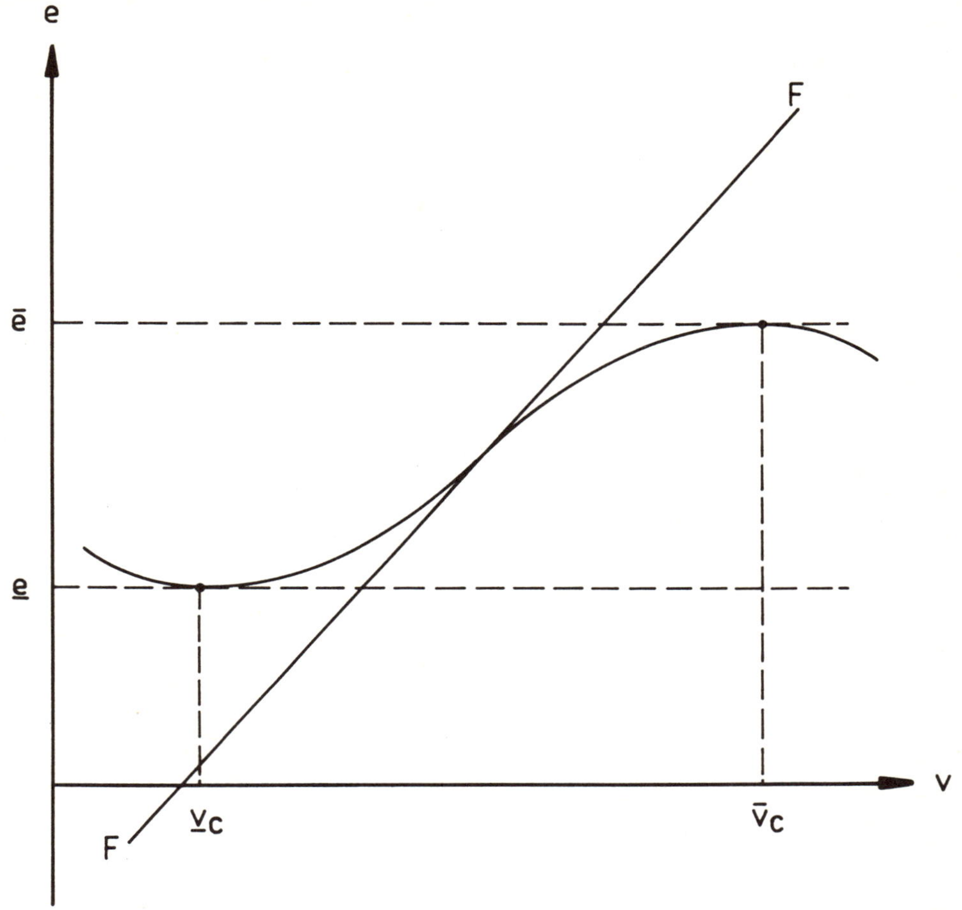

Figure 3

7 COMPETITIVE BANKING WITH FRACTIONAL RESERVES AND REGULATIONS

Benjamin Bental, Zvi Eckstein and Dan Peled

I. INTRODUCTION

Institutions providing demand-deposit-like services have been singled out among financial intermediaries, because demand deposits, unlike an insurance contract, must be paid solely upon its owner's demand. Therefore, when demand deposits are backed by fractional reserves, self-fulfilling panics may occur, so that banks become inherently unstable (Friedman (1959)). Rolnick and Webber (1985) present the conventional view that inherent instability in banking means that bank panics can occur without economy-wide real shocks that directly disturb aggregate economic activity. They, and Smith (1986), emphasize the usual explanation for how this can happen through a local real shock that propagates by the actions of incompletely informed depositors. In the face of this instability governments have found it necessary to intervene and regulate the banking industry. However, there is no agreement concerning the desirability, or even feasibility of the actual policies adopted by various governments.

In this paper we attempt to address some of the above issues within a modified version of the model proposed by Diamond and Dybvig (1983) and Bryant (1980).[1] In that model confidence crises associated with a fractional reserve banking system may arise. In fact there is a multiplicity of Pareto ranked Nash equilibria corresponding to a wide range of self-fulfilling beliefs of agents about future banks payments. However, it is not clear how agents make decisions involving trading via the banking system without knowing which of the possible equilibria will prevail, and therefore it is not clear what governments can do to influence agents' actions. To overcome this problem we assume that depositors' expectations about banks' future payments are influenced by the realization of an extraneous random shock, (a "sunspot"). This extraneous shock is economy-wide and is simultaneously and immediately

---

[1]This paper is based on Bental, Eckstein and Peled (1989).

observed by all agents including the government. Accordingly all trades and policies can be made contingent on its realization. In our analysis we distinguish between confidence crises and bank runs. The former term describes a particular pessimism on the part of depositors which occurs in conjunction with a realization of some adverse real or extraneous shock. When it occurs, depositors' behavior towards the banks is characterized by basic mistrust. Bank runs, on the other hand, are **actual** massive withdrawal of deposits, above and beyond the regular volume of withdrawals, which is motivated in a self-fulfilling way by a confidence crisis. This distinction between confidence crises and actual runs is important because the former are exogenous events, while the latter are equilibrium phenomena, affected, at least partially, by the strategies pursued by banks and depositors in equilibrium, as well as by policies adopted by the government . Maintaining this distinction allows us to examine the functioning of banks when all involved parties are aware of the risks of a confidence crisis, and choose their actions accordingly. In contrast, a simple Nash equilibrium concept, such as the one used by Diamond and Dybvig, requires that agents know in advance which equilibrium will prevail.

The main conclusion from our analysis is that occasional outbursts of lack of confidence among depositors need not result in actual runs in equilibrium, despite the particular illiquid nature of banks' portfolios and the severe restrictions on demand deposit contracts (namely, payment "on demand"). When banks choose the structure of returns on deposits that maximizes depositors' ex-ante expected utility subject to those "exogenous" fears, there are no runs in equilibrium, even though the resulting allocation is state-dependent. Banks can achieve this equilibrium by counteracting confidence crises with suitably chosen interest rates on early withdrawals while avoiding a total "suspension of convertibility". What is crucial for obtaining this result is that banks will be able to observe the factor that triggers depositors' sudden lack of confidence and act upon it, be it a real or an imaginary shock.

The banking equilibrium proposed here is not Pareto optimal. The relatively low returns on early withdrawals under a confidence crisis, which are needed to deter runs on the banks and provide resources to pay the increased debt service, entail a welfare cost that is not implied by the economy's resource constraint. Yet, by themselves, banks have no ability to offer demand deposit contracts that will avoid this inefficiency. We show that a government insurance program that guarantees an appropriately chosen return on short term deposits and is backed by taxes on future output can restore the Pareto optimal allocation. However, if the guaranteed return is set at a level which is "too high" the economy deteriorates to a steady-state which is inferior to the autarky situation, in which no banks can exist. It is crucial, therefore, that the government chosen guarantee be correctly set.

Section II of the paper presents the environment whose equilibria are examined in this work. We characterize the (unique) Pareto optimal allocation which will serve as a reference for evaluating the banking equilibria in the sequel. In section III we review banking models that to a large extent share the characteristics of our model. Section IV provides a formal definition of our equilibrium concept. Section V contains the actual characterization of a banking equilibrium, and in section VI we analyze a government insurance program which can restore optimality. Section VII concludes the paper.

II. THE ENVIRONMENT

The population of the economy consists of three period lived agents who belong to one of two groups which differ in their preferences. The periods are denoted by $t = 0,1,2$. One group of agents, labelled group A, is characterized by its members caring for consumption during their middle period only, according to the strictly concave and increasing function $u(c_1)$. Members of the other group, labelled B, care for consumption in their middle and last period, and are completely indifferent between sum-preserving combinations of these two periods consumption levels. Their preferences over consumption in these two periods are represented by $u(c_1 + c_2)$, where c_1 and c_2 represent middle and last period consumption levels, respectively.

During their first life period, agents are unaware of their type, but correctly perceive their type to be A with probability α, and B with probability $1-\alpha$. The resolution of this individual uncertainty occurs at the beginning of the middle period. But even when it occurs, it is <u>private information</u>, so that in the middle period no agent knows the type of any other agent but himself. Individual prior beliefs are correct in the sense that in aggregate the ratio of type A to type B agents is $a/1-a$. Agents seek to maximize their expected lifetime utility. Each agent is born endowed with one unit of a local non-tradable resource (e.g. labor) which can be converted into a single consumption unit by using two alternative production technologies.

An inferior technology converts one unit of the resource into one unit of the consumption good, and requires no other inputs. This production process yields output in the same period it is employed, and can be used in any period of the agents' lives.

A second technology is also available, which involves two gestation periods. Intermediate output of this technology after one period is just one unit of output per one unit of the local resource. However, no intermediate recovery of the imported input is possible in this process. This technology is described as a fixed proportion constant returns to scale process producing at period 2, R x units of the consumption good for x units of the resource invested at $t = 0$, where $R > 1$.

We are ready now to describe the sets of (stationary) feasible and optimal consumption allocations for this economy. Let c_i^h denote the ith period consumption of an agent of type h, $h \in \{A,B\}$, where $i = 1$ and $i = 2$ correspond to the middle and last period of the agent's life, respectively. During the middle period the maximal per capita amount of consumption good available is 1, so that c_1^A and c_1^B are constrained by:

$$ac_1^A + (1-a)c_1^B \leq 1 \tag{1}$$

The last period constraint is given by:

$$ac_2^A + (1-a)c_2^B \leq R[1 - ac_1^A - (1-a)c_1^B]. \tag{2}$$

The argument on the r.h.s. of (2) is the output from the more productive technology, given the withdrawals of local resources at $t = 1$.

Finally, an allocation $\{(c_1^A, c_2^A), (c_1^B, c_2^B)\}$ must be incentive compatible, given the private information nature of agents' types. That is, the allocation of a type A agent cannot be more attractive to a type B person than his own, and vice versa, namely:

$$c_1^A + c_2^A \leq c_1^B + c_2^B$$
$$c_1^A \geq c_1^B. \tag{3}$$

Any allocation $\{(c_1^A, c_2^A), (c_1^B, c_2^B)\}$ for which (1), (2) and (3) hold is a feasible allocation. The ex-ante Pareto optimal allocation can be found by maximizing: $\{\alpha u(c_1^A) + (1-\alpha)u(c_1^B + c_2^B)\}$ by choice of $\{c_1^A, c_2^A, c_1^B, c_2^B,\}$ subject to (1), (2) and (3).

The assumed preferences and specification of the superior technology (R > 1) imply that any solution to this problem will have $c_2^A = c_1^B = 0$. With these variables predetermined, the optimal allocation, denoted (c_1^{A*}, c_2^{B*}), is the solution to the pair of equations:

$$u'(c_1^A) - R\,u'(c_2^B) = 0 \tag{4}$$

and

$$(1-\alpha)c_2^B = R(1 - \alpha c_1^A) \tag{5}$$

where (5) obtains from (2) using the predetermined variables. These two equations will always have a unique non-negative solution which satisfies (1). It follows from (4), and the assumption that $R > 1$ that (3) is also satisfied. This completes the description of the feasible and optimal allocations in this economy without a banking sector and its associated riskiness. It can be shown (see section 3) that in the Pareto optimal allocation $c_1^{A*} > 1$ if and only if $u'(1) > R$. A sufficient condition for this is the case where the degree of constant relative risk aversion is greater than 1. If $u(c) = \log c$ then $c_1^{A*} = 1$ since there is no incentive for risk sharing. In that case, agents of type A have the same consumption as in the case where the superior technology is not used at all, and only agents of type B enjoy the gains from using the better technology.

III. REVIEW OF BANKING MODELS

The Pareto optimal allocation described in the previous section involves the sharing of idiosyncratic risks which take the form of preference shocks. Agents who end up impatient, type A, receive at t=1 a higher rate of return than they could obtain on their own, while the others earn a return which is somewhat smaller than that generated by the superior technology. One market mechanism which is potentially capable of attaining this allocation as a competitive equilibrium is a banking institution offering demand deposits. A demand deposit made at t=0 is an obligation of the bank to redeem any portion of it on demand, at period t=1 or t=2, at the depositor's discretion, according to interest rates which are announced at the time the deposit is made. Such an instrument can achieve the desired risk sharing between agents of different types provided that the announced repayment schedule is compatible with the agents' privately known types. Specifically, banks can invest the resources deposited with them at t=0 in the superior technology. The (gross) interest payable on t=1 and t=2 withdrawals can be set to c_1^{A*} and c_2^{B*}, respectively, where (c_1^{A*}, c_2^{B*}) is the Pareto optimal allocation. As long as only impatient agents (of type A) withdraw at t=1 this mechanism will attain the optimal allocation as an equilibrium.

Diamond and Dybvig (1983) pointed out that the mechanism of demand deposits is vulnerable to a self-fulfilling belief on the part of depositors that the banks will not be able to pay back the promised returns at t=2. Such beliefs will be self-fulfilling because if depositors of type B, in addition to those of type A, attempt to withdraw at t=1, the return structure that supports the optimal allocation is no longer feasible. Banks have no way of preventing massive withdrawals at t=1, should they arise, without violating the terms of the demand deposit contract as defined above.[2]

[2]The way in which we have specified demand deposit contracts rules out interim trade in them. In particular, if a unit deposited at t=0 is withdrawn at t=1 then no further returns are available on it at t=2. In contrast, Jacklin (1987) considered an extended definition of demand deposit contracts which allows for some interim payoff at t=1 without foregoing all of the expected t=2 payoffs. As Jacklin has shown, these and other modifications in the asset structure in the economy can eliminate the possibility of a bank run as a Nash equilibrium.

The Diamond and Dybvig framework motivated several researchers to propose different extensions of the basic model as a way to analyze the existence of demandable debt with fractional reserves and their implications on the possibility of bank runs. For example, Jacklin and Bhattacharya (1988) emphasize the asymmetry of information between depositors and intermediaries (banks) with respect to both the liquidity needs of the depositors and the solvency of the intermediaries as the reason for the existence of constrained Pareto optimal equilibria with demand deposits which are not fully backed by reserves.

Chari and Jagannathan (1988) analyzed a Diamond and Dybvig type model which is similar to that of Jacklin and Bhattacharya. In Chari and Jagannathan too depositors are asymmetrically informed about the liquidity of the intermediary. In addition, the proportion of agents with early liquidity needs is random. As a result, when uninformed individuals observe an "unusually" large queue of agents who want to liquidate their deposits, they infer (possibly wrongly) that the bank is insolvent, and decide to join the queue. Since bank-runs involve liquidation costs, avoiding such runs is likely to be socially preferable. Therefore, a properly designed suspension of convertibility in case of high early withdrawals may improve the allocation of resources.

The fact that suspension of convertibility may prevent bank-runs was already observed in the original contribution of Diamond and Dybvig. However, a misspecified suspension of convertibility may cause more harm than good. Under imperfect information compounded by uncertainty about the types in the economy, such a misspesification is likely to take place. Furthermore, suspension of convertibility may fail to prevent bank-runs if the number of periods is greater than three (Engineer (1989)). On the other hand, if a policy which restricts aggregate withdrawals to a prespecified proportion of the population can improve the allocation, it is not clear why such a policy does not become part of the deposit contract offered by the banks in equilibrium. The role of the government in this framework was also discussed by Diamond and Dybvig. For the case of aggregate uncertainty with respect to the distribution of the types of agents in the economy, Diamond and Dybvig suggested that the government establish a deposit insurance program. This program involves the imposition of a tax on early withdrawals which is contingent on the realized fraction of agents who withdrew. If the tax is designed correctly, there will be no unnecessary early withdrawals, the tax will never be imposed and optimality will be restored. However, the Diamond and Dybvig scheme assumes that the government possesses information which banks do not have, for otherwise their scheme is not feasible (see also Wallace (1988)).

Another attempt to deal with the government's role is that of Bhattacharya and Gale (1985). They have multiple Diamond and Dybvig-like banks. While the aggregate proportion of early withdrawers is known, every single bank may face a different proportion of depositors with liquidity needs. Therefore, there should be interbank lending and borrowing. However, the realization of the preference shock at each bank is private information of the bank itself. Therefore, banks have an incentive to invest only in the high-yielding, long-term asset. Under these circumstances, there is room for intervention by a central bank-like institution which will, on the one hand, lend to banks at a low interest rate (lower than the return on the long-term asset) and, on the other hand force banks to lend to it at the same low interest rate.

The papers mentioned above emphasized the liquidity and the risk sharing aspects of the demand deposit that is offered by banks. A different issue is addressed by Calomiris and Khan (1989). They show that in an enviroment with asymmetric information between depositors and bankers, the liquidity of the demand deposits provides the correct incentive for investment in institutions that have an advantage in evaluating good investment opportunities on the one hand, and a credible threat to prevent bankers from acting against the interest of the depositors on the other. Moreover, the sequential service constraint, that played a minor role in the Diamond and Dybvig model, provides an incentive, for particular depositors, to closely monitor the banks. The agents who monitor the banks receive a reward in case of a run and this fact lends them credibility.

In Diamond and Dybvig, as well as in most of the literature which came afterwards, there are two separate Nash equilibria: One in which all agents withdraw their deposits before the maturity of the high yielding technology, thereby forfeiting its benefits, and another which attains the optimal allocation. According to this concept, agents know in advance which of the Nash equilibria will prevail and behave accordingly. Obviously, such knowledge can have a profound effect on the agents' willingness to participate in the game, namely, whether or not to deposit resources with the banking system. We adopt the modeling strategy of Bental, Eckstein and Peled (1989) which follows the literature on sunspot equilibria (see Azariadis (1981) and Cass and Shell (1983), among others). This approach allows us to incorporate explicitly the uncertainty associated with runs on banks into the decisions of all agents who conduct trade via the banking system.[3]

The equilibrium concept suggested by us associates certain known probabilities with each of the (extraneous) events that determine agents' expectations about the banks.[4] We view each of the two pure Nash equilibria discussed by Diamond and Dybvig as corresponding to a particular realization of an extraneous shock. However, since our equilibrium formulation incorporates this randomness into agents' decision problems, the resulting equilibrium <u>does not</u> amount to a randomization over these pure Nash equilibria. In particular, the following differences emerge: First, banks may be eliminated altogether as a viable option for depositors who have direct access to production technologies by the introduction of uncertainty associated with the banking system. Second, banks can offer interest on deposits which depends on the expectations forming shock, thus potentially deterring premature withdrawals in equilibrium. Third, investment levels (in the long term technology) must be set prior to the resolution of this uncertainty, and hence, with risk averse agents, these investments will in general differ from their expected value under the pure Nash equilibrium outcomes.[5]

---

[3]The reader should be aware that the extraneous shocks impact directly on some agents' decisions (withdrawals). This is to be contrasted with previous analyses of sunspot equilibria in which extraneous shocks affect the equilibrium only through their impact on prices.

[4]General characteristics of models that lead to the existence of "sunspot" equilibria in which the occurrence of of extraneous event matters are still not agreed upon. However, the works of Azariadis (1981), Cass and Shell (1983) and Spear and Srivastava (1986) suggest that some market incompleteness is essential for that result.

[5]Another reason to consider extraneous events as instigating bank panics stems from certain observations on historical panics in the U.S. Some authors (Sprague (1910), Rolnick and Webber (1984)) state that there was no real reason for the panic, neither due to the banks' conduct or

IV. BANKING EQUILIBRIUM

We now define formally the precise operation of the banking system and agents' withdrawal decision process. At period zero, before individual types and the state of the economy (the aggregate shock) are realized, agents generally face three alternatives for using their endowment of one unit of the local resource: (i)Private investment in the superior technology; (ii)Private investment in the inferior technology which produces one unit of the good at $t=1$ for each unit of the resource invested at $t=0$; (iii)Purchasing a demand deposit from a bank which can be withdrawn at any subsequent period at the depositor's complete discretion. Per unit withdrawn at period i, = 1,2, the bank promises to pay $r_i(s)$ units of the good, where s is the state of the economy which is realized at $t=1$.

One of the issues to be examined is whether banks will indeed offer state-dependent interest rates, and what impact will the offered rates have on the possibility of runs in equilibrium. As we show below, depositors' welfare is maximized when banks offer state-dependent interest rates even though fixed interest rates are also feasible. These rates have the additional property that they deter runs on the banks even under conditions of a confidence crisis.

We consider two possible states of the economy, indexed by $s=0$ and $s=1$, and occurring with probabilities ϕ^s which are known to all agents. We shall further let $\phi^0 = \phi > 0$ and $\phi^1 = 1 - \phi > 0$.

Thus, the decision problem faced by an agent at $t=0$ can be formulated as:

---

no real reason for the panic, neither due to the banks' conduct or reserves level, nor due to general economic conditions. That view, if taken seriously, suggests that at least some depositors reacted in an exaggerated and unwarranted way to an isolated random event, thereby instigating the contagious process of a "run on the bank" which ultimately justified the initial "exaggerated" response. Although we do not model here the process of contagion itself, our approach can be interpreted as a simple form of "instantaneous contagion," whereby some shock to a particular sector of the economy is perceived by depositors to imply the probable collapse of the whole banking system. This preserves the absence of any real cause for panics which nonetheless can occur because of depositors' extreme sensitivity to particular, commonly observable realizations of random extraneous shocks.

$$\text{Max } \Sigma_s \phi^s[\alpha u(c_1^A(s)) + (1-\alpha)u(c_1^B(s) + c_2^B(s))] \tag{6}$$

s.t.

$$\begin{array}{lll}
\text{(i)} & c_1^A(s) \leq (1-d) + dr_1(s), & s \in \{0,1\} \\
\text{(ii)} & c_1^B(s) \leq W_B(d,s)r_1(s), & s \in \{0,1\} \\
\text{(iii)} & c_2^B(s) = (1-d) + (d - W_B(d,s))r_2(s) & s \in (0,1\}
\end{array}$$

where d is the level of demand deposit chosen, and $W_B(d,s)$ is the amount withdrawn by a patient agent (type B) at $t=1$, after knowing both his type and the state s of the economy.

As discussed above, when $s=1$ occurs, withdrawal decisions are made solely on the basis of the relative levels of first and second period returns, so that

$$W_B(d,1) = \begin{cases} 0, & \text{if } r_2(1) \geq r_1(1) \\ d, & \text{if } r_2(1) < r_1(1) \end{cases} \tag{7.1}$$

On the other hand, $s=0$ is interpreted by depositors as the signaling of a massive withdrawal of deposits at $t=1$. We refer to this state ($s=0$) as a <u>confidence crisis</u>. A bank faced by a total withdrawal by all its depositors can only pay back 1 unit or less per unit of deposit, since the superior technology does not mature until $t=2$. Consequently, in addition to requiring a higher return for postponing withdrawal until $t=2$, a depositor of type B wants to be assured that when $s=0$ the bank is not over committed in case of total withdrawal. Thus we have:

$$W_B(d,0) = \begin{cases} 0, & \text{if } r_2(0) \geq r_1(0) \text{ and } r_1(0) \leq 1 \\ d, & \text{otherwise} \end{cases} \tag{7.2}$$

The deposit level which solves problem (6) with withdrawals given by (7.1) and (7.2) will, in general, depend on the promised returns, $r_i(s)$, $i = 1,2$, $s=0,1$. Banks, in competition with each other, will offer a return structure which maximizes depositors' ex-ante expected utility, subject to profits being non-negative and the withdrawal behavior assumed in (7.1) and (7.2), (see, for analogy, the equilibrium concept of Rothschild and Stiglitz (1976)). Thus banks choose, per unit of deposit a term structure of returns on deposits, $r_1(s)$, $r_2(s)$, $s \in \{0,1\}$ that solves the following problem:

$$\text{Max}\{\phi[\alpha u(1-d(1-r_1(0)) + (1-\alpha)u(W_B(d,0)r_1(0) + (1-d) + (d-W_B(d,0))r_2(0))]$$

$$+ (1-\phi)\ [\alpha u(1-d(1-r_1(1))) +$$

$$(1-\alpha)u(W_B(d,1)r_1(1) + (1-d) + (d-W_B(d,1))r_2(1))]\}$$

subject to:

d being the solution to problem (6) under (7.1), (7.2), and

$$r_1(s)[\alpha d + (1-\alpha)W_B(d,s)] \leq d, \qquad s \in \{0,1\} \tag{8}$$

$$(1-\alpha)r_2(s)[d-W_B(d,s)] = R[d-(\alpha d + (1-\alpha)W_B(d,s))r_1(s)] \qquad s \in \{0,1\} \tag{9}$$

Constraint (8) assures that first-period returns do not exceed the resources available at s = 1, before the superior technology matures. The l.h.s. of (9) is the per-capita outlays at t=2, state s, and the term of the r.h.s. of (9) is the t=2 output from the resources left invested in the superior technology. We refer to any solution to the banks' problem as a banking equilibrium.

Note that a feasible option of our banking choice problem is to deny any payment on early withdrawals when s=0, that is, to suspend convertibility. In the Diamond and Dybvig framework, such a policy is an effective deterrent of early withdrawals on the part of patient depositors when banks can tell when an excessive amount of withdrawals requests is accumulating. As these authors point out, however, if there is aggregate uncertainty about the proportion of agents' types in the economy, this method of monitoring becomes insufficient, rendering the policy ineffective. Under our formulation banks do not need indirect monitoring devices of depositors' conduct since they directly observe the expectations forming shock. Thus, the feasibility of such a policy is not affected by aggregate uncertainty about the relative group size of different depositors. It does not follow, however, that a policy of denying any withdrawal privileges when a confidence crisis occurs is the one that best serves depositors' interests. Indeed, as we show below, the optimal solution to the banks' problem entails withdrawal privileges to all depositors under all states.

It is immediately clear that if a confidence crisis can never occur, i.e., $\phi = 0$, the banking equilibrium is unique and supports the optimal allocation. In particular, $r_1(1)$ and $r_2(1)$ can be set equal to c_1^{A*} and c_1^{B*}, respectively, in which case the optimally chosen individual deposit is 1, and y is determined accordingly. Obviously, the state $s=0$ policy is irrelevant in this case.

It is also clear that whenever $\phi = 0$, the setting of $r_1(0) = c_1^{A*}$ and $r_2(0) = c_2^{B*}$ cannot hold in any banking equilibrium. This return structure would activate total withdrawal of deposits at $t=1$, $s=0$, by (7.2). Consequently, we conclude that no banking equilibrium can support the optimal allocation when $\phi > 0$.

It is interesting to note that the ability to choose state-dependent interest rates is not necessarily the feature which eliminates runs in equilibrium here. Even when banks are restricted to choose state-independent interest rates the equilibrium would not display runs (in the sense of $W_B(d,0) = d$). This follows simply from the fact that if $r_1(0) = r_1(1) = r_1 > 1$ then $W_B(d,s) = d$ for both $s=0$ and $s=1$, which is as good as autarky, since in this case no-one enjoys the superior technology. This leaves only one possibility for the state-independent rates: $r_1(s) = r_1$, $r_2(s) = r_2$ for $s=0,1$, with $r_1 \leq 1$, and $1 < r_2 < R$. In this case banks provide no liquidity insurance. Even though this policy is clearly feasible for the banks, and deters runs, it turns out to be suboptimal.

In the next section we characterize the banking equilibrium and examine whether the optimal banks' policy involves state-dependent interest on deposits, whether it supports state-dependent consumption, and whether it involves runs on the banks under a confidence crisis.

V. COMPETITIVE BANKING UNDER CONFIDENCE CRISIS

The banks' ability to adjust interest rates according to the state of nature allows them to prevent "runs" from ever occurring, even when a confidence crisis does occur. This result is achieved by lowering the first period interest rate when s=0 sufficiently, so as to make the banks safe even if all deposits are withdrawn. Moreover, an optimal policy must be such that type B agents refrain from withdrawing at t=1 despite their concerns about their investment. This is so because if type B agents choose to withdraw, feasibility implies $r_1(0) \leq 1$, and optimality implies $r_2(0) = 0$. However, it can be shown that any payment scheme which is consistent with $W_B(d,0) = d$ can be dominated (in the sense of the Banks' problem objective) by another scheme. This other scheme does not affect payments to type A agents but offers $r_2(0) \geq r_1(0)$, (see Appendix A). This higher level of $r_2(0)$, coupled with $r_1(0) \leq 1$, (which holds since by hypothesis everyone withdraws at t=1 in the original scheme), is enough to convince agents of type B to leave their deposits in the bank until t=2, according to (7.2). The maintained deposits of type B allow the banks to invest in the superior technology resources which would otherwise have to be held in reserves to meet t=1 withdrawals, thereby (at least weakly), improving the allocation. In equilibrium, therefore, the banks interest payments are such that the panic is not self-fulfilled. However, as we show next, the potential for panic prevents the banks from offering the optimal interest payments. In fact, the banks hold a completely safe portfolio in case of a confidence crisis.[6]

Next, we characterize the competitive banking equilibrium.

---

[6]Friedman (1959) recommended that banks should be obliged to hold 100% reserves against demand deposits. In our economy, competition among the banks makes them perfectly safe and no additional regulation is required.

<u>Proposition 1</u>: The competitive banking equilibrium with a confidence crisis occurring with probability ϕ, $0 < \phi \leq 1$, is characterized by

$$r_1(1) = r_1^*,\ r_2(1) = r_2^*,\ r_1(0) = 1,\ r_2(0) = R. \tag{10}$$

<u>Proof</u>: See Appendix B.

In addition, we show that in equilibrium with a return structure given by Propositions 1, agents deposit **all** their t=0 resources with the banks (d=1).

<u>Lemma</u>: For the equilibrium configuration of returns given by (10) the optimal deposit d that solves the agent problem (6) is equal to one.

<u>Proof</u>: The partial derivative of the objectives at (6) with respect to d, evaluated at a returns structure that satisfies (10), is given by:

$$\phi[\alpha u'(c_1(0))(r_1(0)-1) + (1-\alpha)u'(c_2(0)(r_2(0) - 1)]$$

$$+ (1-\phi)[\alpha u'(c_1(1)(r_1(1)-1) + (1-\alpha)u'(c_2(1))(r_2(1)-1)] =$$

$$\phi(1-\alpha)u'(c_2(0))(R-1) + (1-\phi)\alpha u'(c_1(1))(r_1(1)-1)$$

$$+ (1-\phi)(1-\alpha)u'(c_2(1))(r_2(1)-1) > 0$$

where $c_i(s) = dr_i(s) + 1 - d$, $i = 1,2$, $s=0,1$. Therefore, d=1.

□

VI. <u>GOVERNMENT INSURANCE</u>

In order to analyze the role of the government, we extend our model by embedding it in an overlapping generations framework. In particular, a new generation of equal number of agents appears at every even date. All generations are identical with all the features described above. We assume that the government can borrow internationally at a given interest rate δ per period, and repay the debt by taxing the output of future generations. Our goal here is to analyze whether the government can use its ability to tax future generations (agents that currently do not deposit their resources in the bank) in order to stabilize the banking system.

According to our specification, a crisis may occur at state 0 if type B agents find out that the banks do not have sufficient resources to back <u>all</u> demand deposits if they are withdrawn, so that

$$W_B(d,0) = \begin{cases} 0 & \text{if } r_2(0) > r_1(0) \text{ and } r_1(0) \leq 1 \\ d & \text{otherwise} \end{cases} \tag{7.2}$$

Accordingly, if the government stands ready to transfer to the banks' resources in case the need should arise, type B agents take this into account when they assess the banks' ability to honor their obligations. Specifically, suppose the government is willing to guarantee a return of up to r_g on short-term deposits, and that this guarantee is credible. Then (7.2) can be modified to

$$W_B(d,0) = \begin{cases} 0 & \text{if } r_2(0) \geq r_1(0) \text{ and } r_1(0) \leq \max\{1,r_g\} \\ 1 & \text{otherwise} \end{cases} \tag{7.3}$$

The condition for no early withdrawal in (7.3) reflects the confidence in the banks' ability to pay up to the government guarantee, when that guarantee exceeds what banks are able to pay on their own.

We assume that if the government has to enact its guarantee, it nationalizes the banks, takes their resources and borrows any amount that is necessary. Accordingly, in order to finance its guarantee, the government borrows abroad a per-capita amount of:

$$F = r_g(\alpha d + (1-\alpha)W_B(d,s)) - d \tag{11}$$

and imposes a tax τ on each member of the next generation to repay the debt so that its budget is given by

$$\tau = (1 + \delta)F. \tag{12}$$

The banks take as given the government's guarantee and choose $\{r_1(s), r_2(s)\}$, $s \in \{0,1\}$ so as to maximize depositors' utility, given their deposits and the depositors' withdrawal decisions. In particular, banks must decide whether the government's guarantee should influence their behavior.

Suppose first that $1 < r_g < r_1^*$. Then a simple modification of proposition 1 is needed.

PROPOSITION 2: If $1 < r_g \leq r_1^*$ and $(1 + \delta)(r_g - 1) < 1$, then $d = 1$ and the competitive banking contract is

$$r_1(0) = r_g,\ r_2(0) = R(1-\alpha r_g)/(1-\alpha),\ r_1(1) = r_1^*,\ r_2(1) = r_2^*.$$

The condition requiring $(1+\delta)(r_g-1) < 1$ means that the guarantee is feasible in terms of future available resources. The condition that $r_g > 1$ implies that the government increases the rate of return for the early withdrawal at the state $s = 0$. The remaining steps of the proof follows the proof of proposition 1 (see Appendix B).

COROLLARY: If $1 < r_g \leq r_1^*$ and $(1+\delta)(r_g-1) < 1$ no taxes need be imposed to back the guarantee.

PROOF: Since the policy is credible, $W_B(d,0) = 0$ and the banks' payments amount to $\alpha r_g d$. However, $r_g < r_1^*$ implies $\alpha r_g < 1$, since $\alpha c_1^{A*} < 1$. Hence, no government help is required.

Clearly, then, the government is capable of restoring Pareto optimality. If it guarantees r_1^*, type B agents will not panic, and the guarantee will not have to be exercised.

Suppose next that $r_g > r_1^*$, but $(1+\delta)(r_g-1) < 1$. Then the banks may consider triggering the government guarantee by offering contracts of $r_1(s) = r_g$, $r_2(s) = 0$, $s \in \{0,1\}$. This policy is optimal only if

$$u(r_g) > \alpha u(r_1^*) + (1-\alpha)u(r_2^*). \tag{13}$$

Let $\bar{r}_g$ satisfy (13) as an equality (see figure 1).

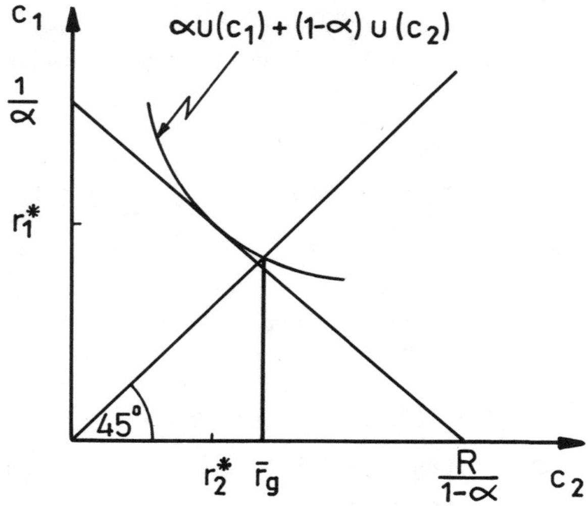

F i g u r e 1:

Determination of $\bar{r}_g$.

Accordingly, we have,

PROPOSITION 3: If $r_1^* < r_g \leq \bar{r}_g$ and $(1+\delta)(r_g-1) < 1$, then $d=1$ and the banks offer $r_1(s) = r_1^*$, $r_2(s) = r_2^*$, $s \in \{0,1\}$.

According to Proposition 3, even if the government's guarantee is a "little" too high, it will not be abused. However, the situation changes if $r_g > \bar{r}_g$. Then we obtain the following result:

PROPOSITION 4: If $r_g > \bar{r}_g$ and $(1+\delta)(r_g-1) < 1$, then

$$r_1(s) = r_g,\ r_2(s) = 0,\quad s \in \{0,1\}.$$

According to Proposition 4 the banks may find it optimal to increase the interest rate they offer on short-term deposits to the level guaranteed by the government. In this case they induce type B withdrawals, and force the government to activate its guarantee and borrow abroad. We show next that the steady state of the economy is inferior to that which would emerge under autarky.

<u>PROPOSITION 5</u>: If $r_g > \bar{r}_g$ and $(1+\delta)(r_g-1)$ then $r_g d_\infty < 1$ where d_∞ is the steady state deposit which is given by $d_\infty = \frac{1}{1+(1+\delta)(r_g-1)}$, and in steady state the economy is worse off than in autarky.

<u>PROOF</u>: Let period 1 be the first time the government guarantee is activated. Then, at period 1 the government borrows abroad $F_1 = r_g - 1$. The tax imposed on every young agent at $t=2$ is $\tau_1 = (1+\delta)(r_g-1)$. Therefore, every young agent deposits $d_1 = 1 - (1+\delta)(r_g-1)$. If the bank offers again $r_1(s) = r_g$, $r_2(s) = 0$, $s \in \{0,1\}$ the government must borrow at $t=3$ $F_2 = (r_g-1)d_1 = (r_g-1)[1-(1+\delta)(r_g-1)]$. The taxes on the next generation amount to $\tau_2 = (1+\delta)(r_g-1)[1-(1+\delta)(r_g-1)]$ so that they deposit $d_2 = 1 - \tau_2$, etc. At steady state we obtain that $\tau_\infty = (1+\delta)(r_g-1)d_\infty$ and $d_\infty = 1 - \tau_\infty$. Therefore, $d_\infty = \frac{1}{1+(1+\delta)(r_g-1)}$. Since $r_g > 1$, it follows that $r_g d_\infty < 1$ and agents are worse off than in the autarky case.

VII. <u>CONCLUDING REMARKS</u>

In this paper we have briefly surveyed some of the literature explaining the existence of demand deposits backed by fractional reserves. The starting point is the papers by Bryant (1980) and Diamond and Dybvig (1983). In this framework confidence crises having no foundations in real events in the economy may occur. Such crises cause misallocations of resources, and should therefore be avoided. We have reviewed some of the policy recommendations arrived at in previous research regarding the banking system itself as well as the government, aimed at solving the problems associated with the inherent instability of the fractional reserves banking system.

Our own contribution to this issue is an analysis of a deposit insurance program operated by the government which is based on the government's ability to tax future resources. We have shown that if the government sets a guaranteed return on short-term deposits at a level which is not too high, optimality can be restored. However, if the government guarantee is set too high, the banks will have an incentive to abuse it, and the government will have to enact its program. As a result the economy deteriorates in steady state to an allocation which is inferior to the autarky allocation (without a banking system).

APPENDIX A

Here we prove that any payment scheme which induces early withdrawal by agents of type B can be dominated by another solution to the Banks' problem in which $W_B(d,0) = 0$, and hence cannot be an equilibrium.

Consider a feasible solution to the Banks' Problem $\{r_1(0), r_1(1), r_2(0), r_2(1)$, such that $r_2(0) = 0$ and $W_B(d,0) = d$. Our claim is that there exists another feasible solution to the Banks' problem, which differs from the above **only** in having $r_2(0) = r_1(0)$ and $w_B(d,0) = 0$. That is, we have to show that

$$(1-\alpha)r_1(0)d + R(1-\alpha r_1(0))d \tag{A.1}$$

This is clearly true because $r_1(0) \leq 1$, and therefore

$$(1-\alpha),\ r_1(0) \leq (1-\alpha) < R(1-\alpha) \leq R(1-\alpha r_1(0)).$$

□

APPENDIX B

PROOF OF PROPOSITION 1.

The banks' problem for this case is to maximize

$$\phi[\alpha u((r_1(0)-1)d+1) + (1-\alpha)u((r_2(0)-1)d+1]$$

$$+ (1-\phi)[\alpha u((r_1(1)-1)d+1] + (1-\alpha)u((r_2(1)-1)+1) \quad \text{(B.1)}$$

by choice of $r_1(0)$, $r_2(0)$, $r_1(1)$, and $r_2(1)$, subject to:

$$r_1(0) \leq 1; \quad \text{(B.2)}$$

$$\alpha r_1(1) \leq 1; \quad \text{(B.3)}$$

$$(1-\alpha)r_2(s)d + R(1-\alpha r_1(s))d; \quad s = \{0,1\}. \quad \text{(B.4)}$$

Clearly, (B.3) holds as an inequality while (B.4) holds as an equality for all s at the optimum.

If $r_1(0) < 1$, we obtain as first order conditions:

$$u'(c_1(0)) = Ru'(c_2(0))$$

and

$$(1-\alpha)c_2(0) = R(1-\alpha c_1(0))$$

which yields the Pareto optimal allocation, i.e. $c_1(0) > 1$. However, this contradicts $r_1(0) < 1$. Therefore $r_1(0) = 1$ and $r_2(0) = R$, while $1 < r_1(1) < r_2(1) < R$.

REFERENCES

Azariadis, C., "Self-fulfilling Prophecies", *Journal of Economic Theory* (Dec. 1981), 380-96.

Bental B. , Eckstein, Z. and Peled, D. "Competitive Banking with Confidence Crisis and International Borrowing ", mimeo Tel-Aviv University, (July 1989).

Bhattacharya, S., and D.Gale, "Preference Shocks, Liquidity and Central Bank Policy," University of California at Berkeley, 1985.

Bryant, J., "A Model of Reserves, Bank Runs, and Deposit Insurance," *Journal of Banking and Finance*, Vol.4, 1980.

Calomiris , C.W. and Kahn, C.M " The Role of Demandable debt in structuring Optimal Banking Arrangements" mimeo, University of llinois at Urbana - Champaign, (March 1989).

Cass, D., and Shell, K., "Do Sunspots Matter?" *Journal of Political Economy* 91 (April 1983), 193-227.

Chari V.V. and Jagannathan , R. "Banking Panics, Information, and Rational Expectations Equilibrium ", *The Journal of Finance* Vol. XLIII (July 1988): pp.749-763.

Diamond, D.W. and P.H.Dybvig, "Banks Runs, Deposit Insurance and Liquidity," *Journal of Political Economy* 91, No.3 (June 1983), 401-419.

Engineer, N., "Bank Run and the Suspension of Deposit Convertibility," (1989), forthcoming, *Journal of Monetary Economics*.

Friedman, M., A Program for Monetary Stability, New York, Fordham University Press (1959).

Jacklin, C.J., "Demand Deposits, Trading Restrictions and Risk Sharing," In: *Contractual Arrangements for Intertemporal Trades*, E.Prescott and N.Wallace, eds., Minnesota Studies in Macroeconomics, Vol.1, University of Minnesota Press, Minneapolis, 1987.

Jacklin, C.J., and S.Bhattacharya, "Distinguishing Panics and Information Based Bank Runs: Welfare and Policy Implications," *Journal of Political Economy* ,96 (June 1988), 568- 592.

Postlewaite, A., and Xavier, V., "Bank Runs as an Equilibrium Phenomenon," *Journal of Political Economy*, Vol.95 No.3 (1987), 485-491.

Rolnick, A.J., and W.E.Webber, "The Causes of Free Bank Failure: A Detailed Examination," *Journal of Monetary Economics*, 14 (October, 1984).

——————————, "Banking Instability and Regulation in the U.S. Free Banking Era," Federal Reserve Bank of Minneapolis, *Quarterly Review*, Summer (1985).

Rothschild, M., and J.E.Stiglitz, "Equilibrium in Competitive Insurance Markets: An Essay in the Economics of Incomplete Information," *Quantitative Journal of Economics* 90, (1976), 624-249.

Smith, B.D., "Bank Panics Suspensions and Geography: Some Notes on the 'Contagion of Fear' in Banking", mimeo., Carnegie-Mellon University, May, 1986.

Spear, S., and S.Srivastava, "Indeterminacy of Sunspot Equilibrium in Stochastic Overlapping Generations Model," Working Paper, GSIA, Carnegie-Mellon University, June 1986.

Sprague, D.M.W., *A History of Crises under the National Banking System*, U.S. Government Printing Office, Washington 1910.

Wallace, N. , " Another Attempt to Explain an Illiquid Banking System: The Diamond and Dybvig Model with Sequential Service Taken Seriously", Federal Reserve Bank of Minneapolis, *Quarterly Review*, (Fall 1988).

COMPETITIVE BANKING WITH FRACTIONAL RESERVES AND REGULATIONS

by: B.Bental, Z.Eckstein and D.Peled

Discussant: Yair E.Orgler

This paper belongs to the interesting literature that has evolved in the last decade, in which an attempt is made to model bank panics as economic phenomena and analyze their implications for the role of the central bank, the deposit contract and the behavior of depositors and bankers. The articles in this area can be roughly divided into those assuming that bank assets are risky, such as Bryant (1), Chari and Jagannathan (2) and Gorton (4) and the ones which assume that assets are riskless such as Diamond and Dybvig (3). The paper by Bental, Eckstein and Peled belongs to the second category in which bank runs occur because of consumption needs of customers holding demand deposits that are backed by fractional reserves and are subject to a sequential service constraint on cash withdrawals. Hence, bank panics are caused by liquidity rather than solvency crises, where the central bank plays a major role as lender of last resort.[1] The main contribution of this paper, which is based on the Diamond and Dybvig model, is the analysis of a deposit insurance program which guarantees a small positive return on short-term deposits. Assuming confidence in the government-backed guarantee, it is shown that a Pareto optimal solution is obtained where bank runs do not occur.

Since the underlying Diamond and Dybvig model has been extensively discussed and since its extension in this paper is properly executed and explained, I will concentrate my comments on the more general issue of the relevance of this approach to bank runs. For this purpose, let us consider three major runs that took place in the U.S. in the 1980s and one "no-run" that is still in effect in this country. The first run was generated by large depositors of Continental Illinois who did not renew their time deposits despite generous interest rate premiums because of

[1]It should be noted that with modern liability management, the likelihood of a liquidity crisis, especially when assets are assumed to be riskless, is quite remote.

most of the underlying assumptions of the model do not apply in this case. The other runs occurred at state-insured savings institutions in Maryland and Ohio. In both instances the main reason for the widespread depositors' panic was concern about the credibility of the insurance system. On the other hand, the inexistence of runs on virtually bankrupt but federally insured savings and loan associations is explained by confidence in the explicit and implicit backing of these institutions by the U.S. government. The same explanation applies to other countries that do not have a formal deposit insurance scheme, yet bank runs were avoided because of depositors' confidence that the central bank or the government will bail out any failed depository institution.

The lesson that can be learned from these cases is that the main factor affecting bank panics is the deposit "insurance" system and depositors' expectations about government behavior whether or not such a system formally exists. It is interesting, therefore, to observe that the treatment of deposit insurance in the recent literature on bank runs is quite different from the "traditional" literature on this subject. In this respect, the paper by Bental, Eckestein and Peled provides some improvement although its relevance is rather limited due to the assumption that bank assets are riskless. A further analysis of the relationships between bank panics and deposit insurance under more realistic assumptions would be both interesting and relevant to a very important economic issue.

REFERENCES

Bryant, J., "A Model of Reserves, Bank Runs, and Deposit Insurance," *Journal of Banking and Finance* 4 (1980), 335-44.

Chari, V.V. and R.Jagannathan, "Banking Panics, Information and Rational Expectations Equilibrium," *Journal of Finance XLIII* (July 1988), 749-63.

Diamond, D.W. and P.H.Dybvig, "Bank Runs, Deposit Insurance and Liquidity," *Journal of Political Economy* 91 (June 1983), 401-19.

Gorton, G., "Bank Suspension of Convertibility," *Journal of Monetary Economics* 15 (March 1985), 177-93.

8 A CASE FOR REFORMING FEDERAL DEPOSIT INSURANCE[1]

John H.Boyd and Arthur J.Rolnick

Federal deposit insurance has long been regarded as one of our most successful government programs. It is now in need of serious repair. Established in 1933 to stem an instability problem in banking, deposit insurance succeeded as well as Congress could have hoped. More recently, however, as federally insured institutions have become less regulated, a problem with deposit insurance has surfaced. In order to allow banks to survive in a more competitive environment, Congress and bank regulators, over the past eight years, have relaxed the regulatory reins. But they did not, as some advised, reform deposit insurance.[2] As a result, banks have become more competitive but at the expense of taking on considerably more risk. In effect, a fundamentally difficult problem with deposit banking has been exchanged for one with deposit insurance.

Over the years, many economists have warned of a problem with the federal deposit insurance system. While protecting depositors, deposit insurance encourages banks to take on more risk than they otherwise would. This is the so-called "moral hazard" problem that is inherent with almost all insurance policies. However, because the deposit insurance system appeared to work so well and because so few banks failed, these warnings went unheeded. Proponents of bank deregulation argued that the supervisory agencies were well-equipped to contain moral hazard and that the low bank-failure rate provided strong support for this point of view.

Something is now amiss. The low bank-failure rate did not continue into the 1980s. Since the beginning of this decade over 800 banks have failed, including a few of the largest in the industry. Many more are facing some financial difficulties. A much worse situation has

---

[1]The views expressed in this paper are expressly those of the authors; they are not intended to represent a formal position of the Federal Reserve System.

[2]The point that reform should logically precede further deregulation was forcefully made as early as 1983 by Karaken.

developed in the savings and loan industry, which is protected by its own federal deposit insurance. This industry has demonstrated just how high the cost of moral hazard can be. Estimated losses to the Federal Savings and Loan Insurance Corporation (FSLIC) now range up to $100 billion or higher, a cost that will likely be borne by the taxpayer. No longer does it appear that those who warned of moral hazard were crying wolf.[3]

There is now an obvious need to reform the way banks are regulated and depositors are protected. What is not so obvious is the best way to reform. Some suggest that banks be constrained to holding only safe assets. Others argue that closer monitoring and pricing of bank risk will solve the problem. Still others believe troubled banks should be closed before their net worth becomes negative. An examination of such reforms, however, suggests that they won't work and/or are extremely costly.

The reforms, we think, that will be effective involve a larger role for market involvement. And they reflect what we see in private insurance contracts that are successful in containing moral hazard. In particular, private market experience suggests that the costs of containing moral hazard will have to be shared by the insured. Depositors will have to bear some risk of loss -- and bank owners a greater share than they do now. This, in turn, will mean the banking system will be potentially more prone to depositor instability. Nevertheless, given the problems with the current banking system, some tradeoff is warranted.

THE FEDERAL DEPOSIT INSURANCE SYSTEM IS IN NEED OF SERIOUS REPAIR

Before federal deposit insurance was in place, the banking system was in periodic turmoil. Bank panics, a large number of bank failures caused at least in part by a general loss of confidence in the banking system and accompanied by a major economic contraction, were a regular feature of the U.S. economy. Such panics occurred in virtually every

---

[3]This essay deals with bank regulation in general, and the Federal Deposit Insurance Corporation (FDIC) in particular. But, most of our policy recommendations would be equally applicable to the savings and loan industry and their insurer, the FSLIC. What is not discussed here is the current financial crisis of the FSLIC, a problem which is (thankfully) unique to that institution.

decade following the passage of the National Banking Act of 1863. The panic of 1907 finally convinced Congress that more direct government involvement was necessary. While federal deposit insurance was discussed, it was ultimately rejected. In 1913 Congress created the Federal Reserve System to be the lender-of-last-resort: a central bank that commercial banks could turn to when depositors' confidence waned. Nevertheless, less than 20 years later, the United States experienced its worst banking panic as over one-fifth of U.S. commercial banks suspended operations (Friedman and Schwartz [1963, p.299]).

To build depositor confidence and help prevent bank panics, Congress established the Federal Deposit Insurance Corporation (FDIC). On January 1, 1934, the FDIC went into business insuring deposits up to $2,500 in banks that had chosen to become members of this new government corporation (on July 1 the maximum coverage was raised to $5,000). Over the years the fraction of total deposits that the FDIC insured has gradually increased, as more depositors chose insured banks and maximum deposit coverage was raised. (See Table 1.) Today the FDIC insures deposits up to $100,000 per account, and this insurance covers over 75 percent of all bank deposits. But even so-called "uninsured deposits," those in accounts that exceed $100,000, have almost always been protected as well. Consider that of the 184 banks that failed in 1987 only 14 percent of the uninsured deposits were not paid in full.[4] Because of the FDIC, most depositors no longer have any reason to withdraw their funds based on fears and rumors that their bank is failing. Indeed, widespread bank panics (of the sort experienced in the 1930s) have become interesting curiosities in banking history, rather than contemporary policy problems.

ONE PROBLEM SOLVED, ANOTHER INTRODUCED

Deposit insurance solved an inherent problem with deposit banking, but it introduced an inherent problem with insurance. Most insurance has a potentially costly side effect called "moral hazard," which is

[4]Data for uninsured deposits in failed banks that were purchased by other banks are not available. We estimate uninsured deposits as the difference between total assets and total insured deposits, based on the assumption that equity of failed banks is zero.

well-known in the industry. People who are insured against a particular risk have an incentive to change their behavior. Consider the owners of a factory who purchase fire insurance. Prior to this purchase, they would have to bear the entire cost of a conflagration. Once insured,

TABLE 1: INSURED DEPOSITS, 1934-1987

Year*	Maximum Dollar Insurance Coverage Per Account	Deposits in Insured Banks[1] (in millions of dollars) Total Deposits	Insured Deposits	Percentage of Insured Deposits
1934-39	5,000	48,662	21,815	44.8
1940-44	5,000	94,536	38,512	40.7
1945-49	5,000	153,994	73,789	47.9
1950-54	10,000	186,232	101,299	54.4
1955-59	10,000	229,432	128,854	56.2
1960-64	10,000	300,326	169,874	56.6
1965-69	15,000	442,915	262,955	59.4
1970-74	24,000	690,630	425,963	61.7
1975-79	40,000	1,048,224	691,832	66.0
1980	100,000	1,324,463	948,717	71.6
1981	100,000	1,409,322	988,898	70.2
1982	100,000	1,544,697	1,134,221	73.4
1983	100,000	1,690,576	1,268,332	75.0
1984	100,000	1,806,520	1,389,874	76.9
1985	100,000	1,974,512	1,503,393	76.1
1986	100,000	2,167,596	1,634,302	75.4
1987	100,000	2,201,549	1,658,802	75.3

[1] Deposits in foreign branches are omitted from totals because they are not insured. Insured deposits are estimated by applying to deposits at the regular Call dates the percentages as determined from the June Call Report submitted by insured banks.

Source: Annual Report of Federal Deposits Insurance Corp. 1987.

*Data reported for the years 1934-1979 are annual averages.

though, a great part of the cost will be borne by the insurance company. For a fixed annual fee the owners' concern about such a loss is significantly alleviated, which is the obvious benefit of insurance. Consequently, the insurance company should expect the insured to take more risks than they would have without the insurance. The insured can now afford to be a little less cautious about the disposing of flammable materials such as old paint cans or chemical containers. If the insurance company hopes to remain in business, it must take account of such behavioral changes when pricing and administering policies.

The federal deposit insurance system suffers from this sort of problem. Other things equal, deposit insurance encourages banks to hold riskier portfolios than they otherwise would. This follows immediately from the protection provided by FDIC insurance: once insured, depositors have no reason to worry about the riskiness of their bank's activities. Regardless of how the bank invests their funds, insured depositors' claims are guaranteed. Depositors, therefore, do not require a risk premium; and banks, therefore, have an incentive to invest in riskier projects. If these riskier projects are successful, the bank owners reap the higher returns; if not, the government insuring agency bears most of the loss. Depositors' funds earn the safe rate of return and are secure in either case.[5]

One might question whether the moral hazard problem is really that serious in banking because bank owners and managers are not protected by deposit insurance -- depositors are. Indeed, the owners can lose their equity if the bank's loans go sour, and managers can lose their jobs. Such losses, therefore, would seem to offset the effects of moral hazard.

This view, although intuitively appealing, misses the point. Equity is an integral part of the moral hazard problem, and the owners of the bank are the ones who benefit from having a high-return/high-risk portfolio. Moreover, some bank owners are able to diversify much of this risk by having only a small fraction of their total resources invested in any one bank. Consequently, owners could very well behave as if they were risk neutral; that is, they may simply seek to maximize expected return. If this is the case, we would expect such banks not just to take on more risk than otherwise, but in fact to seek as much

---

[5]The moral hazard problem is, in fact, more extreme with deposit insurance than it is with many forms of private insurance. The FDIC does not prohibit troubled banks from buying more insurance (that is, acquiring more deposits). This is analogous to allowing the owners of a factory to buy more fire insurance when their factory is on fire.

risk as possible.[6]

MORAL HAZARD KEPT IN CHECK BY PROTECTIVE SUBSIDY

Policymakers were aware of moral hazard from the beginning. Historically, the response to this problem has been heavy supervision and regulation of banking activities. This approach mitigates the moral hazard problem in two ways: first, by limiting risky bank activities, and second, by protecting banks from competition.

Direct limitations of risky activities have taken a variety of forms. For example, bank risk is monitored by three federal agencies and each state's chartering authority. National banks are examined regularly by the Comptroller of the Currency; state-chartered banks are examined by the FDIC or the Federal Reserve (if they are a member), as well as the state in which they are chartered. All bank holding companies are examined by the Federal Reserve. Besides formal examinations, banks have been restricted in the types of businesses they can own and operate, in how much lending they can do with one person or one company, in what types of loans they can make, and in how much of their portfolio must be in liquid reserves.

Regulatory impediments to bank competition have included constraints on the number of bank charters, on where banks could do business, on how many branch offices banks could maintain, and on the interest rates banks could pay. In addition, nonbank financial firms were prohibited from offering traditional bank products.

How successful has this strategy been in limiting the effects of moral hazard? Until recently, the record looked quite good, and banks appeared as safe as the government-insured deposits they offered. Over the 40-year period 1940 to 1979, for example, on average less than seven banks failed per year (see Table 2.) In fact, there were so few failures that many economists argued that the government was

[6]While bank stock owners may be able to effectively diversify their risks, this is much more difficult for the senior management of banks. That is so because when a bank fails it may reflect on their skill as managers, and thus on the value of their human capital. This point is sometimes raised as an important force countervailing the incentive effects of moral hazard. However, if bank owners genuinely want managers to pursue high-risk strategies, it seems they can get their wish. One obvious way is to pay managers sufficiently high current salaries to offset their risk of loss should bankruptcy occur in the future.

over-regulating banks. They claimed that banking, like other industries, needed to weed out its inefficient firms. What was lost in efficiency, though, was gained in safety. With relatively few exceptions, the U.S. banking industry appeared safe and sound.

The most effective part of this supervisory and regulatory strategy was to isolate the banking industry from competition, allowing it to earn high rates of return. Banks themselves were confined to well-specified geographic locations via interstate and intrastate branching restrictions. And nonbank financial firms could not offer transaction accounts. In addition, for many years banks were prohibited from paying interest on checkable deposits and limited in the rates they could pay on time and savings accounts (Regulation Q). With few competitors and few restrictions on the rates banks could charge on loans and earn on investments, banking was a lucrative business even without taking much risk. Short-term, self-liquidiating commercial loans and well-collateralized, long-term loans, along with government securities, were the standard type of bank assets.[7]

These high rates of return, as reflected in the market value of a bank charter, presumably provided the bank with a strong disincentive to take on too much risk. While the bank could have earned more by taking on more risk, the cost of bankruptcy was substantial; that is, the cost of losing a bank charter may have far outweighed the gain from a risky portfolio strategy. The value of a bank's charter, therefore, reflected the subsidy that was the *quid pro quo* for not taking too much risk. This protective subsidy effectively reversed the risk-return tradeoff facing the banker. The subsidy was high enough so that incurring more risk would lower -- not raise -- the banker's expected return.

The protective subsidy was the cost of successfully containing moral hazard in banking. This cost was manifested by the lack of competition in bank services. What has been labeled 3/6/3 banking characterized the industry for decades -- borrow at 3 percent, lend at 6 percent, and be on the golf course by 3 p.m. -- a good life that

---

[7]The high potential earnings in commercial banking were undoubtedly dissipated, in part, by subsidizing loan rates and by non-price competition for depositors. But the monotonously low failure rate through the 1970s strongly supports the notion that bank owners were still doing well.

presumably few were willing to risk losing, despite the incentives created by deposit insurance.[8]

...BUT THE PROTECTIVE SUBSIDY HAS BEEN ERODED BY COMPETITION

Since 1980 the protective subsidy appears to have lost its effectiveness. Over 800 banks have failed, 522 in the last three years. And a significant part of the savings and loan industry, first-cousin to banking, is facing bankruptcy. (According to unpublished Federal Home Loan Bank reports, on June 30, 1988, 16 percent of all savings and loans were bankrupt on an adjusted regulatory capital basis).

Table 2 clearly illustrates the problem that beset the banking industry in the '80s. As noted earlier, from 1940-79, this country averaged less than seven bank failures per year. By contrast, from 1980-88, an average of about 92 banks failed per year. The data also suggest that most failures prior to 1980 involved relatively small banks. Beginning in 1980 that was no longer true, and in fact a few of the largest banks were getting into trouble. For example, from 1945-54, total assets of closed banks averaged about $5.8 million annually. From 1980-87, total assets of closed banks averaged about $6.2 billion annually. The figures for deposits of closed banks tell the same story. Of course, part of the increase in failed bank asset and liabilities simply reflecs the effects of inflation. But, some of the largest problem banks in the 1980s were reorganized with government assistance, and thus are not included in the Table 2 data.

What went wrong? Why had a previously well-managed problem become difficult to control? What had happened to the protective subsidy? These are complex questions that we may not be able to answer satisfactorily for many years. Nevertheless, at least part of the explanation is clear now. The double-digit inflation experienced in the 1970s opened the door to nonbank competition and within a few years eroded the value of bank charters.

Competition from nonbank financial firms came quickly on the heels of inflation. With higher rates of inflation came higher rates of interest. Once market rates exceeded the maximum rates banks could

[8]The protective subsidy notion is more fully discussed and defended in Benveniste, Boyd and Greenbaum (1988).

offer their depositors, a host of nonbank competitors emerged. Thrift institutions were ammong the first to challenge the commercial banks' monopoly on transaction accounts. Until the mid-1970s it was easy for the public to differentiate banks from

TABLE 2: NUMBER, DEPOSITS AND ASSETS OF INSURED BANKS CLOSED BECAUSE OF FINANCIAL DIFFICULTIES, 1934-1988

		(in millions of dollars)	
Year*	Banks Closed	Total Deposits	Total Assets
1934-39	52.5	49	57
1940-44	17.0	41	47
1945-49	3.0	6	6
1950-54	3.0	12	6
1955-59	3.2	9	8
1960-64	3.2	13	17
1965-69	5.6	44	52
1970-74	4.8	551	1,083
1975-79	10.4	475	564
1980	10	216	236
1981	10	3,826	4,859
1982	42	9,908	11,632
1983	48	5,442	7,027
1984	79	2,883	3,276
1985	120	8,059	8.741
1986	138	6,471	6,992
1987	184	6,282	6,851
1988	200	n.a.	n.a.

Source: Federal Deposit Insurance Corporation.
* Data reported for the years 1934-1979 are annual averages.

thrifts. Banks offered checking accounts and savings accounts; the thrifts offered only savings accounts. In 1972, however, two New England states permitted their mutual saving banks to offer a checking deposit that became known as the NOW account (Negotiable Order of Withdrawal). Several important court decisions supported the view that banks could not be granted a monopoly on the issue of three-party negotiable instruments payable upon demand (i.e., checks). While there were initially limitations on withdrawals, these NOW accounts, unlike demand deposits at banks, paid interest. Not surprisingly, they were an overnight success, as is clearly shown in Table 3. Between 1976 and

1981 NOW accounts grew from $2.7 billion to $78.5 billion. Over the same period demand deposits at banks increased only about 5 percent.

About the same time, the large brokerage houses saw opportunities in this area and began to offer money market mutual funds. In the late 1970s they added checkwriting privileges. Typically, these money market accounts carried a higher rate of interest than NOW accounts but had more restrictions on withdrawals. Table 3 illustrates the success of these funds, which grew from $3.4 billion in 1976 to over $188 billion by 1981.

TABLE 3: BANK DEMAND DEPOSITS AND SUBSTITUTE INSTRUMENTS 1976-1987 (in millions of dollars)

Year	Demand Deposits at Banks	NOW Accounts	Money Market Mutual Funds
1976	231,300	2,700	3,400
1977	247,000	5,000	3,800
1978	261,500	8,400	10,200
1979	270,100	17,000	42,900
1980	274,700	27,400	76,600
1981	243,400	78,500	188,600
1982	246,200	104,100	236,300
1983	251,000	132,200	181,400
1984	253,000	148,200	230,200
1985	276,900	180,900	241,000
1986	314,400	237,300	292,400
1987	298,500	261,600	310,700

Source: Federal Reserve Bulletin, various dates.

New competition hit banking from the asset side of the business as well as the liability side. In the 1970s, foreign commercial banks began capturing a growing share of the U.S. commercial loan business. Many large corporations abandoned banks for their borrowing needs by going directly to the commercial paper market. And nonfinancial firms such as the auto manufacturers and large retailers began a concerted effort to expand their share of the consumer loan markets.

This increased competition did not go unnoticed by the policymakers. To allow banks to compete on a more equal basis, Congress passed the Depository Institutions Deregulation and Monetary Control Act of 1980 (DIDMCA), which called for the most radical changes in banking regulation since the 1930s. The act contained several major provisions designed to allow banks to compete more effectively with their nonbank competitors. Interest rate ceilings on bank deposits were to be phased out over the next several years, and federal reserve requirements were lowered across the board and imposed on all institutions offering insured transaction accounts. (To allow the savings and loan industry to compete, Congress passed the Garn-St.Germain Depository Act of 1982 which allowed a savings and loan to make commercial loans as well as home mortgages.)

In addition to DIDMCA, regulators expanded allowable bank activities. Many states permitted their state-chartered banks to own subsidiaries in other lines of business. The Federal Reserve also was more lenient with bank holding company activities, and an increasing number of securities activities were permitted.[9]

All this competition has had the expected effect on the market value of bank charters. Explicit charter values are not available, but they can be estimated. Since charter values are included in the market value of bank equities and not included in the book value (under standard accounting procedures), the ratio of market to book reflects to some extent the value of a bank charter. As shown in Figure 1, and as expected, the market value of bank equities exceeded the book value from the early 1950s until the early 1970s when the ratio began to decline. By the mid-1970s, market value actually fell below book value where it remains today. Of course, charter values can never fall below zero and, therefore, there must be ome other reasons why bank equities have been selling at such low prices. Most probably, this is due to an overstatement of some book assets due to unrealized loan losses. Nevertheless, several recent studies have documented the decline in bank charter values, and one has presented evidence that banks with below-average charter values have above-average willingness to take risk

---

[9]Continuing this trend, on January 18, 1989, the Board of Governors ruled that five major banking firms could underwrite and deal in corporate debt. The Board also indicated at that time that (if all went well with debt underwriting) it would consider permitting banking concerns to underwrite corporate equities within about a year. In a previous decision (April 30, 1987), the Board approved applications to underwrite commercial paper, mortgage-backed securities, municipal revenue bonds and consumer-related receivables. Even earlier, discount brokerage was determined to be a permissible activity for banking organizations on January 7, 1983.

(Keeley [1988]).

In summary, as banking became less protected from competition and less regulated, the incentive to take on risk increased. Moral hazard, long latent, started to be a force and the results were as expected: banks began reaching for profits by reaching for risk. Even though banks continued to be monitored and supervised by a plethora of government agencies, such regulation proved ineffective in the face of increased competition and the loss of the protective subsidy.

Figure 1
Ratio of Market Value of Equity to Book Value of Equity, 1952-1987

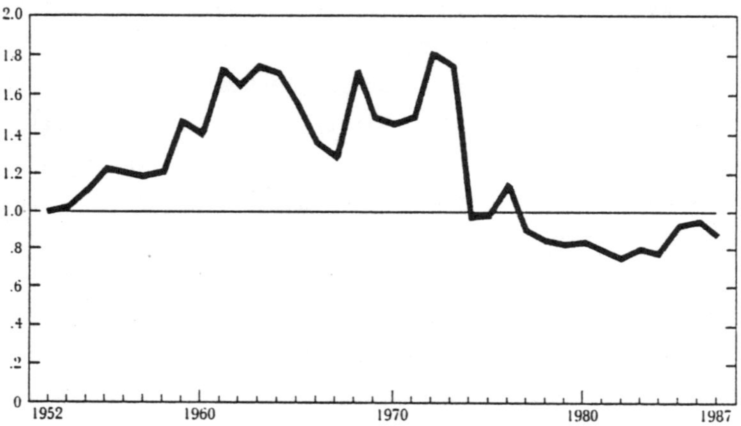

The 25 largest bank holding companies.
Data provided by Federal Reserve Bank of San Francisco.

FIXING DEPOSIT INSURANCE: NO EASY CHOICES

With inflation, competition, deregulation and the resulting decline in the protective subsidy, moral hazard has emerged as a serious concern. Addressing this problem is neither going to be easy nor inexpensive. The approach which appears the most logical, reimposing the regulatory structure that produced the halcyon years before deregulation, is not realistic. Once the doors to competition are opened, closing them is extremely difficult. It would require a severe retrenchment of the entire financial industry.

A realistic solution requires some recognition of the tradeoff between the two inherent problems: the instability in deposit banking versus the moral hazard in deposit insurance. This tradeoff cannot be ignored. Avoiding moral hazard is difficult if deposits are insured, and avoiding depositor instability is difficult if they're not. Because of this tradeoff, there are no perfect or easy answers to either problem. The first-best solution is simply unattainable. Policy proposals which claim to have first-best solutions are simply misguided. Nevertheless, there is a much better answer than our current regulatory framework.

To better understand the choices facing policymakers, consider the two polar options: full-coverage insurance (where all deposits are fully protected), or none at all. The former eliminates instability, but results in moral hazard in the extreme. The policies we have in place today are closest to this option. The latter option eliminates moral hazard, but results in depositor instability in the extreme. This was the policy before 1934, but as noted, the banking system was subject to periodic panics.

Having seen the results of these polar options, we think neither is correct. Rather, the best policy solution lies somewhere between these alternatives. Before presenting our concept of what such a more moderate system might entail, however, we first discuss some recent reform proposals that we view to be ineffective, extremely costly or both. These include 100 percent reserve banking, closing banks before they fail, and risk-adjusting capital or insurance premiums. Then, we turn to proposals that we think are better.

100 PERCENT RESERVE BANKING

One proposal that has been around at least as long as deposit insurance is 100 percent reserve banking. Known today as the narrow banking concept, it takes the regulation of banking to its very limit.[10] Under narrow banking, banks could only invest in safe, liquid assets. (Holding 100 percent cash reserves would obviously satisfy this requirement.) The narrow banking concept would also allow banks to hold short-term Treasury debt as well as noninterest-bearing reserves. On the surface, this proposal appears to solve both the moral hazard

---

[10] 100 percent reserve banking was proposed by Simons (1936) and later by Friedman (1959).

problem and the depositor instability problem at once. Moral hazard is simply regulated away because banks cannot invest in risky assets. Instability is overcome because deposits are 100 percent backed by safe assets -- there is no reason for depositors to lose confidence or to ever fear a bank failure.

Appearances are deceptive. While the narrow banks would be safe, what would happen to all the intermediation (that is, matching of borrowers and lenders) that they did previously as "wide banks"? Intermediation services would still be demanded, and presumably other financial institutions would fill the gap -- operating much like the old wide banks. As such, the new institutions would be prone to depositor instability if they were not insured and moral hazard if they were. The problem, in other words, would not be solved but only shifted to a different part of the financial sector. And if the regulators were able to prevent this shifting, most of the borrowing and lending that was historically performed by banks would be eliminated, a cost that would surely exceed the benefits of narrow banking.

CLOSING BANKS BEFORE THEY FAIL

Another proposal that looks like it would solve both moral hazard and instability with very little cost is to close troubled banks before they go bankrupt (Shadow Financial Regulatory Committee, 1988). The idea here is that if banks are closed when their net worth is close to zero, the insurer's exposure (the administrative costs of closing the bank and selling its assets) is relatively small. Presumably, if banks know they will be closed that quickly, they will also be less prone to take risks. The moral hazard problem then is solved (since the FDIC never takes losses) and depositors' funds are always safe.[11]

Like the narrow banking proposal, the costs of such an arrangement are much greater than they might appear. It's one thing to say troubled banks should be closed before they are bankrupt, but another to put this principle into practice -- that is, to determine precisely when any particular bank should be closed. Regulators currently monitor the net worth of banks; through call reports and formal bank examinations they

---

[11]In theory, at least, the incentive effects of closing banks before they fail are much like those of the protective subsidy.

determine the net worth of banks at least four times a year, an expensive process. And even these data are subject to errors. Evaluating the value of assets that are not traded in a secondary market (such as most commercial loans) is open to considerable uncertainty and sometimes quite arbitrary. Under the proposal to close banks quickly, one would have to monitor banks more frequently and more accurately than we do now, and the costs could well be prohibitive.

Further, the information problem is more complex than identifying low-quality loans. By the very nature of banking, many loans are worth relatively little if sold on the market today, but are in fact good loans with high future payouts. Only if regulators were able to gather the same quality of information the banks have could they make the distinction between short-run and long-run values. This would not only be expensive, but inefficient as well because it would entail a replication of information costs that banks have already incurred.[12]

RISK-ADJUSTED INSURANCE PREMIUMS OR RISK-ADJUSTED CAPITAL REQUIREMENTS

Risk-adjusted insurance premiums or risk-adjusted capital requirements are proposals that also appear to solve the moral hazard problem while keeping deposits safe. In addition, these proposals appear to be market-oriented, for presumably private insurers would charge their riskier customers a higher premium or require larger deductibles. On closer examination, however, the costs of effectively administering such policies would likely be prohibitive, even for private insurers.

To administer a risk-adjusted insurance policy requires some way of accurately assessing risk. And again, there is the cost of some very expensive information. What do private insurance companies do in this situation? In practice, insurance companies generally engage in limited monitoring of risk behavior. Physical examinations, drivers' tests and property inspections are typically required before the insurance is granted, but rarely will the insurer continually monitor the health of a

[12]We are not suggesting that banks should be kept open when all available information indicates that the value of their liabilities exceeds the value of their assets. This policy invites end-gaming strategies on the part of bankrupt institutions, and is in large part to blame for the recent losses of the FSLIC.

patient or the condition of a factory. Given the cost of monitoring, it is likely that private insurers of banks would not operate much differently. Regular monitoring of banks' behavior toward risk is labor-intensive and expensive. And even if the risk could be measured accurately, pricing this risk without market data on the value of bank loans would be difficult and arbitrary.

That is not to say some broad-risk categories could not be established and priced (as age is used, for example, with health and auto insurance). Indeed, the new capital standards established under the Basle Agreements of 1988 feature this sort of rough-and-ready risk categorization.[13] While the new capital standards are surely an improvement over the old, there are still continuing problems. For one thing, by definition, they favor bank investment in some asset categories over others. There is always the danger that these standards may become politicized (here, or in other countries), which could result in a significant misallocation of resources. Moreover, the new capital standards invite loophole exploitation on the part of banks, which have a natural incentive to find (or create) assets which have had their true risk underestimated. In fact, this process is already beginning, and the effectiveness of the capital standards will depend substantially on the authorities' zeal in finding and plugging loopholes. This approach will not help much with the moral hazard problem. Too many arbitrary decisions have to be made, and too many loopholes have to be closed.

NEED TO RELY MORE ON PRIVATE MARKET INVOLVEMENT

We have questioned those proposals that don't face up to the tradeoff between moral hazard and depositor instability. Each of the

---

[13]In 1988, new capital guidelines were announced for banks in the United States and a number of other countries, pursuant to an international agreement in Basle, Switzerland. The Basle Agreement calls for minimum capital of 7.25 percent of assets by the end of 1990 and 8 percent of assets by the end of 1992. The new capital requirements are risk-progressive, at least in terms of asset risk. Five risk classes are established for assets and off-balance sheet items. Each is weighted from 0 to 1.0 with cash and short-term U.S. Treasury bills receiving the lowest weight, whereas most bank loans receive the highest weight. All other assets are assigned weights of 0.1, 0.2, or 0.5, depending on their assessed risk. For a detailed discussion of the Basle Agreement risk classifications, see Federal Reserve System (1988).

above proposals attempts to reduce moral hazard without affecting the safety of bank deposits. That is not possible, at least not at any reasonable cost. These proposals either require exorbitant information costs or don't, in fact, avoid the tradeoff. An effective solution must recognize that there is a tradeoff. The current state of the system is near one extreme; it minimizes the possibility of bank runs at the expense of maximum moral hazard. Since there appears to be no panacea, the tradeoff necessarily means accepting somewhat more depositor instability than is now the case.

The problem, then, is to reform deposit insurance so that there is a better balance between moral hazard and depositor instability. Because the private market tends to allocate resources efficiently, the way to do this is to redesign deposit insurance so that it incorporates features found in most private insurance contracts -- higher deductibles and some degree of co-insurance. This in turn will mean more market discipline of banks and private bearing of risk.

INCREASING THE DEDUCTIBLE

The deductible is one way most insurance contracts are designed to limit the insurance company's loss. Required bank capital, at least from the FDIC's point of view, is the deductible in deposit insurance -- the higher the capital, the lower the FDIC's exposure.

Raising capital requirements would also help reduce moral hazard. It would do this in two ways, and the first is fairly obvious. To the extent that bank owners are risk-averse and cannot completely diversify their investments, more capital helps to offset the incentive to risk-taking because owners have more at stake. The second effect is less direct and considerably more subtle. Other things equal, a higher capital requirement will reduce the expected losses of the FDIC, effectively reducing the net subsidy to banking due to deposit insurance. Reducing this subsidy will cause some shrinkage of the banking industry -- either as banks cut back on marginally profitable lending or as marginally profitable banks are driven out of business. To the extent the industry is made smaller as the insurance subsidy is reduced, so is the moral-hazard problem.

Furthermore, raising capital requirements will bring capital-asset ratios closer to their pre-deposit insurance levels, levels that presumably reflect a more prudent amount of bank capital. Consider the historical bank capital ratios shown in Figure 2. Before 1933, banks held much more capital than they do now. In fact, from 1844 to 1900, average capital ratios exceeded 20 percent of assets. In recent years, the average has been around 6 percent. Figure 3 shows contemporary capital ratios for banks (actually consolidated bank holding companies) in comparison with other financial intermediary firms in different industries. The other industries are generally less regulated than banking and none have deposit insurance. The capital ratios of the nonbank firms are in all cases much higher than in banking. Both data comparisons suggest that were it not for deposit insurance, banks would most likely hold much more capital.

ESTABLISHING CO-INSURANCE

In searching for other ways to mimic a private-market solution to moral hazard, we found an answer in co-insurance.[14] This technique is often used by private insurance companies to control moral hazard. It makes the insured bear some of the cost of a bad outcome and encourages safe behavior. In banking, this will mean some loss of depositor confidence, since only a percentage of deposits would be insured. The tradeoff, as we have noted, however, is unavoidable. At least with co-insurance the tradeoff would be made explicit and the ability to manage the tradeoff should be enhanced.

In many private insurance arrangements there is at least some risk-sharing, which can take a variety of forms, but the most typical is co-insurance. With medical insurance, for example, the insured (after some deductible) may be covered for only 90 percent of expenses. The incentives created by such co-insurance are obvious. The insured are more likely to consider the costs of medical problems. Just as important, the incentives encourage the insured to consider health

[14]We claim no originality for this proposal. In fact, it has some historical precedent. Co-insurance was part of the original deposit insurance plan that was to go into effect on July 1, 1934 (FDIC, p.44). Deposits up to $10,000 for each depositor were to be fully insured, over $10,000 but under $50,000 were to have 75 percent coverage, and over $50,000 only 50 percent coverage. This plan, however, was superseded by a new plan that was part of the Banking Act of 1935 which provided only full coverage up to $5,000.

Figure 2
Commercial Banking Industry Capital/Assets Ratio: 1834–1986

Notes: Series (1) and (2) are from *Historical Statistics of the United States Colonial Times to 1970*. U.S. Dept. of Commerce. USGPO. 1975 which provides a detailed discussion of these data. Series (3) is obtained from the *Federal Reserve Bulletin*, and *FDIC Annual Statistics*, various dates. The definition of the capital account has changed somewhat over time, and it is not possible to construct an absolutely consistent series from 1834 to the present. Generally, however, the capital account includes capital, surplus, net undivided profits, reserves for contingencies, and certain other reserve accounts.

Figure 3
Median Ratio of Equity to Assets, 1971–1984
Bank Holding Companies and Other Financial Firms

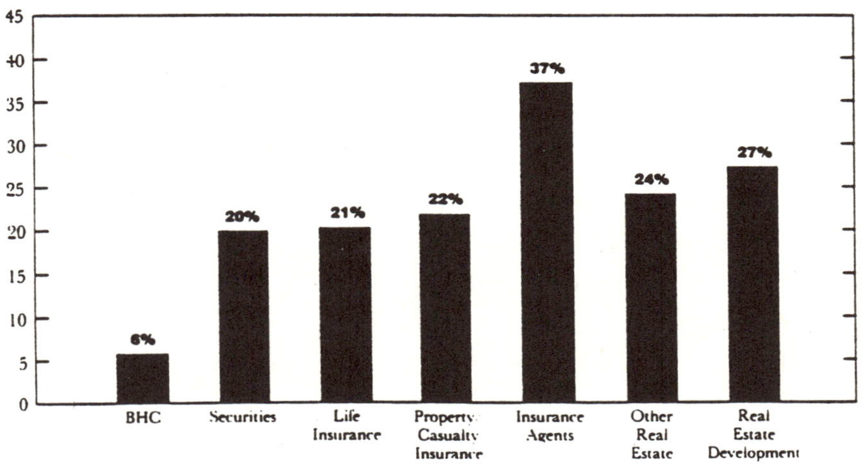

Note: Average ratios are computed for each firm: Medians are reported for each industry.
Source: Boyd and Graham (1988, p. 12)

programs that reduce the need for medical care in the first place.

Co-insurance in banking wouldn't work exactly as it does in the health industry, but the incentive effects would be similar. If deposits were insured only up to 90 percent, for example, all depositors would have an interest in the financial health of their bank. To be competitive with banks that hold relatively safe portfolios, banks that chose riskier portfolios would have to offer their depositors a higher rate of return. Consequently, because risk would now be priced, banks would have less incentive to choose such portfolios and the moral hazard problem would be reduced.

Co-insurance could also be designed to totally protect small savers. For example, the first $10,000 of savings could be 100 percent insured. To avoid the brokering of deposits, this 100 percent insurance limit would apply to the individuals, not to accounts. An individual would be able to identify only one account anywhere that would have this coverage, and anything over this limit (and all funds in other accounts) would be subject to co-insurance.

Some might argue that if we simply enforced the insurance system we have in place today, with its $100,000 ceiling, we could achieve the same result. Of the billions of dollars in deposits, about 23 percent are large, uninsured deposits. In practice, however, regulators have been extremely reluctant to let these relatively few large depositors bear the brunt of a bank failure -- especially when many of them are, themselves, commercial banks.

Two major advantages exist in adopting co-insurance over simply putting teeth in the present $100,000 limit. First, it is a very different situation when all depositors suffer small losses than it is when a few depositors suffer large losses. The likelihood of failures transmitted from one bank to another is greatly reduced. And second, modifying the formal structure of the deposit insurance system would send a strong message to the marketplace (and, for that matter, to regulators) that a real change was taking place. Just announcing a "get tough" policy under the present insurance system is a strategy that has been tried, with very limited success.

TIME INCONSISTENCY: A POLICYMAKER'S DILEMMA

The limited success of the get tough policy is symptomatic of a more general problem. If co-insurance is to mitigate moral hazard, policymakers must confront what is known as the "time inconsistency" dilemma: A policy that is best for the long run may not be best for the short run, and vice versa.[15] Consider the dilemma as it arises with deposit insurance. Once a bank is on the verge of failing, it often appears that the best policy is to protect all depositors, both insured and uninsured. The FDIC can protect all depositors by arranging the purchase and assumption of a troubled bank by a healthy one. For decades this approach was often used because it minimized the FDIC's cost of handling a failing bank. This was the low-cost method, at least partly because in a purchase and assumption transaction the charter value is captured by the FDIC. This approach (or publicly announcing that all depositors will be protected) has the additional advantage that actual or potential bank runs are halted, allowing the reorganization to proceed in an orderly manner.

While such policies may indeed minimize the cost of any particular bank closure, they do not necessarily represent the best long-run policy. That's because the uninsured depositors will learn over time that, whatever is the announced policy, their deposits are actually safe. When that happens, "uninsured depositors" no longer care about bank risk and market discipline is lost. Consequently, there are more bank failures than there would have been, had uninsured depositors not been protected.

Time inconsistency is also a problem in the treatment of large, troubled banks. The current announced policy is that all bank failures are handled under the same set of regulations and general principles. But the announced policy is clearly time-inconsistent, because regulators fear the financial havoc that could result if a large bank were allowed to fail. Quite predictably, the announced policy has not been followed; and just as predictably, it is now widely perceived that all depositors in large banks are fully protected under virtually all circumstances. This market perception confers a significant (albeit unintended) competitive advantage on the largest banks.

For present purposes, the point is obvious. If co-insurance is to

[15]The seminal work on time inconsistency is Kydland and Prescott (1977). For a less technical discussion of this problem, see Chari (1988).

be made effective, it must be time-consistent. That is, the authorities must not protect the uninsured portion of depositors' accounts, whether they're in small banks or large ones. With a system of higher capital ratios and co-insurance, however, FDIC losses would be fewer than with the current system. Thus, the short-run cost advantage of purchase and assumption transactions would be reduced. As far as failing large banks are concerned, losses would be spread across a wide spectrum of depositors, and not concentrated in a relatively few large, uninsured ones. Of course, any depositor's maximum loss would be bounded by the co-insurance percentage limit. Thus, the likelihood of catastrophic losses for a few depositors would be greatly reduced.

Perhaps more important, market discipline would work both before and after the fact. By this we mean that depositors would be more careful, paying some attention to the financial condition of their banks in good times as well as bad. In net, this would tend to concentrate deposits in well-run, lower-risk institutions, unlike the present system. Smaller banks would be more careful about leaving balances of several times their capital in correspondents, and so on. For all these reasons, the dangers of permitting a large bank failure would be greatly reduced.

CONCLUSION

We have argued that deposit insurance should be reformed to better reflect private insurance principles and to encourage market discipline. This implies more direct market involvement in bearing bank risk. Through higher deductibles (capital requirements) and co-insurance, shareholders and depositors will have an increased stake in the soundness of their banks.

This proposal has the significant advantage of gradual implementation with modification to the present system. As Professor Robert Lucas, University of Chicago, once observed,

> ... attempting various policies that may be proposed on actual economies and watching the outcome must not be taken as a serious solution method: Social experiments on the grand scale may be instructive and admirable, but they are best admired at a distance. (Lucas, [1983, p.288].)

Our proposed changes can be implemented on a small scale and carefully, thus avoiding the obvious risks of massive regulatory upheaval. Capital requirements can be raised gradually and with advance warning to the industry. Similarly, co-insurance can be phased in as deemed appropriate. For example, we could adopt a system of 100 percent deposit insurance up to $10,000 and co-insurance for any greater deposit balances, say 2 percent the first year and increasing by a percent or so each year after that. The point is, the initial co-insurance burden of depositors would be small (raising their risk consciousness a bit) but hardly reducing their insurance coverage. An important and difficult question is: How large should the fractional co-insurance burden of depositors ultimately become? We do not pretend to know the answer, and it will surely require an analysis beyond the scope of this essay.

WHO WOULD GAIN AND WHO WOULD LOSE

This proposal, even if fully successful in containing moral hazard and correcting a potentially costly problem, will not necessarily benefit everyone. Some will benefit more than others, and some will be worse off than they are under the current system. Who would gain and who would lose? Those made better off would include the FDIC, the taxpayers and some commercial banks. The FDIC would be an obvious winner, since its insurance liabilities would be directly reduced. How would this benefit the taxpayers? As the U.S. public is in the process of painfully discovering, the taxpayers ultimately stand behind federal deposit insurance, the $100 billion estimated loss of the FSLIC being a case in point. Since our recommended changes would make the FDIC stronger and less likely to become insolvent, all taxpayers would benefit. Moreover, since an essential aspect of our proposal is that all banks operate under the same capital and co-insurance rules -- meaning that no bank is too big to fail -- smaller banking organizations, which currently are confronted with unfair and unfortunate competition, would also benefit.

All banks would lose to the extent the expected losses of the FDIC were lowered, thus reducing the net susidy to the banking industry. Banks, and of course depositors, would also lose the blanket insurance protection now offered depositors, making them less competitive with the myriad of uninsured savings instruments. With a better system of deposit insurance in place, though, bank powers could be expanded with less concern about soundness issues, that is, less concern that moral hazard was being spread to nonbank lines of business.

On balance, the benefits of this proposal far outweigh the costs. That there will be costs and that they cannot be avoided should be clear. We see no way to make progress on moral hazard without increasing the potential for depositor instability. If the experience in the savings and loan industry, however, is any indication of the potential problems in banking, some tradeoff is warranted.

REFERENCES

Association of Reserve City Bankers, 1988. *Beyond Capital Regulation: Strengthening the FDIC Insurance Fund and Systematic Liquidity.* Recommendations of the Special Task Force, Asset Liability Committee (March), Chicago.

Benveniste, Larry, John H.Boyd and Stuart Greenbaum, 1988. Bank Capital Regulation. Monograph prepared for Association of Reserve City Bankers, Banking Research Center, Conference on Bank Capital Issues, December 14-16, Northwestern University, Evanston, Ill.

Boyd, John H. and Stanley L.Graham, 1988. The Profitability and Risk Effects of Allowing Bank Holding Companies to Merge with other Financial Firms: A Simulation Study. *Quarterly Review*, Federal Reserve Bank of Minneapolis (Spring), 3-20.

Chari, V.V., 1988. Time Consistency and Optimal Policy Design, *Quarterly Review*, Federal Reserve Bank of Minneapolis, (Fall), 17-31.

Federal Deposit Insurance Corporation, 1984. *The First Fifty Years.* Washington, D.C.

Federal Reserve System, 1988. Capital: Risk-Based Capital Guidelines. 12CFR Part 225, Appendix B [Regulation Y: docket #R-0628].

Friedman, Milton, 1960. *A Program for Monetary Stability.* New York, New York, Fordham University Press.

Friedman, Milton and Anna J.Schwartz, 1963. *A Monetary History of the United States, 1867-1960*, Princeton, New Jersey, University Press.

Kareken, John H., 1983. Deposit Insurance Reform or Deregulation is the Cart not the Horse. *Quarterly Review*, Federal Reserve Bank of Minneapolis (Spring), 1-9.

Keeley, Michael, C., 1988. Deposit Insurance, Risk, and Market Power in Banking Working Paper No.88-07, Federal Reserve Bank of San Francisco.

Kydland, Finn, E. and Edward, C.Prescott, 1977. Rules Rather than Discretion: The Inconsistency of Optimal Plans. *Journal of Political Economy* 85 (June), 473-91.

Lucas, Robert E.Jr., 1981. *Studies in Business-Cycle Theory.* Cambridge Massachusetts, The MIT Press.

Shadow Financial Regulatory Committee. An Outline of a Program for Deposit Insurance Reform. December 5, 1988. Statement No.38. Mid America Institute for Public Policy Research, Chicago.

Simons, Henry, 1936. Rules Versus Authorities in Monetary Policy. *Journal of Political Economy*, 44 (February), 1-30.

A CASE FOR REFORMING FEDERAL DEPOSIT INSURANCE

by: John H.Boyd and Arthur J.Rolnick

<u>Discussant</u>: Dan Peled, Technion

I am glad for the opportunity to discuss Art's paper, which you might want to know, is on my required reading list in a graduate course on Financial Intermediation. Boyd and Rolnik (B&R hereafter) have presented a careful and quite thorough review of the possible alternatives facing a government backed deposit insurance, and came up with some interesting suggestions that rely on experience gained with insurance in other markets.

But, regardless of how much you like B&R's recommendations, and I have some reservations that I will discuss later, you must admire the crystal clear exposition in that paper of the inherent dilemma in deposit insurance: "Avoiding moral hazard is difficult if deposits are insured, and avoiding depositors' instability is difficult if they are not."

Can this vicious cycle be broken? Should the fight to break it go on? The one thing that comes out loud and clear from B&Rs analysis is that you cannot continue with the current FDIC and deregulate the banks. The incentive conflict has just become too costly.

As I see it, there are three basic questions pertaining to deposit insurance:

1. Should demand deposits be insured?
2. If so, how such insurance should be managed?
3. Should the government be providing that insurance?

I will briefly discuss the main ingredients of B&Rs solutions, and then go on to comment more generally on the above questions, in light of what theory has to tell us, and by taking one step further the idea of drawing analogies from another field where government involvement is massive, albeit different.

B&R provide many insights on the second question, after a short discussion of the first, which essentially relies on the bank panics that have occurred between 1863 and 1907 to derive a positive answer to it. They hardly touch upon the third question. In a sense, their answer is: 'Yes, deposit insurance is necessary for maintaining stability of the banking system, but its risk-invariant premium tends to exacerbate the problem it tries to resolve. Preventing these adverse incentives by the government would be too costly - so let us pass the buck to the public directly. Let us have co-insurance features in deposit insurance, which will provide the public with sufficient incentives to monitor banks' portfolios, thus reducing the FDIC direct insurance liabilities, as well as, hopefully, reducing the risks it is insuring depositors against.'

I am not sure that this solution is all that effective: If there are any increasing returns in monitoring banks' portfolios, and I think a case can be made for that viewpoint, then spreading these costs over a large number of uncoordinated depositors is surely not going to reduce monitoring costs. And if one assumes that the public will not invest the necessary resources to learn enough about banks' portfolios, then we haven't achieved anything.

The second major component of their proposal is, raising the required capital to assets ratio in commercial banks. Here, the figures reported by B&R comparing C/A ratios across different types of financial intermediaries are really striking: 7% in banks, vs. over 20% on other financial firms. Could it be that banks can attract deposits and be profitable despite having such a low C/A ratio, because the FDIC induces confidence in depositors' hearts, confidence that would require much higher C/A ratio absent the FDIC?

It seems to me that the conclusion thus far is: If you want deposit insurance at a premium that is independent of portfolio risks - you should have tough regulations accompanying it. But do you want deposit insurance in the first place? Here I have more questions than answers.

Basically there are two distinct, although related, risks that a banking system faces. One is the idiosyncratic risk that every business faces, that of mistaken decisions by corporate officers. In the case of banks these can be innocent mistakes, mistakes due to incompetence, or malicious and criminal actions by bank officers, primarily in the selection of bank assets. However, once such a bad portfolio causes the collapse of a particular bank - other banks, or for that matter, other businesses not connected with that particular bank, need not be affected in a serious way. Viewed in this way this risk seems insurable, and in fact might be more easily insured the smaller are the banks in the system, the more independent they are, and the larger is their number, (here are some arguments in favor of no-branching policy).

The second type of risk has to do with the inherent instability of the whole banking system, and here the reason is simply the fractional reserve nature of such depository institutions. A case can be made for government or other central intervention in reducing this risk, but it should be kept distinct from the first. A casual look at other countries will suggest that some form of government backing of banks exists in most countries. And more often than not, this backing is implicit. A combined insurance system that aims at mitigating both risks simultaneously is rather rare. Admittedly, as banks become more interdependent, the two types of risks become more entangled, but I still think that it is important to keep the two conceptually distinct.

Still, some important questions about the need to protect depository institutions remain open in my mind: There is almost a continuum of types of transaction accounts: demand deposit, transferable time deposits, money market mutual funds, government securities mutual funds with check writing privileges, corporate bonds mutual funds with similar privileges, etc. Why single out one extreme end of these accounts for special insurance?

Second, recent theoretical work on deposit insurance does not seem to converge on any answer to the first question above, and certainly not to the third one. You have theoretical models demonstrating that deposit insurance is a distortion, and bank regulation just limits its size (Bryant and Wallace, JPE 1980, Kareken and Wallace, J. of Bus. 1978). Then you have other works showing how useful deposit insurance can be, and that the government may be the only one to be able to deliver it (Diamond and Dybvig, JPE 1983, Bryant, J. of Banking and Finance 1980). Along comes Jackline (1985) and shows that if you generalize Diamond and Dybvig's model slightly, you lose not only the role for government insurance, but also demand deposits altogether. Then comes more work that argues that if you take the "first-come-first-served" feature of banks seriously, the government is incapable of insuring demand deposits (Wallace, Mpls.Fed.Quart.Rev. 1989), while others who abandon that feature entirely (Bental, Eckstein and Peled 1989) come up justifying some sort of governmental intervention. It is obvious that theory alone will not be able to tell us which of the theoretical setups fits more closely the world in which we live, and hence theory alone will not tell us which conclusion about deposit insurance, and who should provide it, is more appropriate.

But let us follow B&R, in examining the practice of medicine and health related insurance markets, to see if there are any lessons to be learned there. Although not completely analogous, some implications may be enlightening:

1. A large part of medical insurance in the U.S. is provided privately in various forms.

Implication: deposit insurance can be provided privately.

A possible objection may be related to the contagious nature of bank failures, which, of course, contradicts the statistical independence of the insured events which underlies any insurance business. Too little is known about validity of this contention, although a casual look at history certainly suffices for not dismissing it. The problem with historical anecdotes is that they rarely involve pure experiments, and the same episode can have different meanings interpreted in light of different models.

Somehow we want to protect ourselves against massive bank panic, yet avoid the apparent incentives such insurance provides for too risky banks' portfolios. Maybe we should separate the two risks, and let the private sector handle the insurable one, and the government the uninsurable one. In any case, the possibility of private provision of deposit insurance, at least monitoring, merits some consideration. This is especially true for the U.S., with over 14,000 commercial banks (resulting no doubt from no-branching regulation), and private corporations specializing in evaluating fixed commitments and their issuers.

2. The government licenses physicians regulates what they do and how they do it, but does not feel obliged to back or subsidize their liability insurance.

Implication: the government can regulate banks without insuring them.

3. Do we see too little medical care resulting from absent government mal-practice insurance? Even the observation that such insurance

premiums have sky-rocketed has found adequate answers by the private sector, for instance in the form of HMOs.

Implication: we may have too much by way of checkable deposits now. Is it necessarily good that S&L liabilities are federally insured?

4. Co-insurance may be effective in controlling routine excessive medical expenses. But when it comes to major procedures, insurance companies want to evaluate the situation themselves, not delegate the monitoring to the patient.

Implication: small co-insurance incentives to depositors may help the weeding out of obvious frauds which are easy to detect anyway. More subtle problems with bank asset management may still require professional monitoring.

Finally we should remember the overall picture with government-guaranteed loans - the "$5 trillion bailout shock" as Newsweek has recently labelled it. Farmers, homeowners, students, S&L depositors, etc. are presenting the government with ever-increasing insurance liability which is inadequately reported in the government budget, but poses a serious threat in any one's mind. The B&R proposals to limit deposit insurance liabilities are certainly in the right direction. They just do not seem to go far enough.

9 MONETARY CONTROL AND EXCHANGE MARKET MANAGEMENT: GERMAN POLICY EXPERIENCE FROM THE 1985 PLAZA AGREEMENT TO THE 1989 SUMMIT OF THE ARCH

Hermann-Josef Dudler

I. DOMESTIC MONETARY MANAGEMENT UNDER EXTERNAL CONSTRAINTS AS A "LEITMOTIV" OF GERMAN CENTRAL BANKING

For more than three decades, apparent conflicts between domestic and external requirements of monetary management have been a recurrent topic for debate on central bank policy-making in Germany. While such issues are not unfamiliar to other major central banks, German experience in this field has tended to exhibit specific national characteristics. Administered by a central bank, which enjoys a rare degree of legal and factual political independence, German monetary policy has traditionally aimed at a particularly ambitious degree of domestic price stability as its overriding ultimate objective. During the first 40 years of its existence the Deutsche Mark lost only 2.7% of its domestic purchasing power per annum, while its external value rose by 130% since 1950. Together with a small number of other countries with comparable policy preferences, notably Japan, Switzerland and the Netherlands, this low inflation standard placed post-war Germany within a short time into an internationally exposed position.

Unlike Japan, Germany abandoned administrative methods of monetary control and most restrictions on external capital flows at an early stage and soon became a leading world exporter in the post-war reconstruction period. This produced a high degree of "openness" of the economy already since the late 1950s. At the same time, Germany was too small to impose its policy preferences on the rest of the world like a US-style "dominant player"; however, unlike Switzerland and the Netherlands, it was at the same time too big to see its national policy choices in the field of domestic and external monetary management readily tolerated by the international community. This placed the Federal Republic and the Deutsche Bundesbank frequently into the position of a conspicuous international <u>"island" or "fortress" of stability</u> and strongly influenced monetary policy-making procedures in

Germany since about the second half of the 1950s. During the past three decades, domestic monetary management generally aimed at preserving the integrity of the Deutsche Mark as a "hard currency" in the longer-run, while yielding temporarily to the impact of huge capital inflows or exchange rate pressures, especially when rigid internal monetary control appeared to conflict with domestic employment concerns or political commitments in the field of international financial diplomacy.

Under the Bretton-Woods adjustable-peg system Germany's conservative financial policies, the rapid rebuilding of an efficient industrial base and its exceptional cost and price performance favored the generation of "chronic" current account surpluses. Already in the second half of the 1950s exports of goods and services claimed close to 20% of Germany's output, and its current external surplus was equivalent to around $2\frac{1}{2}\%$ of GNP. Due to early steps towards financial liberalization and the growing international role of the Deusche Mark, German money and capital markets quickly became a target of interest-rate induced and speculative "hot money" inflows and the main harbor for funds leaving the US dollar during the terminal stages of the Bretton-Woods system. The Bundesbank was thus confronted with recurring dilemma situations in which the efficient control of domestic monetary conditions and inflation was rendered more and more difficult due to excessive increases in Germany's real foreign balance, direct price arbitrage in goods and services traded with high-inflation economies, and destabilizing capital inflows. The economy experienced major "stabilization crises" triggered typically by the spectre of "imported inflation" in 1956-57, 1960-61, 1968-69 and 1970-71. Such developments typically prompted temporary departures from conservative practices of monetary control, massive sterilized foreign exchange purchases, the introduction of partial capital import restrictions, and revaluations (1961 and 1969) or unilateral floating episodes (1969 and 1971) of the Deutsche Mark (see Emminger (1976)).

The subsequent period of "managed floating", for which the collapse of the traditional key currency role of the US dollar in 1972-73 paved the way, removed the rigid constraints on domestic monetary management inherent in the fixed parity system. The Deutsche Mark was allowed to move flexibly in response to apparent changes in economic fundamentals and lasting "underlying" market pressures. This served, in particular, to avoid a continued tendency of the German price level to adjust to the higher world inflation rate and to ward off persistent capital inflows.

Reconciliation of domestic policy priorities with exchange rate constraints or commitments, nevertheless, remained a permanent and often complicated task for the bundesbank after 1973 (cf. Deutsche Bundesbank 1983). The authorities recognized that floating exchange rates could not completely insulate the domestic economy from international price, demand and financial shocks. They even had to admit that floating rates developed disconcerting signs of inherent, medium-term instability. The real external value of the Deutsche Mark went up by more than 40% against the US dollar and by $7\frac{1}{2}\%$ against all major currencies between early 1973 and end-1979, and it declined again by more than 50% and 20% respectively from early 1980 until March 1985. In relation to freely floating major currencies, predominantly the US dollar, heavy official exchange market interventions were therefore undertaken and discretionary monetary policy adjustments made from time to time to smooth out erratic exchange rate movements and counteract tendencies of the real exchange rate of the Deutsche Mark to over or undershoot its presumed longer-run "equilibrium level". As a further reaction to the excessive volatility of floating rates, formal exchange rate agreements and commitments were undertaken by Germany and its closest trading partners within the framework of the European bloc-floating ("snake") arrangements and, since 1979, the European Monetary System (EMS). These institutional innovations also gave rise to sizeable movements in official exchange reserves (see illustration 8) and significant modifications in domestic monetary policy-making. Moreover, during the past 10 to 15 years money, capital and exchange markets were increasingly characterized by short-run forward-asset-pricing behavior, rapid dissemination and processing of relevant economic and political "news", and a far-reaching process of deregulation and global integration of national financial systems.

In response to these post-1973 challenges, the Bundesbank developed an innovative framework for monetary policy-making based on explicit and flexible monetary targeting techniques. Following the collapse of the Bretton-Woods system, it attempted to systematically exploit the advantages of floating exchange rates in order to re-establish its credibility as a low-inflation and tight-money institution in accordance with traditional German standards. Germany's subsequent commitments in the framework of the EMS were, on the whole, not inconsistent with this objective. The Deutsche Mark appreciated, on average, vis-a-vis other EMS currencies by about 4% per annum, i.e. broadly in line with Germany's better inflation performance (see illustration 11). Severe external policy constraints originated, however, from the excessive medium-term gyrations of the Deutsche Mark/US dollar rate (see illustration 10) and the changing behavior of financial markets. These influences forced the Bundesbank to adjust its monetary control procedures quite substantially during the ten years preceding the recent period of intensified international monetary cooperation.

By about the mid-1980s the Bundesbank's monetary targeting framework, which had been modified almost continuously in a "trial and error" process, appeared to be sufficiently robust so as to allow the authorities to combine the control of the money stock and longer-run "core" inflation with temporary discretionary reactions to external disturbances and other exogenous shocks (see Schlesinger (1985)). The policy period following the Group of Five Plaza Agreement of September 1985 and the Louvre Accord of February 1987 did, therefore, not represent a departure into hitherto uncharted territory, it rather prompted a flexible - albeit somewhat extreme - use of existing policy arrangements. Before reviewing the recent policy episode (section III) and the prospects for better international coordination of exchange rate and monetary management (section IV), the main features of established domestic monetary control procedures and their reconciliation with the requirements of exchange market management will be described in the following section II.

II. THE EVOLUTION OF POLICY PROCEDURES UNTIL THE MID-1980s

a. The Basic Policy Framework

Shortly after the transition to floating exchange rates, i.e. at the end of 1974, the Bundesbank started as the first central bank the practice of publicly announcing annual monetary growth targets. This partly reflected a subtle impact of the monetarist doctrine on the thinking of German central bankers and their economic advisors. The more immediate causes of this shift in policy regime can, however, be traced back to the Bundesbank's desire to visibly regain control over internal monetary conditions, the domestic inflation rate and the general price climate. Due to massive capital inflows, the destablizing impact of rising global inflation, the repercussions of the first oil shock, and unchecked domestic wage and price pressures, the Bundesbank's reputation as an efficient "guardian of the currency" had suffered badly during the final years of the fixed parity system. In 1973-74 the cost of living index rose by 7% (an inflation rate last recorded during the 1951 Korean war crisis in Germany), and wages and salaries advanced at double-digit rates (far in excess of the 3% trend growth in productivity). By publishing an intelligibly tight, intermediate monetary objective for 1975 (see illustration 3), the Bundesbank demonstrated its firm resolve to gradually wind down the rate of inflation and break the public's anticipation of a never ending price/wage spiral. Apart from facilitating public monitoring of the non-accommodating conduct of monetary management, the newly established targeting framework served to gain the cooperation of both sides of industry and the government in the common fight against inflation.

The apparent stabilization gains derived from this approach after 1975 and the particular appeal it had to an inflation-averse German society may help to explain, why its basic features could be retained until today. Unchanged principal elements of the original framework include the following points:

- the explicit derivation of annual growth objectives for the broadly defined money stock from medium-term macroeconomic relationships (the estimated increase in real potential output, a normative - "unavoidable" or "tolerable" - inflation rate, and structural changes in velocity);
- temporary, discretionary departures from the medium-term "rule" facilitating the absorption of large exogenous shocks;
- a two-stage implementation procedure, in which short-run manipulations of key money market rates and bank reserves serve to achieve annual monetary objectives and the ultimate policy goal of noninflationary growth.

Accidental and technical features of the Bundesbank's policy base, such as the definition of the broad money stock (see illustration 4), the numerical presentation of annual objectives, and control procedures in the money market, changed over time. Moreover, the binding nature of the targeting framework was sometimes called into question, in particular during periods, when the Bundesbank attached particular weight to external policy concerns. However, each time the economy was confronted with serious inflation risks (i.e. the years 1975-76, 1979-80 and 1989-90) the Bundesbank successfully exploited its basic monetary targeting procedures for launching an anti-inflationary policy campaign and evoking the consensus spirit of the German public.

b) Reconciliation of Domestic and External Policy Requirements

As already indicated, the Bundesbank often had to take exchange rate disturbances as well as international financial commitments into account when implementing its basic policy approach after the transition to a floating rate regime. To this end it partly resorted to - largely "sterilized" - exchange market intervention.

1. Intervention policies

"Active" or discretionary intervention has taken place almost exclusively in the US dollar/Deutsche Mark spot market, in which the Bundesbank and the US monetary authorities jointly or separately intervene. Two main purposes of such foreign exchange operations may be discerned:

(i) Short-lived "smoothing" operations. These aim at the maintenance of orderly market conditions. Given their limited scale and duration, such transactions do not normally conflict with domestic monetary management.

(ii) Sustained massive purchases or sales of US dollars. These were sometimes made in order to dampen pronounced tendencies of the Deutsche Mark to overshoot or undershoot its desired level (cf. illustration 7). Such intervention activities, for which the DM 35 billion dollar purchases in 1977-78 and the DM 40 billion dollar sales in 1980-81 provided characteristic examples, are typically combined with policies of domestic monetary ease and restraint respectively, with the latter addressing the macroeconomic disturbances originating from excessive currency appreciation or depreciation (see section II.b.2 below).

"Passive" or quasi-automatic intervention can result from obligatory official sales and purchases of EMS currencies, whenever these reach their stipulated upper or lower limit vis-a-vis the Deutsche Mark, or results from voluntary, so-called intramarginal, official Deutsche Mark dealings (see illustration 8). The latter operations are initiated by EMS central banks other than the Bundesbank and normally bypass its books, since they are mostly effected with the help of official Deutsche Mark deposits held in the Euromarket. At least until the mid-1980s, sizeable EMS interventions tended to be rather short-lived or reversible; the conduct of domestic monetary management was therefore rarely seriously hampered by Germany's participation in the exchange rate mechanism (ERM) of the European Monetary System.

2. Monetary policy adjustments

The Bundesbank never felt that largely "sterilized" exchange market intervention could, by itself, exert a lasting impact on the exchange rate or break underlying market trends strongly working in the direction of apparent over or undershooting of the Deutsche Mark. In order to effectively cope with destabilizing exchange rate pressures or shield domestic monetary management from undesired external repercussions, the Bundesbank therefore had to develop sufficiently flexible policy implementation procedures.[1] To this end, the Bundesbank adopted a number of "tactical" expedients (to deal with minor external irritations) and a "mixed" strategy of "conditional" monetary targeting (for absorbing large real exchange rate shocks). "Tactical" adjustments in day-to-day monetary policy-making have generally been confined to technical modifications which leave the traditional targeting framework unimpaired. In contrast, "mixed" strategies typically entailed sustained discretionary or pre-announced deviations from the Bundesbank's medium-term monetary growth rate norms.

"Tactical" policy adjustments can, to some extent, be made quite readily in the Bundesbank's familiar targeting framework. The Bundesbank has always tended to tolerate short-run aberrations of monetary growth from the projected target path, and annual monetary objectives were often announced in the form of 2 to 3 percentage point target ranges (see illustration 3). Such implementation practices leave

[1] An early empirical framework for money stock control in an open economy was presented in Deutsche Bundesbank (1983). This was updated in several respects by Dudler (1988).

considerable elbow-room for transitory exchange rate pressures to be reflected in domestic monetary conditions. Moreover, the Bundesbank shifted the choice of policy instruments deliberately away from its traditional heavy weapons (discount and lombard rate, minimum reserve requirements, rediscount quotas) and, instead, preferred the flexible use of short-term open market operations (see illustration 1). Shifts in money market rates and bank reserves (see illustrations 2 and 6) can now be engineered in miniscule increments, more frequently and with weaker announcement effects, and official foreign exchange transactions sterilized more smoothly. These innovations at the instrument level also took account of the fact that forward-looking international money and exchange markets have become quite sensitive to changes in monetary policy and in many cases react excessively to any type of relevant new information or "surprise".

"Mixed" policy strategies, which combine long-term money stock control considerations with short to intermediate-run exchange rate concerns, were adopted repeatedly by the Bundesbank, when monetary policy was confronted with sustained, pronounced fluctuations of the real US dollar/Deutsche Mark rate and the real trade-weighted value of the Deutsche Mark. Depending on the initial or prevailing macroeconomic conditions, real exchange rate shocks sometimes tended to throw the domestic economy off course, entailing the clear risk that the authorities could miss their ultimate medium-term objectives for noninflationary growth. In such circumstances, i.e. when abnormal appreciation or depreciation pressures distorted the real exchange rate, the Bundesbank tolerated a lasting overshooting of annual monetary targets (1977-78 and 1986-87) or monitored monetary growth consistently towards the lower end of wide annual target ranges (1980-81).[2] The main purpose of these adjustments was to apply stabilizing monetary "countershocks" mitigating the deflationary or inflationary repercussions of lasting exchange rate aberrations on the domestic economy while simultaneously influencing the exchange rate in a desired

[2]From 1979 until 1983 the Bundesbank specified the domestic and external conditions in advance under which it was prepared to gear monetary growth toward the upper or lower limits of annual target "corridors", with the middle of the range corresponding to a medium-term "rules-guided" policy.

direction.

Such "strategic" shifts in monetary policy were rarely made in direct response to exogenous disturbances, such as real interest rate or monetary growth rate changes abroad, international fiscal imbalances or oil price shocks; nor did the authorities commit monetary management to pursuing numerically specified exchange rate objectives. Policy-makers hesitated to react as long as there seemed to be a chance that exogenous disturbances or the concomitant real exchange rate movements could reverse themselves within a reasonable time. Moreover, the authorities were always aware of the fact that pronounced departures from their medium-term monetary norms could entail credibility losses and destabilizing side-effects in the long-run, if "activist" policy moves were not reversed in time. Only when it became clear to the Bundesbank and the general public that real exchange rate aberrations were threatening to seriously disrupt domestic economic developments through violent shifts in foreign trade prices, international competitiveness and real incomes, monetary policy was conducted in a shock-absorbing manner. Despite these cautious official attitudes, "activist" externally motivated policy shifts were not always entirely free from "overreactions" on the part of policy makers and, in some instances, partly reflected the influence of public opinion and international "peer pressures".[3]

III. POLICY EXPERIENCE AFTER THE 1985 PLAZA AGREEMENT

a. Monetary Policy on a "tight-rope walk"

The framework for Bundesbank policy-making presented in the previous section was seriously strained in the wake of the heavy exchange rate disturbances characterizing the second half of the 1980s. During much of this period the Bundesbank had to attach increasing weight to external policy considerations. It overshot its monetary targets for three consecutive years, namely in 1986, 1987 and 1988, a period during which the Deutsche Mark for a long time threatened to appreciate excessively. By reacting to these pressures with a prolonged policy of monetary ease, the Bundesbank partly responded also to

[3]A well-known example is discussed by Putnam and Henning (1989).

domestic recession fears, since turbulences in the exchange market contributed to a temporary breakdown of business confidence in 1986-87 (see illustration 12).

This scenario closely resembled macroeconomic conditions prevailing ten years previously, which the Bundesbank had, at the time, countered with a "mixed" expansionary monetary strategy. Since the earlier policy experiment was followed somewhat later by an inflationary boom and entailed some loss of reputation for the monetary authorities, they were initially reluctant to duplicate such an exercise in the latter half of the 1980s. Policy coordination efforts at the Group of Seven (G-7) and European Community (EC) levels and international "peer pressure" served to mitigate the Bundesbank's reservations.

The G-5 Plaza Agreement of September 1985, the G-7 Louvre Accord of February 1987 and its subsequent restatements as well as European efforts to strengthen the EMS (Basle/Nyborg 1987) inaugurated an era of intensified economic and monetary cooperation among governments and central banks of major industrial countries. The authorities essentially agreed, on the one hand, to promote long-run noninflationary growth and to reduce major external imbalances through mutually consistent macro and microeconomic policies. On the other hand, efforts were made to cooperate closely in the exchange market.

This was, on principal grounds, a desirable development, since incompatible policy approaches, destabilizing monetary and fiscal policy combinations, and external strategies of "benign neglect" among the largest economies had greatly contributed to the outbreak of exchange rate disturbances in the course of the 1980s. The Bundesbank was determined, however, to reject binding exchange rate commitments which would have forced major central banks to indefinitely defend narrowly perceived target ranges for the biggest currencies. Given its traditional skepticism as to the effectiveness of pure exchange market intervention, the political uncertainties attaching to general economic and budgetary policy commitments in the framework of G-7 "multilateral surveillance" and the empirical vagaries of exchange rate determination, the Bundesbank firmly defended the principle that domestic price stabilization should unambiguously be regarded as the primary task of monetary policy. In practice, German monetary policy attempted to strike a reasonable balance between the longer-term requirements of inflation and domestic monetary control and short-run pressing needs for coordinated exchange rate management and the promotion of internal demand growth.

This "balancing act" implied that the Bundesbank continued to set annual monetary targets in accordance with traditional medium-term norms, although chances for implementing them successfully were generally small during the years 1986-1988 in view of the existing external constraints. By sticking to familiar monetary yardsticks, the authorities wished to ensure that long-run inflation risks associated with a prolonged period of excessive monetary growth would not be overlooked. At the same time, domestic cost and price developments continued to be monitored closely. Moderate developments in world raw material prices, the decline of the US dollar, the 1986 oil price collapse, domestic wage moderation and unutilized capacity margins helped to restrain immediate inflation dangers during most of the period (see illustration 13). With changes in the cost of living index receding to -0.1% (in 1986), +0.2% (in 1987) and + $1\frac{1}{4}\%$ (in 1988) and Germany's underlying inflation rate hovering around, perhaps, some $1\frac{1}{2}\%$ to 2%, the Bundesbank saw some lasting leeway for easy monetary policies.

Between early 1986 and the end of 1987 the Bundesbank lowered its key lending rates to unusually low levels. At $2\frac{1}{2}\%$ the discount rate touched an all time record low in the history of nation-wide German central banking (see illustration 5). However, long-term interest rates exhibited a high degree of downward "stickiness". The average yield on domestic bonds oscillated around the 6% level during the years 1986-1988, and in the first half of 1988 the spread between short and long yields widened abnormally to more than 3 percentage points. Broadly starting in 1986, domestic holders of financial wealth ceased to newly invest in longer-term Deutsche Mark-instruments while private and public long-term borrowers preferred to raise funds at fixed coupon rates at the long end of the home market. These "liquidity trap" phenomena suggest that the Bundesbank's policies of sustained monetary ease were not received with a high degree of credibility at home and that the central bank's attempts to stimulate domestic demand in order to facilitate the international adjustment process may not have been very successful.[4]

As a consequence, the main short-run impact of the "mixed" expansionary strategy pursued after 1985 probably ran through the exchange rate. Together with net foreign exchange purchases of Deutsche Mark 40 billion in 1987, monetary relaxations contributed to a gradual return of confidence in the functioning of the global exchange rate system especially after the Louvre Accord and the 1987 stock exchange crash. Moreover, large-scale interventions in EMS currencies and visible attempts at closer coordination of monetary policies among participants of the ERM served to impart a high degree of stability to the EMS, which saw its last realignment in January 1987. These factors are likely to have strengthened business confidence and encouraged a recovery of corporate investment in Germany.

On the other hand, the policy-induced reduction of exchange rate risks, the build-up of excess liquidity in Germany and the maintenance of low German interest rates in the face of monetary tightening abroad contributed to the subsequent prolonged period of "abnormal" weakness of the Deutsche Mark.[5] Between the end of 1987 and mid-1989 the real overall depreciation of the Deutsche Mark amounted to 6%, that against the US dollar alone $13\frac{1}{2}\%$ and that against EC currencies 4%. This maladjustment pushed up import cost in the course of 1988 and improved Germany's international competitiveness. Both effects were embarrassing, since a sharp rise in German exports to European trading partners had already led to an unexpected, slightly inflationary rise in demand pressures in 1988 and a renewed rise in Germany's current external surplus to DM 85 billion.

b) Forward-looking policies of restraint

With international and domestic demand pressures clearly exceeding initial expectations, the Deutsche Mark weakening, and monetary growth remaining buoyant, the Bundesbank initiated a policy of forward-looking restraint around the middle of 1988. In order to avoid earlier unstable

---

[4]Recognized major econometric models of the German economy, as a rule, show nominal and real bond yields to affect interest-sensitive expenditures, while short-term rates influence the exchange rate.

[5]The announced introduction in early 1989 of a 10% withholding tax on interest income also contributed temporarily to the weakening of the Deutsche Mark.

policy configurations, in which corrective restrictive measures had been delayed too long and sharp monetary restraints coincided with lagged upward shifts in cost and price inflation, the authorities launched a gradual strategy of preemptive corrective strikes in order to nip potential inflation pressures "in the bud". To this end, the Bundesbank geared its policies essentially to four classes of indicators:

(i) the current rate of monetary growth and the liquidity overhang from previous years, which were regarded as early financial signals of future inflation risks;

(ii) current and future measures of demand growth and overall capacity utilization;

(iii) the effective exchange rate as a vehicle of "imported inflation" and the development of domestic wage claims

and the resulting

(iv) cost and price forecasts (rather than changes in concomitant price indices).

Examining longer-run developments in this complex set of data, the authorities felt compelled to tighten up step by step between mid-1988 and the autumn of 1989. The Bundesbank - like most other observers - more or less continuously underestimated the strength of foreign and home demand, monetary upward pressures and the underlying weakness of the Deutsche Mark in the exchange market. Price risks tended to be temporarily large in the first few months of 1989, when higher import costs were passed on, indirect taxes raised by an equivalent of 0.5 to 0.7 percentage points of the cost of living index and long-term wage contracts threatened to be renegotiated prematurely.

Although the Bundesbank was partly criticized for acting too cautiously, the stabilization results achieved by the end of 1989 seemed to justify the forward strategy adopted. For the first time in several years, the Bundesbank's 5% annual growth target for the broadly defined money stock (M3) was achieved fairly smoothly. Growth of domestic demand and real GNP was faster than the 2 1/2% potential output rate, but entailed a still tolerable degree of capacity pressure. Following a temporary acceleration at the beginning of 1989, annualized 6-month rates for industrial producer and consumer prices stood at around 2% (or slightly less) towards the end of the year. Moreover, the Deutsche Mark passed its lower turning point in July 1989 and appreciated in an orderly manner in the second half of the year.

The policy approach followed since mid-1988 inevitably implied that monetary management placed the main emphasis again on longer-run domestic stabilization concerns. Many European trading partners felt compelled to raise their interest rates more or less in unison with German official rates in order to prevent their currencies from depreciating. These reactions were, however, more or less predictable and deemed not to conflict with the Bundesbank's ultimate policy goals and its international obligations. Rising rates of capacity utilization in Germany largely reflected buoyant growth of exports to booming European neighbors. The authorities therefore felt that interest rate increases induced outside Germany through Bundesbank action would serve appropriate stabilization purposes for the Community as a whole and improve the chances for steadying self-sustained noninflationary growth in the area for the near-term future.

IV. INTERNATIONAL COORDINATION OF EXCHANGE RATE AND MONETARY MANAGEMENT

The foregoing discussion of German monetary policy-making would seem to permit one preliminary conclusion: The Bundesbank's basic policy framework, as it evolved since 1973 and during the mid-1980s, does not rely on radical "corner solutions" in reconciling the requirements of exchange rate and domestic monetary management.[6] Massive "sterilized" exchange market intervention or tight control of capital movements are not regarded as "missing instruments" with which the exchange rate could be managed efficiently and independently from domestic monetary management and general economic policy-making. The Bundesbank does not see itself as a "dominant player" who could effectively impose Germany's characteristic policy preferences in the field of monetary and inflation control on the rest of the world in a noncooperative "Stackelberg game."[7] Performing itself an "anchor"

---

[6]See on this point also a recent contribution by Frenkel/Goldstein (1989), which contains a fairly balanced evaluation of official thinking in this field in major industrial countries.

[7]This notion has been borrowed from game-theoretic interpretations of international policy coordination efforts. For recent contributions to this type of analysis see Bryant/Portes (1987).

function in the EMS and considering Germany's relative economic and financial strength, the Federal Republic is, on the other hand, like Japan too big to assume the role of a pure "follower" of US monetary policy, although the Federal Reserve may, at times, be able to substantially influence German monetary policy, with policy-induced movements in the real US dollar/Deutsche Mark rate acting as a powerful "leadership" transmission channel. The latter feature of the present international monetary system, which, in a similar way, affects also Japan, could be regarded as an element of potential weakness, since it has tended to synchronize "cyclical" monetary policy behavior in the three largest industrial economies.

On the evidence of presently available knowledge, a system of freely fluctuating exchange rates does not seem to be able to ideally cushion differences in policy preferences, socioeconomic structures and dynamic adjustment properties among the larger industrial countries. Independent "managed" floating and harder or softer forms of international monetary cooperation thus remain the only alternative policy options for larger open economies in the position of Germany. As already indicated in the previous sections, German monetary policy has chosen cooperative solutions and fully participated in the strengthening of international monetary arrangements since the mid-1980s. At the global - G-3 or G-7 - level "soft" forms of monetary cooperation have generally been preferred and are now well established in the framework of G-7 "multilateral surveillance". At the European level, "hard" forms of regional policy coordination are incorporated in the ERM rules system of the EMS and can be expected to be developed further in "stage one" of the envisaged European economic and monetary union.

In the global context, the Bundesbank has been quite skeptical from the outset, whether ambitious "target zone" approaches to cooperative monetary and exchange rate policies should be seriously considered by policy-makers in the larger countries. This concerns in particular proposals of the Williamson/Miller (1987) type. Policy blueprints which oblige monetary policy primarily to keep a country's nominal exchange rate within a narrow band, with the largest central banks pursuing a short-term real interest rate objective compatible with optimum world demand, are obviously at variance with the Bundesbank's traditional policy framework. It is true, as shown in the previous section, that the Bundesbank, together with other major central banks, has been ready in recent years to contribute to orderly conditions in exchange markets and to promote the real international adjustment process. However, viewed from a German perspective, the largest central banks' main function lies in the fact that they collectively influence the "world inflation rate" and that each individual major bank is primarily responsible for the long-run stability of the purchasing power of its home currency. Monetary policies of the major industrial countries should therefore provide a reliable nominal "anchor" - preferably in the form of binding monetary objectives or medium-term price norms - in order to stabilize world-wide inflationary expectations. Nominal exchange rate commitments among the largest countries cannot, by themselves, perform a disciplining or stabilizing function. They could, on the contrary, even act as a vehicle of collective monetary policy errors, if the leading central banks pursue procyclical or inflationary strategies in a synchronized or collusive way.

"Target zone" blueprints of the McKinnon (1984, 1988) type - which envisage the joint symmetrical control of the world money stock or world price level by the largest three central banks under a regime of fairly tight nominal exchange rate commitments - may be thought to conform distinctly better with the Bundesbank's revealed policy preferences. But a critical look at the relevant stylized facts would suggest that "quasi-currency-union" links of the McKinnon type could also not be readily established among the largest economies. The degree of "openness" of their goods, labor and financial markets is significantly different (see illustrations 14 and 15), and trade and financial integration links between them vary greatly (see illustration 14). Structural and dynamic adjustment properties of domestic goods, factor and financial markets in these countries are far from being homogenous or perfectly flexible, and their monetary and fiscal policy concepts as well as policy decision-making procedures are hardly compatible. It is therefore difficult to see how these countries could undertake consistent and credible international policy commitments or be effectively controlled through "multilateral surveillance" or mutual "peer pressure" procedures. In the given circumstances, sizeable real exchange rate changes between the US dollar, the Japanese yen and the

Deutsche Mark, "flanking" appropriate domestic policy adjustments, may be needed from time to time to smoothly absorb unavoidable real and financial shocks affecting and separating the largest economies.

At the European level, prospects for tighter forms of international cooperation in the field of exchange rate and monetary management seem to be more promising from the viewpoint of Bundesbank policy-making. Close trade and financial linkages, the planned creation of a large single market for goods, capital, labor and services by 1993, widely shared basic convictions in the field of economic and monetary policy and the fairly smooth functioning of the EMS have encouraged European policy-makers to launch a European economic and monetary union. During the past two years, European countries adhering to ERM rules already appear to have de facto been on a fixed exchange rate system with highly synchronized national monetary policies. It is difficult to predict whether these favorable conditions can last and when they could be extended to other EC member countries. Germany's massive current account surplus equivalent to 5% of GNP and the remaining national differences in inflation and growth performance could become a source of tensions in the EMS. Moreover, the macroeconomic repercussions of the realization of the internal market program and of the envisaged complete financial integration process on individual member economies are not easy to project. It would therefore seem preferable to enter the first stages of the union with a flexible policy framework, in which nominal and real exchange rate changes are still considered as adjustment instruments of last resort, while domestic monetary policies primarily aim at converging, low medium-term national inflation goals.

REFERENCES

Bryant, R.C. and Portes, R. (eds.), *Global Macroeconomics: Policy Conflict and Cooperation* (London: Macmillan, 1987).

Deutsche Bundesbank, "Intervention Policy, Monetary Management and the Final Goals of Economic Policy," Background paper prepared for the seven-country *Report of the Working Group on Exchange Market Intervention* (Jurgensen Report), March 1983.

Dudler, H.J., "Monetary Policy and Exchange Market Management in Germany," in BIS, *Exchange Market Intervention and Monetary Policy* (Basle: March 1988), 65-96.

Emminger, O., "Deutsche Geld-und Wahrungspolitik im Spannungsfeld zwischen innerem und ausserem Gleichgewicht (1948-1975)," in Deutsche Bundesbank, *Wahrung und Wirtschaft in Deutschland, 1876-1975* (Frankfurt: Knapp, 1976), 485-554.

Frenkel, J.A. and Goldstein, M., "Monetary Policies, Capital Market Integration, and the Exchange Rate Regime," paper prepared for the Bank of France - University Conference on "Monetary Policy in its International Environment," Paris, November 29-December 1, 1989.

McKinnon, R.I., *An International Standard for Monetary Stabilization* (Washington, D.C.: Institute for International Economics, 1984).

————————, "Monetary and Exchange Rate Policies for International Financial Stability: A Proposal," *Journal of Economic Perspectives*, Vol.2, Winter 1988, 83-104.

Putnam, R.D. and Henning, C.R., "The Bonn Summit of 1978: A Case Study in Coordination," in The Brookings Institution, *Can Nations Agree?* (Washington, D.C.: 1989), 12-140.

Schlesinger, H., "Zehn Jahre Geldpolitik mit einem Geldmengenziel," in Gebauer, W. (ed.), *Offentliche Finanzen und monetare Okonomie* (Frankfurt: Knapp, 1985), 123-147.

Williamson, J. and Miller, M.H., *Targets and Indicators: A Blueprint for the International Coordination of Economic Policy* (Washington, D.C.: Institute for International Economics, 1987).

List of Ilustrations

Illustration 1

INSTRUMENTS OF MONETARY POLICY IN GERMANY

I. Longer-run adjustments	II. Fine-tuning measures
(a) Interest rate policy	
Discount rate	Bill rate[1]
Lombard rate	Bidding/allotment rates[2]
(b) Bank liquidity management	
Compulsory reserves	Issue and premature redemption of Bundesbank "mobilisation" or "liquidity" paper "
Rediscount/lombard ceilings	
Outright purchases/ sale of long-term bonds	Repurchase agreements in trade bills and foreign claims
	Foreign exchange swaps
	Deposit policy[3]
Security-based repurchase agreements[4]	

1 Selling rates set for bill-type Bundesbank "mobilisation" or "liquidity" paper (under Sections 42 and 42a respectively of the Bundesbank Act) act as a floor for the call-money rate.
2 Minimum bidding and allotment rates fixed for security-based repurchase agreements influence the determination of short-term money-market rates (especially through expectations).
3 Redepositing of Federal Government cash balances held with the Bundesbank in the money market (according to Section 17 of the Bundesbank Act).
4 Repurchase agreements in fixed-interest securities are used for "fine-tuning" banks' reserve position during calendar months and for satisfying banks' longer-run refinancing needs on a "roll-over" basis.

Central bank money stock* and control variables in the money market

Illustration 2

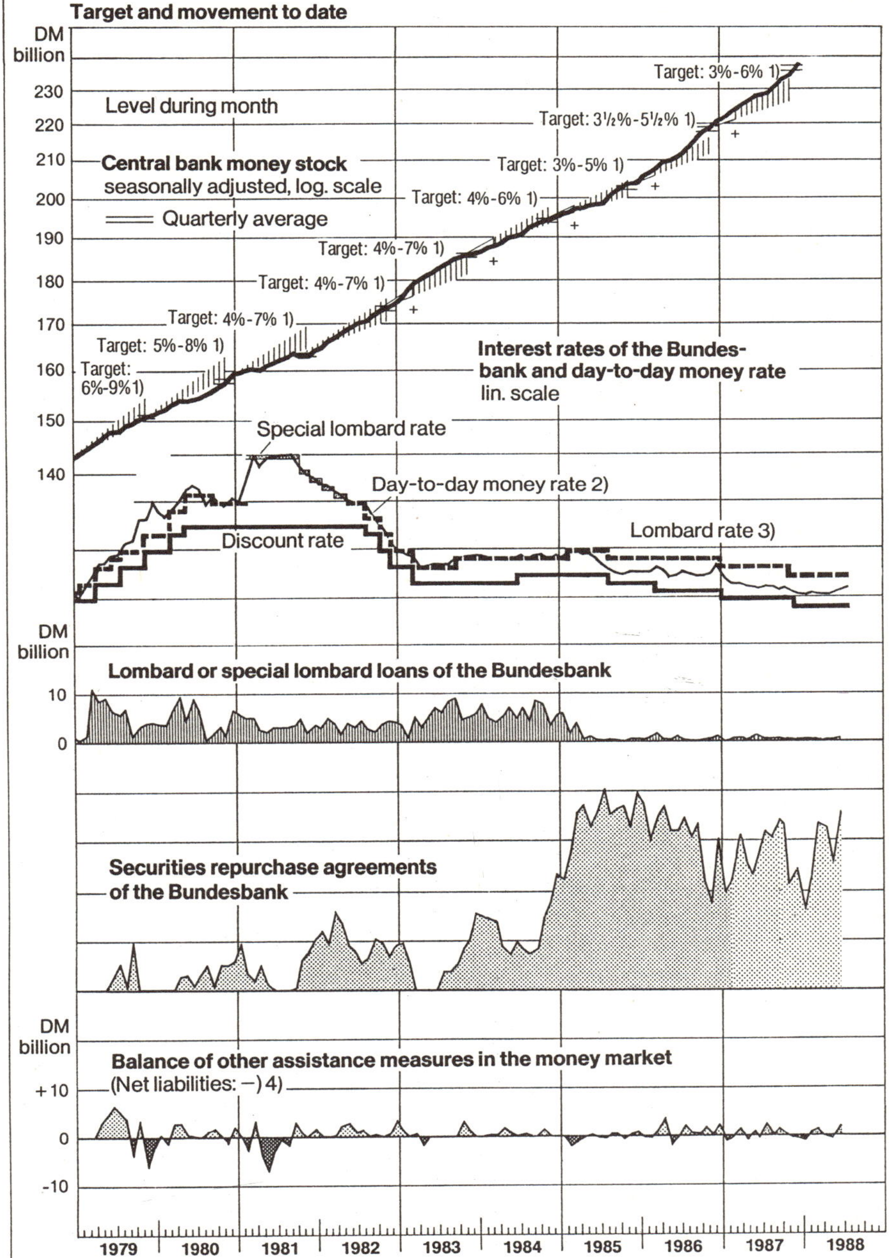

*Currency in circulation plus required minimum reserves on domestic liabilities (at constant reserve ratios, base: January 1974); excluding bank bonds subject to minimum reserve requirements.- 1) Between the 4th quarter of the previous year and the 4th quarter of the current year.- 2) Monthly averages.- 3) From February 20, 1981 to May 6, 1982 lombard loans were not granted to the banks at the lombard rate.- 4) Open market transactions in trade bills under repurchase agreements, foreign exchange swaps and foreign exchange transactions under repurchase agreements, shifts of Federal balances under section 17 of the Bundesbank Act and short-term sales of Treasury bills.- + For the first time in 1984 (and retroactively for 1983) the target corridor until March was not shaded because the growth of the central bank money stock is generally subject to sharper random fluctuations around the turn of the year. According to calculations made by the Bundesbank, from the spring onwards the average deviation of these random variations from the trend no longer exceeds the width of the corridor.

BBk

Illustration 3

The monetary targets and their implementation

%

Year	Target: growth of the central bank money stock resp. M3 [2]			Actual growth (rounded figures)		Target met
	in the course of the year [1]	on an annual average	Concretising of target in the course of the year	in the course of the year [1]	on an annual average	
1975	8	–	–	10	–	no
1976	–	8	–	–	9	no
1977	–	8	–	–	9	no
1978	–	8	–	–	11	no
1979	6 – 9	–	Lower limit	6	–	yes
1980	5 – 8	–	Lower limit	5	–	yes
1981	4 – 7	–	Lower half	4	–	yes
1982	4 – 7	–	Upper half	6	–	yes
1983	4 – 7	–	Upper Half	7	–	yes
1984	4 – 6	–	–	5	–	yes
1985	3 – 5	–	–	5	–	yes
1986	3 1/2 – 5 1/2	–	–	8	–	no
1987	3 – 6	–	–	8	–	no
1988	3 – 6	–	–	7	–	no
1989	5	–	–	5	–	yes
1990	4 – 6	–				

1 Between the fourth quarter of the preceding year and the fourth quarter of the current year; 1975: December 1974 to December 1975.
2 Since 1988: M3.

Illustration 4

Money stock and central bank money stock

Change from previous year in %, quarterly

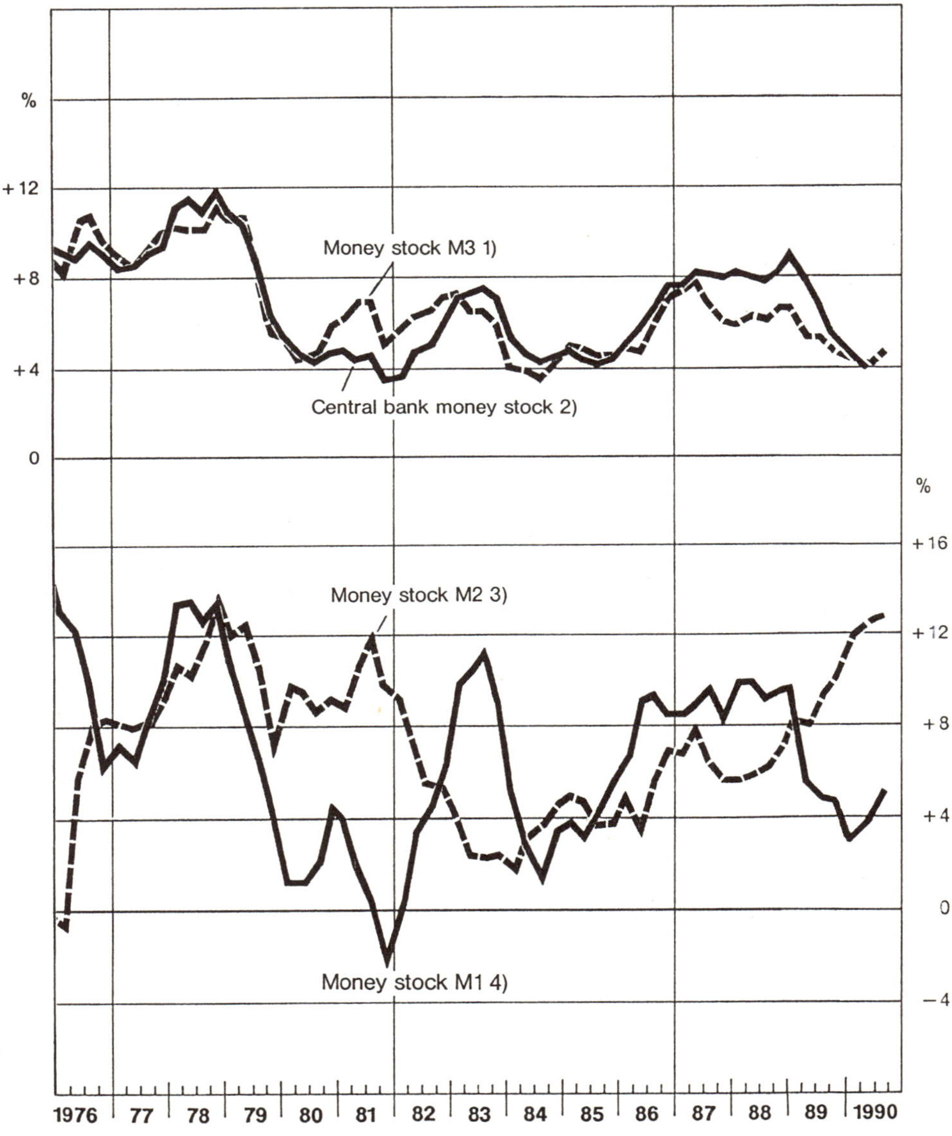

1) M3 = currency, sight deposits, time deposits for less than 4 years, savings deposits at statu - tory notice.- 2) Central bank money stock = currency in circulation plus required minimum re serves on domestic deposits (calculated at constant reserve ratios, base: January 1974).- 3) M2 = M3 excluding savings deposits at statutory notice.- 4) M1 = currency and sight deposits.

BBk

Illustration 5

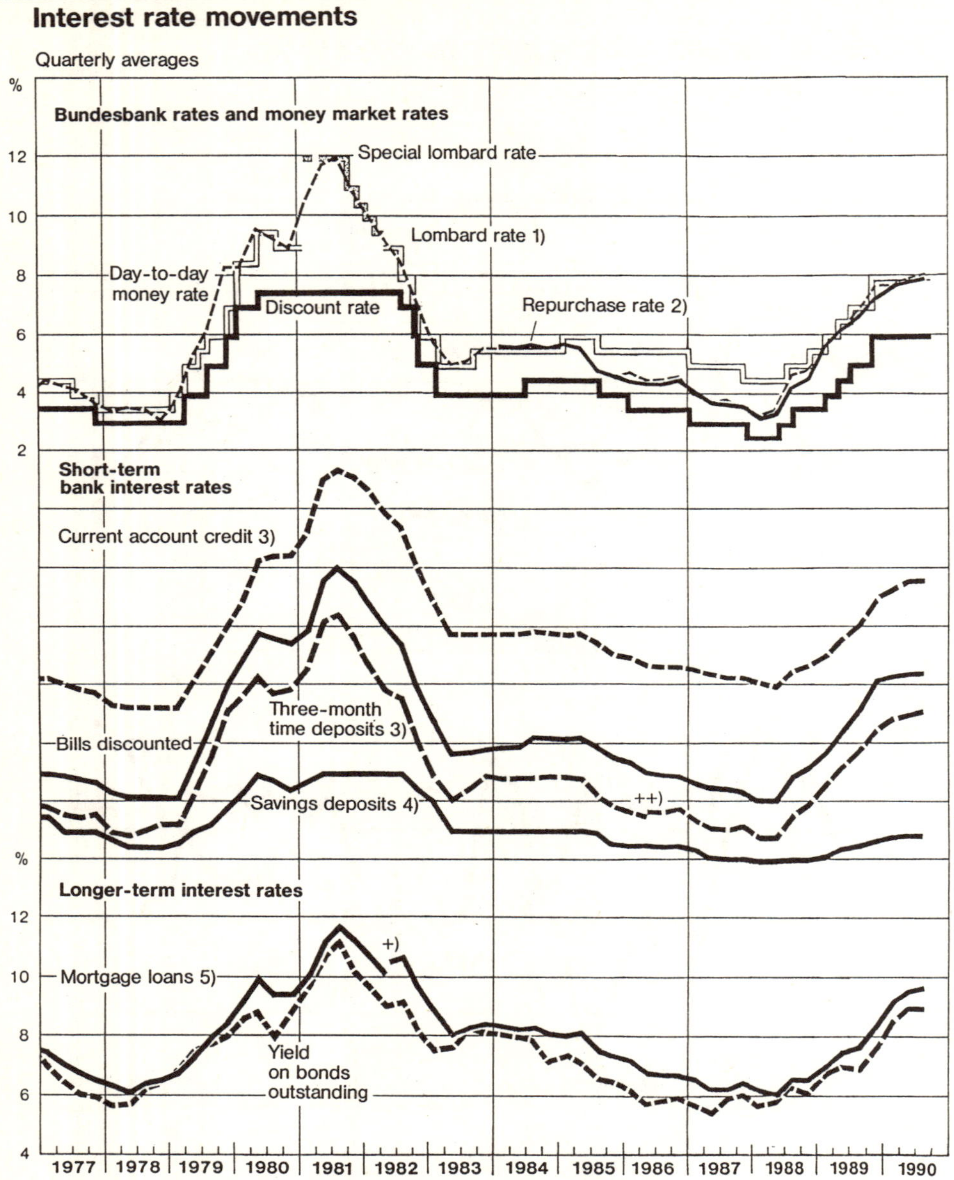

1) From February 20, 1981 to May 6, 1982 lombard loans were not granted at the lombard rate; during that period the Bundesbank provided special lombard loans at a special lombard rate as and when required.- 2) Rate for open market transactions under repurchase agreements in securities (since 1984).- 3) Of less than DM 1 million.- 4) At statutory notice.- 5) On residential real estate, effective rate of interest.- + From June 1982, only average rate for floating-rate mortgage loans; data comparable with earlier figures only to a limited extent.- + + From June 1986, rate for time deposits from DM 100,000 to less than DM 1 million.

BBk

Illustration 6

German money-market rates

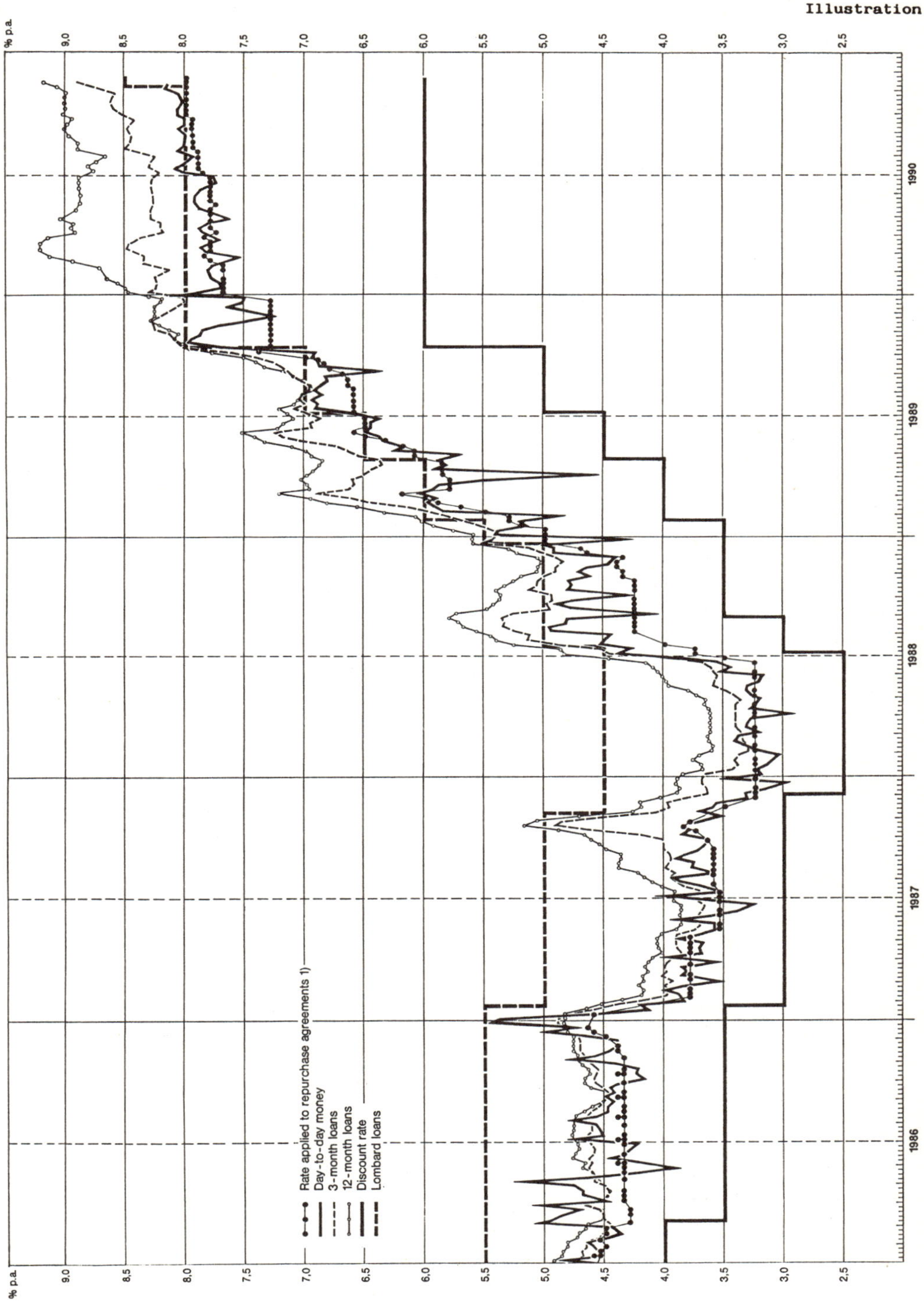

1) Fixed rate (volume tender) or allotment rate (interest rate tender) for open-market transactions under repurchase agreements in securities on the date the transaction is credited.

Illustration 7

Changes in the net external position of the Deutsche Bundesbank
due to operations in the foreign exchange market and other foreign exchange movements *) r)

DM billion

Period	Operations in the exchange market 1)					Other foreign exchange movements	Total change in net external position
			DM operations in the ERM 2)				
	Total	Deutsche Mark/ Dollar market	Total	Inter- ventions	Debt settle- ment 3)		
A. By calendar years							
1973 April-December	+ 7.9	- 0.4	+ 8.3	+ 8.3	-	- 1.3	+ 6.6
1974	+ 0.2	+ 0.0	+ 0.2	+ 0.2	-	- 1.8	- 1.6
1975	- 2.4	- 0.6	- 1.8	- 1.8	-	+ 0.3	- 2.2
1976	+ 19.5	+ 2.5	+ 17.0	+ 17.0	-	- 10.6	+ 8.6
1977	+ 12.4	+ 10.9	+ 1.5	+ 1.5	-	- 2.0	+ 10.5
1978	+ 32.0	+ 24.1	+ 7.9	+ 7.9	-	- 11.8	+ 20.1
1979	+ 15.5	+ 7.3	+ 8.2	+ 8.2	-	- 23.3	- 7.8
1980	- 28.8	- 18.3	- 10.5	- 10.5	-	+ 3.4	- 25.4
1981	- 7.8	- 21.5	+ 13.7	+ 15.0	- 1.3	+ 3.3	- 4.5
1982	- 3.0	- 6.6	+ 3.7	+ 3.7	- 0.1	+ 6.2	+ 3.2
1983	- 22.5	- 14.7	- 7.8	- 7.8	-	+ 18.5	- 4.0
1984	- 21.7	- 23.1	+ 1.4	+ 3.6	- 2.2	+ 16.3	- 5.4
1985	- 16.7	- 16.5	- 0.2	- 0.2	-	+ 19.4	+ 2.7
1986	- 5.8	+ 2.5	- 8.4	- 6.6	- 1.8	+ 11.1	+ 5.2
1987	+ 28.2	+ 10.0	+ 18.1	+ 25.4	- 7.3	+ 13.9	+ 42.1
1988	- 27.5	- 21.3	- 6.1	-	- 6.1	- 8.1	- 35.6
1989	- 28.6	- 28.6	-	+ 3.0	- 3.0	+ 9.5	- 19.1
B. By selected periods							
October 15, 1987 to January 14, 1988 Dollar under marked downward pressure; Deutsche Mark strong within the ERM	+ 17.6	+ 7.6	+ 10.0			+ 7.6	+ 25.2
January 15, 1988 to March 8, 1988 Recovery of the dollar; easing of tensions within the ERM	- 6.1	-	- 6.1	-	- 6.1	+ 0.8	+ 5.3
March 9, 1988 to May 12, 1988 Further slight strengthening of the dollar; weakening of some partner currencies within the ERM	+ 0.6	+ 0.6	-	-	-	+ 0.0	+ 0.6
May 13, 1988 to August 23, 1988 Sharp rise in the dollar; easing of tensions within the ERM	- 21.4	- 21.4	-	-	-	- 8.8	- 30.2
August 24, 1988 to December 19, 1988 Dollar weaker; some ERM currencies repeatedly under downward pressure	- 1.5	- 1.5	-	-	-	- 0.9	- 2.3
December 20, 1988 to March 20, 1989 Renewed recovery of the dollar; weakening of the Danish krone	- 7.8	- 7.8	-	-	-	0.5	- 7.3
March 21, 1989 to March 23, 1989 Dollar unchanged; Danish krone at lower intervention point	- 0.2	- 0.2	-	-	-	+ 0.1	- 0.1
March 24, 1989 to October 10, 1989 Dollar strong; quiet markets within the ERM	- 20.9	- 20.9	-	-	-	+ 5.7	- 15.3
October 10, 1989 to January 8, 1990 Dollar under downward pressure; Danish krone at lower intervention point	- 0.6	- 0.6	0.0	+ 3.0	- 3.0	+ 3.0	+ 2.5
January 9, 1990 to November 1, 1990 Dollar unchanged until mid-year, then under heavy selling pressure; Italian lira and Spanish peseta strong within the ERM	- 3.1	- 1.5	- 1.6	- 1.6	- 0.0	+ 11.1	+ 8.0
November 2, 1990 to November 19, 1990 Dollar under continued downward pressure against the Deutsche Mark; recovery of the Deutsche Mark within the ERM	-	-	-	-	-	+ 1.6	+ 1.6

*) Excluding liquidity swaps. Recorded at current exchange rates and according to the date on which the transaction was conducted; this results in discrepancies between these figures and those of the balance of payments statistics.
r) Revised.
1) Including operations by other central banks, where they affect the external position of the Bundesbank.
2) Incl. Spain and United Kingdom as from June 19, 1989 and October 8, 1990, respectively.
3) Deutsche Mark repayments to the Bundesbank or to the EMCF by ERM partners.

Discrepancies in the totals are due to rounding.

Illustration 8

Net ERM interventions in Deutsche Mark by types of transactions *) r)

DM billion

Period	Obligatory	Intramarginal	Total	Memo item: Impact on banking liquidity in Germany 1)
A. By calendar years				
1979 2)	- 3.6	- 5.4	- 9.0	+ 9.2
1980	+ 5.9	+ 4.9	+ 10.8	- 10.5
1981	- 15.0	- 4.7	- 19.7	+ 13.7
1982	- 3.0	- 3.4	- 6.4	+ 3.6
1983	+ 8.4	+ 6.2	+ 14.5	- 7.8
1984	- 4.7	+ 21.4	+ 16.6	+ 1.4
1985	- 0.4	- 1.6	- 2.0	- 0.2
1986	+ 14.8	- 40.4	- 25.5	- 8.4
1987	- 15.0	- 13.9	- 28.9	+ 18.1
1988	-	+ 10.5	+ 10.5	- 6.1
1989	- 5.0	+ 11.8	+ 6.8	-
B. By selected periods				
October 15, 1987 to January 14, 1988 Dollar under marked downward pressure; Deutsche Mark strong within the ERM	-	- 20.6	- 20.6	+ 10.0
January 15, 1988 to March 8, 1988 Recovery of the dollar; easing of tensions within the ERM	-	+ 9.9	+ 9.9	- 6.1
March 9, 1988 to May 12, 1988 Further slight strengthening of the dollar; weakening of some partner currencies within the ERM	-	- 6.0	- 6.0	-
May 13, 1988 to August 23, 1988 Sharp rise in the dollar; easing of tensions within the ERM	-	+ 10.4	+ 10.4	-
August 24, 1988 to December 19, 1988 Dollar weaker; some ERM currencies repeatedly under downward pressure	-	- 4.3	- 4.3	-
December 20, 1988 to March 20, 1989 Renewed recovery of the dollar; weakening of the Danish krone	-	+ 8.2	+ 8.2	-
March 21, 1989 to March 23, 1989 Dollar unchanged; Danish krone at lower intervention point	- 1.7	+ 0.3	- 1.4	-
March 24, 1989 to October 10, 1989 Dollar strong; quiet markets within the ERM	-	+ 14.3	+ 14.3	-
October 10, 1989 to January 8, 1990 Dollar under downward pressure; Danish krone at lower intervention point	- 3.4	- 8.3	- 11.6	-
January 9, 1990 to November 1, 1990 Dollar unchanged until mid-year, then under heavy selling pressure; Italian lira and Spanish peseta strong within the ERM	+ 1.5	+ 30.4	+ 32.0	- 1,6
November 2, 1990 to November 19, 1990 Dollar under continued downward pressure against the Deutsche Mark; recovery of the Deutsche Mark within the ERM	-	- 3.4	- 3.4	-

*) DM interventions by other central banks participating in the ERM and ERM interventions by the Bundesbank. Incl. Spain and United Kingdom as from June 19, 1989 and October 8, 1990, respectively.
r) Revised.
1) Indicates the extent to which DM interventions in the ERM and the settlement of creditor and debtor positions in the EMCF affected the net external position of the Bundesbank and thus the banks' provision with central bank money;
+ = Expansionary impact owing to DM sales; - = Contractionary impact owing to DM purchases.
2) As from the beginning of the EMS on March 13, 1979.

Discrepancies in the totals are due to rounding.

Illustration 9

Changes in money stock during speculation periods and subsequent months*

Speculation period / Subsequent period	Bundesbank intervention 1 2 8	Changes in money stock during period against preceding months: M2		M3		Non-bank sector inflows 2 4
	DM billion	DM billion 2	% 3	DM billion 2	% 3	DM billion
1973 Febr./March	+ 21,9	+ 7,5	+ 18,8	+ 6,9	+ 18,2	+ 10,1
April/May	- 2,5	+ 10,3	+ 10,4	+ 8,8	+ 6,1	+ 3,3
1976 Febr./March	+ 9,6	+ 2,6[5]	+ 13,4[5]	+ 2,1[5]	+ 11,0[5]	+ 6,0[5]
May/June	- 2,0[7]	+ 8,9	+ 13,9	+ 10,2	+ 12,2	+ 0,2
1977 Oct./Febr. 1978	+ 15,6	+ 17,3	+ 9,9	+ 33,6	+ 8,8	+ 11,6
March/July 1978	- 3,7	+ 15,3	+ 10,7	+ 18,7	+ 10,0	- 2,8
1978 Aug./Nov.	+ 13,4	+ 38,6	+ 23,2	+ 43,0	+ 15,8	+ 10,9
Dec./Jan. 79	+ 1,2	- 18,4	- 4,3	- 4,8	+ 1,4	- 5,9
1983 Febr./March[9]	+ 13,3	- 6,1	+ 6,1	- 2,4	+ 9,9	+ 4,7
April/May[9]	- 19,3	+ 6,7	- 3,9	+ 7,9	+ 2,5	- 9,1
1985 Dec./April 86 10	- 0,7	- 11,6	+ 5,8	+ 8,3	+ 6,2	+ 14,9
April/May 10	- 9,5	- 1,3	- 3,0	- 0,3	- 2,1	- 3,3
1987 Jan./Febr.	+ 16,5	- 16,9	+ 15,9	- 10,9	+ 12,5	+ 18,3
March	- 0,2	- 8,9	- 2,3	- 9,0	+ 1,2	+ 3,1

* Length of subsequent period, as a rule, corresponds to length of preceding speculations period (except for periods in which renewed speculation occurred).- 1 Incl. interventions in EEC currencies and by Federal Reserve within swap arrangements.- 2 Unadjusted.- 3 Seas. adj. annual rates.- 4 Changes in net foreign assets of banking system (incl. Bundesbank).- 5 Lagged by one month against speculation period.- 6 Interventions in December and January.- 7 Interventions in April and May.- 8 Excluding swap transactions with domestic banks.- 9 Interventions from February 1 to March 18 (before realignment) and from March 21 to April 30 (after realignment).- 10 Interventions from Dec. to April 4 (realignment) and April 7 to the end of May.

Nominal and real external value of the Deutsche Mark

Illustration 10

End-1972 = 100, half-yearly, log. scale

1) Weighted external value.- 2) External value after adjustment for the differing rates of inflation (on the basis of prices of total expenditure).- 3) Excluding Greece, and Portugal. Figures prior to the start of the EMS in March 1979 calculated retroactively.- e Estimated.- ● Latest position: July-mid Dec. 1990.

Illustration 11

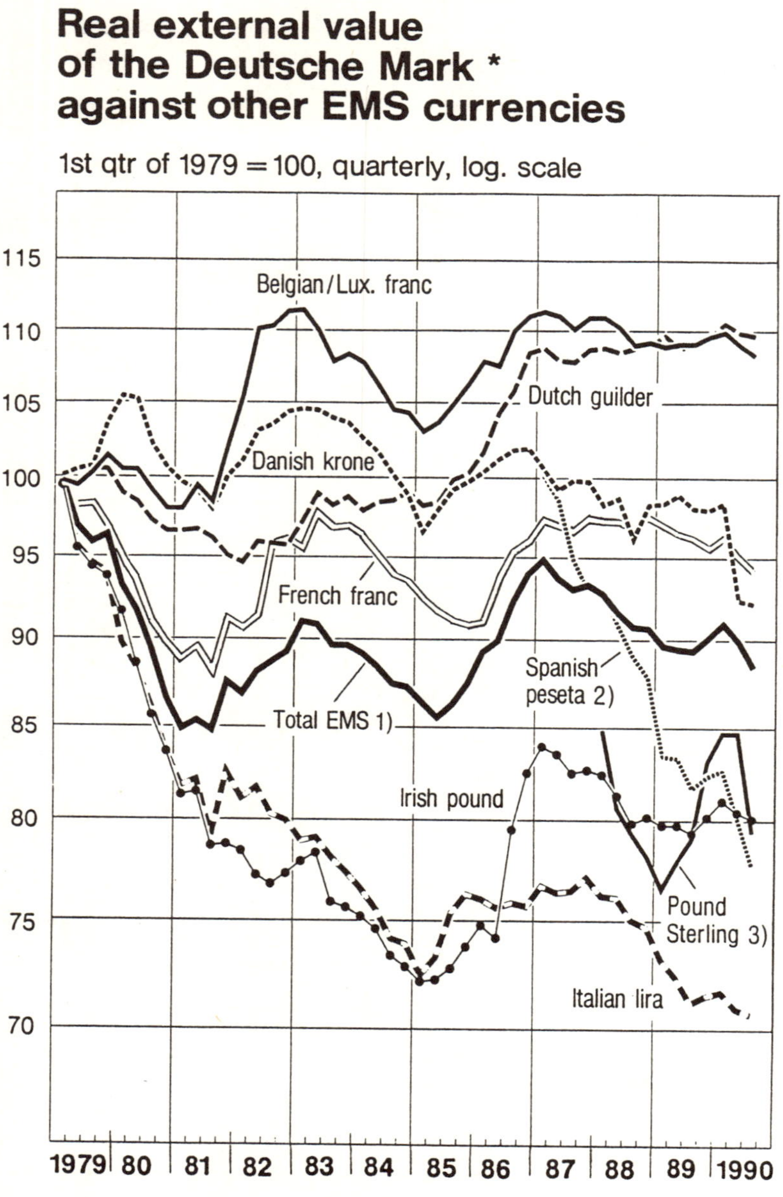

* Weighted nominal external value, adjusted in each case for the differing overall price movements (measured by the prices of total expenditure).- 1) From July 1989 including Spanish peseta, from October 1990 including Pound Sterling.- 2) Has participated in the exchange rate mechanism of the EMS since June 19, 1989.- 3) Has participated in the exchange rate mechanism of the EMS since October 8, 1990.

BBk

Illustration 12

Business conditions in Germany *

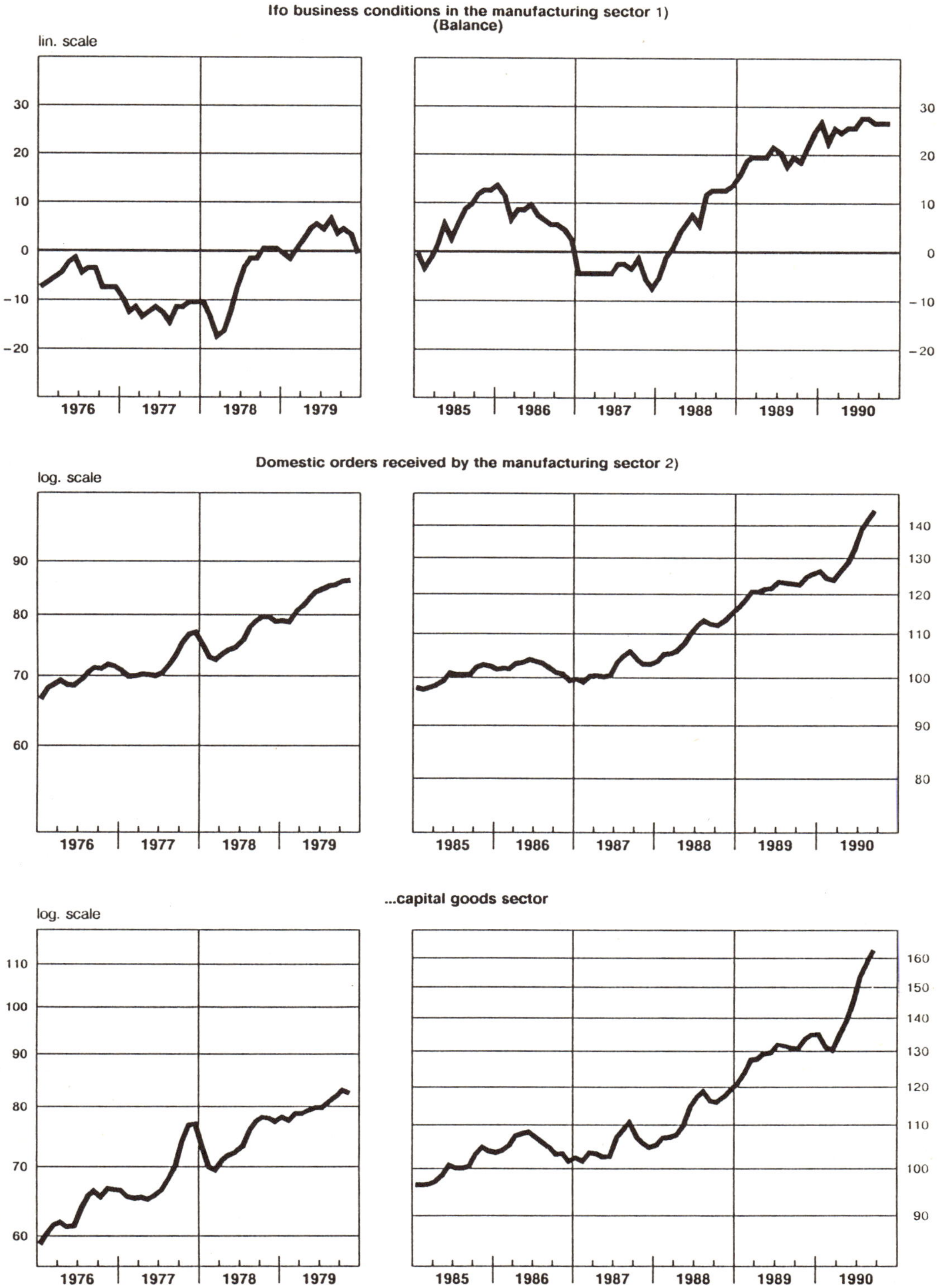

* Seasonally adjusted.- 1) Excluding food, drink and tobacco industry.- 2) 1985 = 100, 3-months moving averages.

Illustration 13

External value of the Deutsche Mark and price and wage development in Germany

(changes from previous year as a percentage)

	Real external value of the Deutsche Mark 1	Import prices 2	Wages and salaries 3	Unit labour costs 4	Cost of living index
1974	- 1.5	28.7	11.5	9.8	7.0
1975	- 3.2	- 1.8	7.2	5.7	5.9
1976	- 0.3	6.1	7.9	1.3	4.3
1977	1.9	1.6	6.6	3.7	3.7
1978	1.5	- 3.8	5.6	2.9	2.7
1979	0.7	11.7	5.9	3.2	4.1
1980	- 4.8	14.9	6.9	6.5	5.5
1981	- 9.9	13.6	5.2	4.5	6.3
1982	0.9	2.3	4.2	3.5	5.2
1983	0.3	- 0.3	3.8	0.4	3.3
1984	- 4.6	6.0	3.4	0.2	2.4
1985	- 1.8	1.4	3.1	1.8	2.0
1986	8.1	- 15.7	3.8	2.5	- 0.1
1987	4.8	- 5.3	3.1	2.2	0.2
1988	- 2.5	1.3	3.1	0.1	1.3

1 Against the currencies of eighteen industrial countries (adjusted by prices of total sales).
2 Index of prices in foreign trade.
3 Wages and salaries per capita.
4. Labour costs divided by real GNP.

Illustration 14

United States, Japan, Germany: Foreign Trade Weights and Mutual Trade Linkages[1]

A. Share of exports and imports in GNP (in %)[2]

	export/GNP	import/GNP
United States	11.2	12.7
Japan	13.0	10.0
Germany	32.6	26.9

B. Mutual trade linkages between US, Japan and Germany
(Share of total exports or imports in %)

		export	import
United States,			
trade with	Japan	11.7	20.2
	Germany	4.5	6.0
Japan,			
trade with	US	34.0	22.6
	Germany	6.0	4.3
Germany,			
trade with	US	8.0	6.6
	Japan	2.3	6.4

1 Figures for 1988.
2 Goods and Services.

Illustration 15

External financial links of three major industrial countries*

Percentage of total

Year	United States	Japan	Federal Republic of Germany
1980	4.7	6.6	11.4
1981	1.5	6.0	10.7
1982	1.7	3.8	8.1
1983	3.6	5.6	7.7
1984	3.1	7.0	15.2
1985	3.5	10.6	18.9
1986	5.6	13.5	23.6
1987	7.6	12.0	17.8
1988 pe	...	...	16.0

* Financial asset acquisition and borrowing by non-residents as a percentage of the total financial asset acquisition and borrowing in each country.-
pe Partly estimated.

Source of basic data: Capital finance account of the Bundesbank and OECD Financial Statistics.

10 THE BALANCE-OF-PAYMENTS OFFSET TO MONETARY POLICY: AN EXAMINATION OF THE ISRAELI CASE*

Leora (Rubin) Meridor and Shula Pessach

The adoption of a stabilization program in July 1985 marks a turning point for the Israeli economy, ending a decade of high inflation -- since then, the economy has functioned at annual inflation rates of around 15-20 percent.

One of the program's central features was the pegging of the exchange rate to a basket of currencies of Israel's main trading partners. The Israeli inflation rate did not converge to the rates prevailing in these countries, so that expectations emerged for devaluation at some unspecified time. Although the authorities tried to avoid it, there has been some devaluation since the stabilization program, and on at least one occasion it was fully expected.[1] As a result the last three years (1986-89) have been marked by large capital inflows and outflows, in spite of the controls to which the capital account is subject. Confronted by the implications of the new exchange rate regime, the monetary authorities had to revise their policy so that issues concerning the role of monetary policy and its effectiveness were brought into the open.

The effectiveness of monetary policy depends largely on the exchange rate regime and on the substitutability of domestic and foreign assets. In the short run it also depends on the mobility of capital, which in turn depends on the extent of controls. It is by now widely accepted that portfolio considerations add to the monetary authority's ability to determine domestic interest rates and the money supply, and

---

* We would like to thank the participants in the seminar in international trade and market structure at the Institute for Advanced Studies at the Hebrew University and during the seminar held by the Research Department of the Bank of Israel, and in particular Joshua Aizenman, Giora Hanoch, Nissan Liviatan, and Rafi Melnick for helpful comments on an earlier draft. We would also like to thank Avigdor Shwartztein for research assistance, Susanne Freund for editorial help, and Chava Reich for typing the manuscript. All errors, omissions, and opinions remain our own.

---

[1] The devaluation of the end of 1988.

there is a close link between the degree of integration with the international capital market and the speed with which monetary disturbances are reversed namely both substitutability of different assets and mobility of capital flows affect this speed. The extent to which monetary policy actions are offset by induced capital flows is measured by an "offset coefficient."

A great deal of empirical work has been done on the extent to which world financial markets undermine the ability of monetary authorities to conduct an independent monetary policy. The pioneers in this area are Argy and Kouri (1974) and Kouri and Porter (1974). They were followed by Herring and Marston (1977), Obstfeld (1980b, 1982) and others. The results vary from very low offset coefficients in Mexico (Kamas (1986)) of about 0.04 to very large long-run coefficients of 0.75 in West Germany during the 1970s (see Obstfeld (1982)).

In examining monetary policy, the concurrent fiscal policy must be taken into account. In particular, budget deficits and the way they are financed are the context within which monetary authorities operate. Most of the empirical work done along the lines mentioned focused on monetary policy with respect to the balance of payments and tended to overlook the effect of budget deficit. Our paper follows the offset-coefficient line of research but deviates from it by explicitly introducing the government budget constraint. This enables us to throw some light on the relationship between monetary and fiscal policy.

Furthermore, instead of solving the model for the conventional balance-of-payments equilibrium, we solve it for domestic bond market equilibrium. We thus end up with a different model specification, which is equivalent to the traditional one. The new equation enables us to estimate the offset coefficient from monthly data.

Some points of interest emerge from our analysis:

1. The short and long run offset coefficients for monetary policy in Israel estimated here averaged 0.5 and 0.7 respectively; the difference between the two is attributable to the fact that the money and bond markets differ in speed of adjustment to long-run equilibrium.

2. The offset coefficient depends heavily on the money multiplier. Since the latter declined substantially throughout the period investigated, the offset coefficients are now above their average magnitudes.

3. The offset varies considerably across fiscal policy actions -- this is so in theory and is also strongly supported by the empirical evidence. In particular, when the budget deficit is financed by issuing bonds the effect on the foreign reserves differ from that of deficit financing by money creation. Moreover, there is a difference between a monetary policy carried out by open market operations and one involving only money creation. In the latter case, the offset is higher due to the lack of indirect effect on interest rates.

Section 1 presents the theoretical model taking into account some prominent characteristics of the structure of the Israeli financial markets. Section 2 discusses the problem of simultaneity that may arise when the central bank operates according to a given reaction function; section 3 presents the empirical results for the period from September 1985 to March 1989. Section 4 sums up and draws some conclusions.

1. THE CONCEPTUAL FRAMEWORK

The monetarist approach to the balance of payments provides a theoretical framework for an analysis of capital movements within which a clear-cut connection is determined between them and monetary policy: monetary policy has no effect whatsoever on domestic financial markets and its entire impact is therefore passed on to the foreign reserves. The portfolio approach, on the other hand, makes it possible to analyze capital movements without a priori determination of the magnitude of the effect of monetary policy and permits substitution between domestic and foreign assets, thus enabling domestic interest to respond to monetary policy even in a small and open economy maintaining a fixed exchange rate.

The portfolio approach has served empirical research that estimates the effect of monetary policy on capital movements. There are two ways of deriving the relationship between them: through equilibrium in the money and foreign-exchange markets; or through equilibrium in the money and domestic bond markets. As will be shown, these methods yield two different but equivalent equations, so that the conclusions are independent of the method used.

We present a simplistic model which somewhat extends the one used by Kouri and Porter (1974) (henceforth K&P).[2]

The model is for a small open economy with a fixed exchange rate. There are three financial assets: money, held by the nonfinancial private sector; domestic bonds denominated in domestic currency, also held by foreigners as well as by the domestic nonfinancial private sector; and foreign bonds also held by foreigners and the nonfinancial private sector. Formulating the model in this way permits analysis of less than perfect substitution between domestic and foreign assets. Since the model focuses on financial relationships, we make the conventional assumption that the real economic variables (especially GNP and the current account) are not determined within this framework, that is, they are exogenous to the model (see also K&P).

The equations of the model are:

(1)	$M^d = L(r, \pi^e, i^*, \hat{e}^e, w, y, P)$	money demand
(2)	$M^s = \frac{1}{\theta}(ER + D + C_g)$	money supply
(3)	$M^s = M^d$	money-market equilibrium
(4)	$B^d = B(r, \pi^e, i^*, \hat{e}^e, w, y, P)$	domestic demand for domestic bonds
(5)	$J^d E = J(r, \pi^e, i^*, \hat{e}^\ell, w, y, P)E$	domestic demand for foreign bonds
(6)	$F^d E = F(r, \pi^e, \hat{e}^e, w^*, y^*, P^*)E$	foreign demand for domestic bonds
(7)	$B^s = B_g - D - C$	supply of domestic bonds
(8)	$B^s = B^d + F^d E$	domestic bond market equilibrium
(9)	$w = (M + B^d + J^d E)/P$	private financial wealth (in real terms)
(10)	$K = \Delta F - \Delta J$	capital account (in foreign currency)
(11)	$\Delta R = K + CA$	change in foreign reserves (in foreign currency)
(12)	$G - T = \Delta B_g + \Delta C_g$	budget deficit
(13)	$C = (1 - \theta)M^s$	bank credit

[2]The model ultimately goes back to Tobin 1969.

Notation

Unless otherwise stated, all variables are set in nominal terms and in domestic currency.

B	-	domestic bonds held by the domestic public (private nonfinancial sector)
B_g	-	government bonds
C	-	bank credit to the nonfinancial private sector
CA	-	surplus in the current balance-of-payments account (in foreign currency)
C_g	-	central-bank credit to the government
D	-	government bonds held by the central bank
E	-	exchange rate (domestic units per foreign unit)
$\hat{e}^e$	-	expectations for exchange-rate changes
F	-	domestic bonds held by foreigners (translated into foreign currency)
$G-T$	-	budget deficit
i^*	-	nominal world interest rate
J	-	foreign bonds held by the domestic public (in foreign currency); J may be negative
K	-	capital imports (in foreign currency)
M	-	quantity of money
P	-	domestic price level
P^*	-	foreign price level
r	-	real domestic interest rate
R	-	foreign reserves held by the central bank (in foreign currency)
w	-	real domestic private financial wealth
w^*	-	real foreign private financial wealth (in foreign currency)
y	-	real domestic GNP
y^*	-	real foreign GNP (in foreign currency)
π^e	-	domestic inflationary expectations

The first three equations describe the money market assuming that $\frac{1}{\theta}$ is the money multiplier. In equation (2) we distinguish between government bonds held by the central bank and direct credit given to the government, where the latter is determined by the government (equation

(12)). Equations (4), (6), (7), (8), (12), and (13) describe the domestic bond market. The bonds are held at home and abroad.

The supply of bonds to the private nonfinancial sector is net, i.e., total bonds issued net of bank credit C. Domestic bonds are issued by the government to finance its deficit (equation (12)). The central bank, for its part, trades these bonds in the secondary market (ΔD). Thus ΔD represents open-market operations, which is the monetary policy tool. Note that $\Delta D > 0$ decreases the supply of bonds and increases the money supply.

The third asset held by the domstic public is foreign bonds. The demand for them is represented by equation (5), and since the economy is small and open, the supply is perfectly elastic at the world interest rate.

The demand functions are of standard form and bear the usual features. The following conditions therefore hold:

$$
\begin{aligned}
&L_w + B_w + J_w E = P \\
&L_p + B_p + J_p E = w \qquad\qquad (C.1)\\
&L_j + B_j + J_j E = 0, \qquad \forall \; j \neq w, P
\end{aligned}
$$

where A_j is the partial derivative of A with respect to j ($A = B$, L, F, J).

Equation (9) is the private wealth identity. It is easy to see that in the absence of capital gains the change in private wealth is identical with the sum of the budget deficit, which generates domestic assets, and the surplus on current account, which generates net assets abroad:[3]

$$\Delta w = (CA \cdot E + G - T)/P - w\,\frac{\Delta P}{P} + \frac{E(R + J - F)}{P}\,\frac{\Delta E}{E}. \qquad (14)$$

Capital imports, K, is equal to the difference between purchases of domestic bonds by foreigners and the purchase of foreign bonds by the

[3]This is obtained by substituting equations (2) and (8) into equation (9), taking differences, and using (10)-(12).

domestic public (equation (10)). Equation (11) represents the balance of payments. Equation (13) relates bank credit to money supply, using the bank's balance sheet.

For convenience, it is assumed that:

A.1 the exchange rate, E, is fixed, and without loss of generality $E = 1$

A.2 the foreign variables w^*, P^*, and y^* are fixed

A.3 the vector of rates of return other than r is $x = (\pi^e, i^*, \hat{e}^e)$.

The standard solution used by K&P derives from money-market equilibrium and capital flows, and does not explicitly use the domestic bond market (by Walras's Law).

The money-market equilibrium derived from equations (1)-(3) can be presented by differentiation, as follows

$$\Delta L(r,x,w,y,P) = \frac{1}{\theta}(\Delta R + \Delta D) - \frac{\Delta\theta}{\theta}M^s. \tag{15}$$

Solving from ΔR in equation (15) and using the balance-of-payments equations (10) and (11), we obtain

$$\begin{aligned}\Delta r = \epsilon_1[&CA + \Delta D + \Delta D_g - M\Delta\theta - (\theta L_x + J_x - F_x)\Delta x - (\theta L_w + J_w)\Delta w \\ &- (\theta L_y + J_y)\Delta y - (\theta L_p + J_p)\Delta P],\end{aligned} \tag{16}$$

where $\epsilon_1 = (\theta L_r - F_r + J_r)^{-1} \leq 0$.

Substituting (16) into equation (15) and using (11) to solve for K, we obtain

$$\begin{aligned}K= &-(1-L_r\theta\epsilon_1)CA - (1-L_r\theta\epsilon_1)(\Delta D - M^s\,\Delta\theta) - (1-L_r\theta\epsilon_1)\Delta C_g \\ &+ [\theta L_w - L_r\theta\epsilon_1(\theta L_w + J_w)]\Delta w + [\theta L_x - L_r\theta\epsilon_1(\theta L_x + J_x - F_x)]\Delta x \\ &+ [\theta L_y - L_r\theta\epsilon_1(\theta L_y + J_y)]\Delta y + [\theta L_p - L_r\theta\epsilon_1(\theta L_p + J_p)]\Delta P.\end{aligned} \tag{17}$$

Note that the coefficient of CA in equation (17) (the effect of the current account on capital movements) is identical with the coefficient of monetary policy ($\Delta D - M^s\Delta\theta$). A lot of empirical work has been done based on equation (17) and on the assumption that exogenous current account and fixed private wealth ($\Delta w = 0$), since wealth does not change in the short run (see Obstfeld 1980b, for a comprehensive survey). These studies include financing the budget deficit through money creation (ΔC_g) as part of the monetary policy and indeed in equation (17) ΔC_g has the same coefficient as does monetary policy.

By the second method of solution, the final equation is derived from the money and bond markets. The interest rate is derived by differentiating the bond-market equilibrium equation with equation (13) plugged in. Hence

$$\begin{aligned}\Delta r = \epsilon_2\{-\Delta B_g + \Delta D - M\Delta\theta + [B_x + F_x + (1-\theta)L_x]\Delta x \\ + [B_w + (1-\theta)L_w]\Delta w + (B_y + (1-\theta)L_y]\Delta y + [B_p + (1-\theta)L_p]\Delta P\}\end{aligned} \tag{18}$$

where $\epsilon_2 = -[(1-\theta)L_r + B_r + F_r]^{-1}$. As can be seen, $\epsilon_1 = \epsilon_2$ according to condition (C.1).[4] Substituting equation (18) into the money-market equilibrium equation, (15), yields

$$\begin{aligned}\Delta R = &-(1-L_r\theta\epsilon_1)(\Delta D - M^s\Delta\theta) - L_r\theta\epsilon_1\Delta B_g - \Delta C_g \\ &+ \{\theta L_x + L_r\theta\epsilon_1[B_x + F_x + (1-\theta)L_x]\}\Delta x \\ &+ \{\theta L_w + L_r\theta\epsilon_1[B_w + (1-\theta)L_w]\}\Delta w \\ &+ \{\theta L_y + L_r\theta\epsilon_1[B_y + (1-\theta)L_y]\}\Delta y \\ &+ \{\theta L_p + L_r\theta\epsilon_1[B_p + (1-\theta)L_p]\}\Delta p.\end{aligned} \tag{19}$$

The coefficient of monetary policy ($\Delta D - M^s\Delta\theta$) is identical with the coefficient derived in the previous approach [equation (17)].

---

[4]We have $\epsilon_2 = -(B_r + L_r + F_r - \theta L_r)^{-1} = -(F_r - J_r - \theta L_r)^{-1} = \epsilon_1$.

Nevertheless, equation (19) differs from equation (17) since some of the variables are different: the issue of bonds by the government (which in a way represents fiscal policy) appears, while the current-account variable does not.

The fact that the current account variable does not appear in equation (19) implies that there is no need for the assumption of the exogeneity of this variable. Such an assumption may cause problems in empirical work since export and import flows are affected by the real interest rate and expectations for exchange-rate changes. Moreover, excluding the current account while using ΔR as the dependent variable enables us to let both the capital and current accounts offset the effect of monetary policy.

We have chosen to estimate the offset coefficient of monetary policy by equation (19). This estimation allows us to use monthly data for Israel, for which there are no monthly data on the current account and capital imports, while monthly data for changes in the foreign reserves and for govrnment bond issues are available. Monthly estimation is important because the period during which the rate of exchange was fixed is short.[5]

Equation (19) brings out a number of noteworthy points. Monetary policy is represented by $(\Delta D - M^S \Delta \theta)$, the effect of monetary policy on the money base through two instruments, D and θ. The offset coefficient is $-(1 - L_r \theta \epsilon_1)$, which is the coefficient of monetary policy, and it is easy to see that it lies between zero and unity. The balance-of-payments flows offset the effect of monetary policy on the money base, and therefore on the quantity of money. The magnitude of the offset depends on the rate of substitution between domestic and foreign assets. In the case of perfect substitution, F_r and J_r tend to infinity and therefore $\epsilon_1 = 0$. The offset coefficient is then -1, and there is full offset. In other words: monetary policy is completely ineffective. In the opposite extreme case, where there is no substitution between domestic and foreign assets and F_r and J_r tend to zero -- the offset coefficient is zero: the economy resembles a closed economy and monetary policy is fully effective. Full

[5]It is easy to show that Walsras's Law implies the equivalence of equations (19) and (17). A formal proof can be obtained from the authors on request.

substitution is not a necessary condition for full offset, which can also occur under imperfect substitution if money demand is not sensitive to domestic interest ($L_r = 0$). The offset coefficient will then be -1, and monetary policy is ineffective.

Under imperfect substitution, the offset coefficient of monetary policy, $(1 - L_r\theta\epsilon_1)$, also depends on θ, itself a function of both the required reserve ratio [6] and the ratio of cash to deposits held by the public. This means that the offset coefficient is a function of monetary policy itself as well as of the rate of substitution between domestic and foreign assets. To be precise, the offset coefficient is a direct function of the money multiplier $1/\theta$. The lower the multiplier, the lower the offset coefficient. The economic explanation arises from the relationship between the money base and the demand for money. When, for instance, the monetary authority adopts a contractionary monetary policy by reducing D and there is perfect substitution, the domestic interest rate will not change, so that in order to restore money-market equilibrium, the foreign reserves must rise by exactly the same amount as the drop in D. If, on the other hand, there is imperfect substitution, the contractionary policy will raise the domestic interest rate and reduce money demand. Hence the rise in the reserves is a function of the change in money demand weighted by θ and it must be smaller than the change in D.

In Israel, where there have been numerous changes in liquidity ratios, the offset coefficient is not constant, and this must be taken into account in the estimation.

Equation (19) raises another important point: A distinction must be drawn between deficit financing and open-market operations as a means of changing the quantity of money. This distinction implies that monetary and fiscal authorities' intervention in the bond market differed in their effects. As stated, the coefficient of the monetary policy, $(\Delta D - M^S\Delta\theta)$, is $-(1 - L_r\theta\epsilon_1)$ (note that ΔD represents open-market operations). However, the fiscal authority also affects the money base if it chooses to finance the budget deficit by central-bank

---

[6] In the model, θ represents the actual and not the required reserve ratio. However, the two are related by actual θ=f (required θ,...). It can thus be assumed without loss of generality that θ is the required θ, i.e. a policy instrument.

credit (that is, by money creation), ΔC_g. The effect of such credit on the foreign reserves is -1 so long as wealth is given, that is, there is full offset independently of the rate of substitution. Interestingly, this difference was pointed out by Meltzer (1951) in relation to a closed economy:

> Whether the rate r_0 is a real rate or a monetary rate depends, as I have indicated earlier, upon the nature of the monetary disturbance. If the disturbance is of the first type -- that is, if it is a change in the quantity of money associated with the purchase or sale of securities by the central bank it will ... accordingly change the equilibrium in interest rates. ...On the other hand, if the monetary disturbance is of the second type, which consists of an increase or decrease in the quantity of money without any offsetting changes in other assets, it will ... not permanently change the interest rate (p.339).

In a closed economy a change in the money base while the interest rate remains fixed will be reflected in a matching change in the price level. In our open economy model, it will be reflected by a full offset through a change in foreign reserves.

This result implies that the effect of the monetary authorities' intervention in the bond market differs from the effect of the fiscal authority's intervention. In fact, the coefficient of monetary policy is $-(1 - L_r\theta\epsilon)$, while the coefficient of deficit financing through the bond market, ΔB_g, is $-L_r\theta\epsilon$.

Monetary policy carried out by open market operation (ΔD) alters both the amount of money and the amount of bonds (and therefore also the interest rate). These two elements affect the foreign reserves, so that the effect of the offset coefficient can be divided into two parts: (a) the direct effect of the money supply which is always -1; and (b) $-L_r\theta\epsilon_1$, the effect of the bond market and the interest rate. In contrast, fiscal policy, ΔB_g, works only through the bond market and has no effect on the quantity of money, which leaves only the second effect $(-L_r\theta\epsilon_1)$. It is thus easy to see that deficit financing through ΔB_g which is offset by open-market operations turns out to be financing through money creation and is fully offset by reserve flows.

Partial Adjustment in the Financial Markets

We have so far assumed instantaneous equilibrium in the financial markets. However, this is somewhat too strong an assumption, particularly with regard to short periods (one month). An alternative, more appropriate, assumption is therefore needed: asset holders adjust their holdings toward their long-run equilibrium level at a rate $0 < \delta < 1$, so that if B^s denotes actual, as distinct from desired (B^d, F^d), asset holdings, we have

$$B^s - B^s_{-1} = \delta(B^d + F^d - B^s_{-1}), \tag{8'}$$

where δ is the bond-market adjustment coefficient, which is the same for domestic and foreign holders (following Obstfeld (1982)). Similarly

$$M^s - M_{-1} = \lambda(M^d - M_{-1}), \tag{3'}$$

where $0 < \lambda < 1$ is the money-market adjustment coefficient.

Substituting equations (3′) and (8′) for equations (3) and (8) in the model yields equation (19′):

$$\begin{aligned} \Delta R = & -(1-\theta\epsilon L_r\lambda)(\Delta D - M^s\Delta\theta) - \theta\epsilon L_r\lambda\Delta B_g - \Delta C_g + (1-\delta)\theta\epsilon L_r\lambda\Delta B_{g-1} \\ & -(1-\delta)\theta\epsilon L_r\lambda(\Delta D_{-1} - M^s_{-1}\Delta\theta) + \theta[(1-\lambda)+(1-\theta)\epsilon L_r\lambda(\lambda-\delta)]\Delta M_{-1} \\ & +\theta\lambda(\{L_x + L_r\epsilon[B_x+F_x + (1-\theta)L_x]\}\Delta x + \{L_w+L_r\epsilon[B_w+(1-\theta)L_w]\}\Delta w \\ & +\{L_y + L_r\epsilon[B_y + (1-\theta)L_y]\}\Delta y + \{L_p + L_r\epsilon[B_p + (1-\theta)L_p]\}\Delta P), \end{aligned} \tag{19'}$$

where $\epsilon = -[\delta(B_r + F_r) + (1 - \theta)\lambda L_r]^{-1}$.

At this point the long and short run offset coefficients in equation (19′) can be distinguished. The long-run offset coefficients (expressed as a positive quantity) is

$$k_\ell = \left[1 - \frac{\theta L_r}{(F_r - J_r)} \right]^{-1},$$

while the short-run offset coefficient is

$$k_s = \left(1 - \frac{\theta \lambda L_r}{\delta(F_r - J_r)} \right)^{-1} \geq 0.$$

Denote $b_s = -\lambda L_r / \delta(F_r - J_r) \geq 0$; then $k_s = (1 + \theta b_s)^{-1}$, the short-run offset coefficient. Similarly, it is easy to see that the long-run offset coefficient is $k_\ell = (1 + \theta b_\ell)^{-1}$, where $b_\ell = -L_r/(F_r - J_r) = (\delta/\lambda) b_s$.

Thus it is easy to see that the long-run offset coefficient is greater (smaller) than the short-run coefficient according as λ is smaller (greater) than δ.

Denote $\Delta MBI = \Delta D - M^S \Delta\theta$, the monetary policy variable. Hence, (19′) yields:

$$\begin{aligned} E\Delta R = & -k_s \Delta MBI + (k_s - 1)\Delta Bg - \Delta Cg + (k_s - 1)(1 - \delta)\Delta MBI_{-1} \\ & - (k_s - 1)(1 - \delta)\Delta Bg_{-1} + [(1 - \lambda) + (k_s - 1)(1 - \theta)(\lambda - \delta)]\theta \Delta M_{-1} \qquad (20) \\ & + \theta a_1 \Delta x + \theta a_2 \Delta y + \theta a_3 \Delta P + \theta a_4 \Delta w. \end{aligned}$$

2. THE REACTION FUNCTION OF THE CENTRAL BANK (THE PROBLEM OF SIMULTANEITY)

A central problem in the estimation of an equation such as (17) or (19) arises because of the probable endogeneity of policy variables such as D and B_g. As mentioned, a considerable part of the empirical research on offset coefficients was on West Germany for the 1960s and early 1970s; these studies have provided a bewildering range of estimates of the offset coefficient.

With the exception of the Argy and Kouri (1974) study -- which, significantly, yields the lowest offset coefficient -- the reduced-form studies treat domestic monetary policy as an exogenous determinant of capital movements. However, the exogeneity assumption ignores the possibility of systematic sterilization operations that result in a negative correlation between changes in the central bank's domestic and foreign assets and so introduces a potential simultaneous-equation bias towards unity into the result. These suspicions appear to be confirmed by a detailed econometric model of the West German financial sector constructed by Herring and Marston (1977) (henceforth H&M). Simulation of the H&M model indicates an offset coefficient similar to those found by K&P. But the H&M offset is a long-run coefficient, since they permitted partial adjustment in the financial markets. These points were made by Obstfeld (1980b, 1982) who also distinguished between the short and long-run offset coefficients, and found the short-run offset coefficient to be very small (between 0.07 and 0.15), while the long-run coefficients were slightly below those of K&P (between 0.50 and 0.63). These findings suggest that the simultaneity bias in the standard approach of K&P is apparently due not only to the sterilization, but also to the distinction between the short run and the long run.

Recently, the possibility of a bias in the opposite direction has been raised. Roubini (1988) discusses the issue of the offset coefficient with an optimizing central bank and shows that when the central bank is concerned more with smoothing the interest rate than with stabilizing the foreign reserves, a negative correlation between the central bank's domestic and foreign assets will in fact be observed. However, if the foreign reserve objective is dominant, this correlation will be positive. Using the same argument, it can be shown that there will also be a positive correlation between the two types of assets if total net domestic credit,[7] $NDC = M^S - R$, is set as an intermediate monetary target. Such a positive correlation biases the estimate of the offset coefficient towards zero.

The simultaneity problem should be dealt with by a two-stage-least-squares (2SLS) procedure. The direction of the bias, however, depends on the monetary policy, and this may, of course, cause problems of estimation if the monetary authority changes its targets or its instruments during the period examined. Since the introduction of the stabilization program, there have been several changes in targets

---

[7]The domestic component of the quantity of money.

and instruments, suggesting that the period reviewed is largely one of transition and learning which may manifest itself in an unstable and unidentifiable reaction function. We have been able to identify only a sterilization policy around the time of the December 1988 devaluation.

3. THE EMPIRICAL FINDINGS

The analysis of section 2 indicated that the equation to be estimated is (20). It was estimated under the assumption that $\Delta w = 0$. The change in output is Δy (as measured by the index of industrial production); θ (which is subsumed in ΔMBI) and k are each a function of reserve requirements on deposits and credit and the cash-deposits ratio. In order to use θ as an exogenous variable, we calculated it using the cash-deposits ratio lagged one month. There was a substantial change in θ during the period (from 0.53 in September 1985 to 0.34 in December 1988). The change in the cash-deposits ratio was relatively small (from 0.49 to 0.45).

Finally, the vector Δx consists of inflationary expectations and the change in the rate of return on foreign-currenty denominated bonds. Neither inflationary expectations nor ΔP, the change in the price level, were significantly different from zero in any of the subsequent results. This is theoretically possible, since a_3 and a_1 can be zero.

The other component of Δx is the change in the rate of return on foreign-currency denominated bonds: $\Delta(i^* + \hat{e}^e)$. There are no direct data on the expectation for change in the exchange rate. We therefore use a proxy derived from the black market for dollars.[8]

Estimation of equation (20) requires a nonlinear method, since k_s is a function of θ. However, we have run linear regressions as well in order to avoid some econometric problems that may emerge in nonlinear estimation. A linear regression gives the flavor of the results by approximating the offset coefficient assuming constant θ.

We are, however, also interested in deriving offset coefficients

---

[8]This variable is stated in percentage points, and its coefficient indicates the change (in NIS million) in foreign reserves that results from a 1 percentage point change in the foreign rate of return. For further details on the data, see appendix available from the authors upon request.

implied by the low reserve ratios to be expected on the basis of declared monetary policy. Therefore k must also be estimated as a function of θ. In order to estimate the offset coefficient as a function of reserve ratios, we also present nonlinear estimates by estimators of b and derive an estimator of k.

The relationship between the coefficients in equation (20) enables us to impose the same b on all the coefficients. Alternatively, b can be estimated in two ways in order to give a range for the offset coefficient. We decided to calculate two b estimators, one derived from the coefficient of ΔMBI (denoted by BMI), and one derived from the coefficient of ΔB_g (denoted by BG).

Equation (20) holds when the exchange rate remains fixed. Since the introduction of the stabilization program in July 1985, a fixed exchange-rate regime has been maintained -- at first against the dollar and since August 1986 against the basket of currencies of Israel's main trading partners; there have been just two discrete changes: a 10 percent devaluation in January 1987 and one of 13.4 percent at the end of December 1988. It is for this reason that this study centers on the period following the stabilization program, September 1985-May 1989.

Following others we tested whether the policy variables are endogenous or exogenous so that an OLS procedure is sufficient to ensure an unbiased coefficient. A specification test for the presence of simultaneous-equation bias along the lines discussed in Godfrey (1984)[9] yields low t statistics (1.1 for the linear estimation and 1.4 for the nonlinear one). A 2SLS procedure is therefore not required. However, monetary policy was not, as mentioned, homogenous during the sample period. In particular, at the time of the 1988 devaluation, the Bank of Israel took steps to sterilize these flows in order to prevent the capital flows effect on domestic interest rates. We therefore allowed the monetary-policy coefficient to vary during the sterilization period, which was identified as October 1988-February 1989, using a dummy to measure the difference in the monetary-policy coefficient (DUM).

Results of the Linear Estimation

Results of the linear estimation of equation (20) by linear OLS procedure gave the following results:

---

[9] A test that is equivalent to a Hausman (1978) test.

$$\underset{(0.90)}{E\Delta R = 67.32} \; - \underset{(-2.61)}{0.428\Delta MBI} - \underset{(-4.92)}{0.579\Delta B_g} - \underset{(-14.67)}{0.937\Delta C_g} - \underset{(-3.14)}{0.266\Delta MBI_{-1}} \qquad (21)$$

$$+ \underset{(2.95)}{0.403\Delta B_{g-1}} + \underset{(0.26)}{0.139M_{-1}} - \underset{(-1.76)}{112.39\theta\Delta\hat{e}^e} + \underset{(1.74)}{61.45\Delta Y} - \underset{(-1.91)}{0.323DUM}$$

$$\bar{R}^2 = 0.873 \qquad DW = 2.22$$

(numbers in parentheses are t values).

Almost all of the coefficients are significant and have the right sign as required by equation (20). The constant does not differ significantly from zero, as required. The ΔC_g coefficient is close to -1 as required and does not differ significantly from it. Proxies for $\Delta\pi^e$ and the variable ΔP are omitted as they were not significantly different from zero and did not alter the results.

According to equation (20), the sum of the coefficients of ΔMBI and ΔB_g should be -1. In the estimation it falls slightly below -1, but it is not significantly different from it.

Note that omission of the change in financial wealth from the equation might bias the coefficient of the wealth components, ΔB_g and ΔC_g.[10] However, the fact that ΔC_g coefficient is so close to -1, and that the coefficients of both ΔB_g and ΔMBI sum to -1 suggests that there is no such bias.

The most important result of equation (21) is the short-run offset coefficient of monetary policy which measures the fraction of domestic monetary expansion offset by capital outflow in the current month. The short-run offset coefficient is -0.43. However, the DUM variable represents the additional effect of monetary policy during the sterilization period. Its coefficient of -0.32 and its significance show that sterilization was in fact carried out during October 1988-February 1989.

Results of Non-Linear Estimation

As stated, the non-linear estimation is important not only because it makes it possible to relate the offset coefficients to the various reserve ratios, but also for the derivation of the adjustment coefficients for the financial markets.

---

[10] It should be emphasized that the offset coefficient of monetary policy is not biased, as it represents only a change in the wealth mix and not its

We make the following assumptions:

B.1. BMI is the estimator of the b that appears in the coefficients of ΔMBI, ΔMBI_{-1}, and ΔM_{-1}.

B.2. BG is the estimator of the b that appears in the coefficients of ΔBG and ΔBG_{-1}.

B.3. BDUM is the estimator of the coefficient of DUM.

B.4. We allow direct estimation of δ and λ.

The results are presented in Table 1. The constant A does not differ significantly from zero; $\delta = 0.36$ (the same as the value of δ derivable from the OLS estimation), and $\lambda = 0.74$. Table 2 presents monthly long-run and short-run offset coefficients; during 1989 they averaged respectively 0.71 and 0.54.

The coefficient of ΔC_g is -0.95 and it does not differ significantly from -1. The estimate of BG is 4.07 and the coefficient of ΔB_g therefore averages -0.62, greater (in absolute value) than the coefficient found in the OLS estimation. This might be due to omission of the change in wealth; if so, the coefficient of ΔC_g would also be biased -- but since, as mentioned, it does not differ significantly from -1, the bias cannot be large.

Theoretically, BMI and BG should be identical; if we impose this relation, the results of Table 3 are obtained. An F test for this restriction implied that the restriction cannot be rejected. In this case, the estimator of b is higher and the offset coefficients are therefore somewhat lower, -0.49 for the short run at the end of the sample period and -0.63 for the long run. Table 4 presents the monthly short and long run offset coefficients for the entire period.

4. CONCLUSION

This paper has dealt with issues of monetary policy in Israel since July 1985. It does not go into the important and interesting question of the effect of monetary variables (such as money supply, interest rates, and credit) on other macroeconomic variables. Rather it concentrates on the question of whether monetary policy has an effect on monetary variables in Israel, which is an open economy with a fixed

---

value.

exchange rate and capital flows under control.

The offset coefficients were estimated through a reduced-form equation. However, we did not use the standard equations; instead, from the same basic model, we derived a different specification which enabled us to employ monthly data. Moreover, this specification emphasizes the effect of fiscal policy on the monetary side of the economy. In particular, we distinguish between money creation and traditional monetary policy such as open-market operations. The former is always fully offset, and this was verified by the empirical estimates. The offset coefficient of monetary policy is the standard offset coefficient; it was here found to average 0.5 for the short run and 0.7 for the long run. This seems rather high given the extensive measures taken by the authorities to reduce capital flows and given the high real domestic interest rate relative to the world rate. Thus Israel's relatively high real interest rate may reflect, at least in part, the extraordinary institutional structure of the Israeli financial system.

TABLE 1: RESULTS OF THE NONLINEAR ESTIMATION (BG $\neq$ BMI)

Variable	Estimate	S.E.	t value
A	87.86	58.60	1.50
BMI	2.73	1.50	1.82
BG	4.07	2.00	2.05
ΔC_g	-0.95	0.06	-14.75
λ	0.74	0.24	3.02
δ	0.36	0.21	1.72
a_1	-100.65	61.62	-1.63
a_2	61.78	35.56	1.74
BDUM	10.71	9.37	1.14
	$\bar{R}^2$ = 0.8933	DW = 2.315	

TABLE 2: SHORT AND LONG RUN OFFSET COEFFICIENTS (ACCORDING TO TABLE 1)

	k_s	k_ℓ
1985		
September	-0.40781	-0.58753
October	-0.40966	-0.58939
November	-0.41004	-0.58977
December	-0.40866	-0.58839
1986		
January	-0.41506	-0.59477
February	-0.41953	-0.59919
March	-0.42878	-0.60825
April	-0.43187	-0.61125
May	-0.44302	-0.62196
June	-0.45378	-0.63214
July	-0.45121	-0.62972
August	-0.45171	-0.63019
September	-0.45593	-0.63415
October	-0.46074	-0.63863
November	-0.46553	-0.64307
December	-0.46697	-0.64440
1987		
January	-0.46617	-0.64365
February	-0.48556	-0.66129
March	-0.50231	-0.67613
April	-0.48988	-0.66515
May	-0.46871	-0.64599
June	-0.46966	-0.64687
July	-0.46879	-0.64606
August	-0.46477	-0.64236
September	-0.46378	-0.64145
October	-0.46614	-0.64363
November	-0.46592	-0.64343
December	-0.46548	-0.64302
1988		
January	-0.46800	-0.64535
February	-0.47541	-0.65212
March	-0.50754	-0.68069
April	-0.50919	-0.68213
May	-0.51087	-0.68358
June	-0.51469	-0.68688
July	-0.51555	-0.68762
August	-0.51625	-0.68822
September	-0.51628	-0.68825
October	-0.54111	-0.70923
November	-0.53553	-0.70457
December	-0.53273	-0.70222
1989		
January	-0.53905	-0.70751
February	-0.54557	-0.71291
March	-0.55975	-0.72451
April	-0.55857	-0.72356
May	-0.55600	-0.72146
Mean	-0.48	-0.65

TABLE 3: RESULTS OF THE NONLINEAR ESTIMATION (BG = BMI)[a]

Variable	Estimate	S.E.	t value
A	7.06	57.02	0.12
BG = BMI	3.56	1.55	2.29
ΔC_g	-0.93	0.06	-15.62
λ	0.76	0.22	3.42
δ	0.43	0.18	2.43
a_1	-112.38	58.82	-1.91
a_2	54.85	33.76	1.62
BDUM	8.54	6.35	1.35
	$\bar{R}^2 = 0.892$	DW = 2.277	

a An F test for this restriction yields $F_{1,37} = 0.47$.

TABLE 4: SHORT AND LONG RUN OFFSET COEFFICIENTS (ACCORDING TO TABLE 3)

	k_s	k_ℓ
1985		
September	-0.34618	-0.48569
October	-0.34792	-0.48761
November	-0.34827	-0.48800
December	-0.34698	-0.48657
1986		
January	-0.34299	-0.49318
February	-0.35720	-0.49777
March	-0.36594	-0.50274
April	-0.36887	-0.51039
May	-0.37948	-0.52170
June	-0.38977	-0.53255
July	-0.38731	-0.52997
August	-0.38779	-0.53046
September	-0.39184	-0.53470
October	-0.39646	-0.53952
November	-0.40109	-0.54431
December	-0.40248	0.54574
1987		
January	-0.40170	-0.54494
February	-0.42052	-0.56415
March	-0.43694	-0.58055
April	-0.42475	-0.56840
May	-0.40416	-0.54747
June	-0.40508	-0.54842
July	-0.40423	-0.54755
August	-0.40035	-0.54354
September	-0.39940	-0.54246
October	-0.40168	-0.54491
November	-0.40147	-0.54470
December	-0.40104	-0.54426
1988		
January	-0.40348	-0.54677
February	-0.41065	-0.55412
March	-0.44209	-0.58563
April	-0.44372	-0.58723
May	-0.44538	-0.58886
June	-0.44916	-0.59256
July	-0.45001	-0.59339
August	-0.45071	-0.59407
September	-0.45073	-0.59409
October	-0.47552	-0.61789
November	-0.46992	-0.61257
December	-0.46711	-0.60990
1989		
January	-0.47344	-0.61593
February	-0.47999	-0.62212
March	-0.49433	-0.63551
April	-0.49313	-0.63440
May	-0.49052	-0.63198
Mean	-0.41	-0.56

REFERENCES

Argy, Victor, and Pentti, J.K.Kouri (1974), "Sterilization Policies and the Volatility in International Reserves." In *National Monetary Policies and the International Financial System.* Edited by Robert Z.Aliber. Chiago and London: University of Chicago Press, pp.209-230.

Bank of Israel Economic Review, No.60 (January 1988).

Cumby, Robert E., and Maurice Obstfeld (1981). *Capital Mobiliby and The Scope for Sterilization: Mexico in the 1970s.* (Working Paper Series No.770). Cambridge, Mass.: National Bureau of Economic Research.

Dornbusch, Rudiger (1980). *Open Economy Macroeconomics.* New York: Basic Books.

Godfrey, L.G. (1984). "On the Uses of Misspecification Checks and Tests of Non-Nested Hypotheses in Empirical Econometrics," *Economic Journal*, 94 (supplement), 69s-81s.

Hausman, J.A. (1978). "Specification Tests in Econometrics," *Econometrica*, 46 (No.6, November), 1251-1272.

Herring, Richard J., and Richard C.Marston (1977), *National Monetary Policies and International Financial Markets.* (Contributions to Economic Analysis 104). Amsterdam: North-Holland.

Kamas, Linda (1986). "The Balance of Payments Offset to Monetary Policy: Monetarist, Portfolio Balance, and Keynesian Estimates for Mexico and Venezuela," *Journal of Money, Credit and Banking* 18 (No.4, November), 467-481.

Kouri, Pentti, J.K. (1975). "The Hypothesis of Offsetting Capital Flows: A Case Study of Germany," *Journal of Monetary Economics*, 1 (No.1, January), 21-39.

——————, and Michael G.Porter (1974). "International Capital Flows and Portfolio Equilibrium," *Journal of Political Economy*, 82 (No.3, May/June), 443-467.

Leiderman, Leonardo, and Assaf Razin (1988). "Testing Ricardian Neutrality with an Intertemporal Stochastic Model," *Journal of Money, Credit and Banking*, 20 (No.1, February), 1-21.

Magee, Stephen P. (1976). "The Empirical Evidence on the Monetary Approach to the Balance of Payments and Exchange Rates," *American Economic Review: Papers and Proceedings*, 66 (No.2, May), 163-170.

Metzler, Lloyd A. (1951). "Wealth, Saving, and the Rate of Interest," Journal of Political Economy, 59 (April), 93-116. Reprinted in *Monetary Theory and Policy*, Edited by R.S.Thorn, New York: Random House, pp.324-327.

Neuman, Manfred J.M. (1978). "Offsetting Capital Flows: A Reexamination of the German Case," Journal of Monetary Economics, 4 (No.1, January), 131-142.

Obstfeld, Maurice (1980a). "Imperfect Substitutability and Monetary Policy Under Fixed Exchange Rates," *Journal of International Economics*, 10 (May), 177-200.

——— (1980b). *Sterilization and the Offsetting Capital Movements: Evidence from West Germany, 1960-1970.* (Working Paper Series No.494.) Cambridge, Mass.: National Bureau of Economic Research.

——— (1982). "Can we Sterilize" Theory and Evidence," *American Economic Review: Papers and Proceedings*, 72 (No.2, May), 45-50.

——— (1982). "The Capitalization of Income Streams and the Effects of Open-Market Policy under Fixed Exchange Rates," *Journal of Monetary Economics*, 9 (No.1), 87-98.

Roubini, Nouriel (1988). *Offset and Sterilization under Fixed Exchange Rates with an Optimizing Central Bank.* (Working Paper Series No.2777.) Cambridge Mass.: National Bureau of Economic Research.

Tobin, James (1969). "A General Equilibrium Approach to Monetary Theory," *Journal of MOney, Credit and Banking*, 1 (No.1, February), 15-29.

11 ISRAEL'S POST-STABILIZATION RECESSION: MONETARY FACTORS

Assaf Razin and Efraim Sadka

I. OVERVIEW

For more than a decade after the Yom-Kipur war, Israel muddled through a high inflation, balance-of-payments crises with almost no growth. In July 1985, the government launched a comprehensive stabilization program. Inflation was brought down sharply, almost overnight, from a three-digit annual level to 15-20 percent. At the same time, the accelerated increase in Israel's external debt was brought to an end and Israel's financial standing in the international capital markets improved significantly. These accomplishments are still in place today, five years later.

About the same time, several Latin American countries faced with problems similar to Israel launched stabilization programs. In some countries the stabilization program looked promising initially, but after a while, failed completely (Argentina and Brazil). In others (Bolivia, Chile and Mexico) the stabilization programs proved successful. However, as in the case of Israel, there still remains a hard core of inflation in the order of magnitude of about 15-20 percent per annum.

In the first two years after the launch of the stabilization program Israel recorded exceptional rates of growth of output and productivity, and a relatively low rate of unemployment. However, the post-stabilization boom was short lived. It was caused by once-and-for-all factors: the sharp decline in the rate of inflation, the pullout of the Israeli forces from Lebanon and the fall in energy prices. A slide into a recession could have been detected already in the second half of 1987. The recession continued at least through the first half of 1989. The temporary post-stabilization boom alluded policy-makers away from the emergence of a recession. This late diagnosis led to a longer and deeper recession.

We analyze key monetary factors and the economic policy-making processes which led to the 1988-1989 recession. The recession is deeply rooted in the pegged exchange rate policy and high rates of interest that prevailed in 1987 and 1988. Moshe Nissim (The Finance Minister) who is charged by law on the exchange rate policy, opted for not changing the exchange rate for reasons of price stability and preceived public credibility. Michael Bruno (The Governor of the Bank of Israel) in charge of the monetary and interest policy, was in effect the architect of the exchange rate policy. He stuck rigidly to a policy of using the exchange rate as a monetary anchor for price and wage stability, even when the fundamentals were inconsistent with that policy. It was not before mid-1988, 18 months after a complete freeze of the exchange rate, in the face of an almost 30 percent increase in the price level during that period, that the Governor sought to realign the exchange rate. This rather belated attempt to sway the Finance Minister in the direction of adjusting the exchange rate failed, due to the approaching national elections (November 1988). After the elections, the new government took a sharp turn in the economic policy.

The launching of the stabilization program dictated a sharp cut in the rate of expansion of the nominal monetary aggregates, and this was in fact done. (In theory, a one-shot expansion of the supply of money, followed by a fall in the money growth rate, would have been the desired policy. However, in practice, the initial monetary expansion may have generated inflationary expectations with failed stabilization). Monetary restraint, at a time when the demand for money rose as inflationary expectations abated, caused in turn a sharp rise in real interest rates (particularly on unindexed local-currency credit). This rise deterred the Bank of Israel from continuing the sharp monetary restraint, consistent with the one-digit inflation rates in Israel's trading partner countries. At the same time, the central bank and the Ministry of Finance adhered to a declared and determined policy of freezing the exchange rate, which in turn further reduced the Bank of Israel's ability to check the rate of growth of the monetary aggregates. The real appreciation of the shekel against the currency basket which followed from the policy, further cut into the business sector's profitability (especially in the sectors producing tradeables, for export and import substitution, such as manufacturing industry, agriculture, and others). This sector had already been hurt by the higher interest rates. To these factors one should add the rise in the cost of raising capital, due to the tighter restrictions on capital imports imposed for fear of a "monetary flood" which might have been caused by the freeze on the exchange rate. The erosion of profitability in the business sector, which was further damaged by the increase in the effective tax burden on the business sector stemming from the decline in inflation, made it difficult to roll over long-term credits by raising fresh long-term loans. The business sector was increasingly forced to turn into "distress borrowing", especially in the unindexed local-currency credit segment, in order to roll over loans as well as to cover current losses. Consequently, the demand for unindexed domestic credit rose and became less elastic. In market conditions far from perfectly competitive, as they are in Israel's banking sector, these developments facilitated the rise in lending rates together with the widening of the financial margins.

The initial rise in interest rates apparently was an unavoidable by product of stabilizing the economy which had experienced rampant inflation. But the monetary policy pursued subsequently, especially since it included the freezing of the exchange rate without succeeding in checking the nominal expansion of the monetary aggregates to one-digit levels, severely reduced business sector profitability and left short-term real interest rates at a relatively high level. The high rates of interest further aggravated the erosion of profitability. In this broader sense, monetary policy is viewed as a fundamental driving force of the recession which actually began as early as the second half of 1987, and was further deepened by the Intifada and the rise in the effective tax burden.

The Intifada, the uprising in the territories which exploded on 9th December, 1987, had an immediate and direct effect on the employment of Arab workers in Israel. Exports of labor services from the West Bank and Gaza fell as a result of threats issued by the leadership of the Intifada and preventine curfews imposed by the Israel Army. The decline in the labor supply was mainly in the form of infrequent appearances in work places and reduced hours worked per employee. However, consequent on the decrease in the supply of labor was a rise in real wages. Thus, income earned by workers from the territories in Israel did not fall significantly in the first year after the commencement of the Intifada. Furthermore, the 1988 olive crop (which is subject to a two-year cycle) in the West Bank was record high. Thus, no significant fall in the West

Bank GDP was recorded either. The picture was different in the Gaza Strip where a significant decline in income occurred. Investments (especially, public) in both the West Bank and the Gaza Strip fell sharply, and this will hamper growth prospects in the coming years.

II. TWO YEARS AFTER THE STABILIZATION: A RECOVERY THAT FADED AWAY

First signs of economic recovery became apparent soon after the launching of the July 1985 stabilization program and its accompanying policy measures. After an initial GDP decline of about 4 percent per annum in the second half of 1985, compared to the first half of the year, GDP rose in 1986 by 3.6 percent, and the business sector product increased even more impressively - by some 5.7 percent. The economic upswing continued at an even more rapid rate in the first half of 1987, when GDP grew at an annual rate of about 6.5 percent and the business sector product by some 8 percent annually over the second half of 1986. These are the highest growth rates experienced by the Israeli economy since the Yom Kipur War. Since 1985, after many years of stagnation and even decline, business sector productivity recorded a substantial rise of about 4 percent per annum - unquestionably an exceptional growth by comparison with the earlier record in Israel as well as by international standards. In the second half of 1986 and the first half of 1987 this was accompanied by a substantial increase in fixed investment (15 percent and 6.7 percent in annual terms, respectively), coming after sharp declines of 11.3 and 7.8 percent, respectively in 1984 and 1985. Immediately after the implementation of the stabilization program the unemployment rate rose moderately but began to fall by mid-1986, with the decline continuing into 1987. The short-lived boom did not result in a deterioration of the balance of payments - certainly not at the time. In 1985 and 1986, current account surpluses of 1.1 and 1.6 billion current dollars, respectively, supported by the U.S. emergency grant of $1.5 billion and the decline in the world price of oil, were recorded for the first time in Israel's economic history. Among the principal causes of GDP growth was an exceptional productivity increase, resulting from a combination of factors. First, the drastic reduction of inflation (and particularly the narrowing of the random fluctuations in its monthly rate) shifted work effort away from financial activities (chiefly designed to afford protection against the inflationary erosion of monetary assets, or to generate inflation profits which contributed nothing to real GDP) to real productive activities. Second, the drop in world energy prices raised the value added of local production, expressing itself in a rise of productivity. Third, the withdrawal of the Israel Defence Forces from Lebanon eased the burden of military reserve duty and its disruptive effect on work. However, these factors had a one-time effect on productivity, and had run their course already in the year or two following the stabilization program. The inflation rate became more or less stable and its random fluctuations became much more moderate. Even a further decline in the inflation rate to a level comparable to that prevailing in OECD countries will not significantly affect the business sector's burden of inflation-induced financial activities, and will therefore also have no significant impact on productivity. In the period under discussion, oil prices were relatively low in real terms in comparison to their level after the oil crises of 1974 and 1979-80, and did not subsequently decline further, nor is it likely that they will continue to fall significantly in the future.

Despite the remarkable performance, a number of unsolved problems remained and others emerged, becoming increasingly prominent in subsequent years:

a) The rise in productivity was due to non-recurrent factors, such as the one-shot drop in inflation.

b) The inflation rate remained high in comparison to that prevailing in Israel's trading partners. The stabilization program and the curbing of inflation were associated with a fixed nominal exchange rate (except for a slight correction in January 1987). A continuing erosion of the real exchange rate (i.e., a real appreciation of the shekel) therefore developed, causing a steady fall of profitability in the business sectors producing for export or import substitution (manufacturing, tourism, etc.).

c) The high real interest rates, (serving as an important instrument of curbing domestic demand within the framework of the stabilization program), did not decline in the period under discussion to levels permitting a renewal of economic growth. On the contrary, the high level of interest rates aggravated the financial crises of various enterprises and economic sectors.

d) The decline in the national saving rate, due to a sharp drop in the private saving rate, despite the rise in the public sector saving rate which resulted principally from the narrowing of the government deficit and its turning into a budgetary surplus. The drop in the national saving rate, from 21.7 percent of total income in 1985 to 16.5 percent in 1987, inhibited the accumulation of wealth, required for sustained growth.

e) The sharp erosion of real wages in the business sector in the second half of 1985, immediately after the stabilization program. For 1985 as a whole, real wages contracted by 6.4 percent over 1984, despite the rise in real wages in the first half of 1985. Real wages rose again in 1986 and 1987 - by 9.1 and 8.1 percent, respectively. These wage increases exceeded the rise in the value of the marginal product of labor as measured by the change in labor productivity, and as such contributed to eroding returns to capital in the business sector.[3] This was partly offset by the rise in total productivity, over and above the growth in labor productivity, which contributed to an increase in the returns to capital. However, in total, returns to capital in the business sector were eroded substantially, just when the cost of capital rose. This reduced the profitability of investment in the business sector (see Appendix I).

Table 1 presents the calculation of the changes in returns to capital in 1986 and 1987, when returns to capital declined by 12 and 7.9 percent, respectively.

TABLE 1. WAGES, RETURNS TO CAPITAL AND PRODUCTIVITY IN THE BUSINESS SECTOR, 1986-87*
(Percent rate of change)

	1986	1987
(P_T) Total Productivity	3.8	4.1
(P_L) Labor Productivity	3.5	3.0
(g_W) Wages	9.1	8.1
(g_S) Returns to Capital	-12.0	-7.9

Source: Bank of Israel 1988 Annual Report, p.78. Based on the assumption that the respective shares of capital and labor in product are 25 and 75 percent.

3. THE SLIDE INTO RECESSION: A RETROSPECTIVE DIAGNOSIS

The impressive expansion of GDP and economic activity which marked the early period following the July 1985 stabilization program (the year 1986 and the first half of 1987) came to an abrupt end in the second half of 1987 (see Table 2). In 1986, GDP grew by 3.9 percent and the business sector product by 5.7 percent. In the first and second quarter of 1987, the business sector product rose at annual rates of 7.4 and 14.8 percent, respectively. However, in the second half of 1987, before the outbreak of the uprising in the territories, business sector product as well as total GDP began to decline. The unemployment rate, which in the year following the stabilization program had risen temporarily (from about 6 percent in the first half of 1985 to 6.4 percent in the first half of 1986), later fell back to the low level of the pre-stabilization period. Unemployment remained low also in the second half of 1987 and the first half of 1988, and began to rise only in the second half of 1987, reaching 9.3 percent in the second quarter of 1989.

Early diagnosis of an illness is crucial in medicine for proper treatment. The same holds for economic policy. A real-time identification of turnabouts in economic trends is vital for updating and revising economic policies. However, several factors impede the timely observation of trends. First, most data on the economic variables (such as GDP, unemployment rate, level of investment, etc.) appear naturally with the significant delay of a quarter or even a whole year. Secondly, a change of trend in the level of economic activity is not immediately reflected in all economic indicators. A fall in demand for a product does not immediately lead to a decline of output, because initially there is a tendency to accumulate inventories in the wishful hope that the contraction of demand is temporary, and also because in part, some production costs are in the short run a sunk cost. A decline in output also does not express itself in Israel in an immediate contraction of employment, since firms do not rush into shedding workers immediately after a cut in output due to high costs (financial and others), which layoffs would require in Israel. Thus, for example, despite the fact that the slack in economic activity began already in the second half of 1987, no significant rise in the unemployment rate appeared until the second half of 1988.[1]

In retrospect, it seems that policymakers were late in perceiving that economic trends were headed towards recession. The Bank of Israel's periodic report on economic developments, published in September 1987 said:[2] "The turnaround in domestic economic activity began in the second half of 1986, as the economy emerged from the standstill during the first year after the adoption of the emergency stabilization program." At the time there was a guarded assessment that the economy was about to move towards the resumption of economic growth.

TABLE 2. ECONOMIC ACTIVITY, 1985-89
(Annual percentage changes, seasonally adjusted)

Quarter		GDP	Business Sector Product	Unemployment*
1985	I	-0.8	7.4	
	II	26.2	14.8	
	III	-16.8	-20.3	
	IV	- 0.8	22.5	
Annual	Average	3.9	5.3	6.5
1986	I	7.0	2.0	
	II	- 0.4	2.0	
	III	4.5	8.2	
	IV	13.4	12.6	
Annual	Average	3.6	5.7	7.1
1987	I	0.8	2.4	
	II	13.0	22.5	
	III	- 0.8	- 2.0	
	IV	- 2.4	- 8.9	
Annual	Average	5.2	7.0	6.1
1988	I	14.8	19.3	
	II	-15.8	-16.1	
	III	6.6	2.0	
	IV	6.1	7.8	
Annual	Average	1.6	1.1	6.4
1989	I	-12.4	-19.6	8.1
	II	7.3	- 7.3	8.8
	III	-5.4	0.0	9.2
	IV	5.8	0.0	9.0
Annual	Average	-2.0	-6.8	8.8

* Percentage of unemployed out of (civilian) labor force.

[1] It should be noted that higher public sector employment also moderated the rise in unemployment.

[2] See: "Economic Developments in Recent Months" No.42, Bank of Israel, September 1987.

The aforementioned Bank of Israel's report stated: "Another important feature of recent developments is the growing indication of the beginning of structural change in the economy - a change which, if continued, will bring forth accelerated stable growth." The authors of the National Budget for 1988 judged that there would be no return to the impressive growth rates in GDP and business sector product of 1987, but still believed that the "GDP will grow by 3.7 percent and the business sector product by 4.6 percent" - growth rates that are far from indicating a beginning of recession. Even by March 1988, the Bank of Israel was still hesitant whether economic activity was clearly turning towards recession: "The slowdown in business activity that made itself felt in the last quarter of 1987 followed a steady and rapid expansion during the three preceding quarters. The question that therefore poses itself is what caused activity to slow in the last quarter, and whether this is a temporary phenomenon or indicates a reversal of the expansionary trend that marked business activity during 1986 and, even more so, the first three quarters of 1987."[3] The Bank of Israel's Annual Report for 1987, published at the end of May 1988 (English version published in August 1988), after the Central Bureau of Statistics had published data on the economic growth of 1987, was clearly on an optimistic note: "Following the initial shocks caused by the stabilization program, a process set in of progressive adaptation to the changed economic environment. This process has apparently not yet run its course. So far, three stages are discernible in it: (a) a sharp drop in the inflation rate, and a large cut in the budget deficit, with a slowdown in economic activity; (b) the consolidation of stability and a surge in domestic demand; and (c) a rise in business sector activity and employment, associated with changes in the structure of demand and product..." In mid-1988, when the Annual report was published, the Bank of Israel had not yet perceived that the third of these stages had in fact come to its end by the third quarter of 1987. This significant delay (of nearly a year) in diagnosing the turnaround in the economy held back decisions to adopt corrective policy measures and caused the recession in economic activity to accelerate, as

---

[3]See: "Economic Developments in Recent Months", No.43, Bank of Israel, March 1988.

witnessed in 1989.[4]

3. CAUSES OF THE RECESSION

The recession actually took policymakers by surprise. In contrast to the 1966-67 recession, which was policy-initiated, and intended to check adverse balance of payments trends that had developed, the recent recession was unplanned. Policymakers did not perceive it as the price to be paid for those policies. On the contrary, as stated in the previous section, their assessment was even that the prevailing policy would gradually bring forth economic growth.

It may in fact be said that the recession was primarily caused by the distortion of several key relative prices, namely, the real exchange rate and real short- and long-term interest rates, which are affected by monetary policy. The first signs of slowdown surfaced already in the third quarter of 1987, before the outbreak of the intifada. The uprising was therefore not the factor that pushed the Israeli economy into recession; it merely deepened it.[5] The economic impact of the intifada may, in any event, be regarded as a one-time adverse shock to the level of GDP; it cannot explain a continuing fall in GDP growth rates.

Monetary policy, as is well known, has three interrelated

---

[4]This prolonged lag in recognizing the change of trend by economic policymakers was not shared by others in the business and academic community. Thus, for example, the evaluations and forecasts of the Economic Models Ltd. company, published in July 1987 stated: "The leading indicators for the first half of 1987 indeed point to a substantial rise in industrial production, exports, investment and private consumption. However, in our view, this is a temporary phenomenon, and a slowdown is expected in the second half of 1987, compared with the first half of the year." In September 1987, even before the outbreak of the Intifada, the same company made the assessment that the previous twelve months' acceleration of economic activity had in fact ended, and "since the conditions for structural change had not yet materialized, especially in the industrial sector, economic activity returns to a path of moderate growth, of a 2-3 percent per annum." (See "Macro-economic and Sectorial Trends," July 1987 and September 1987, Economic Models Ltd.)

[5]For the effects of the intifada on the economy see Chapter 4 in Amnon Neubach, Assaf Razin and Efraim Sadka (1990), Challenges to the Economy of Israel: Aliya, Growth and Integration into the World Economy, Maariv Press, Chapter 4.

dimensions - monetary aggregates, interest rates, and the exchange rate. Until the end of 1988, monetary policy was characterized by a freeze of the nominal exchange rate (except for a slight correction in January 1987) and a high rate of increase (tens of percentage points per annum) in the money supply, at current prices. The money supply measure relevant for issues of monetary policy is customarily taken to be the M_3 aggregate, which comprises cash held by the public, demand deposits with the banks, unindexed short-term shekel deposits (such as Pakam, short-term time deposits and Pahak, CDs, etc.), and short-term foreign-currency indexed deposits (Patam, local residents' foreign currency deposits, etc.). For a better understanding of the mechanism of monetary expansion, it should be pointed out that in an examination of the assets side in the banking system's balance sheets, this definition of M_3 in fact equals the shekel value of the Bank of Israel's net foreign currency reserves,[6] plus net domestic credit extended by the banking system to the public and the government (see Appendix II). Note that in order to describe the interrelationships between the money supply and price levels, wages and interest rates, it is necessary to look at the nominal rather than the real changes in the money supply.

A. Monetary Expansion

It is well known that intervention in the foreign currency market by the central bank in order to peg the exchange rate impairs the Bank's control over the money supply. Under a regime of foreign currency controls and a fixed exchange rate, capital imports (which the central bank in this case is obliged to convert without limit into local currency) automatically increase the money base (the reserves of the commercial banks and cash held by the public). This leads to an increase in the money supply, through the money-credit multiplier (which is greater than 1). Therefore, when the Bank of Israel announces a stable exchange rate policy, and the public becomes convinced that the bank will adhere to that policy, while domestic nominal interest rates are higher than abroad, there will, of course, be capital inflows - cheap loans will be taken up abroad and invested in Israel at high

---

[6]Net of the Bank of Israel's liabilities to the rest of the world.

returns. As a result, the money supply increases. Such a process actually developed in the course of 1986-87. Bank of Israel's data show that the M_3 aggregate increased between 1985 and 1986 by a nominal 45 percent, and by another 32 percent between 1986 and 1987. These expansions are made up of increases in the central bank's foreign reserves, by 61 and 56 percent, respectively, in 1986 over 1985 and in 1987 over 1986, and increases in net domestic credit of 34 and 16 percent, respectively, in the same years.

The slowing of inflation and the relative price stability that followed the July 1985 stabilization seem to have caused a substantial change in the public's behavior as regards the holding of unindexed financial assets. It is plausible that the demand for money expanded significantly in this period. The increased money supply of 1986 therefore served at least in part to satisfy this larger demand for money.

Since 1987, however, there has been no substantive change in the inflation rate, nor are there reasons to assume that there were further significant changes in the demand for money. The continued rise in the money supply therefore exerted, pressure on the price level. On the other hand, if economic policy is not consistent[7] with freezing the exchange rate for a long period, expectations of devaluation are aroused. These expectations generate capital exports. Such capital exports express themselves in a fall in the Bank of Israel's foreign reserves, automatically shrink the money base and with it, all the financial aggregates. This, in fact, occurred in the second half of 1988.

As expectations of devaluation strengthened in 1988, the rate of nominal M_3 growth declined to an average of 18 percent. Most of the slowdown occurred in the second half of 1988, when the annual rate of M_3 expansion was only about 10 percent, as against 19 percent in the first half of the year.[8]

---

[7]The loss of control over net domestic credit, which is a principal component of monetary policy, is particularly important in this context.

[8]The growth rate of GDP was indeed lower in 1988 than in 1987, but even if the expansion of M_3 is adjusted for the growth of GDP, there still is a slower increase of M_3.

As stated earlier, the M_3 aggregate is in fact equal to the sum of the shekel value of the Bank of Israel's net foreign reserves and the net domestic credit extended by the banking system to the public and the government. It is noteworthy that despite the 1988 decline in the growth rate of M_3, its net domestic credit component, which is supposed to be the Bank of Israel's principal policy instrument, expanded at an accelerated rate. From an expansion of no more than 16 percent in 1987, net domestic credit grew by some 30 percent in 1988. The expansion rate of net domestic credit spiralled in the second half of 1988 to an annual rate of 60 percent. This expansion actually financed the public's stepped-up foreign currency purchases, caused by expectations of an impending devaluation. As we show later in this section, the expansion of net domestic credit was a result of the Bank of Israel's reaction to the rise in the interest rates in the short-term unindexed segment of the credit market, in view of the Bank's inability to force down these rates by other means. The mirror image of the accelerated growth of net domestic credit, which contrasted withfffe relatively moderate expansion of M_3, was the sharp decline in the foreign currency reserves.

B. Exchange Rates and Wages

An excessive money supply expresses itself in price increases. The frozen exchange rate limits price increases of tradeable goods, such as manufactured goods and tourism services, which are exposed to competitive imports. Prices of such goods rise at a rate approaching the average world rate of inflation. In contrast, prices of nontradeable goods (mainly services), which are not exposed to competitive imports continue to rise. These price increases are of course accompanied by wage increases in these sectors. Competition for workers causes wage increases to spread also to industries facing competition from imports or which produce for export (such as manufactured goods and tourism services), despite the slower rate of increase in their prices. As a result, profit margins in these industries are reduced, and firms are compelled to contract.

Figure 1 shows the changes in real wages (nominal wages deflated by the price index of the sector's product) for two sectors - manufacturing, which mainly represents internationally tradable goods, and the commerce and services sector, which produces mainly nontradeables.[9] Real wages in manufacturing, in terms of manufacturing prices, rose between 1984 and 1988 by a cumulative 20 percent, while wages in the services and commerce sector, in terms of the respective sector's prices, declined in the same period by 5 percent. The foregoing discussion clearly indicates the adverse effect of the prevailing economic policy on industry, a leading sector of the economy (the product of the manufacturing sector accounts for about 30 percent of the business sector product). Such a high wage rise (in terms of cost to the employer) - nearly twice the increase in labor productivity - severely cut into the profitability of manufacturing.

It is therefore no surprise that this sector's product was among the first to be hurt by the prevailing economic policy. Figure 2 shows that the growth of industrial production was arrested in the third quarter of 1987, and then began to decline. Due to the close intput-output type of interrelations between manufacturing and the other economic sectors, damage to manufacturing necessarily sparks a chain reaction in all economic sectors, with feedbacks to manufacturing itself. The index of industrial production, which is published with a relatively short lag (some three months) should serve as a leading indicator of economic trends, so that it ought to have switched on, in nearly real time, a red light for policymakers. This is particularly so because a theoretical economic analysis of the effects of the economic policy could have indicated the possibility of damage to the profitability of manufacturing. Another available indicator is the index of industrial exports which is published with a very short lag (no more than one month).

It has variously been argued, in the Finance Ministry and the Bank of Israel, that one of the principal causes of the recession was an exogenous wage rise. One explanation offered for such a wage increase was that "employers were prepared to accede to wage demands in the (erroneous) hope that they would eventually be extricated by an appropriate government policy, such as the continuation of a policy of

---

[9]Services are evidently mainly nontradeables. The product of the commerce sector is the local value added which serves to prepare goods for marketing them to the domestic consumer. This sector therefore also represents mainly nontradeables.

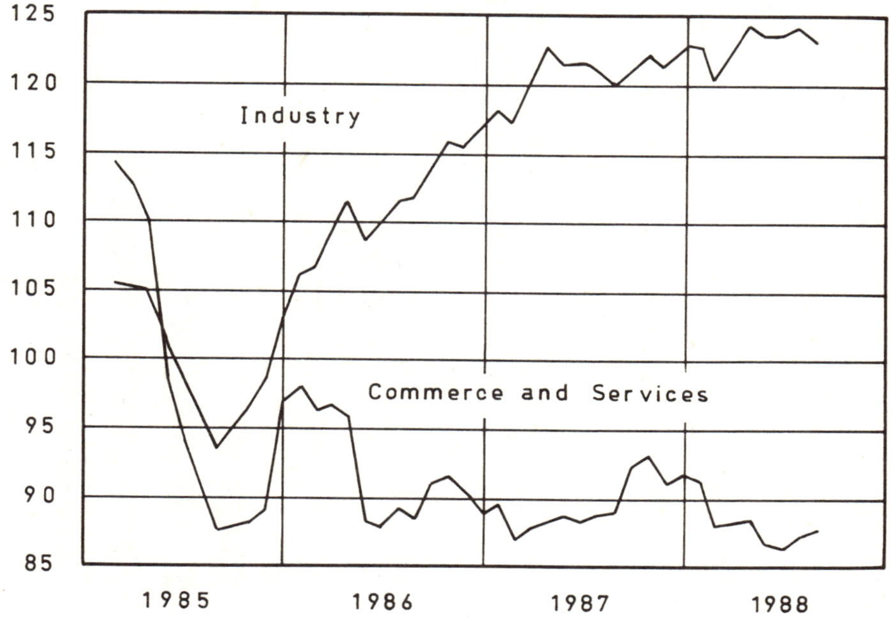

Figure 1. Index of Real Wages, 1985-88.

(Nominal wages deflated by industry price indexes)

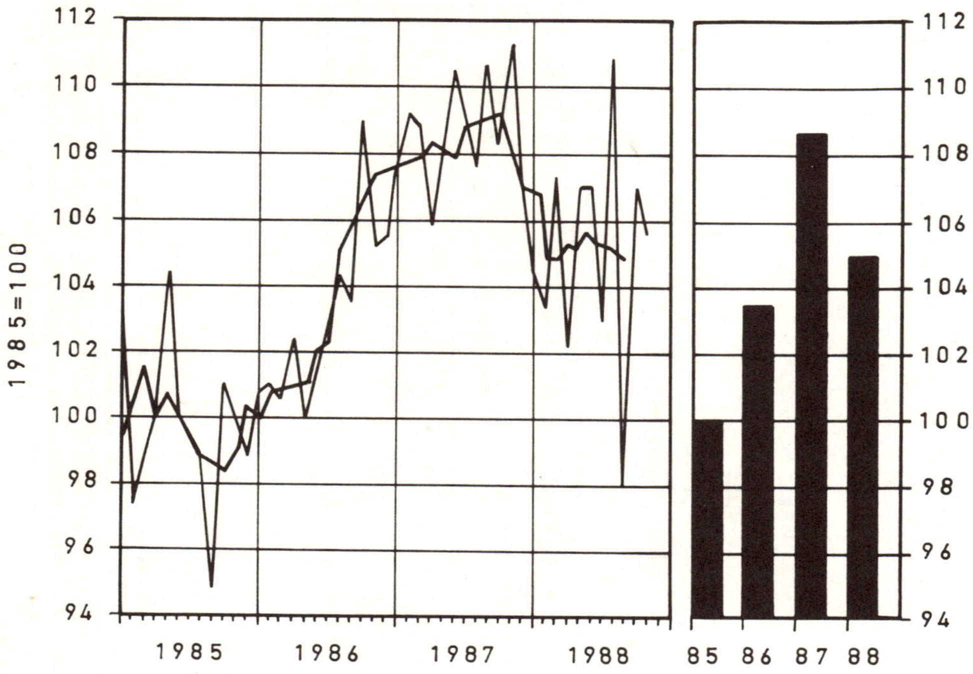

Figure 2. Index of Industrial Production, 1985–88 .

(Monthly and annual averages)

devaluations."[10] Expectations of future price increases, including those following devaluations, under a regime in which the cost-of-living allowance is neither immediate nor compensates fully for price increases, no doubt encourage workers' demands for higher wages, and induce employers to accede to such demands. It is, however, unreasonable to assume that the expectations of workers and employers can be systematically and irrationally erroneous and upward-biased for such a long period. A fixed exchange rate had been a key component in a policy announced and pursued determinedly for two years - from January 1987 to the end of 1988. Moreover, it may be said that the government adhered to a stable exchange rate policy at nearly any cost almost since the launching of the stabilization program in July 1985. The only exception were the modest devaluation of January 1987 and the fact that when the stabilization program was adopted the shekel was pegged to the dollar, which weakened against the other currencies in the basket, and caused a devaluation of the shekel against the currency basket. It is implausible that in such an environment employers sysetmatically continued to expect that the government would bail them out from their own acquiescence in excessive wage increases.

The argument that expectations of workers and employers can be systematically erroneous (which means continuing to believe that the government would come to their aid with a devaluation) is also not supported by the data on nominal wage increases in the various industries. If this argument were true, nominal wage increases would have been higher in sectors where devaluation has a greater impact on prices as perceived by firms (i.e., the sectors producing tradeables), and lower in sectors producing nontradeables. Thus, for example, nominal wage increases in manufacturing should have been greater than those in the personal services sector and others like it. The data, however, indicate the opposite: between the second half of 1985 and the second half of 1987, nominal wages in mansufacturing rose by 89 percent, whereas in the sectors of personal services and other nontradeables, money wages rose by 97 percent.

Although the government adjusted the exchange rate against the currency basket only partially to the movements of wages and domestic

---

[10]See Michael Bruno, "Economic Recovery in Historical Perspective," Economic Quarterly (Hebrew), No.141, July 1989, 113-189.

prices, the argument has still been raised that even this partial adjustment was unnecessary. This reasoning is based on the assumption that the sole function of a devaluation is to erode real wages, so that it is preferable to endeavor to achieve a direct cut in nominal wages rather than devalue the currency. The problem with this line of argument is that it ignores the fact that devaluation changes relative prices as between different sectors, especially as between tradeables and nontradeables. It thus affects real wages (in terms of producer prices) differentially in the various sectors. In the tradeable industries, in particular, devaluation reduces real wages more than in the sectors producing nontradeables. However, nominal wages are determined by the competition of all sectors for workers, and therefore vary according to occupation, seniority, etc., and not in accordance with an industry breakdown. Mechanical engineers with similar qualifications, for example, earn more or less the same in all industries. Therefore, even if a restrictive monetary policy and other macroeconomic measures, and particularly tripartite wage negotiations between government, employers and the trade unions could bring about a downward pressure on nominal wages without devaluation (which is difficult to assume under circumstances of less than full employment), it must be assumed that such wage cuts would spread more or less evenly over the various sectors. The distortion of relative real wage levels in the various sectors would remain unaffected, as can be seen from Figure 1.

One factor which clouded the picture of economic developments and, in particular, made it difficult to "read the map" as regards the effects of economic policy, was the development of exports, especially industrial exports. On industrial exports, the Bank of Israel's 1988 Annual Report (p.198) says: "The 1988 exchange rate freeze against the dollar did not prevent significant expansion in industrial exports to the U.S. and an increase in their share in total exports." In the first half of 1987 total industrial exports rose in real terms, seasonally adjusted, by 5 percent over the second half of 1986, and by an additional 8.4 and 6.5 percent, respectively, in the second half of 1987 and the first half of 1988. When economic activity slows down, exports obviously tend to rise, diverting supply from the slack domestic market to international markets which are unaffected by the level of domestic activity. But an hysteresis effect was apparently also at work, preventing the decline in profitability caused by the freezing of the exchange rate from promptly affecting the level of exports.[11]

Exchange rate policy also had a recessionary effect through its impact on fixed investment. An exchange rate freeze, and particularly expectations of continued erosion of returns to capital in the business sector, depress business firms' propensity to invest. Exchange rate policy therefore dampened domestic demand through the investment mechanism. In addition, since capital goods are mainly imported, the low exchange rate lowered their prices relative to other domestic prices and the cost of domestic inputs. Although in general this increased the relative profitability of investment, it had an even stronger effect in diverting investment demand to foreign markets, thus reducing domestic demand. Thus, for example, the share of investment in transport equipment (which is predominantly imported) in total nondwelling investment rose from 14.5 percent in 1986 to 19.5 percent in 1987 and 21.5 percent in 1988.

C. Interest Rates

Short- and long-term interest rates are among the principal facets of monetary policy. The short-term interest rate is directly affected by the supply of the monetary aggregates. In the long run, these aggregates have only a marginal effect on real long-term interest rates, although they may have some effect in the short-run. But monetary policy has a direct effect on short- and medium terms interest rates, via administrative restrictions and tax barriers to international capital movements (such as prohibitions, imposts or ceilings on interest rates of capital imports). Interest rates are, of course, also directly affected by the capital market policies, particularly through the gap (or the financial margins) between lending and borrowing rates.

---

[11]Hysteresis exists because there are sunk costs in the entry into and exit from foreign markets. Therefore, as long as exporters believe that there is a reasonable chance that the erosion of profitability will cease in the future, they will postpone a decision to get out of their foreign markets. A similar phenomenon occurred in Japanese exports to the U.S. Despite the strengthening of the Yen, Japanese exporters did not quickly raise the dollar prices of their products and continued to export at lower Yen prices. For an explanation of this phenomenon, see Avinash Dixit, "Hysteresis, Import Penetration, and the Exchange Rate Pass-Through," Princeton University, 1988.

1. *Short-Term Interest Rates (The Unindexed Shekel Segment)*

The drastic fall of the inflation rate, accompanied within a short time by a downward adjustment of inflationary expectations, also led to an increase in the demand for money to a higher steady-state level. Such an increase exerts upward pressure on the short-term real interest rate. This pressure became even stronger as a result of the monetary restraint that was a necessary component of the stabilization program, and reduced the nominal expansion of the monetary aggregates from their pre-stabilization rates of growth.

Such a rise in interest rates seems to be inevitable in practice, and was typical of similar stabilization programs in the world. Theoretically, it would be possible to think of a careful and credible combination of two monetary measures which would bring about price stabilization without entailing a sharp rise in real short-term interest rates. This might be achieved by a one-time increase in the money supply, which would satisfy the higher demand for money (as a result of the fall in the expected inflation rate), and immediately afterwards, a drastic reduction of the growth rate of the money supply, which would cut the inflation rate and be in line with the lower inflationary expectations. In practice, however, it is difficult to make such a policy credible among the public, because on the one hand it would increase the money supply, and on the other, promise to reduce its rate of expansion immediately afterwards. In practice, it would therefore seem to be unavoidable to start a stabilization program with an immediate monetary restraint and pay the price for that by a rise in real short-term interest rates, at least for some time.

Several other factors contributed to the rise in real interest rates and, in particular, to their stabilization on a higher level. In consequence of the sharp initial rise of interest rates that followed the stabilization program, as well as the erosion of the real exchange rate, enterprises and various economic sectors experienced financial difficulty. The banks become exposed to a higher risk level in lending to the public. The risk premium raised lending rates, especially for short-term credit.[12]

---

[12]This phenomenon is particularly noticeable in the case of short-term credit (overdraft facilities), because the rolling over of long-term credits for firms in difficulty (and therefore in arrears in servicing their debt) is shifted to short-term accounts.

An additional cause of the rise in real short-term interest rates (in the unindexed shekel segment) seems to be related to high concentration of the banking industry. The Israeli financial market is far from being regulation free and competitive. The restraints on market freedom (for example, the restrictions on the minimum period for which indexed credit may be granted), which are set by the government and the Bank of Israel establish in effect two financial sectors - an indexed and an unindexed sector, which differ both in the level of their borrowing and lending rates and in the financial margins prevailing in each. The unindexed shekel segment is generally under looser regulatory control, and in this segment the commercial banks have more discretion in adjusting interest rates to the demand for credit. When long-term credits fall due, and firms in financial difficulty are hard put to roll them over by taking fresh long-term loans, their demand for short-term credit <u>increases</u> and becomes less elastic (Figure 3 in fact indicates a continuing decline in the net medium-and long-term credit flows, relative to business sector product). When the supply of credit is concentrated in a relatively small number of big banks, with significant market shares, and therefore characterized by the absence of effective competition, higher and less elastic demand for credit will express itself in high levels of lending rates and a larger spread between lending and borrowing rates. (For a detailed explanation of this phenomenon, see Appendix III.) Figure 4 demonstrates the determination of the financial spread between borrowing and lending rates in a less than competitive market. Figure 5 indicates the substantial rise in importance of unindexed short term credit following the stabilization and Figure 6 illustrates the rise in the ratio of local currency short term credit.

Table 3 presents time series of interest rates in the unindexed shekel segment. The sharp rise in average lending rates in 1984-85 is prominent. Since then, interest rates have fallen, but their level still remains high in comparison to the 1970s and the early 1980s. The table also indicates a very sharp increase in the gap between lending and borrowing rates and in the financial margins in 1984-85 which, as said earlier, are due to the high degree of concentration in the banking sector, the decline in the elasticity of demand for credit, and the

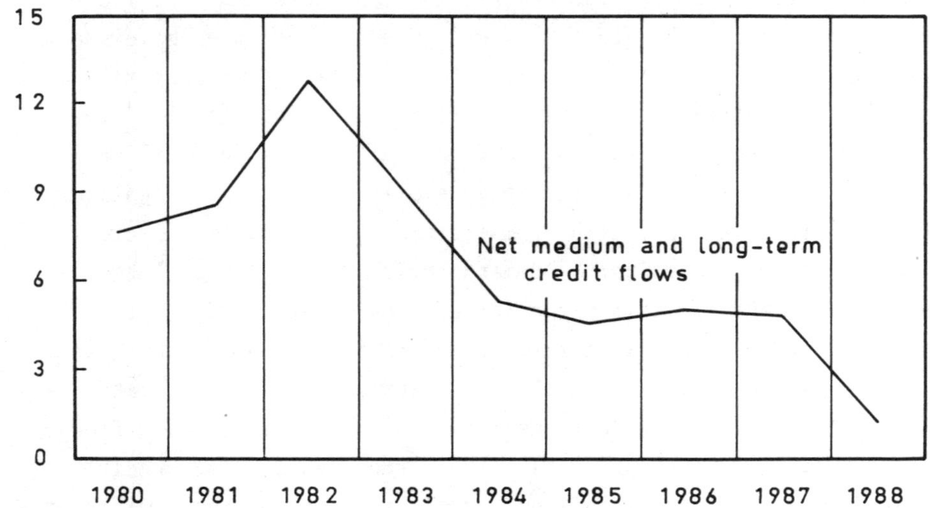

Figure 3. Net Medium-and Long-term Credit Flows as a Percentage of Business Sector Product, 1980-88.

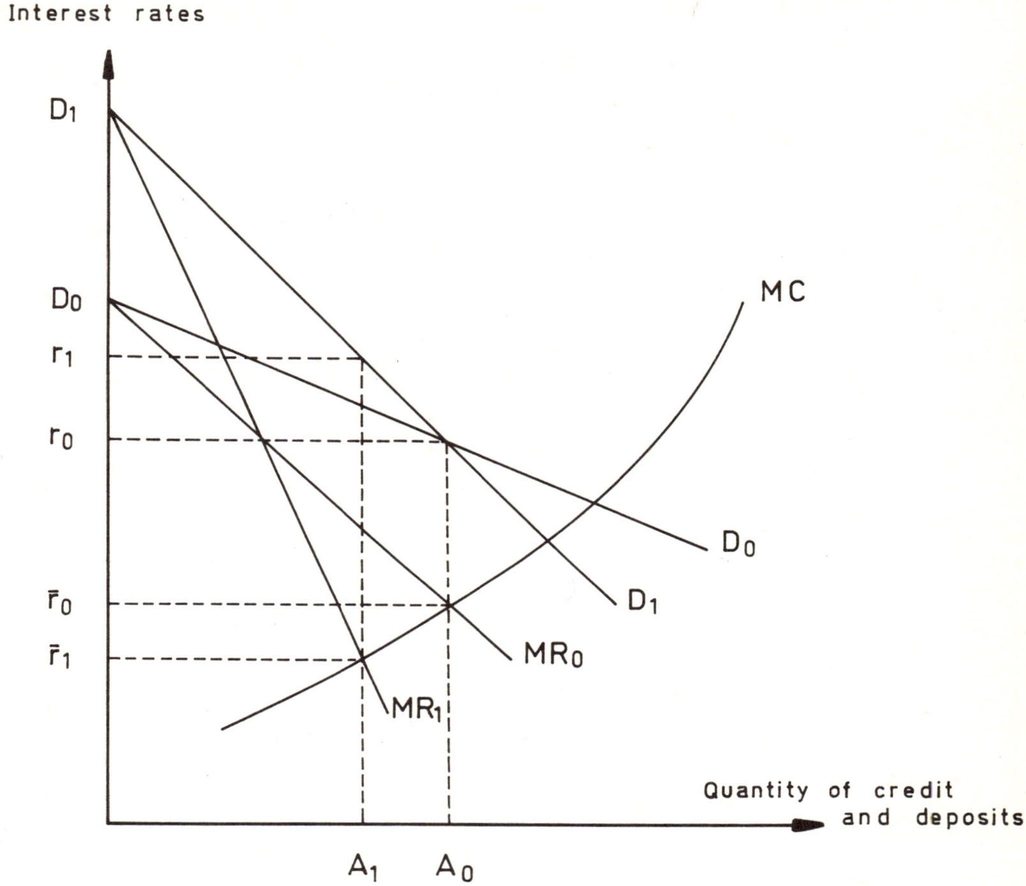

Figure 4. Determination of the Gap between Borrowing and Lending Rates in a Monopolistic Market .

$\bar{r}_1$, $\bar{r}_0$ –Borrowing rates .

r_1 , r_0 –Lending rates .

D_0D_0, D_1D_1–Demand curves of the public for credit confronting the bank .

MR_0, MR_1–Marginal revenue curves (from interest on credit) of the bank .

MC –The bank's marginal cost of mobilizing deposits .

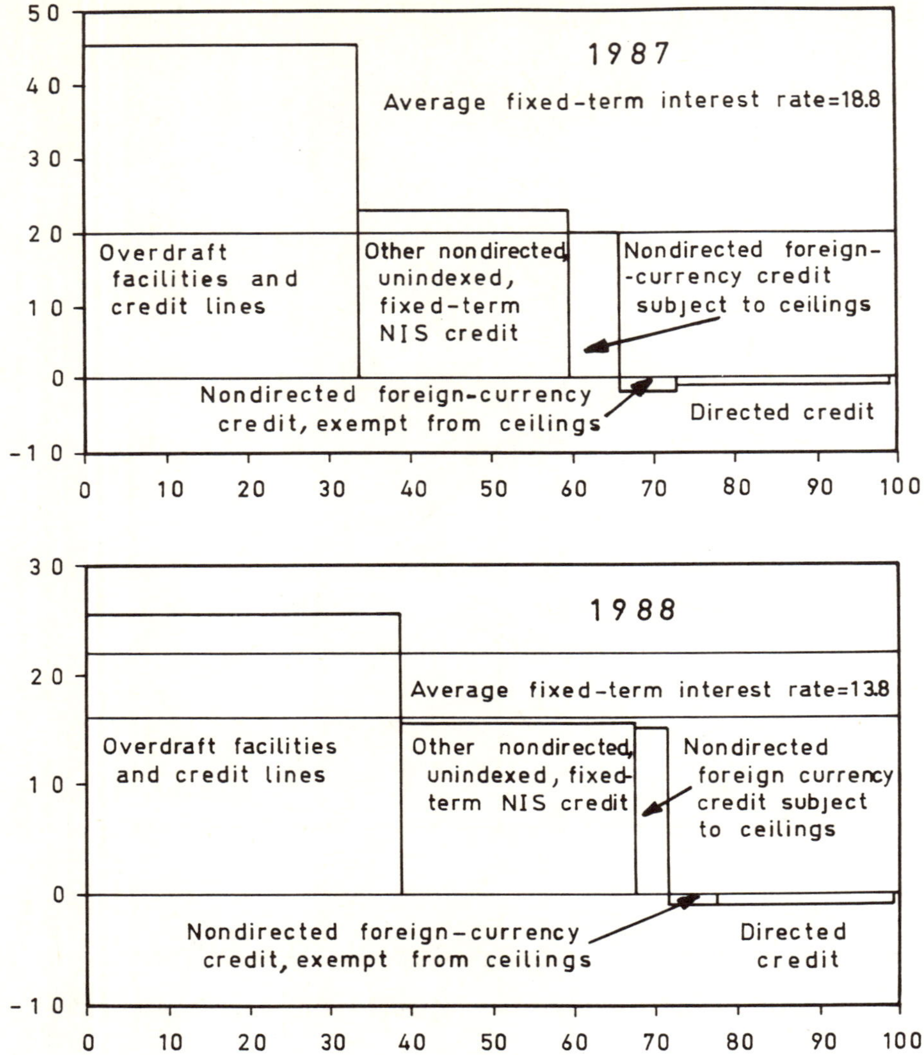

Figure 5. Real Short-Term Interest Rates by Shares of Credit Components, 1987-88, percent per annum *

* The average fixed-term interest rate is based on weighted monthly averages. It therefore differs from the average rate of interest obtained from the weighted quarterly averages shown in the diagram.

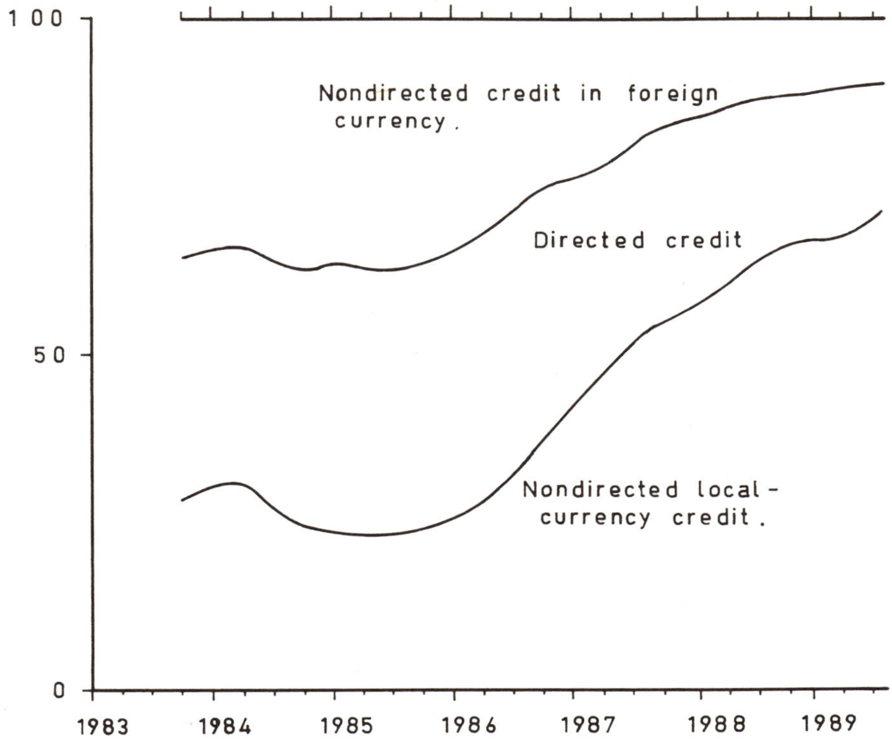

Figure 6. Total Short-term Credit by Type, 1982–89.

Source: Yoram Ben-Raveh, The Interest Burden of Short-term Bank Credit, 1983 89, Bank of Israel. Discussion Paper No. 89.07, July 1989 (Hebrew).

higher risk premium.[13] Noteworthy are also the temporary fluctuations in shekel interest rates which are due to expectations of price rises in general, and devaluation in particular. The shekel interest rate thus includes, in addition to the risk premium (which also exists for indexed credit), a premium for expectations of price changes, including devaluations. Thus, when expectations of devaluation rise, demand increases for shekel credit destined to finance purchases of foreign currency made in order to profit from the expected devaluation. Such an increase in demand for credit of course raises nominal interest rate, as in fact happened towards the end of 1988 when expectations of devaluation strengthened. After the devaluations, interest rates resumed the downward trend that characterized the year 1988.

The rise in the interest rate on short-term local-currency credit has various effects on the economy. First, companies which suffered a severe profit erosion in real operations (also as a result of the factors mentioned earlier) were compelled to cover their accumulated losses by turning to the short-term credit market. For such enterprises, the higher interest rates in that segment were "the straw that broke the camel's back" (for example, Carmel Carpets, the Horowitz Brothers, Kibbutzim, Moshavim, Koor, Solel Boneh, and others). The financial burden aggravated the critical situation which these firms had reached and accelerated the cutbacks in output and employment. Secondly, in all sectors the rise in short-term interest rates increasedthe cost of holding inventories, and thus caused them to contract. In other words, firms found it more difficult (or less profitable) to absorb a fall in demand by increasing their inventories (for example, Soltam, Ordan, Tadiran, and others), and had to adjust their current activities more rapidly to the fall in demand. Analysis of investment in inventories in recent years in fact indicates a certain downward trend

[13]The financial margins are lower than the spread between lending and borrowing rates because the former take account of the central bank's reserve requirements, which oblige the banks to redeposit, at a relatively low interest rate, part of the public's deposits with the central bank. Thus, for example, although the difference between borrowing and lending rates was in 1987 39.8 percent, this does not represent the banks' profit from lending because they are not able to use all the funds they borrow from the public at the (negative) lending rate of -1.2 percent in order to grant credit at 38.6 percent, but have to deposit part of these funds with the Bank of Israel at the relatively low interest fixed by the central bank.

TABLE 3. UNINDEXED SHEKEL CREDIT: REAL INTEREST RATES AND FINANCIAL MARGINS, 1970-88

	1970-1975	1976-1977	1978-1983	1984-1985	1986	1987	1988
A. Real short-term interest on unindexed shekel credit							
1. Lending rate[a]	0.4	- 0.1	7.0	77.8	33.4	38.6	25.4
2. Deposit rate[b]	-8.7	-14.1	-23.4	-9.5	-2.1	-1.2	-4.1
3. Interest rate spread (2-1)	9.1	14.2	30.4	87.3	36.8	39.8	29.5
4. Financial margins	4.5	5.7	17.5	33.8	15.1	18.4	16.0[c]
B. Average real interest rate on total short-term bank credit[d]			3.7	22.5	8.2	18.8	13.8

[a] From 1978, on overdraft facilities.

[b] CDs or overnight deposits.

[c] Estimate.

[d] For the purpose of illustration, details of this aggregate for 1987 and 1988 are given in Appendix III.

Source: Bank of Israel Annual Report, 1988, p.243 (English version).

in inventories relative to business sector product (see Table 4). It must, however, be kept in mind that investment in inventories is also influenced by other factors, such as expectations of higher prices and devaluation, the tax code and actual inflation (the tax code does not regard business inventories as fixed assets, so that, ceteris paribus, the higher the actual inflation rate, the more profitable is the holding of inventories).

TABLE 4: CHANGE IN INVENTORIES AS A PERCENTAGE OF BUSINESS SECTOR PRODUCT, 1980-1988

1980	+1.0
1981	-1.7
1982	+0.9
1983	+0.2
1984	+1.6
1985	+0.6
1986	+3.4
1987	+0.2
1988	0.0

2. *Capital Imports and the Long-Term Cost of Funds*

The economic policy of the Ministry of Finance and the Bank of Israel closed the economy, by dministrative restrictions, to free capital movements. Under such conditions, domestic interest rates can obviously differ from those prevailing in international capital markets. In practice, the marginal cost of long-term credit from domestic sources was substantially higher (as a result of effective restrictions on capital imports) than the cost of raising funds abroad. At the same time, returns on certain financial investments abroad are higher or appear safer than the return obtained by Israeli savers (as a result of effective restrictions on capital exports). For the purpose of the present section, the relevant cost is that of long-term credit for domestic firms (whether selling in domestic or foreign markets). As said earlier, due to the administrative and tax restrictions, developments in international capital markets alone do not affect the cost of domestic credit. The latter is also influenced by domestic demand, private and public, for investment and consumption.

The freeze on the exchange rate (accepted as credible policy by the public) required a fairly rigid enforcement of the restrictions on capital imports in order to prevent a "monetary flood." When the nominal local-currency interest rate is much above the nominal, foreign-currency denominated interest rate abroad, and when this is accompanied by official declarations of intent to adhere to a stable exchange rate regime, it is evidently profitable to import capital (to borrow at low interest rates abroad and invest the funds in Israel for a high nominal yield). This remains profitable so long as the public does not expect a devaluation in the near future and therefore does not fear exchange rate losses that would offset the profits arising from the difference between domestic and foreign interest rates. The justified fear of a "monetary flood" that would occur if unlimited capital imports were permitted required a strict enforcement of the restrictions on them, particularly so on short-term, but also on long-term capital imports.

The restrictions on capital imports were tightened, among other things, by the imposition of a 3 percent surcharge on credits taken up abroad, increasing the business sector's cost of raising funds abroad and caused domestic long-term interest rates to go up (in the same manner as when customs duties on goods are levied, enabling domestic producers to set higher domestic prices). A ceiling was also imposed on the borrowing rate on credits taken up abroad, which eliminated segments of Israeli firms from the market. In addition, there were factors at work which augmented domestic demand for long-term credit - an increase which cannot at present be supplied by credit from abroad, and which therefore necessitated a rise in the cost of domestic credit. One of the principal factors which increased the demand for credit was the higher demand for consumption goods (especially durables such as automobiles, VCRs, etc.[14]), which was due to a too low real exchange rate. The resulting increase in demand for credit was, it might be noted, in part moderated by restraint in public consumption.

As a result of the high dispersion of long-term credit among different borrowers, the different purposes for which such credit is taken up and granted, it is difficult to arrive at a precise estimate of the marginal cost of long-term credit. Nevertheless, in this credit segment the differences between borrowing and lending rates are relatively small. This permits taking the changes in real yields on long-term financial assets as an approximation of the business sector's real cost of raising capital. Figure 7 indicates a substantial rise in the yields on long-term (risk-free) financial assets soon after the adoption of the stabilization program. Although subsequently there was a clear downward trend in these yields (and the 3 percent impost on

[14]To avoid complicated diagrams, we purposely ignore the possibility that the bank can also act as a monopsonist towards its depositors. This possibility in fact increases the interest rate gap even more.

capital imports was abolished), it was only towards the end of 1988 that these yields began to approach their level in the 1970s. The high cost of raising capital eventually, albeit with a lag, depressed investment and contributed to the onset of recession (see above for the hysteresis effect).

5. CONCLUSIONS AND FUTURE OUTLOOK

The initial rise in interest rates apparently was an unavoidable accompaniment of stabilizing an economy which had experienced rampant inflation, but the monetary policy pursued subsequently, especially since it included the freezing of the exchange rate without succeeding in checking the nominal expansion of the financial aggregates to one-digit levels, severely reduced profitability in the business sector and left real interest rates at a relatively high level. This further aggravated the erosion of profitability. In this broader sense, monetary policy was a fundamental in the onset of a recession which actually began as early as the second half of 1987.

The slump in economic activity in Israel, which had begun in the second half of 1987, and deepened significantly in 1988, lasted through the first half of 1989. The new national-unity government, formed in December 1988, implemented a series of economic measures which constituted a sharp turn from previous policies. Among these measures are: two realignments of the exchange rate; a new cost-of-living adjustment clause in the wage pact which sterilized the direct effect of devaluations on prices from the cost-of-living adjustment; investment promoting tax changes such as accelerated depreciation and reduced corporate tax rates; some gradual lifting of controls on international capital flows; and moral persuasion, to reduce interest rates and financial margins in a concentrated banking industry. These new measures and the economic recession brought about major changes in some key relative prices: the <u>real</u> exchange rate, the <u>real</u> wage, and the <u>real</u> interest rates. The turnabout in policy succeeded in bringing down trend of the economy into a halt in the second half of 1989 and even into a slow start of an upward trend. In February 1990 the government implemented additional policy measures, consistent with the turnabout in policy that took place in December 1989. The new measures include: a 6 percent devaluation with sterilizing its price effects from the cost of

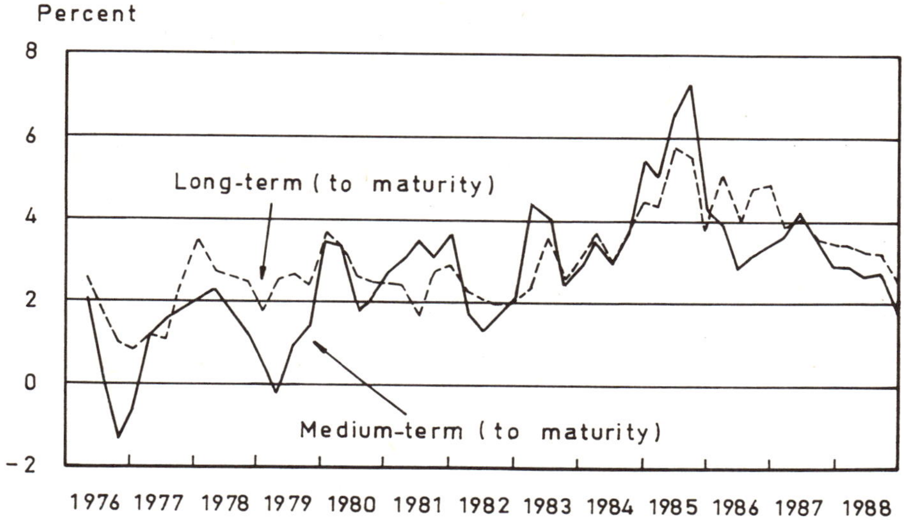

Figure 7. Real Rates of Return on Government Bonds, 1976–88[a].

living allowance, a reduction in export subsidies, and additional liberalization measures concerning international capital flows. These measures further contributed to the upturn in activities witnessed in 1990.

The major regime changes taking place nowadays in the Eastern Bloc countries following Mikhail Gorbachev's Glassnost coupled with stricter quotas imposed by the United States government on Jewish immigration from the Soviet Union, generated a new wave of Jewish Aliya (immigration) from the Soviet Union to Israel. The new Olim (immigrants), relatively rich in human capital, tend to have a relatively large labor force participation rate among women. Thus, the new Aliya can become a leverage for renewed growth of the Israeli economy. The economic estimate for 1990 is a 5-6 percent growth rate of GNP. If the new wave of Aliya continues at the present rate also in the coming years, a 8-10 percent growth of GNP is expected in subsequent years. Nevertheless, the growth in output will not be reflected in a significant drop in the rate of unemployment because the labor force is expected to increase more than usually due to several factors: the Aliya itself, the entrance of the Post Six-Day War baby boomers to the labor market (after army service), and the ongoing trend of a larger labor force participation rate among women from the existing population. A successful absorption of the new Aliya wave as a leverage for a new long-lasting economic growth is one of the main challenges for the Israeli economy in this decade.

The lion's share of Israel's international trade in goods is the European Community. Israel is not a member of the European Community, but has a preferential trade agreement with the European Community. The creation of a single market in Europe of 1992 puts forward another challenge for the Israeli economy in the 1990s. In contrast to trade in goods, Israel has no special agreements with respect to capital flows and financial services. The chance of a "Fortress Europe" scenario in this area is therefore real for Israel, unless a process of capital market liberalization is advanced in Israel. Obviously, international capital market integration affects the real side of trade and thereby growth.

In a country like Israel, poor in natural resources, there is a special significance for human capital in the growth process. The tax structure in Israel does not encourage investments in human capital. Furthermore, the policy of direct government's financing of this kind of investment is inadequate and inefficient. As a matter of fact, the policy even restricts investments in human capital among several major groups of the population. A major reform in the government's policy towards investment in human capital and in the tax treatment of such investment is urgently needed. Parallel to the need of investments in human capital, there is a need for significant measures to enhance the efficiency of investments in physical capital and private savings. The aim is to channel investments to the most efficient projects, while simultaneously increasing private savings as a source for funding private investments. Accordingly, a special emphasis must be placed on the privatization of the banking industry. The most important aspect of meeting the challenge of a long-lasting economic growth is new policies concerning the volume and efficient allocation of investments in human and physical capital.

APPENDIX I: WAGES AND PRODUCTIVITY

This appendix will clarify the connections between changes in the marginal product of labor, overall and labor productivity, and the returns to capital, and reports on the developments in these variables in the short-lived boom period.

Assume that output (Y), is produced by two production factors, labor (L), and capital (K), according to the following production function :

$$Y = F(K, L, T) \tag{1}$$

where T is total productivity. Denote the changes over time in the variables Y, L, and K by g_Y, g_L, and g_K, respectively. Differentiating (1) we obtain

$$g_Y = a_K g_K + a_L g_L + P_T \tag{2}$$

where P_T is the total productivity of production factors.

In the above equation, a_K and a_L measure the respective shares of labor and capital in output, as determined by their respective marginal product, namely:

$$a_K = MP_K K/Y = MP_K/AP_K \tag{3}$$

$$a_L = MP_L L/Y = MP_L/AP_L, \tag{4}$$

where MP_i and AP_i are the marginal and average product of production factor i $(i = K, L)$. Assuming constant returns to scale, it is known that

$$a_K + a_L = 1. \tag{5}$$

Labor productivity (P_L) is defined as the rate of change in the average product of labor, and is equal to the rate of change in output minus the rate of change in the labor input:

$$P_L = g_Y - g_L. \tag{6}$$

Equations (2), (5) and (6) yield the relationship between total productivity and labor productivity:

$$P_T - P_L = g_Y - a_K g_K - a_L g_L - (g_Y - g_L) = a_K(g_L - g_K). \tag{7}$$

In other words, total productivity is greater than labor productivity if, and only if, the rate of change in the labor input is greater than the rate of change in the capital input.

In the various measurements of productivity it is usually assumed that the production function is of the Cobb-Douglas type, i.e.:

$$F(K,L,T) = TK^{a_K}L^{a_L}. \tag{8}$$

In this case, the respective shares of capital and labor in output (a_K and a_L) are constant, and a constant ratio is also maintained between the marginal and the average product of the two production factors. It follows that labor productivity is equal to the rate of change in the value of the marginal product of labor.

In 1986 and 1987, labor productivity increased by 3.5 and 3 percent, respectively. As stated in the text, real wages in the business sector rose in these two years by 9.1 and 8.1 percent, respectively, i.e., real wages increased more than the value of labor's marginal product.

With returns to capital (equity) being the residual product after deduction of wages paid to labor, the returns per unit of capital are equal to:

$$s = (Y - WL)/K, \tag{9}$$

where W is the real wage. Hence, by differentiating and using equations (2), (5) and (7), it can be seen that

$$g_S = \left[P_T - a_L P_L - a_L(g_W - P_L)\right]/a_K. \tag{10}$$

Thus, a wage increase in excess of labor productivity growth reduces real returns to capital. There is, of course, another factor which may act in the opposite direction, namely a rise in total productivity in excess of the growth of labor productivity (multiplied by labor's relative share in total product), which would contribute to an increase in the real returns to capital.

APPENDIX II: COMPOSITION OF MONETARY AGGREGATES

The monetary aggregate M_3 is conventionally defined, by using the liabilities side of the banking system's balance sheets, as currency in circulation (C_a), shekel-denominated demand and time deposits (D_1) and dollar-denominated deposits (D_2). That is

$$M_3 = C_a + D_1 + D_2$$

Ignoring the Bank of Israel's equity, a stylized version of its balance sheet is

<u>Bank of Israel</u>

Assets	Liabilities
R	C_a
B_g	C_b
B_{p1}	
B_{p2}	
H	H

where:

C_b - Commercial banks' reserves;

R - International reserves (net of external indebtedness)

B_g - Bank of Israel's credit to the public sector;

B_{p1} - Bank of Israel's credit to the private sector;

B_{p2} - Bank of Israel's credit to commercial banks;

H - Money base.

From the balance sheet we get:

$$H = C_a + C_b = R + B_g + B_{p1} + B_{p2} \tag{11}$$

Ignoring commercial banks' equity, a stylized version of their balance sheet is:

<u>Commercial Banking System</u>
<u>(Consolidated Balance Sheet)</u>

Assets	Liabilities
C_b	B_{p2}
	D_1
B_{p3}	D_2

where B_{p3} denotes commercial banks' credit to the nonbanking private sector and the public sector.

Hence, from the balance sheet we get:

$$D_1 + D_2 + B_{p3} = C_b + B_{p3}. \tag{12}$$

Equations (11) and (12) yield:

$$M_3 = C_a + D_1 + D_2 = R + B \tag{13}$$

where $B = B_g + B_{p1} + B_{p3}$ is the net domestic credit of the banking system (central and commercial) to the nonbanking private and public sectors. That is, the money supply is equal to the shekel value of the international reserves plus net domestic credit.

APPENDIX III: THE DETERMINATION OF INTEREST RATES IN A NON-COMPETITIVE MARKET

In order to clarify which factors basically influence the gap between borrowing and lending rates, we shall present an extreme case of non-competitiveness on the supply side, namely, that the market consists of a single bank. For simplicity, we further assume that there are no reserve requirements and no discount-window lending by the Bank of Israel, so that the borrowing rate paid to depositors represents the bank's marginal cost of raising funds. We assume that the initial demand for credit which the bank faces is D_0D_0 in Figure 4, and the marginal revenue (receipts of interest on credit) is MR_0. His marginal cost curve (namely, borrowing rate) is MC. In this situation, the bank will set its borrowing rate at $\bar{r}_0$ and its lending rate at r_0.[15] The quantity of credit (and deposits) will then be A_0 and the gap between borrowing and lending rates will be $r_0 - \bar{r}_0$. Now, if the elasticity of

[15]To avoid complicated diagrams, we purposely ignore the possibility that the bank can also act as a monopsonist towards its depositors. This possibility in fact increases the interest rate gap even more.

demand for credit declines (around the quantity A_0), the new steeper demand curve for credit will be D_1D_1 and the marginal revenue curve will be MR_1. The quantity of credit (and deposits) will then decline to A_1; the borrowing rate will fall to $\bar{r}_1$, the lending rate will rise to r_1, and the gap between the two rates will rise to $r_1 - \bar{r}_1$.

12 TAX SMOOTHING AND TESTS OF RICARDIAN EQUIVALENCE: ISRAEL 1961-1988

Edward K. (Akiva) Offenbacher[1]

I. INTRODUCTION

The way that private consumption responds to changes in fiscal variables, especially taxes, has important implications for monetary policy. For example, a tax cut that is regarded as temporary (say, because it is enacted about a year before elections) and that is financed by the issue of interest-bearing debt, may well induce a Keynesian central bank Governor to expand the money supply in an attempt to reduce the expected shift in the composition of private expenditure from investment to consumption. The Ricardian equivalence theorem asserts that an increase in the public's demand for consumption is not to be expected after such a tax cut since the public fully anticipates the taxes that will have to be imposed in the future to repay the new debt. A Governor who believes in Ricardian equivalence would shun expansionary monetary policy on the grounds that the increased deficit will not raise real interest rates. Any observed increase in nominal rates following a tax cut may be attributable to expectations of higher inflation, perhaps due to the public's fear of unnecessarily expansionary monetary policy! More generally, the Ricardian equivalence theorem (to be denoted sometimes by RET) has been one of the most controversial and interesting issues in macroeconomics in the past 15 years, spawning a vast literature that involves both micro and macro theory, as well as issues that are at the forefront of time series econometrics.[2]

---

[1] Senior economist, Research Department, Bank of Israel. I am grateful to Levis Kochin, who took time from his vacation to convince me that this work was worth trying, and, for helpful comments, to participants in this conference and in a seminar at the Bank of Israel's Research Department, especially to Michael Beenstock, Yaakov Lavi, Rafi Melnick, Mordechai Frenkel and Leora Meridor; Nurit Malchin provided excellent research assistance and Chava Reich competently typed several drafts. All the usual disclaimers apply."

[2] The literature on Ricardian equivalence has become so voluminous that even the list of survey articles is getting pretty long. Some relatively recent surveys are Bernheim (1987), Leiderman and Blejer (1988) and Barro (1989).

The development of the budget deficit and of private consumption in Israel in the last two decades seems to provide a fertile and favorable testing ground for the RET. The variability of the budget deficit as a percent of GDP has been very high but the effect of this variability on the national savings rate appears to have been largely offset by movements of private consumption in the opposite direction. These stylized facts are summarized neatly in Figure 1, a diagram that has appeared regularly in recent issues of the Bank of Israel's Annual Report and that was featured by Robert Barro in a recent summary of the "Ricardian Approach to Budget Deficits" (1989).

Diagrammatic presentation of stylized facts is not a substitute for careful econometric analysis and, not surprisingly, a number of such studies have been carried out using Israeli data. Results of these studies have yielded conflicting results: Meridor (1985) finds strong support for RET, Leiderman and Razin (1988) find somewhat weaker support while Elkayam, Tal and Yariv (1988) reject RET.

The main purpose of the present paper is to assess the RET in the Israeli case on the basis of a related and more recent development in the public finance literature, the tax smoothing hypothesis. Briefly, this hypothesis asserts that if the tax authorities follow an optimizing rule that is described more fully below, then the time path of the average tax rate will be a random walk. This implies that the current tax rate is the best predictor of future tax rates and that additional information on the history of the economy, including data on the budget deficit or on government spending, is not useful for predicting future taxes. Conventional tests of the RET are based on the assumption that variables other than current tax rates, such as budget deficits or government spending, are important for predicting future taxes. Thus, the tax smoothing literature asserts that if the tax smoothing hypothesis cannot be rejected, conventional tests of the RET are not appropriate. Any empirical work on the RET should first test to see whether tax smoothing holds and may proceed only if tax smoothing is rejected. The tests of tax smoothing that are carried out in this paper for the Israeli case show quite conclusively that the tax smoothing hypothesis cannot be rejected. Thus, the conflicting results about RET contained in previous work on the Israeli case are, in some sense, reconciled.

Another feature of the present paper is the use of a more appropriate set of data than the data used in previous work. I use annual data for a fairly long time period (by Israeli standards), 1960-1988, and these data have been adapted historically for the switch in the national income accounts to the UN System of National Accounts. Annual data seem more appropriate than higher frequency data for testing the RET since one does not expect the forces posited by the RET to operate over relatively short time intervals. Also, the sample period includes a number of years after Israel's Economic Stabilization Program of July 1985.

The remainder of the paper is organized as follows: The next section presents the various strands of theory that motivate the paper's empirical work, along with a review of the previous literature on the Israeli case. Section III presents the tax smoothing argument and its implications for conventional tests of Ricardian equivalence. Section IV describes the empirical work and section V concludes the paper.

II. RICARDIAN EQUIVALENCE IN ISRAEL: A CRITICAL REVIEW OF THE LITERATURE

The Ricardian equivalence theorem on public debt is "the proposition that shifts between debt and tax finance for a given amount of public expenditure ... have no first-order effect on the real interest rate, volume of private investment, etc." (Barro, 1979, p. 940). The RET stands in sharp contradiction to the Keynesian view that a shift from tax to debt finance causes an increase in real interest rates, crowds out private investment and has an expansionary effect on total output. The key assumption needed to derive the RET is that members of the public do not regard government bonds as part of their net wealth because they fully anticipate the taxes that must be levied in the future to retire the debt and act as if the taxes were being levied presently. Appeal to an intergenerational bequest motive (usually, but not necessarily, viewed as altruistic) deals with the objection that the debt may not be retired in the lifetimes of the current taxpayers. In addition, RET requires that capital markets not be too imperfect and that neither uncertainty nor tax induced distortions are too important. Precise statements of these assumptions and criticisms thereof abound in the literature but our concern is with tests for the empirical validity of the implications of Ricardian equivalence.

There have been three empirical studies of Ricardian equivalence in Israel which have yielded conflicting results. The first study is by Meridor (1985), who followed the early and influential approach of Kochin (1974) and regressed current consumption on current income, lagged consumption and alternative measures of the fiscal deficit. The presence of lagged consumption as an explanatory variable is derived by applying the Koyck transformation to a geometric distributed lag specification for permanent income. Kochin found that the deficit has a significant negative effect on consumption and attributed this effect to the anticipation of future taxes. Subsequently, more precise tests for a complete offset were developed, involving restrictions on the coefficients of current income, taxes and government expenditure in the consumption equation. The refined approach was applied to the Israeli case by Meridor. Using annual data from 1955 - 79, a period that excludes some of the worst excesses of government largesse as well as the subsequent Economic Stabilization Program, Meridor was unable to reject the restrictions implied by Ricardian equivalence.

The second study, by Elkayam, Tal and Yariv (1988), focused on stocks, rather than flows. Rather than specifying consumption as a function of the flows of permanent income and government budget variables, they specified consumption as a function of labor income and of non-human wealth, and tested whether net government liabilities should be included as part of private sector wealth. In particular, Ricardian equivalence suggests that the domestic component of government debt should have no effect on consumption since the future tax liability to be imposed on the public at large fully offsets the asset value of government bonds to their holders. On the other hand, the external component of government debt is a net liability of the private sector since the local citizenry has no asset to offset the future taxes. Adopting a general specification in which consumption is regressed on labor income, the internal debt, the private sector capital less its liabilities to foreigners and the public sector's foreign debt net of its capital stock, these authors clearly reject Ricardian equivalence in favor of the Keyensian approach: the internal debt has a significantly comprehensive theoretical framework that provides a very clear interpretation of their results, problems with the data used and with some of the results themselves qualify the support that was found for Ricardian equivalence.

Empirical tests of Ricardian equivalence have been criticized on numerous grounds. Perhaps the most common criticism is the simultaneity problem, namely that variables such as income, taxes and even government spending are not likely to be exogenous. The current state of the debate on the empirical evaluation of Ricardian equivalence was summarized succinctly in the general discussion of Bernheim's (1987) survey article. "Robert Barro questioned Bernheim's claim that the empirical evidence provides strong support for the Keynesian view. There are so many problems in the empirical studies that their results are uninformative" (p. 313).

The present study focuses on another important criticism of empirical work on Ricardian equivalence with radical implications for interpreting conventional tests. Broadly speaking, the criticism begins by asserting that expectations of future taxation and government spending have not been dealt with adequately in the earlier literature. One recent striking example is the implications of political developments in the U.S.S.R. and Central Europe for U.S. defense spending. These events may already be affecting private consumption in the U.S. while government consumption data certainly do not yet reflect these events. The studies by Meridor and by Elkayam, Tal and Yariv make to attempt whatsoever to project future tax liabilities beyond inclusion of the current deficit or the current national debt, measures which do not reflect future government spending. Leiderman and Razin are concerned with the future path of government spending but their projection is also subject to criticism that will be elaborated below. The next section shows that when a somewhat more systematic forward-looking approach to Ricardian equivalence is adopted, it is possible that the Keynesian and Ricardian approaches become indistinguishable in conventional tests.

III. TAX SMOOTHING AND ITS IMPLICATIONS

Equation (1) presents the forward looking, intertemporal government budget constraint, as in Barro (1986):

$$\int \tau(t)y(t)e^{-rt}dt = \int g(t)e^{-rt}dt + b(0) \qquad (1)$$

where

$\tau(t)$ = average tax rate, defined as tax receipts from all sources relative to income

$y(t)$ = current real income

r = interest rate

$g(t)$ = current real value government expenditure

$b(0)$ = real value currently outstanding debt

The left-hand-side of (1) is the present value of current and future tax receipts which must equal the present value of all current and future expenditures including debt retirement, as stated on the right hand side. (Integration here and elsewhere in the paper is from the present, t=0, to the infinite future.) Within this framework, the RET simply asserts that the public is indifferent to alternative time paths for $\tau(t)$ for a given value of the right hand side of (1).

A major difficulty in constructing "forward-looking" empirical tests of Ricardian equivalence is that the time path of future government expenditures, $\{g(t)\}_{t=0}$, is unknown at t=0 and expectations of this time path for some, presumably relevant, information set available at t=0 are hard to assess. Specifically, the estimation of any particular forecasting equation for government expenditures using some historical data set, which may include a wide variety of time series, will generally be subject to the powerful criticism of being arbitrary and of ignoring relevant information. For later reference, the problem of obtaining values for the expected future path of government spending will be termed the "observational quandary".

One possible escape from this observational quandary is based on the tax-smoothing hypothesis, introduced by Barro (1979). This approach was originally proposed as an attempt to explain the behavior of tax rates over time in an environment where individuals behave according to Ricardian equivalence so that rational policy makers would not expect to get any benefit to the macro-economy from re-distributing taxes and deficits over time for a given path of expenditures. The tax smoothing hypothesis asserts that the path of tax rates should be set to maximize economic efficiency (or social welfare) subject to the government's budget constraint. If there are increasing marginal costs associated with increasing tax rates, say because higher tax rates generate greater activity to evade or avoid taxes, then efficiency considerations suggest that at any point in time the tax rate should be a constant, set at the level that just finances the present value of expected government spending. Specifically, $\tau(t)$ should be set at the constant rate, τ, that satisfies

$$\tau = [\int g^e(t)e^{-rt}dt + b(0)] / \int y^e(t)e^{-rt}dt \tag{2}$$

where $g^e(t)$ and $y^e(t)$ are rational expectations of $g(t)$ and $y(t)$. Furthermore, if we define permanent levels of g and y, denoted by g^* and y^*, respectively

$$\begin{aligned} g^*/r &= \int g^e(t)e^{-rt}dt \\ y^*/r &= \int y^e(t)e^{-rt}dt \end{aligned} \tag{3}$$

then tax smoothing implies that

$$\tau = [g^* + rb(0)]/y^* \tag{4}$$

It is easy to infer from equation (4) that the average tax rate will be a good proxy for the permanent level of government spending if the government adheres to the principle of tax smoothing.

At any point in time, g^* will represent the best estimate of permanent government spending given all relevant information. As time evolves, new information becomes available, leading to revisions in the expected path, $g^e(t)$, and hence to revised values of g^*. But since new information arrives randomly, the revisions of g^* and, hence, of τ, will be random. Thus, the testable implication of the tax-smoothing hypothesis is that the average tax rate follows a random walk, or that the current tax rate is the best estimate of future tax rates.

We are now ready to present the key implication of tax-smoothing for the present purposes, namely that if a policy of tax smoothing is followed, then conventional tests cannot distinguish between the Keynesian and Ricardian theories. This implication is called the problem of observational equivalence. The Keynesian approach argues that consumption will respond to all tax changes, whether or not these tax changes are associated with changes in the permanent level of government spending, while the Ricardian approach suggests that private consumption responds only to tax changes that are associated with changes in g^*. Kochin, Benjamin and Meador refer to tax changes that are not associated with change in g^* as arbitrary tax changes and point out that the implication of the Keynesian and Ricardian approaches differ only with regard to arbitrary tax changes. However, if the authorities follow a policy of tax smoothing, there are no arbitrary tax changes--all tax changes are associated with changes in g^*. In this case, the tax series do not provide the type of observations that are capable of distinguishing between the two theories. On the other hand, if the authorities do not follow a policy of tax smoothing, some tax changes are arbitrary and it should be possible to distinguish between the two theories.

Conventional tests of Ricardian equivalence do not distinguish between arbitrary and purposeful tax changes, and essentially maintain the hypothesis that all tax changes are arbitrary. Kochin, Benjamin and Meador argue that "If the government is not sufficiently devoted to the cause of scientific investigation so as to in fact vary taxes arbitrarily, the results of this work (i.e., conventional tests of the RET -EO) should not be interpreted as presented." Alternatively, one can infer from the theoretical result of Kochin, Benjamin and Meador, that if one wishes to conduct an empirical investigation of Ricardian equivalence, a prior test should be performed to assess whether or not the tax rate series is consistent with the tax smoothing hypothesis. If the data fail to reject the tax smoothing hypothesis, it is unreasonable to carry out a test of Ricardian equivalence since tax changes cannot be presumed to be arbitrary. The observational quandary is replaced by observational equivalence. However, if the data reject the tax smoothing hypothesis, it is always possible that some other purposive model generates tax rates but until such an alternative is provided, the assumption of arbitrary tax rate changes is not rejected.

IV. TESTS FOR TAX SMOOTHING

A. Data

The data on tax rate series for Israel are for the period 1961-1988. The gross tax rate is the ratio of nominal tax revenue to nominal GDP. Following Kochin, Benjamin and Meador, government revenue from the sale of services is not treated as a tax. We include taxes of the National Insurance Institute (roughly comparable to Social Security in the United States) since a relatively large proportion of these taxes are used to make transfers that are not part of retirement benefits, especially child allowances. The second tax series adds inflation tax revenue to gross tax revenues. The full revenue from money creation is not included because the component that is not due to the inflation tax is more appropriately viewed as a payment for a service provided by the government, namely the provision of a means of payment.[3] The data on GDP and on government consumption are based on National Income Accounting data that use the U.N. System of National Accounts. Official data using this system exist only from 1980 but data for previous years using the old system have been adjusted recently by a team in the Bank of Israel Research Department for the purpose of estimating a macro-econometric model of the Israeli economy.[4]

B. Results

Figure 2 presents the data on the two tax rate series, along with a series on net taxes, i.e., gross taxes less transfer payments. The last series is included only for describing the sources of the movements in the gross tax rate and no tests are carried out on it. The two gross tax rate series are described well by a few stylized facts: (1) The tax rate increased during two distinct episodes, 1967-71 and 1974-76. Each of these episodes started with a major war while the earlier episode also includes a major increase in transfer payments, resulting from some

---

[3] The tests reported were also conducted using the full revenue from money creation, with no appreciable affect on the results.

[4] Details of the differences between the two series are described in the Bank of Israel's Annual Report, 1986. The main difference is in the treatment of non-profit institutions. Previously, all of these institutions were included in the private sector while in the U.N. system, a non-profit institution is regarded as being in the private sector if less than 50% of its budget comes from public funds and it is in the public sector otherwise.

social unrest.[5] (2) During each of the other three time periods, 1961-66, 1972-73 and 1977-present, the tax rate was roughly constant at the rate that had been attained at the beginning of the period. (3) The years 1984 and 1985 are exceptions to the startling constancy of the tax rate during the episodes of no increase but these were years of startlingly exceptional events -- major losses were incurred by the commercial banks associated with the bank stock manipulation and the wild oscillation of inflation generated big Tanzi effects in both directions.[6]

The stochastic properties of the tax rate series are described more formally in tables 1 and 2. Table 1 contains sample autocorrelations for each of the two series, along with a portmanteau test for the joint significance of these autocorrelations. The autocorrelations of the levels of both series indicate that the series are non-stationary. The autocorrelations damp out very slowly and the Q statistic has a very high value. First-differencing each series yields autocorrelations that suggest stationarity of the first differences: For each series only the first-order autocorrelation exceeds its standard error but in neither case is the first-order autocorrelation significant, even at the 10 percent level. For the first-difference of each series, the marginal significance level of the joint test for eight autocorrelations is approximately 50 percent. Thus, adopting the finance literature terminology of tests for market efficiency, we can assert that the Israeli tax rate series pass weak-form tests for tax smoothing.

Table 2 presents results of regressions that test for tax smoothing in a semi-strong form. Specifically, if the tax rate series is a random walk, neither the lagged value $(T/Y)_{-1}$, nor any other variable should have a statistically significant effect on the change, $\Delta(T/Y)$. A significant value for the constant suggests that the random walk has drift. Theoretical literature on tax smoothing allows for some drift, in light of secular changes in the costs of both tax collection and tax avoidance. The results of the semi-strong form tests generally support tax smoothing along with some positive drift over time in the average

[5] The increase in transfer payments and its longer run implications are described succinctly in Bruno (1989), pp. 9-10.

[6] The term Tanzi effect refers to the negative effect of higher inflation on the real value of tax receipts due to the erosion of the value of tax payments during the lag between accrual and payment, and vice-versa.

tax rate, but there is one important exception to this result--the effect of government spending abroad.

The results that support tax smoothing can be summarized briefly. The lagged value of the tax rate is not significant at the 5% level in any of the regressions. With the exception of government (non-interest) spending abroad, none of the additional variables in the regressions are statistically significant. In particular, even the value of Israel's large internal debt does not contribute significantly towards explaining tax rate changes.

The important exception to the results that support tax smoothing is the significance of government spending abroad in regression (5). While it is possible to disregard this result on the grounds that sooner or later, a small sample of data points will by chance yield some significant coefficients, I prefer to regard the result seriously, as reflecting some economic effect. The positive sign on the lagged change in spending abroad suggests that the government has not adjusted domestic taxation as quickly as it should have in response to changes in this type of expenditure. Now, it is well known that Israel has significant expenditures abroad, mainly for the procurement of military equipment, but it also has had considerable income from abroad both in the form of grants and in the form of a loan package. Both the expenditure side and the income side of the government's foreign budget are subject to unusually high degrees of uncertainty, that is not independent of the size of cumulated foreign deficits, i.e., the government's foreign debt. On the expenditure side, the permanent level of military procurements is a function of the regional arms race. Major changes in this race have been associated with re-stocking in the aftermath of the two major wars (1967 and 1973), the timing and magnitude of which having been extremely uncertain. On the income side, both the extent and duration of aid, as well as the degree of "softness" of both governmental and private loans are all subject to great uncertainty. In light of all this uncertainty, it appears that the Israeli government may have adopted some degree of a "wait and see" attitude in adjusting domestic taxes to changes in expected net outlays abroad, but perhaps there is some degree of justification for such an attitude. On the other hand, rational economic agents must make some assessment of the likely implications of past and expected foreign deficits on future domestic taxation. It is possible that this effect may also account for the slightly high values for the Durbin-Watson statistic obtained in all the regressions. In any event, more careful study of this particular and complicated aspect of public finance in Israel is needed before one should conclude that an important violation of tax smoothing has been found.

V. CONCLUSION

The main result of this paper is that data on average tax rates in Israel fail to reject the tax smoothing hypothesis. Therefore, conventional tests of Ricardian equivalence are not applicable to the Israeli case. This result reconciles the conflict among previous studies by asserting that the tests they conducted were not appropriate in the first place.

TABLE 1: AUTOCORRELATION TEST FOR TEMPORAL EFFICIENCY OF TAXATION: 1961-1988

	Without Inflation Tax		With Inflation Tax	
Lag	Level	1st Difference	Level	1st Difference
1	.86	-.26	.87	-.29
2	.75	-.20	.77	-.13
3	.64	.11	.67	.14
4	.54	-.11	.53	-.14
5	.49	-.05	.47	-.06
6	.41	.17	.36	.20
7	.28	-.07	.22	-.08
8	.16	-.24	.12	-.13
Q(8)	**87.9**	**7.4**	**84.3**	**6.9**

Critical chi-square value for Q(8) equals 15.5 for the 5% significance level and 7.3 for the 50% significance level.

TABLE 2: REGRESSIONS FOR SEMI-STRONG FORM TESTS OF TAX SMOOTHING
[Dependent variable: Δ(T/Y); sample period: 1963-1988]

Explanatory variable	(1)	(2)	(3)	(4)	(5)
Constant	0.043	0.056	0.063	0.036	0.024
	(1.48)	(1.23)	(1.98)	(1.14)	(0.69)
$(T/Y)_{-1}$	-0.099	-0.119	-0.147	-0.082	-0.057
	(1.28)	(1.22)	(1.79)	(1.00)	(0.59)
ΔLY_{-1}		-0.073			
		(0.35)			
$\Delta(DEBT/Y)_{-1}$			0.001		
			(1.47)		
$\Delta(GDOM/Y)_{-1}$				0.147	0.209
				(0.65)	(1.00)
$\Delta(GFOR/Y)_{-1}$					0.42
					(2.20)
R^2	0.06	0.07	0.14	0.08	0.26
S.E.R.	0.031	0.032	0.031	0.031	0.029
D.W.	2.53	2.50	2.74	2.57	2.48

Definitions: T = gross tax receipts including inflation tax
Y = gross domestic product (GDP)
LQ = log of GDP
DEBT = internal government debt
GDOM = domestic government expenditures
GFOR = government expenditures abroad
Δ denotes change over time
Numbers in parenthesis are absolute values of t statistics.

REFERENCES

Aschauer, David A., "Fiscal Policy and Aggregate Demand," American Economic Review, 75 (March 1985), 117-127.

Barro, Robert J., "On the Determination of the Public Debt," Journal of Political Economy, 87, (October 1979), 940-971.

_______________, The Behavior of United States Deficits," in Robert J. Gordon (ed.), The American Business Cycle: Continuity and Change, NBER Studies in Business No. 25, Chicago: University of Chicago Press, 1986.

_______________, "The Ricardian Approach to Budget Deficits," Journal of Economic Perspectives, 3 (Spring 1989), 37-54.

Bernheim, B. Douglas, "Ricardian Equivalence: An Evaluation of Theory and Evidence," in Stanley Fischer (ed.), NBER Macroeconomic Annual, Cambridge, Mass., MIT Press, 1989, 263-315.

Bruno, Michael, "Israel's Crisis and Economic Reform: A Historical Perspective," NBER Working Paper No. 3075, August 1989.

Elkayam, David, Daniel Yariv and Itzhak Tal, "The Effect of the Internal and External Public Debt on Private Consumption in Israel," Bank of Israel Economic Review, 63, (1988), 1-19.

Hall, Robert E., "Stochastic Implications of the Life-Cycle Permanent Income Hypothesis Hypothesis: Theory and Evidence," Journal of Political Economy, 86 (December 1978), 971-988.

Kochin, Levis, "Are Future Taxes Anticipated by Consumers?" Journal of Money, Credit and Banking, 6 (August 1974), 385-394.

_______________, Daniel K. Benjamin and Mark Meador, "The Observational Equivalence of Rational and Irrational Consumers if Taxation is Efficient," West Coast Federal Reserve Academic Conference, Federal Reserve Bank of San Francisco, (1985), 103-121.

Leiderman, Leonardo and Mario Blejer, "Modeling and Testing Ricardian Equivalence: A Survey," IMF Staff Papers, 35 (March 1988), 1-35.

_______________, and Assaf Razin, "Testing Ricardian Neutrality with an Intertemporal Stochastic Model," Journal of Money, Credit and Banking, 20 (February 1988), 1-21.

Meridor, Leora, "Deficit Neutrality: The Israeli Case," Bank of Israel Economic Review, 57, (May 1985), 26-36

Figure 1

Gross National Saving out of Total Income of the Economy, and Its Distribution between the Private and Public Sector, 1960–88

(Calculated on the basis of the representative exchange rate)

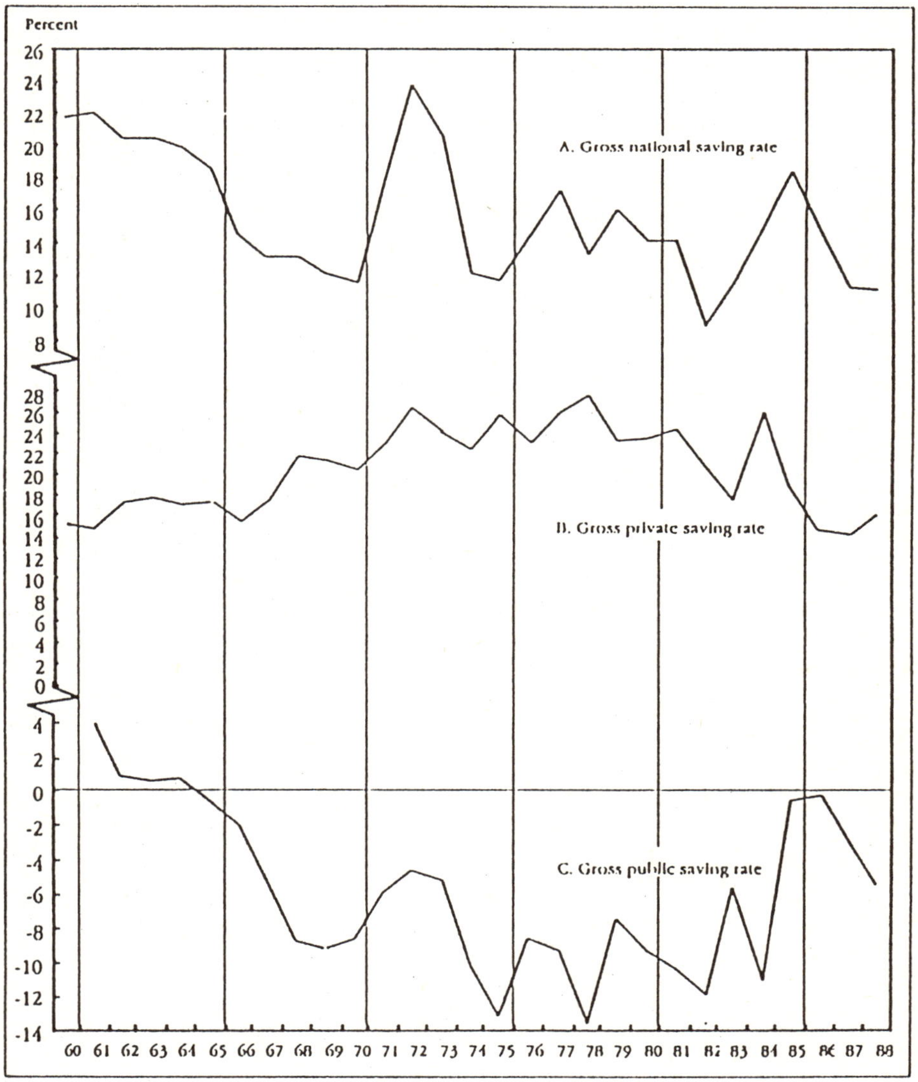

Source: Bank of Israel Annual Report 1988, Figure 2.3. See Source
For definitions of variables plotted.

Figure 2: AVERAGE TAX RATES (T/Y)

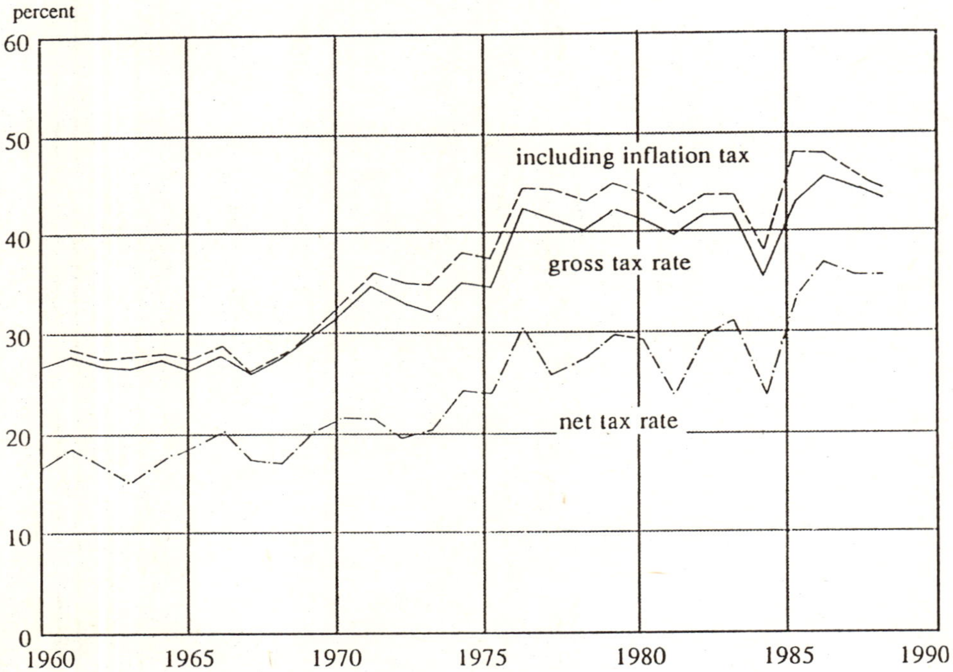

Printing: Druckerei Zechner, Speyer
Binding: Buchbinderei Schäffer, Grünstadt